Dr Adrian Greaves has a PhD in South African history and is the editor of the Anglo Zulu War Historical Society journals. He regularly lectures on the Zulu Wars both in the UK and abroad, and is the author of several books on the subject, including *Isandlwana* and *Rorke's Drift*. He is married with three sons, and lives in Kent.

crossing the buffalo
the zulu war of 1879

adrian greaves

CASSELL

Cassell Military Paperbacks

Cassell
Wellington House, 125 Strand
London WC2R 0BB

1 3 5 7 9 10 8 6 4 2

British Library Cataloguing-in-Publication Data.
A catalogue record for this book is available
from the British Library.

ISBN-13 978-0-3043-6725-2
ISBN-10 0-3043-6725-7

Printed and bound in Great Britain by
Cox & Wyman Ltd, Reading, Berkshire

The Orion Publishing Group's policy is to use papers that
are natural, renewable and recyclable products and
made from wood grown in sustainable forests. The logging
and manufacturing processes are expected to conform to
the environmental regulations of the country of origin.

www.orionbooks.co.uk

Contents

List of Maps

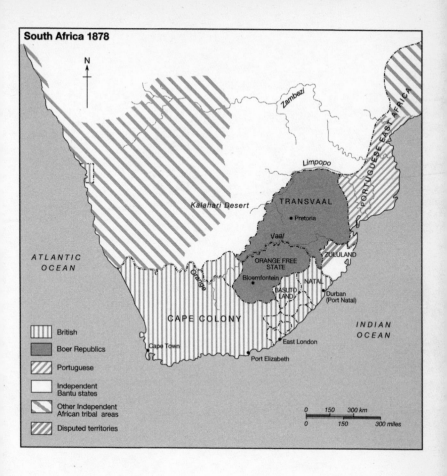

South Africa 1878

ATLANTIC
OCEAN

Kalahari Desert

Zambezi

Limpopo

TRANSVAAL

• Pretoria

PORTUGUESE EAST AFRICA

Vaal

ORANGE FREE
STATE

ZULULAND

Bloemfontein •

Orange

BASUTO
LAND

NATAL

Durban
(Port Natal)

CAPE COLONY

INDIAN
OCEAN

Cape Town •

East London

Port Elizabeth •

British

Boer Republics

Portuguese

Independent
Bantu states

Other Independent
African tribal areas

Disputed territories

| 0 | 150 | 300 km |
| 0 | 150 | 300 miles |

Preface

In 1879 Queen Victoria's military planners and politicians were actively preparing Britain for war in Afghanistan when, without their knowledge or the authority of Parliament, the British Army in South Africa invaded Zululand. The first the home government and people knew of the invasion was when devastating news reached London that part of Lord Chelmsford's well-trained invasion force had been destroyed by the Zulus at the battle of Isandlwana.

The battle lasted less than two hours but 4,000 bodies now lay across the British position. Dead Zulus, many blasted by volley fire and artillery, lay intertwined with slaughtered British soldiers. The ghastly blood-smeared debris of war littered the battlefield; Zulu war shields and spears lay tangled with Martini-Henry rifles, wrecked tents and wagons. Not content with a resounding victory and before the last British soldier had died, the victorious Zulus set about stripping the dead and dying soldiers for their red jackets – then adding to the horror by ritually disembowelling their bodies. When viewed that night by Lord Chelmsford and the passing survivors of his invasion column, the horrific scene seared itself into their memories and ensured the resulting war would be merciless.

Chelmsford's unexpected defeat involved the loss of nearly 1,300 well-trained officers and men, including the near annihilation of the prestigious 1/24th (Warwickshire) Regiment together with many hundreds of supporting colonial soldiers and black Natal auxiliaries. Isandlwana was a military disaster that shocked and outraged the nation; the defeat had to be decisively and swiftly avenged – especially when it was realized that the Zulu army responsible for crushing the experienced invasion force was part-time and ill equipped. With her reputation of invincibility severely shaken, Britain unleashed unconditional war against the previously friendly Zulus and from the outset both sides fought ferocious pitched battles that involved many thousands of combatants. During the vicious six-month-long Anglo-Zulu War, neither side took prisoners and terrible casualties were inflicted on both sides. According to the official history of the war [1] a total of 76 officers and 1,007 British troops were killed in action during the campaign and 37 officers and 206 men seriously wounded; a further 17 British officers and 330 men died of disease and throughout 1879 a total of 99 officers and 1,286 men were invalided 'from active duty for causes incidental to the campaign' which unashamedly included numerous well-documented cases of psychological stress and battle fatigue. Officially, 604 African auxiliaries supporting the British were killed – a figure that is probably grossly underestimated as records relating to the auxiliaries were deficient in every respect; this figure would just about account for their losses at Isandlwana. Equally tragic is the fact that Zulu losses throughout the war can only be estimated, with historians calculating that well in excess of 10,000 warriors were killed with a similar number maimed by Martini-Henry bullets, artillery rounds or by the swords and lances of the cavalry.

In three major engagements, Isandlwana, Ntombe and Hlobane, the British invasion force suffered unexpected and crushing defeats and in each of these battles only a handful of British soldiers survived to tell of their ordeal; conversely, at Rorke's Drift, Khambula, Gingindlovu and Ulundi, it was the turn of the Zulus to suffer overwhelming defeat.

Even today the memory of this conflict is still powerful, especially at the unchanged and haunting battlefields across Zululand. It is easy to visualize disciplined lines of young red-coated British soldiers, hopelessly outnumbered yet bravely standing shoulder to shoulder to defend Queen

Victoria's empire in the depths of uncharted Africa. Its allure is accentuated by the fact that the war was waged against the noblest of all African warriors, those of the Zulu nation. As it developed, the Zulu War became extremely savage in its execution, and brutality abounded even after the final British victory. Though so very different, each side deeply respected the other, a respect that continues through to today, which may explain why the war is still considered to be a 'romantic' war by both the British and the Zulu people. Certainly its unique and enduring popularity has set it apart from all other seventy-two colonial wars involving British soldiers during the sixty-four-year reign of Queen Victoria. There were no flagrant attacks on non-combatants, no concentration camps, very little rape and pillage, and only a little annexation of territory.[2] The war also received greater newspaper coverage from on-the-spot reporters than any previous colonial war.

In order to understand the significance and consequences of the seven major battles that constituted the Anglo-Zulu War, this book will necessarily pivot around the numerous accounts of conspicuous bravery and heroism on both sides. Some participants won medals while others, equally deserving, were deliberately overlooked. Both press and Parliament gloated over their troops' successes, or were appalled by their defeats, and all the while the war that should have served to strengthen Britain's reputation for being all-powerful throughout the world instead revealed serious military weaknesses in her chain of empire. Furthermore it was a war that was as unnecessary as it was unjust; Britain invaded the territory of her friend and ally, King Cetshwayo of the Zulus, much to his everlasting puzzlement. Within six months the war had cost the Zulu people a whole generation of young men and as proof of its being an utterly pointless war, following the final ruthless victory against the Zulus at Ulundi, the British Army about-turned out of Zululand and marched for home. Worse was to come; only weeks later British troops captured King Cetshwayo and exiled him to Cape Town, leaving his leaderless and starving people to the modern African fate of famine and civil war.

Nevertheless, the image of these soldiers, fighting fearlessly for their queen and country in the intense African heat, is immensely powerful and one that is regularly strengthened with each showing of popular and epic films such as *Zulu* and *Zulu Dawn* which depict the two famous battles of Rorke's Drift and Isandlwana; yet there is infinitely more to the Zulu War than these two battles in isolation. What of the daunting Zulu foe so feared and yet so respected by the British soldiers? Why were the British in South Africa, or more to the point, why did they invade Zululand? How was it that at Isandlwana an inexperienced part-time and poorly armed warrior army, which had been at peace for twenty-two years, managed to inflict such a devastating defeat on one of the most modern, well-equipped professional armies in the world? How, indeed, were they able to follow this victory with further triumphs at Hlobane and Ntombe River? Also to be considered is the mysterious role and death in Zululand of the French Prince Imperial while in the service of the British. And having finally routed the Zulu army at Ulundi and laid waste the countryside at such enormous cost to both sides, why did the British then abandon Zululand to its fate?

This book will consider not only these questions but also the whole Anglo-Zulu War in the light of modern research, including that of recent archaeological examinations at the more accessible battlefields. Walking the largely unchanged battlefields of Zululand is always a moving experience and extremely useful when trying to enter the mind of the participants, but much more material can still be discovered by examining primary and secondary sources, including official army maps and volumes of beautifully drawn sketches, and newspaper and journal articles from those hardy news reporters and military artists who accompanied the army during the invasion. Yet it is the official reports and letters from the participants themselves that are most valuable source of fresh material. Both officers and soldiers, at least those who could write, wrote from the heart: of the battles, the conditions and hardships endured, the extremes of weather and of their experiences, fear and terror of pending battle. Even with the lapse of time, all these emotions pour forth from their letters; after all, this was one of the last wars without any form of official censorship. Although many of these letters are now housed in a number of fine military museums, many still remain in private hands, the property of proud descendants of men who took part in the Zulu War. It is due to the generosity of all the guardians of these poignant letters, both official and those still held by the participants' descendants, that new information, different aspects and fresh interpretations of the Zulu War continue to emerge.

This famous war has, remarkably, continued to intrigue successive generations. The ongoing popularity of the Zulu War may well lie in its indisputably exciting battles in a sensationally beautiful country, to which are added the thrilling accounts of bravery and unprecedented awards of medals. Conversely, the true story includes many acts of chilling cowardice, devious betrayal and official cover-ups following some astonishingly serious blunders and disasters; such aspects, previously overlooked or glossed over by authors and historians, are fully examined in their rightful place.

This book is dedicated to the memory of all officers and men, British, Colonial, black Natalian and Zulu, who died in the Zulu War in the honest belief that what they were doing was right.

Acknowledgements

I dedicate this book to my wife Debbie for her unflinching love, encouragement and patience, especially since my accident in 1985 which so dramatically changed our lives.

I also gratefully acknowledge the kind and generous assistance and permissions of the following people without whose co-operation and assistance this work would have been incomplete: Ian Knight for his general technical advice and support; David and Nicky Rattray for the use of their magnificent accommodation at Fugitives' Drift Lodge in South Africa; Dave and Sue Charles for the loan of various artefacts and input of Zulu culture; Major Martin Everett of the South Wales Borderers and Monmouthshire Regimental Museum at Brecon for his generous support and advice; Ron Sheeley for the use of his photographs, and the Anglo Zulu War Historical Society for granting me access to their research material. I also acknowledge Dr Lita Webley of the Albany Museum, Grahamstown, South Africa and my son, Captain Andrew Greaves RA, who provided me with archaeological material and advice relating to the battlefields. Brian Best kindly checked my research of the Victorian period and especially that relating to Zulu War medals; Nicki von der Hyde generously assisted me with her family's drawings of Rorke's Drift.

I especially acknowledge Consultant Surgeon Cliff Stossel and his wife, Katie, for their ongoing support and kindness during the many years of surgery that I have undergone. Last year it was my great pleasure to accompany them around the stunning battlefields of Zululand and introduce them to my many South African and Zulu friends.

Lastly, no one else had any direct control or influence over the final draft – although I respectfully acknowledge and thank Keith Lowe of Cassell for gently and tactfully steering me through the necessary 'house style'; his suggestions always made sense. I alone accept responsibility for any factual errors or omissions although I have always based my conclusions on empirical research and primary sources.

Adrian Greaves

TENTERDEN, 2004

Glossary of terms

amabutho (s. *ibutho*) Age-grade regiments.

amakhanda (s. *ikhanda*) Homesteads belonging to the king.

Bastaards Early Dutch term used around the Cape denoting the children of mixed blood.

battles, names of Battles of the Zulu War are usually named by the British after a local hill or river – the Zulus name these battles after the nearest homestead or settlement. To the Zulus, the battle of Ulundi is known as Nodwengu, although the place of Ulundi, or oNdini, means 'The Heights', a Zulu name for the Drakensberg range. Eshowe is named by the Zulus '*Tshowe*' to sound like a sneeze – as Eshowe overlooks the low-lying coastal plain and is occasionally subjected to cool breezes.

Boer Mainly Dutch-speaking white settlers, with some French, German and other Europeans, originating from the Cape.

Column The British invading columns were known variously as the Coastal or No. 1 Column, the Centre or No. 3 Column and the Northern or No. 4 Column; Colonel Durnford and Rowland's Reserve Columns were the No. 2 and No. 5 respectively.

donga A rift in the ground caused by heavy rain and in depths of between 2 and 50 feet. The bane of early travellers in Zululand; usually occurring when least expected and frequently involving a detour of many miles.

drift A shallow river crossing point.

giya A show of individual prowess during a Zulu war dance.

Helpmekaar or **Helpmakaar** The first spelling is colloquial; the second spelling is the British adaptation.

ibutho (pl. *amabutho*) An age-grade regiment.

ikhanda (pl. *amakhanda*) A homestead belonging to the king or a state barracks where *amabutho* were quartered when in the king's service.

ikwa (pl. *amakwa*) A stabbing spear.

imizi (s. *umuzi*) Zulu homesteads.

impi A fighting body of Zulu warriors.

induna (pl. *izinduna*) An officer appointed by the king.

isicoco The fibrous head-ring worn by married or senior men.

isigodlo The royal enclosure quartering the women of the king's household.

isijula (pl. *izijula*) A throwing spear.

kaffir Used in the historical context only, due to the sensitivity of the word. Commonly believed to be the Arabic word for 'infidel' or 'non-believer', which is odd as the word is not found elsewhere in Africa where the Arab traders flourished. The original usage of the word in South Africa could also have come from the following Zulu and Bantu sources:

a *Kafulwa*, the Bantu name for the early shipwreck survivors 'washed up' along the Cape to Natal coast.

b Following the *umfecane*, those refugees fleeing to the protection of the British Crown were known as the *abakafula*: the 'washed out' or dispossessed.

c *Kafula* also has a modern usage, to denote the 'washing away' of an unhappy memory or washing away a bad taste.

d See *Through the Zulu Country* (Griggs, Durban 1883) by Bertrand Mitford who wrote that 'non Zulu blacks were known as *Amakafula*' which is only a short step from 'kaffir'. Similarly, the *AmaFengu* people later became known as *Fingoes*.

kop or **koppie**. A small hill.

kraal An enclosure for cattle; not to be confused with a Zulu homestead or *umuzi*.

kwa The place of ...

laager A number of wagons formed into a circle to form a defensive perimeter.

lobolo The bride price, normally involving cattle.

mealie Maize.

nek A saddle between two hills.

pont A flat-bottomed punt or boat made of barrels.

sangoma A Zulu diviner.

spruit A small stream or tributary.

uDibi (pl. *izinDibi*) A Zulu boy between the age of 12 and 16 years who supported older relatives on the march or other military tasks.

umfecane or 'crushing': denotes the period of internecine clan fighting pre 1825.

umKhosi or First Fruits. The annual gathering before the king to review the army and to usher in the new harvest.

umuzi (pl. *imizi*) A Zulu homestead – often misnamed as a kraal.

uSuthu The political party of King Cetshwayo – the term was the popular Zulu war cry during the 1879 war.

CHAPTER 1

Early Settlers in South Africa

Due to the remorseless combination of time and the continent's perniciously destructive climate much of the evidence of early human settlement in Africa has been lost. Nevertheless, some of the oldest human remains in the world have been discovered at a number of locations across southern Africa. Archaeological evidence indicates that, from the Holocene era 10,000 years ago, the southern tip of Africa was sparsely populated by a diminutive stone-age people, the San, whose tenacity and simple lifestyle enabled them to survive into modern times as the Bushmen. They lived in small groups hunting wild animals with puny bows from which they fired thin poison-tipped arrows; they supplemented their diet with highly nutritious grubs, termites, locusts, wild berries and roots. Living alongside the San, though rarely in harmony, were groups of pastoralists, the taller and brown-skinned Khoikhoi, meaning 'men of men'. These aboriginal people had originally migrated south from modern-day Botswana; the Boers named them, for reasons unknown, the 'Hottentots'.

Archaeologists and historians still tend to regard today's black African people, the Bantu, as relatively recent incomers to southern Africa, while evidence from sites in KwaZulu Natal suggest that Khoikhoi and San communities were already established in the region by 300 AD. The main Bantu migration did not reach this far south for another 1,000 years but the eventual arrival of this cattle-owning society had an inevitably destructive impact on the indigenous populations; the pastoral Khoikhoi avoided conflict by moving further south while the hunter-gathering San were gradually forced to abandon their fertile grasslands in favour of the more marginal environments of the Qahlamba mountains, later named 'Drakensberg' by the Boers. Large numbers of the San crossed the Qahlamba to seek sanctuary in the inhospitable and arid Kalahari desert.

Over several thousand years the native Bantu people had spread laterally across central Africa from the equatorial West Coast and slowly progressed south and east around the wastes of the Kalahari desert. One Bantu tribe, the Nguni, settled the area known today as Natal, probably between 1500 and 1700. The remaining Bantu, the Xhosa tribe, continued south and eventually reached the Great Fish river, the limit of Boer scouting, in 1769; they were now only 500 miles from the Cape, which unbeknown to them was already in the process of being colonized by the Dutch.

These Bantu people were recognizably similar to the main cultural and linguistic groups who inhabit the area today: the Xhosa to the south, the Sotho and Tswana in the interior, and the Nguni on the eastern coastal strip adjoining the Indian Ocean. This pattern of human settlement was already well established by 1486, though only the Khoikhoi and San groups shared possession of the most southern reaches of the African continent. It was at this crucial point in time that the first Europeans, led by the Portuguese explorer Bartholomew Diaz, landed at the Cape while searching for a southerly route to the East Indies.

For the emerging European empires of Holland, Spain and Portugal, the newly discovered Americas and the East Indies were the lands of opportunity and commercial development. Following Diaz's discovery of the Cape, southern Africa was of little interest to the Europeans; it appeared to have nothing to offer beyond its geographical location. In the name of King John of Portugal, Diaz and his men erected a marble cross at the site of their landfall, today known as Angra Pequena; that cross lay neglected for hundreds of years but today it stands in the Lisbon Maritime Museum, a treasured memory of Portugal's contribution to

Africa's history. It was King John's expectation that the Cape might open a passage from the Atlantic to the Indian Ocean, thence to the Portuguese-controlled East Indies. Ten years later Vasco da Gama landed at the Cape, but only to replenish his water supplies. Curious Khoikhoi gathered to stare in awe at their first white men, only to have one of their number shot dead by a sailor's crossbow bolt. The Khoikhoi fled and the die was cast for future mistrust between the races. Vasco da Gama then sailed further north along the lush coastline, far beyond the point previously reached by Diaz, and on Christmas Day he named the spray-swept coast *Terra Natalis* before sailing on to cross the Indian Ocean. Due to the dangerous currents and treacherous ocean breakers that pounded the African shoreline, the green hills of the interior were to remain unexplored until the mid seventeenth century; before then the only landings made were accidental, usually involving shipwrecks; few survived the surf. In the years that followed, isolated Portuguese stations were established in modern-day Mozambique and it was to these stations that the handful of surviving shipwrecked sailors rendered the first known accounts of the fearsome Bantu people. The stations were usually established on the sites of thriving Arab slave and trading posts. As a consequence, the Portuguese adopted the Arab word for these black people; the word used was *kaffir*, which meant 'unbeliever', and at that time lacked the derogatory connotations of modern times.

While the lucrative East India trade remained the prerogative of the Portuguese the Cape was of little importance; after Spain seized Portugal, Dutch vessels were banned from Lisbon, their main storage and watering station. In 1595 the next eastbound Dutch fleet investigated the Cape and discovered sound moorings and plentiful water supplies. The only other ships known to have entered the Cape bay in this period of time were commanded by Captain Lancaster, who was later to command the first English East India fleet. Using his knowledge, his company ships also used the Cape as a convenient staging post. Meanwhile, ships of the English East India Company regularly used the victualling facilities of Table Bay. Aware of growing foreign interest in the Cape, the dominant seagoing nation of the time, the Dutch, actively discouraged other ships from visiting the area, alleging the dangers of its treacherous shore. Nevertheless, Francis Drake had fully charted the Cape coast in 1580 and the British knew it to be a relatively safe haven; Drake had written:

> We found the report of the Portuguese to be most false. They affirm that it is the most dangerous cape in the world, never without intolerable storms and present dangers to travellers who come near the same. This cape is the most stately thing, and the fairest cape we have seen in the whole circumference of the earth.[1]

As the years went by, the number of trading ships rounding the Cape greatly increased; its natural harbour was ideally suited as a watering point on the long haul around Africa to the Indies, but little more. By 1650 it was common practice for Dutch ships outbound for the Indies to deposit mail at the Cape under a prominent rock where it remained until collected by a homebound vessel, but apart from this strange role as a forwarding post office the Cape saw no immediate further activity.

Then in 1651 the Generale Vereenigde Nederlantsche Geoctroyeerde Oostindische Compagnie, better known as the Dutch East India Company, established the first permanent white settlement in southern Africa. They built a small fortified enclave intended to provide fresh food and water to their ships rounding the Cape en route to their distant destinations. The company was controlled by a powerful council of seventeen members based in Amsterdam and with important commercial interests in Japan, Malaysia, the East Indies and Formosa. As the company's Far Eastern trade increased, a more permanent victualling station at the Cape became essential and a tenacious former ship's surgeon of the company and previous visitor to the Cape, Jan Van Riebeeck, was chosen as the founder leader to develop the Cape settlement. In 1652 Van Riebeeck's growing band of settlers constructed a fortified camp. They duly expanded by trading their European goods with the Hottentots for cattle and sheep and Van Riebeeck's settlement quickly prospered, marred only by attacks from the numerous lion and leopard living on the Cape peninsula. In

1662 the Dutch settlers secured vast tracts of additional land from the Hottentots in exchange for goods worth only £10, and the whole location became known as 'The Cape of Good Hope' after the vessel *Good Hope* that sank in the bay. The first company employees and settlers began arriving from Holland shortly afterwards.

Many of the *Freiburgers*, the familiar term for those pioneer farmers who had worked out their contracts for the Dutch East Indies Company, chose to make their homes around the company settlement of 'Good Hope' rather than return to the uncertainties of life in Holland. Over the years that followed, limited settlement took place and as sovereignty of the Cape changed hands, the vast majority of those displaced by change stayed on as farmers and began to progress further inland. Here there was unlimited land for the taking, blessed not only with better grazing but also with absolute freedom from petty administrators. These people, together with an increasing immigration of French, German and Dutch settlers, created a tough new race; they co-operated with each other and collectively adopted the name 'Boer' to describe their predominantly agricultural way of life. Their farms were vast by European standards as land was free and relatively unpopulated; they had merely to register their property with the supervising chartered company, a process that was nothing more than a simple formality. In due course this influx had grown into a community of over 10,000 settler and refugee families that stretched for 600 miles inland from Cape Town; numerous inter-Boer political disputes followed concerning farmers' land rights and in 1795 matters deteriorated to the extent that the two frontier districts of Swellendam and Graaff-Reinet threatened insurrection. It was to avoid such political restrictions and disputes that the isolationist Boers continued to migrate away from the developing administrative complexity of life at the Cape.

As the Boers moved progressively towards the open lands to the north and east they provided for themselves and obtained those items that they needed, such as lead and powder for their guns, from a growing number of passing traders. These hardy European farmers unwillingly shared the land with the scattered local natives, the San and Khoikhoi, though it was to be another century and a half before they were to come into physical contact with the black-skinned Bantu people living further to the north-east. Limited European contact had been made with the San but due to the latter's wildness and bewildering language of clicks and glottal sounds, trade with them was non-existent; even when captured as children they made impossible servants. Equally disagreeable to the Europeans was the San's nakedness and unusual genitalia, the semi-erect penis and the pronounced female labia; likewise, their propensity not to wash led to the Boer belief that the San were little better than the animals they hunted.

In 1712 the Europeans inadvertently brought smallpox to the Cape, which reduced the white population by a quarter and virtually wiped out the Cape Khoikhoi; it then spread through the San tribes. Yet the few San survivors of the disease were still feared, partly because of their use of poisoned arrow tips for hunting or when defending themselves, and they continued to suffer persecution by black and white alike. By the 1840s the San were so reduced in numbers due to the 'blind eye' policy of open slaughter that they faced extermination; Sunday afternoon 'Bushman shoots' were still a feature of European farming life and only those who fled towards the desolate Kalahari were to survive. It was not until the early twentieth century that Europeans became aware that these primitive people had an appreciation of music and art; fine examples of their delicately coloured wall paintings can still be seen today on numerous rocky outcrops across South Africa, including the eastern face of the Oskarsberg at Rorke's Drift. As the famous African explorer Sir Laurens van der Post wrote of the San, 'they were dealt a rotten hand'.[2]

In 1688 over 200 Protestant French Huguenots arrived. The Huguenots were forced to flee France after the revocation of the Edict of Nantes made Protestant worship unlawful there. The majority fled to Britain, some 50,000 souls in all; others went as far afield as Germany, Scandinavia and Canada to escape savage persecution and torture in their home country. Many smuggled themselves and their children across the border into Holland by adopting disguises or hiding in wine barrels. Those caught by French officials were severely treated: most were imprisoned and the women detained in convents where they were punished with hard labour as well as being roundly abused. Although kindly treated by the Dutch population these religious refugees were not encouraged to remain in Holland but earnestly urged to emigrate to the Cape, and most complied. Within a generation of their arrival at the Cape they had ceased to speak French, yet from those original 200 immigrants, their number multiplied until by the 1970s one million white South Africans could trace their descendants back to the original Huguenots.

The Khoikhoi had lived in the area for over 1,000 years and differed from the San by being taller, and in their appearance were more like the Bantu people but with a distinct coppery brown tinge to their colouring. They lived in family and small clan groupings with an established leadership hierarchy. They kept cattle and although they knew of the bow and arrow, they preferred to use the spear, which enabled them to maintain their dominance over the diminutive San. The Khoikhoi lived predominantly in two distinct groups, the strandlopers or beach dwellers who lived by fishing, and those who lived off the land as nomadic farmers and hunters. It has been estimated that before the smallpox epidemic of 1712, the five known Khoikhoi tribes in the Cape area amounted to no more than 15,000 people, including women and children.[3] Shipborne smallpox returned to the Cape in 1755 with even more serious consequences; in the month of July alone more than 1,100 people died.

As the surviving Khoikhoi gradually displaced the San, so they in turn were displaced by the steady expansion of the Boers. The Khoikhoi were more amenable to change and to trading with the Europeans and, in time, they accepted the role of menial workers; later a few became soldiers, some serving the British and some the Boer cause. Boer men were not averse to associating with Khoikhoi and other slave women, and a significant number of mixed-race children resulted from these liaisons; these offspring were destined for a difficult life of rejection by all other races and in time were collectively known as the 'Bastaards'.

The Boers' appetite for both domestic servants and slaves steadily increased and these had to be imported from the north-eastern coast of Africa and from the Dutch East Indies.[4] Harmony between the Boers and other races was never achieved and in 1739 the Boers undertook a 'Bushman War' with disastrous consequences for both the San and Hottentot peoples; further such wars soon followed. It was not until 1769 that the Cape whites made their first contact with the dark-skinned natives of the eastern Cape area, known today as the Bantu nation; this contact also resulted in tumult and conflict.

The origins of the Bantu are uncertain but archaeological discoveries indicate that they entered central Africa, perhaps from the Middle East, as long ago as 8,000 BC. As their lives had always been based upon cattle they were well suited to a nomadic life and in due course spread south and then west across central Africa, eventually reaching the area known today as the Congo. Their slow thousand-year migration continued south-east around the wastes of the Kalahari desert where they occupied the verdant coastline of the Indian Ocean before expanding further south towards the Cape. It is ironic that a migration of such magnitude and over such a long span of time should have failed to reach the Cape and that Europeans should fill that vacuum at exactly the same point in time. To the Boers' surprise, their own large migration to the north-east came unexpectedly face to face with the foremost Nguni group, the amaXhosa, moving in even greater numbers southwards, the two sides meeting on opposing banks of the Great Fish river in 1769.

Neither side had much experience of the other though the Boers quickly discovered that this new race were far more defiant than the San and Khoikhoi. The amaXhosa fiercely contested attempts by the Boers to cross and settle on their side of the river and ferocious raids and vicious attacks by both sides regularly occurred. The two opposing migrations were competing for the same natural resources and the disputed boundary area created a pattern of conflict between the black and white races that was to shape the future of southern Africa into modern times. The first of these frontier conflicts took place in 1780 when the Boers attempted to drive the local Xhosa tribes from the immediate area. The Boer leader, Van Jaarsveld, adopted a novel approach to the problem: one of his riders would enter the chosen village and throw tobacco onto the ground, and in the ensuing mêlée Jaarsveld and his men approached the scrabbling mass and opened fire, killing over 200 on one occasion. The war ended during July with over 5,000 cattle seized and an unknown number of Xhosa killed. There followed an uneasy peace that deteriorated into the second Frontier War of 1793 when a sizeable horde of Xhosa crossed the river border, murdering settlers and seizing their cattle; severe destruction, brutal retribution and reprisals thereafter caused much suffering on both sides.

In 1794 the Dutch formally assumed administrative control of the Cape but in the same year they were defeated by the French in the Napoleonic Wars, which opened the Cape to French warships. This caused considerable concern to the British Admiralty and Britain promptly responded by seizing the Cape in order to protect her own prosperous sea routes to India.

In 1799 began the third Frontier War which was to be waged for over two years. This particular war saw the surviving Khoikhoi join with the Xhosa against white settlers but again their predictable defeat ultimately favoured the Boer trekkers.

Meanwhile, and several hundred miles north-east beyond the Great Fish river frontier, one Bantu tribe, the Nguni, settled along several coastal rivers that led into the Indian Ocean. This left the main migration, now consisting of the predominantly Xhosa tribe, still steadily moving south. Little more than a generation after the first conflict occurred near the Cape between black and white, the Zulus began to emerge as a new tribe among the northern Nguni. The Zulu kingdom became Zululand, now known as KwaZulu Natal, and consisted of the landmass from the eastern side of the Drakensberg mountains to the Indian Ocean. Before the emergence of the Zulu nation the area was originally populated by a patchwork of independent but minor chiefdoms whose people spoke broadly the same language and followed the same cultural practices.

Along the Great Fish river border the most southerly Xhosa people and the Boers lived uneasily as neighbours; the Xhosa prized Boer cattle and the Boers coveted Xhosa lands. During one Xhosa raid the Boers were forced to abandon more than a hundred farms. Limited Boer retaliation was undertaken, but to little effect; each side remained wary of the other. The struggle for domination of the Great Fish river area finally erupted in the fourth Frontier War of 1811, which resulted in over 20,000 Xhosa being forcibly relocated beyond the far bank of the river.

By 1814 the border was becoming more of an imperial than a Boer problem. Having temporarily seized the Cape in 1806, the British had acquired the Cape Colony for the sum of £6,000,000 and they now sought to resolve the border disputes through the construction of a series of well-defended military fortifications, known as blockhouses, strategically sited along the border. The plan failed and the fifth Frontier War, now termed 'savage warfare' by the troops, broke out in 1818. In 1819 the settlement of Grahamstown, complete with its British garrison commanded by Lieutenant Colonel Willshire, was surrounded by some 10,000 angry Xhosa warriors. The Xhosa were beaten off during a two-hour battle that left over 1,000 dead and dying warriors compared with British losses of three killed and a handful wounded. The British solution to the growing border problem was to 'clear' a vast area of land between the Great Fish and Keiskamma rivers and declare the area neutral territory, which they then filled with land-hungry British settlers who had accepted the home government's generous offer of free land. Such an offer resulted in large-scale emigration from Britain whose working classes were still suffering from widespread agricultural depression following the long war with France. The local Xhosa increasingly resisted European settlement with cross-border raids against the new settlers which resulted in the sixth Frontier War of 1834–5; this was another brutal conflict which left nearly 1,500 Xhosa and 100 colonial fatalities. One noted casualty was Chief Hintsa who surrendered to the British commander; his tribe was given an impossible ransom for his release so he stole a horse and tried to escape.

He was pulled off his horse, shot through the back and through the leg. Desperately he scrambled down the riverbank and collapsed into the watercourse. A scout named George Southey, coming up fast behind him, blew off the top of his head. Then some soldiers cut off his ears as keepsakes to show around the military camps. Others tried to dig out his teeth with bayonets.[5]

Again, no resolution was found and following the murder of a British escort to a Xhosa prisoner who had stolen an axe, the seventh Frontier War, 'the war of the axe', was undertaken throughout 1846. This war ebbed and flowed until the now desperate Khoikhoi, Xhosa and Thembu joined forces in 1850 for the eighth Frontier War. The war was fought over land that was again stricken by drought and in the midst of the starvation and death, a girl gave birth to a two-headed baby. Although the baby died within days, the birth was seen as a sign to continue the war, which lasted for two years and only ended with the battle of Fort Armstrong. The war's end resulted in an even stronger line of defence for the Boers, now fully supported by the British. In 1857 the Xhosa were further decimated when a young girl, Nongqawuse, prophesied that the whites would be driven from their land if the Xhosa slaughtered all their cattle and burned their crops. The Gcaleka chief, Sarhili, ordered his people to fulfil the prophecy; the resultant famine killed thousands of Xhosa while others fled towards the Cape. The famine was used by the British to move waiting German settlers into the region and the whole area was brought under British control.

Meanwhile Dutch influence had long since failed at the Cape which, in 1806, had finally and permanently been annexed by Britain; this coincided with a new British colonial policy of self-finance through taxation, a form of revenue that was alien to both the Dutch traders and the isolated Boer farmers. Even while the Cape Border Wars were raging, new circumstances involving taxation and legislative controls were gradually evolving that would seriously undermine relationships between the British and the Boers, the two dominant European groups at the Cape.

In 1807 slavery was abolished internationally but this and taxation had little immediate effect on the Boers, due both to their isolation and to the distances between their farms and the British administrators. The new Cape legal system relied on the Black Circuit, a system of travelling courts established by the British in an attempt to establish a fair system of justice for all, though the Boers recognized it as being biased against them in favour of natives generally. Matters deteriorated for the Boers when the anti-slavery missionaries recognized the potential of using the system to bring Boer farmers to trial for keeping slaves; one enthusiastic missionary laid twenty different complaints in just six months. This zealousness frequently led to accused Boer farmers having to leave their families and farms unprotected and at the mercy of marauders while they travelled hundreds of miles to answer charges that were frequently of a political or malicious nature.

In 1815 an incident occurred which was to create eternal animosity between Boer and Briton. Two brothers, Frederick and Johannes Bezuidenhout, lived roughly as farmers near Slagters Nek, nearly 100 miles to the north of Port Elizabeth. Frederick kept a Hottentot slave named 'Boy' whom he regularly thrashed. Encouraged by a missionary, Boy made a number of formal complaints to the authorities, alleging illegal rough treatment. Bezuidenhout refused to communicate with the authorities, and in order to get him to answer the allegations the Landdrost (magistrate) eventually issued a summons for his arrest. The summons went unanswered and Bezuidenhout was found guilty in his absence. A British military detachment of one bailiff escorted by two officers, a sergeant, two corporals and a troop of Hottentot soldiers were dispatched to arrest him. An exchange of fire took place and Bezuidenhout was shot dead. The deceased's brother, Johannes, together with a few other like-minded Boers, commenced a feeble insurrection that attracted a disproportionately severe military response. In a brief skirmish, Johannes Bezuidenhout was killed and a number of his fellow conspirators were arrested. They were duly tried and convicted; the five ringleaders received the death sentence, to die on the public gallows at the appropriately named Slagters Nek or Slaughterer's Pass.

The date of execution was fixed for 9 March 1815 and sentence was ordered to be carried out in the presence of the local Boer population under the supervision of the two local Landdrosts, Cuyler and Stockenstrom. When the gallows lever was pulled, four of the five ropes broke simultaneously, dropping four of the accused in a breathless heap. There was much wailing and consternation followed by a delay while fresh rope was sought; during this time the four huddled with their distraught families and friends while others fervently implored for their release on the logical grounds that the broken ropes were an obvious Act of God. The British were not swayed by the argument and persisted with the execution until the hapless four were finally dispatched; one, the 29-year-old Theunis de Klerk, endured four attempts before the rope finally held him. A priest appointed by the authorities to oversee the executions commented that the British would forever regret that day.

After Slagters Nek, revolt fanned through the Boer population and secret meetings went on late into many a night across the veld. The Boers were a hardy new race; they called themselves Afrikaners and they fiercely resented any interference with their way of life, and most of all politically motivated executions. They owed allegiance only to God, themselves and to Africa (hence the name Afrikaners). They were fully aware that the whole of Africa lay to the east and the north; surely it was possible, many asked, to move there and live in peace? Being devoutly religious, they fervently prayed for a solution and, inevitably, the solution stared them in the face. Because they had sought help through prayer, the obvious answer took on a religious significance and many Boers came to believe the trek was ordered by God. The final indignity to be endured, which precipitated the trek, came in 1834 with yet more British legislation, including the Act of Emancipation, which gave equality to all regardless of their race, colour, creed or station in life. As prodigious users of slaves, found this too much and some of the wealthier Boers responded by threatening to sell their farms and head for the uncharted African interior.

Without doubt, the most influential Voortrekker was the aristocratic

Piet Retief who was highly respected by Boers and British alike. Although a failed businessman, he was also a wily politician, a wealthy farmer and a field commandant. His eventual approval of the trek was the spark that ignited the fire of mass disaffection among the Boers. His mind was probably made up with the passing of the 1834 Act of Emancipation, which finally abolished slavery; compensation was offered but payment had to be made in London. No Boer could afford this undertaking and the loss of their slave workforce would have destroyed many Boer businesses and farms. To gain a few months' grace, the Boers designated their slaves as 'apprentices' while they busily prepared for the trek; curiously, the undertaking did not have the blessing of the United Dutch Reform Church.

The purpose of the Great Trek, once under way, was to discover new land where they could establish their own Boer law-abiding state and live totally independent of British rule. It was their overwhelming frustration that led to this extraordinary and carefully considered emigration of nearly 12,000 Boers, probably a fifth of their people, together with a similar number of servants and apprentices. The trek took place over several years and many parties perished at the hands of, firstly, the northern Matabele and then, as they progressed further east and north, the Bantu. Two other large parties perished when they attempted to cross the Kalahari desert; they were never seen again and no trace of their wagons has ever been found. Several influential families initiated the trek and became known as the Voortrekkers or trek leaders. Many names are well known to students of South African history, people such as the Tregardts, who were of Swedish origin, and the Van Rensburgs, who were slaughtered by the Matabele as they entered unknown territory to the north. As the treks progressed three men came to the fore: Maritz, Uys and Retief. Maritz and Uys pressed on, seeking their promised land to the north, while Retief pondered the possibility of his promised land being somewhere east of the Drakensberg mountains.

When Retief left his farm and set off with twenty-five families, their wagons, servants and herds, the news spread rapidly and others rushed to join the Retief column. At the Orange river over 300 trekkers and their entourages joined Retief while others followed the trails left by his wagons. Piet Retief wrote bitterly in his diary of British oppression, which he believed was deliberately biased in favour of non-whites, and added:

> We leave this fruitful land of our birth in which we have suffered enormous losses and continual vexation and are about to enter a strange and dangerous territory. We go relying on merciful God whom we shall fear and humbly endeavour to obey.[6]

On 17 April 1837 his group joined a larger column under the leadership of Gert Maritz. At a trekker meeting, Retief was elected overall leader giving him a command of nearly 5,000 trekkers with over 1,000 wagons and huge herds of cattle and sheep. Retief made strict rules and gave orders to control the multitude, which included instructions that the local clans were not to be molested, native servants were to be properly treated and game was only to be shot for the pot. Order was maintained by a system of field commandants and offenders were punished with fines. His policy towards the native chiefs through whose territory they passed was one of friendship and, while reports from trekkers to the north indicated hostile Matabele, his advance scouts were reporting most favourably on the lands east of the Drakensberg mountains and towards the Indian Ocean, the land of the Zulus.

Retief knew the reputation of the inhabitants there, a little-understood warrior nation, but he was confident that he could negotiate land rights for his people. Accordingly he made plans to cross the Drakensberg mountains to negotiate for settlement land with the Zulu leader, King Dingane. Retief and fifteen Boers travelled to meet the king and by early October 1837 they had crossed the Drakensberg and headed towards the small white settlement on the coast of the Indian Ocean, later to be called Durban. Towards the end of October they arrived to a most cordial welcome from the hundred or so English settlers who were fully aware that a Boer settlement inland would afford them added security against any marauding Zulus. To smooth his route to King Dingane, Retief sent him a warm and friendly letter in which he expressed his wish to discuss the possibility of a peaceful and profitable Boer settlement in the vicinity of the Drakensberg mountains. Retief knew that an English missionary, Francis Owen, lived at the king's *amakhanda* and could translate his letter to King Dingane.

Once they had crossed the Drakensberg mountains, the well-watered grasslands through which Retief and his party travelled appeared ideal for their settlement, being totally devoid of human population. What was unknown to the unsuspecting Boers was the reason for the depopulation, namely the *umfecane*, and the subsequent slaughter of surrounding tribes by King Shaka when he had expanded his empire some fifteen years previously.[7] Little was known of King Dingane except that he was overweight and that he exercised autocratic control over the Zulu people. Although Dingane had killed his famous half-brother Shaka and was known to murder any opponent out of hand, Dingane's reputation may not have unduly perturbed the well-armed Boers but, with all events considered, perhaps more caution should have been used. Dingane was also fully aware that Retief's equally well-armed fellow trekkers to the north were being successfully harassed by the Matabele, with whom the Zulus had been in indecisive conflict in 1830. King Dingane's reply to Retief was nevertheless friendly; he even returned some sheep that had previously been stolen from the trekkers and with Thomas Halstead, a fellow Boer linguist, as his interpreter, Retief set off in anticipation of a successful outcome.

On about 5 November 1837 the party approached King Dingane's *amakhanda* at Mgungundhlovu, near modern-day Ulundi. Retief must have been impressed; the *amakhanda* consisted of a fortification containing over 2,000 huts, each capable of housing twenty people, and with another 300 larger huts for the king's personal use, his wives and his senior *indunas*. He was even more impressed by the eight days of celebration, feasting, dancing and displays which went on endlessly and which must have exhausted and frustrated the Boers. Missionary Owen was present throughout and it is due to his meticulous diary, discovered only in 1922 at the Missionary Hall in London, that we now accurately know of the horrendous events that unfurled.

At the end of the eighth day, King Dingane informed Retief that he would be granted permission to settle where he requested – subject to Retief first recovering cattle that had been stolen from the king by a rival chief, Sikonyela. Retief accepted the arrangement and returned to his settlers who, without his permission, had begun to stake their claims towards the Tugela river. Other trekkers, encouraged by the promising news, were enthusiastically following across the Drakensberg mountains in the anticipation of bountiful grazing. Retief gathered seventy of his best fighting men to undertake the mission against Sikonyela and immediately following the celebration of Christmas, Retief's expedition set out for Sikonyela's homestead, leaving the main party in the care of the youths and elderly Boers, though without instructions for the remaining families to laager or to prepare defensive positions.

Within the week they arrived and, on the pretext of presenting Sikonyela with a bracelet, snapped the chief into handcuffs and held him prisoner while the stolen cattle were collected. Sikonyela was then released and Retief headed back towards King Dingane's *amakhanda* in optimistic mood and with the recovered cattle. Prior to Retief's return to Mgungundhlovu on 3 February 1838, Missionary Owen had observed an unusually large number of young warriors arriving at the *amakhanda*; he also recorded in his diary hearing rumours that the king was annoyed at reports from his spies that Retief had permitted Chief Sikonyela to live. Retief immediately returned the stolen cattle to an apparently appreciative King Dingane whereupon the celebratory feasting recommenced. For several days Retief and his men were obliged to watch the ritual entertainment held in their honour until, on 6 February, following an impressive display of horsemanship and firearms salvoes by the Boers, Retief was finally called before the king. In the presence of the senior *indunas* King Dingane allegedly gave verbal permission for the Boer settlement; everything promised by the king was written down by the Boer scribe, Jan Bantjes, who then translated it back into Zulu for the benefit of the assembled *indunas*. According to Boer legend King Dingane and the three most senior *indunas* then signed the document before Retief placed it in his leather pouch for safety.[8]

As Retief was about to depart he and his men were invited to one final feast. Not wishing to appear discourteous or impatient, Retief reluctantly agreed. The Zulu *indunas* respectfully reminded Retief that it was impolite for anyone to enter the king's *amakhanda* with firearms and Retief readily agreed; all their firearms were stacked outside the enclosure next to their horses. The feast commenced and hundreds of young warriors began their series of dances. Suddenly King Dingane rose to his feet and a chilling silence descended on the multitude. He called out, '*Babulaleni abathakathi*' (Kill the wizards!) and before the unsuspecting Boers realized what fate held for them, they were seized and bound hand and foot with leather thongs. They were then dragged several hundred yards to the hill of execution, deliberately sited by the *amakhanda* main gate to remind residents and visitors of the king's power. Missionary Owen was watching the whole event through his telescope just as a warrior arrived at his house with a reassuring message from the king to the effect that Owen and his family need have no fear for their lives.

At the hill of execution each Boer in turn had his arms and legs broken with knobkerries before being untied and then clubbed to death. Retief was made to watch the orgy of torture and death, including that of his 12-year-old son, before he too was executed. The bodies were then thrown over the cliff for disposal by wild animals and the resident flock of vultures. Owen wrote in his diary that he fainted from the shock, as did his wife.

Also murdered were the thirty or so native servants who accompanied Retief's party; only one escaped, named Lomana, who was guarding the Boers' horses outside the King's *amakhanda*. He escaped the slaughter and lived to tell the tale until he died near Weenen in 1909. Rumours still exist that a number of Boer women were with the party and that they too were murdered. There is no evidence that this was the case though Owen's diary records that those slain included a number of Boer boy riders, 'some under the age of 11'. King Dingane decreed that no Boer, woman or child, should survive on his land. Owen's next diary entry reveals that, 'within two hours, a large impi was gathered and almost immediately departed the king's homestead'.

Disaster of a colossal magnitude was about to befall the unsuspecting Boer families gathering in the area now known as Bloukranze and Weenen; all were totally unsuspecting and eagerly anticipated Retief's return with the promised permission to settle. Under cover of darkness, the Zulu *impi* approached the sleeping Boer families and then launched their merciless attack. Immediately south of the Tugela river the most appalling horror and bloodshed was unleashed. Throughout that Friday night and the following day the trekkers further back from the direct line of attack sought desperately to rally whatever men they could and bring the remaining women and children to the relative safety of wagons hastily drawn up into protective laagers. By dawn on the Sunday, the stabbed and mutilated bodies of 531 elderly Boer men, women and children were spread over an area of 20 square miles. An estimated 300 coloured servants had also died violently at the hands of King Dingane's warriors.

The surviving trek leaders, Maritz and Cilliers, were helpless to prevent thousands of head of cattle, sheep and horses from being driven off by the Zulus. While the survivors surveyed the terrible scenes of death and devastation a Boer scouting party arrived with news that the Zulus had withdrawn. But grieving had to wait; much was to be done to prevent the circling vultures from descending. The days ahead were critical in view of the possibility of a renewed assault and the crucial decision had to be made whether to trek back over the mountains and abandon Natal or take revenge. A clear majority, especially of the women, forcefully insisted on punishment and retribution. The decision of a public meeting late in March was that the combination of the highly respected Boer leaders Potgieter and Uys would be granted equal status, each to command his own men, in order to punish King Dingane.

Early in April the first punitive expedition of 347 well-armed men departed from the main Boer laagers. Across the Buffalo river, at the Italeni valley, the waiting Zulus camouflaged themselves as cattle by hiding under their cowhide shields and easily decoyed Uys and his followers into a carefully planned trap. Potgieter, deeply suspicious, held back; the Uys strategy of rounding up Zulu cattle did not appeal to him at all. Soon encircled by the Zulus, Uys and his men tried desperately to shoot their way clear in order to escape the overwhelming odds but in the process Uys was fatally stabbed and his young son, Dirkie, not wishing to leave his father, also perished.

Potgieter and his men now had to face the waiting trekkers and report their failure. Panic once again set in at the realization of defeat and, even worse, another leader's death; renewed serious thought was given to abandoning Natal. Potgieter was labelled a coward and accused of treason. He left Natal a haunted man and, due to the seriousness of the situation, many others were tempted to follow him back to the Cape.

Once again it was the women who implored their menfolk to remain, this time fiercely demanding that King Dingane should be made to pay personally. Conditions for the Boers were extremely difficult and the constant threat of Zulu attacks forced them to remain in laager. Local grazing was soon exhausted and the Boers' food supplies were minimal. Crisis loomed; Maritz was on his own and within weeks he became desperately ill and died. Like Moses, he saw the Promised Land but was not destined to live in it.

A month or so after Maritz's untimely death another Boer leader, Andries Pretorius, responded positively to a plea to join the trekkers in the vicinity of the Little Tugela near Loskop. The trekkers' situation was extremely grave; Pretorius found a demoralized people and an epidemic of measles raging through the Boer camps. Pretorius was immediately elected Commandant General and within days he set out with another force of 468 well-armed men along with 120 coloured servants and sixty-four battle wagons. Each wagon was drawn by only ten oxen, as they would be very lightly loaded; though cumbersome and slow-moving, they would be absolutely essential for forming a laager. Wherever the scene of battle was likely to be, it would be grassland and therefore it was imperative to prepare 'veghekke', or fighting gates, in order to deny to the Zulus any gaps between the wagons drawn together for protection. Ammunition bags were prepared in order to make reloading of old muzzle-loading muskets quicker; biltong, rusks and coffee were to suffice as rations. A strong disciplinarian, Pretorius demanded total obedience and made it clear that he would not tolerate independent dissidence, the factor that led to the previous undoing of the Boers and which was to prove a problem in future. Proclaiming 'Unity is Strength' (to become the Transvaal Republic motto and later that of the Union), he did not hesitate to take the preacher Sarel Cilliers to task when he volunteered to lead some fifty men into what surely would have amounted to a repeat of the recent rout at Italeni.

Ever the tactician, Maritz had wisely thought to bring with him two of his personal small cannons. These, and a longer-range ship's cannon belonging to Pretorius, were to prove invaluable. On the eve of the battle some 700 oxen and 750 horses along with the wagon leaders and trekkers (among them three Englishmen) were brought into the roughly D-shaped laager. Whip-sticks supporting lanterns were in readiness should the *impi* attack during that night. However, a thick mist prevented the warriors from creeping nearer; but, ironically, the heavy mist seriously alarmed the trekkers as the threat of their gunpowder becoming damp and useless was very real.

The mist lifted at daybreak as the trekkers waited for the inevitable Zulu attack and the fact that it was Sunday gave the dramatically tense situation a special religious significance for them although it was of no consequence to the Zulus. Commanded by Chief Ndlela, the Zulus charged the Boer position but were unable to breach the barrier of wagons. In spite of the din of battle, the animals within the laager did not panic, as the Boers had feared; they could so easily have wreaked havoc by breaking loose and stampeding to escape the confines of a relatively small enclosure. Victory was assured by mid morning as the *impi* fled; released from the defensive position the mounted Boers gave chase and hastened the Zulus' speedy withdrawal.

Although the battle of Blood River has long been considered to be one of the greatest victories in Boer history, the trekkers had, in fact, laid themselves open to siege. How much longer would those animals have behaved under such stressful circumstances without grazing? How much longer would the ammunition, the food and, above all, the water have lasted? The lessons learned after the earlier Boer defeat at Vegkop alerted the Boers to the fact that the Zulus, victorious or otherwise, always drove away stock. Chief Ndlela had been determined to attack the Boers during darkness and in doing so, his plan could possibly have met with success had the night not been so dark and misty resulting in the Zulu army repeatedly losing themselves as they tried to surround the Boers. Fortunately for the Boers, the dawn caught Ndlela's force divided by the river, and at opposing ends of the Boer position.

The official copy of the battle report displayed at the Blood River Museum boldly describes the short battle that followed, and explains how the Ncome river became known as Blood River.

The mist gradually cleared and Sunday dawned bright and clear. Pretorius gave the order to shoot as soon as sights and targets could be distinguished. With a total disregard for danger, the Zulus charged but within a quarter of an hour they were forced to withdraw to a position 500 metres away. When they launched the second attack they were fired upon with deadly accuracy. Once again, the Zulu attack was repulsed and they retreated to a distance of 400 metres. Pretorius now directed the copper cannon towards the hill where the leaders of the Zulu force congregated. The second and third rounds burst among the Indunas and led to a third fierce attack lasting nearly an hour.

Soon after the Zulus had retreated once again a mounted commando of a few hundred men led by Field Cornet Bart Pretorius launched an attack upon them. Twice the commando was driven back but at the third attempt, they managed to split the Zulu force in two. The greater part of the commando force now emerged from the laager and deployed from the north and south along the river where hundreds of fleeing Zulus were shot amongst the reeds and in the river until the river ran red. At this point Ndlela's three thousand crack impis went into action. They attempted to cross the river at the drifts above and below the hippo pool but were swept along by the hordes of fleeing warriors being shot down by the Boers. At last the entire Zulu army took flight in all directions. The pursuit lasted until midday when the commando returned to the laager where 3,000 Zulus lay dead.

Zulu folklore certainly acknowledges a Boer presence at Blood River but not that a major battle took place, nor that they suffered such serious casualties. In 1999 a new Zulu museum was built on the Zulu river bank overlooking the battle site, and as visitors there discover, claims of any Boer victory are strongly rebutted. Disregarding the cross-river interpretation of events, it is curious that the Boers, armed with antiquated firearms, are still believed by their descendants to have accounted for 3,000 Zulu fatalities in the same time-span that the British defenders at Rorke's Drift, armed with sophisticated breech-loading Martini-Henry rifles, also used at point-blank range, accounted for only 351 Zulus. Nevertheless, it was at Blood River that the Zulus learned to avoid a tightly compacted enemy in possession of firearms. They also discovered that the rounds fired by the Boers had a limited effective range. Over a distance of more than 100 yards the Boer low-velocity rounds would bounce off an angled shield. This knowledge resulted in the Zulu belief that their shields were magical, especially when doctored with magic *muti*, a belief strongly held and maintained for the next sixty years until the Zulus met the British at the battle of Isandlwana.

According to Boer history, Pretorius then seized the initiative and, with the Zulus in disarray, he led an élite mounted group of Boers towards the now abandoned and still smouldering ruins at Mgungundhlovu with the intention of giving a Christian burial to the mortal remains of the Retief party, exposed to the harsh extremes of the elements for ten months and under the eyes of an ever-watchful flock of vultures provided with carcasses on a regular basis. Pretorius apparently found Retief's body still with his bag containing the treaty signed by King Dingane. The miraculous recovery of the treaty, together with the eyewitness reports of those who found it, along with the details of its content, were accepted without question until some eighty years later when the account of the battle came under close scrutiny. Then, in 1923, a heated debate ensued; indeed, a Cape judge who had visited Natal in 1843 claimed that 'the deed or writing formally ceding this territory to the emigrant farmers was written out by the Reverend Owen'. Yet on the day previous to Retief's massacre Owen, now an apparent eyewitness to Dingane's treachery and the alleged very writer of that document, must have been in a state of extreme shock when he recorded in his diary:

> Two of the Boers paid me a visit this morning and breakfasted only an hour or two before they were called to eternity. When I asked them what they thought of Dingane, they said he was good; so unsuspicious were they of his intentions. He had promised to assign over to them the whole country between the Tugela and the Umzimvubu [sic] rivers, and 'this day the paper of transfer was to be signed'.[9]

The Reverend Owen made no mention in his diary of having ever written the treaty and certainly did not know that it had been signed two days before. Discrepancies would undoubtedly abound if the treaty could be found and examined – if only in that three Zulu witnesses had allegedly signed their names. Could they write, and if they could, who had taught them? Accounts by the trekkers themselves certainly differ greatly. Was forgery necessary? Perhaps so: the Boers knew that their actions against the Zulus would be questioned by both the London Missionary Society and the British government who would certainly oppose their occupation of Natal. A mutually signed document was imperative to validate the considerable number of Boer claims to settle in Natal. A point of interest is that when the noted Afrikaner G.E. Cory made a public address in Bloemfontein in 1923, he also cast a thoroughly researched doubt on the treaty's genuineness, possibly as a result of the discovery of Owen's diary. The ensuing emotional storm forced him initially to silence then to sanctuary, until the occasion of the opening of Piet Retief's old Cape home, on the eve of the Day of the Vow, 15 December 1923. Addressing the meeting, Cory made a public apology and declared that he had been mistaken in his findings and that the treaty was in fact genuine. And that was the end of that particular matter.

A memorial church was built, today a fine museum housing Voortrekker artefacts including Retief's glass flask bearing the mason's insignia which was purportedly rescued from the scene of mutilation where, according to the accompanying museum description, 'about nine or ten Zulus to each Boer dragging their helpless unarmed victim to the fatal spot where they commenced the work of death by striking them on the head with knobbed sticks'. It is perhaps more likely that this flask was found along with other various items retrieved from what remained of King Dingane's great *amakhanda*. Retief's satchel, having survived intense extremes of weather and protected the treaty so miraculously, then seems to have conveniently disappeared, as did the original treaty, during the Boer War six decades on. The battle of Blood River has nevertheless been a mighty symbol, ruthlessly exploited since 1838, to further the political and religious cause of the Afrikaner. Professor Ben Liebenberg has argued that earlier Afrikaner historians exaggerated the significance of the battle out of all proportion. He wrote:

> This view, that Blood River saved the great trek overestimates the significance of the battle. At that stage, only a section of the Voortrekkers were in Natal. The rest were in the present Transvaal and Orange Free State and they wanted to live there. If the Zulus had won at Blood River, the great trek would, at most, have failed in Natal and not elsewhere. It is therefore not correct to say that the victory at Blood River saved the great trek.[10]

Regardless of events at Blood River, Boer farmers continued to trickle into the more northern reaches of Zululand while the British concentrated on developing Natal and mistakenly left Zululand and the 'Boer problem' to Dingane's successor, King Mpande. Britain annexed Natal in 1844 and it became a British colony the following year; most of the Natal Boers abandoned their farms in protest and set off to rejoin the other fledgling Boer 'republics' seeking independence from British rule. The gathering Boer trekkers began settling on the central plateau. They named the settled area the 'Free Province of New Holland in South East Africa' and its centre of crowded wagons became known as 'Pietermaritzburg' after two Boer notables, Piet Retief and Gert Maritz. At the same time the British formally occupied Port Natal and renamed it 'Durban' after Sir Benjamin D'Urban, Governor of the Cape Colony, and the relationship between the Zulu kings and the British authorities in southern Africa remained sympathetic. In January 1853 and February 1854 respectively, Britain first recognized the Voortrekkers' South African Republic (the Transvaal) and then the Orange Free State; it was a desperate gesture to offload the enormous financial and military burden of protecting these two Boer states. It was also a shrewd political gamble to protect the valuable British coastal colony of Natal from the incessant conflicts of the African interior. By 1878 the problem of white incursion had grown out of control, and the British would be forced to act.

CHAPTER 2

The Zulus,
Defenders of the Buffalo River

A very remarkable people the Zulu.
BRITISH PRIME MINISTER DISRAELI, 1879

Neither Lieutenant General Lord Chelmsford, the senior British military commander in South Africa, nor his political master, Sir Bartle Frere, expected the Zulus to be a match for the British forces being assembled along the Natal border with Zululand. Such a positive attitude reflected an overwhelming confidence in the prowess of the British military, especially when the obvious discrepancies between the two opposing armies were considered. The British force in South Africa was tightly disciplined and well led by experienced officers and NCOs; its soldiers were battle-hardened from the recent Cape Frontier War and they were well armed with modern Martini-Henry rifles and supported by artillery. Opposing this seemingly invincible force was the Zulu army, a part-time, primitively armed native force whose military role was to serve the king as and when required. It was a necessity that had not arisen during the previous twenty-two years.

For an invasion of Zululand to succeed, the British commanders needed the support of Natal's white settler population; civilian volunteers, their wagons, horses and oxen would all be needed to supplement and support the British line regiments that would lead the invasion. A propaganda campaign was set in motion to elicit this support. A 'celibate, man-slaying machine' was Sir Bartle Frere's famous description of the Zulu army, a widely reported comment containing sufficient innuendo to stoke the fears of Natal's European population that their safety, especially that of their womenfolk, was in dire peril from the Zulus. Missionary tales of sexually frustrated warriors lusting for blood helped to create a distorted image of naked raping warriors in the minds of the European civilian population. It was an image that Frere deliberately orchestrated through the press, and he unashamedly used its acceptance by the civilian population to justify his invasion of Zululand. This propaganda was successful because so little was known of Zulu life, or of the structure and purpose of the Zulu army. Anthony Trollope, a visiting British writer who found the Zulus a complaisant people living in sympathy with their time and environment, commented:

> I have no fears myself that Natal will be overrun by hostile Zulus, but much fear that Zululand should be overrun by hostile Britons.[1]

Following the British defeat at Isandlwana, there was one question being asked across Britain that could not be answered: 'Who were the Zulus?'

Like the first Dutch settlers and now the assembling British soldiers, the Zulus had also invaded southern Africa by migrating down the east coast. One Bantu tribe, the Nguni, settled the area known today as Natal, while the remaining Bantu, the Xhosa tribe, continued south, eventually reaching the Great Fish river only 500 miles from the Cape.

The beginning of the nineteenth century had seen the more northerly Nguni chiefdoms immune from the effects of the Cape Frontier Wars. They were, however, not immune from pressure created by their own growing populations, and, resources being limited, internecine violence resulted. Four chiefs, Dingiswayo, Zwide, Matiwane and Mtimkulu, were principally responsible for the resultant catastrophic intertribal warfare and economic destruction that followed as each chief waged war on his neighbour in order to become the paramount chief. This warfare degenerated into virtual genocide of those tribes that suffered defeat and has often, but incorrectly, been attributed to Shaka; it resulted in vast tracts of land being depopulated.

The situation changed between 1816 and 1824 when the Zulu people, whose traditional lands lay on the southern bank of the White Mfolozi river and far beyond the reach of either Boer or British influence, came to dominate their neighbours; their success being due to a powerful combination of astute diplomacy and ruthless military force applied by their legendary leader, Shaka kaSenzangakona. Indeed, by the 1820s, many of the groups south of the Tugela had survived the threat of Zulu attack or of being scattered as refugees only by pledging their allegiance to Shaka. The repercussions from Shaka's autocratic reign spread far and wide. With each Zulu purge or victory, a fresh wave of refugees would fall upon their neighbouring tribe; some would blend to form new kingdoms while others fought for ascendancy. Chief Sobhuza consolidated what became the Swazi kingdom, the Ngwane and Hlubi people encroached upon the Sotho peoples while Chief Sikonyela settled his people along the Orange river; instead of finding peace, these tribes suffered raids by the growing bands of Bastaards, themselves refugees from the Cape. Things were no better to the north; Prince Mzilikazi took his tribe across the Vaal river and established the Ndebele kingdom until his people were forced by Shaka's army to move northwards where Mzilikazi occupied the Tswana chiefdom.

The Zulus were highly civilized; they enjoyed complex social structures, were competent cattle farmers and were able to make implements out of metal which was virtually equal to steel. One of these items, the throwing spear, ensured their ascendancy over any San and Khoikhoi they encountered, and would soon seriously inconvenience the whites. Their social structure valued marriage, a concept orientated more towards property than the values of conventional European marriage; its complex system of dowry payments for a wife, known as *ilobolo*, ensured that a man could not marry until he was established in society and possessed sufficient cattle to pay the required *ilobolo*. The more cattle a man had, the more wives he could buy. It was this Zulu dependency on cattle for the vital *ilobolo*, for social prestige and their subsequent wealth, which was to bring them into permanent conflict with the trekkers. To the Zulus, the Boers had more than sufficient cattle 'for the taking' and cattle-raiding was, after all, a traditional and popular Zulu activity.

Another Zulu ritual that was later to be feared, misunderstood, and which tended to give many a British soldier in southern Africa sleepless nights, was the Zulu post-battle cleansing tradition of disembowelling the enemy, usually with a knife-like weapon – rarely the assegai. To the Zulus it was essential that those slain in battle be ritually disembowelled to free any incarcerated spirit and to protect the victor from absorbing any bad spirits previously possessed by their victim. As a final cleansing rite the victor then had to have intercourse with a woman, not his wife, before returning to his clan. This practice ensured that any remaining trace of evil spirits would be left with the woman, leaving the victor clean and whole to return home. It also ensured that after battle the *impi* would rapidly and enthusiastically disperse from the battlefield for the purpose of religious cleansing.[2] Zulu warriors were only accorded any real status when they had 'washed' their spears in the blood of a defeated enemy. Both medicine and superstition played an important part in Zulu life to the extent that each clan chief was able to maintain complete control through fear by utilizing his witch doctor's ability to 'smell out' dissenters, dissension being a crime punishable with immediate execution of the offender or, in serious cases, his whole family or homestead; there was no possible appeal. Every adult male was a warrior who, on the call from his chief, would join his *amabutho*, a guild or regiment of warriors; collectively, this was a remarkably successful form of national service and bonded each age group to its chief. Zulu military tactics were in their infancy and interclan differences were traditionally resolved by each side engaging in *giya*, a process of hurling threats and some throwing of spears for an hour or two until one side felt they were in ascendancy. Such disputes rarely resulted in more than casual bloodshed but this relatively harmless system of challenge was to be short-lived.

At the time of the Xhosa's first encounter with the Boers, an insignificantly small group of between 100 and 200 Nguni people lived some 300 miles away along the banks of the White Mfolozi river. Their chief, named Zulu, was succeeded by his two brothers who then gave way to Senzangakona. During this embryonic stage of their development the group adopted the title 'Zulu' and had grown in size to well over 1,000. In about 1787 Senzangakona fathered the child of a neighbouring eLangeni chief's daughter, Nandi. Under pressure from her father, Senzangakona reluctantly appointed Nandi as his unofficial third wife but refused to recognize her son, iShaka. When the Zulus were hit by famine Nandi and her children were evicted back to the unwelcoming eLangeni, who responded by treating the family as outcasts.

In 1802 Nandi was forced to flee and sought refuge with the Qwabe clan where she had previously given birth to a son by a Qwabe warrior named Gendeyana. Under Gendeyana's patronage the family again received shelter and the young Shaka developed into such a skilled warrior that Senzangakona eventually sought his return. Shaka's reputation increased and legend records both his fearlessness when hunting wild animals and great prowess with the spear. At the age of 24 Shaka was called to join King Dingiswayo's iziCwe *ibutho*. During the next five years he closely studied the king's strategy of control over other tribes by the use of brutal and aggressive tactics, a policy frequently but incorrectly attributed to Shaka.

Now nearly 30 years of age, Shaka was appointed to lead the iziCwe regiment; he taught his warriors the close combat for which he became famous and caused the ineffective throwing spears to be melted down and recast as the long and sharp, flat-bladed stabbing spear[3] or *ikwa*, the onomatopoeic term for the sucking sound of the blade being withdrawn from a body. He ordered his regiment's traditional large shields to be cut down in size and strengthened, so that in close combat the new shield could be hooked under that of an opponent and, when twisted sideways, revealed the opponent's body exposed and vulnerable to the deadly *ikwa* thrust.

His retrained regiment was soon pitched against the nearby Buthelezi tribe and in due course both regiments lined up for the traditional *giya*. The unsuspecting Buthelezi, led by Shaka's half-brother, Bakaza, commenced to *giya* in expectation of the usual bloodless confrontation. But Shaka rushed upon and instantly killed Bakaza whereupon the iziCwe fell upon the hapless and unsuspecting Buthelezi warriors who fled for their lives. Not content with his victory, Shaka led his warriors into the Buthelezi homestead, firing huts and killing everyone they could find, including women and children.

Shaka then turned his attention to the eLangeni tribe who had treated his mother so severely. On seeing Shaka's approaching force, many of the eLangeni people fled in terror. The tribal elders remained in an attempt to placate Shaka. They failed and were all savagely put to death; the surviving eLangeni people were absorbed into Shaka's alliance of compliant tribes. It was Shaka's ruthlessness that gave him the reputation he enjoyed; in battle he was merciless, to the survivors and their families he was equally pitiless – surviving men were killed, the women and children taken and absorbed into the growing Zulu tribe; other tribes swiftly sought alliance with the Zulus rather than risk being attacked. Impressed by his success, Dingiswayo appointed Shaka to lead the northern Zulu tribe. On Senzangakona's death Shaka learned that another son, Sigujana kaSenzangakona, had been nominated as heir to the Zulu clan; Shaka immediately dealt with the matter by having Sigujana assassinated. Shaka annexed the Zulu clan and disposed of his half-brothers Mhlangana and Mpande; the most threatening half-brother, Dingane, was sent back to his own distant clan, an offshoot of the Qwabe tribe.

Shaka was in his early thirties when he commenced his ruthless reign. Any opponents or dissenters were mercilessly executed, as were warriors who did not reach the exacting physical standards required for a Zulu regiment or *impi*. He perfected the *ikwa* stabbing spear and developed the *impondo zankomo*, the encircling technique known as the 'horns of the bull'. This was a technique formerly used for hunting large herds, whereby the fast-running horns, the *umuva*, of the two flanks encircled an enemy. The main Zulu body, the *isiFuba*, would then engage the surrounded enemy at close quarters with their shields and stabbing spears. Shaka drilled his Zulus remorselessly in order to attack the resurgent and belligerent Buthelezi clan, who appeared to have ignored the lesson of their previous encounter. When the two sides met, Shaka's warriors encircled the Buthelezi and slaughtered them before their distraught onlookers. Shaka then ordered the mass slaughter of the Buthelezi noncombatants. Meanwhile, Dingiswayo was captured in battle by a neighbouring chief, Zwide, and put to death; the defeated tribe fled to Shaka for protection.

By 1818 Shaka's fearsome army had grown to more than 2,000 warriors and his sphere of influence was steadily increasing. The struggle for power now focused on Chief Zwide. Zwide's overwhelming force attacked Shaka at Gqokli hill but the battle was inconclusive and both sides withdrew to their own territory. Shaka's army was still intact and warriors from other clans immediately flocked to swell his ranks. Zwide attacked the Zulus again in the summer of 1819 with a massive army of nearly 20,000 warriors but this time Shaka was even better prepared. Shaka teased Zwide's army into following a number of feints across barren terrain; several days later, when Zwide's men were starving, Shaka attacked and destroyed them.

Thereafter Shaka ruled unchallenged, albeit with constant guidance from his mother, Nandi. His army grew to over 20,000 trained warriors and was based in a heartland that extended from the Indian Ocean to the Drakensberg and from the Pongola river in the north to the Tugela river in the south. Shaka forced his ruthless influence still further and by 1822 his clan had grown into an empire whose influence extended beyond the Drakensberg mountains into the Kalahari desert, north to the shores of Lake Malawi and south to the northern Cape.

Shaka knew of the handful of white men who had recently settled at a small coastal enclave known to the whites as Port Natal and in early

1824 he sent them an invitation to visit his kraal at kwaBulawayo, 'the place of him who kills'. The party consisted of Lieutenant Francis George Farewell RN, Henry Francis Fynn, who was the British Resident in Zululand, and four hardy pioneers, John Cane, Henry Ogle, Joseph Powell and Thomas Halstead, together with a large number of gifts. James King and Nathaniel Isaacs joined the group several weeks later. They were welcomed as a source of exotic trade-goods, including firearms. This meeting was a success and established Farewell's expedition as a client chiefdom at the Bay. It was to this ramshackle beginning that all subsequent British claims to the region owed their origin. The title 'king', as applied to the Zulu leader, appears to have evolved from a spontaneous gesture by Lieutenant Farewell during an early meeting with Shaka. In deference to Shaka, Farewell took a smear of grease from one of his cannon wheel hubs and ceremonially anointed Shaka on his forehead, after which he was referred to as the 'king'.

After various displays and feasts, Farewell and Fynn finally met Shaka and during one of their meetings they sought and were granted trading rights for the Farewell Trading Company. The party returned to Port Natal but without Fynn, who remained at Shaka's request – not as a hostage but to enable Shaka to learn more of the white men. Fynn was residing at the royal *amakhanda* when an attempt was made on Shaka's life. Shaka was stabbed through his left arm and ribs by an unknown assailant and was close to death for a week. During this time Fynn cleaned and bandaged the wound and generally watched over Shaka, who quickly recovered. Shaka believed that members of the distant Qwabe tribe were responsible for the attempt; accordingly, two *impis* were dispatched which captured the Qwabe cattle and destroyed their kraals. The settlers' position was assured and Shaka allegedly signed an agreement granting Farewell nearly 4,000 square miles of land around Port Natal.

Two years later Farewell and Fynn accompanied Shaka's army of over 15,000 warriors on an expedition against the distant Ndwandwe clan that resulted in the total slaughter of the Ndwandwe, an event that distressed even Farewell and Fynn, though Shaka was delighted with the 60,000 captured cattle. Fynn's horror at the post-battle massacre was recorded in his diary:

> The enemy's [Ndwandwe] loss had now become more severe. This urged the Zulus to a final charge. The shrieks now became terrific. The remnants of the [Ndwandwe] army sought shelter in an adjoining wood, out of which they were soon driven. Then began a slaughter of the women and children. They were all put to death. The battle from the commencement to the close did not last more than an hour and a half … Early next morning Shaka arrived and each regiment, previous to its inspection by him, had picked out its cowards and put them to death.[4]

Shaka's total disregard for human life was difficult for the Europeans to comprehend; even in peaceful times a dozen or more daily executions were carried out before Shaka – often for minor indiscretions; it was a custom that continued through to King Cetshwayo's reign. The absolute nature of his power was demonstrated when Nandi suddenly died during 1827. Shaka's grief was so intense that he required every Zulu to experience his loss and ordered a gathering of some 20,000 souls within the royal homestead. Enforced wailing and summary executions commenced and continued throughout the day until well over 1,000 of the multitude lay dead. Shaka then decreed that during the next twelve months no crops could be grown, children conceived, or milk drunk – all on pain of death.

Fynn was present and recorded the event in his diary:

> Those who could not force more tears from their eyes, those who were found near the river panting for water, were beaten to death by others who were mad with excitement. Towards the afternoon I calculated that not fewer than seven thousand people had fallen in this frightful indiscriminate massacre. The adjacent stream, to which many had fled exhausted to wet their tongues, became impassable from the corpses which lay on either side of it; while the kraal in which the scene took place was flowing with blood.[5]

The situation continued for three months until Shaka tired of mourning, whereupon some normality returned. The damage and carnage was such that Shaka's half-brothers, Dingane and Mhlangana, clandestinely agreed that Shaka must die. They waited until the army was on campaign and stabbed Shaka to death during a meeting with his remaining advisers. His body was unceremoniously buried in a pit, weighted down with stones.

Within days the exhausted and anxious Zulu army returned in expectation of Shaka's wrath, only to be relieved when Dingane welcomed the army back, fed them and then authorized their leave. Dingane thus ensured their loyalty and – having meanwhile murdered Mhlangana – he assumed the mantle of king.

Between King Shaka's death in 1828 and the Zulu War, the Zulu kingdom underwent considerable change, as did the power of its monarchy. King Dingane settled into a life of luxury and security. At no more than 30 years of age he enjoyed singing, dancing and clearly had an artistic inclination. Unlike Shaka, King Dingane spent most of his time in the *isigodlo* being entertained with singing and dancing or reviewing parades of warriors and cattle. He reduced the size of the Zulu army and Shaka's previous policy of random butchery ceased, though offenders were still summarily executed without trial or mercy.

Having controlled the advancing Boers, King Dingane decided to re-establish his control over the non-Zulu tribes by undertaking a punitive expedition against a younger half-brother, Mpande, who promptly fled to the Boers for protection with nearly 20,000 of his people. The Boers realized the Zulus were in disarray and mounted a massive counter-expedition, which included Mpande's Zulus in support of the Boers, mainly to recapture their lost cattle and horses. The king sent two ambassadors to plead for a truce with the Boers who were camped at the site of the Blood River battle, but the two were promptly executed out of vengeance for their suspected complicity with Retief's murder. During the protracted skirmishing that followed, the Boers recovered most of their cattle and King Dingane was forced to flee across the northern Pongola river where Zulus loyal to Prince Mpande murdered him.

In a matter of days the news of the king's death swept across Natal and then beyond to the many tribes who had been displaced by Shaka and Dingane. These commenced their own trek back to their homelands, only to discover the Boers were settling on their lands. The Boer Volksraad (Council) decreed that the natives, now starving and homeless, were to be rounded up and moved into a native homeland well away from the Boer sphere of influence. The British at the Cape heard of the plan towards the end of 1841 and forbade the Boer action. British troops reseized Durban and quickly dispatched sufficient administrators to govern the area while the Volksraad endeavoured to regain control over the increasingly contrary Boers, who had even tried, unsuccessfully, to enlist the support of the king of Holland (a wasted exercise, as Holland had no intention of provoking Britain). In 1842 the British formally took control of Natal by force and European immigration into the area thereafter increased which, in turn, resulted in a shortage of good farmland; many newly arrived farmers began to look at the verdant pastures of Zululand.

Britain finally annexed the whole of Natal into the Cape Colony during 1845, including Boer-held territory. Reluctantly the Boer Volksraad acquiesced. They had overreached themselves and, by provoking the British, lost sovereignty over lands won by great sacrifice. Settlers continued arriving from Europe and Durban rapidly prospered as the influence of Pietermaritzburg declined. During the European upheaval in Natal, the Zulus under their new king, Mpande, had decided to avoid further confrontation with the whites and had withdrawn to the north side of the Buffalo and Tugela rivers.

The following period was one of relative peace as King Mpande ruled the Zulu nation fairly but firmly according to Zulu custom; it was also a welcome period of consolidation after the internecine wars of 1838 and 1840. Having been preoccupied with internal politics and the successful rebuilding of his nation, King Mpande was able to turn his attention away from politics and towards the *isigodlo* and feasting, until he became too obese to walk; he was moved about in a small cart. His activities in the *isigodlo* produced nearly thirty sons; the firstborn was named Cetshwayo and was followed shortly by a brother named Mbulazi. As the king aged, schisms developed within the Zulu nation and the subservient chiefs and clans gradually inclined to either Cetshwayo or Mbulazi. The two brother princes were now in their early twenties. Cetshwayo was a traditionalist and much admired the regal days of Shaka whereas Mbulazi was more inclined to intellectual matters, though he was equally devious and powerful. In 1856 both sought to be king and, traditionally, resolution came through bloody conflict, perhaps the worst seen or recorded in South African history. Near Ndondakusuka Hill, Cetshwayo mustered 20,000 warriors, the uSuthu, and pitted them against Mbulazi's 30,000 iziGqoza, who included many women and old men. The confrontation took place on the banks of an insignificant stream, the Thambo, which fed into the Tugela river. The battle lasted no more than an hour, with Mbulazi's army being heavily defeated. In customary Zulu fashion, Cetshwayo gave orders for their total slaughter and only a handful of survivors escaped across the river. Cetshwayo was later song-praised for his victory as being the victor who 'caused people to swim against their will, for he made men swim when they were old'.[6]

Cetshwayo assumed command of the Zulu army, leaving the aged King Mpande a mere figurehead. Cetshwayo had long since observed the underlying tension between the British in Natal and the Transvaal Boers and knew he was in a position of considerable strength. He now had full control of Zululand and in order to strengthen his grip further he astutely courted friendship with the British, whereupon Shepstone, Secretary for Native Affairs, went to King Mpande and suggested that, in the name of Queen Victoria, Cetshwayo should be appointed heir apparent. The king accepted the proposal on behalf of the Zulus though Cetshwayo was aware that his future now depended, to a degree, on British support. King Mpande died in 1872 after thirty relatively peaceful years on the Zulu throne, a reign marred only by his two sons' recent battle by the Tugela.

In 1873, following a traditional wild animal hunt that saw the slaughter of a number of rare black rhinoceros, Prince Cetshwayo became king of Zululand and immediately sought British confirmation of his position. Shepstone readily agreed and, in a sham ceremony on 1 September 1873, Cetshwayo was crowned king of the Zulu nation, in the name of Queen Victoria. The ceremony became lively when a small grass fire swept into the camp. One headman seized the opportunity to steal two dozen bottles of medicine thinking they were gin; he became the first person to be executed under the new regime. King Cetshwayo, now in his mid-forties and perhaps the most intelligent of all the Zulu kings, ruled a united nation; his army was the strongest in southern Africa and the Zulus had a most powerful friend, Queen Victoria, and no apparent enemies. With his military position secure, King Cetshwayo began to strengthen his economic and political control.

Since Shaka, young men had been obliged to serve in the army as a means of binding the nation together; this policy was now rigidly enforced. At the age of 18 all Zulu men were required to serve part-time in the *amabutho* as a form of national service. Each *ibutho* was given a distinctive name and ceremonial uniform of feathers and furs. Their war shields remained the property of the king, being issued only for special ceremonies or to settle disputes and to maintain the *ibutho* bond and identify its own warriors; *ibutho* shields were invariably of a matching colour. An *ibutho* was required to give service to the king only until such time as the men married, when their primary duty reverted to their families and local chiefs. To maximize the time the young men were available to serve them, the Zulu kings had often refused to allow a regiment to marry until the men were in their late thirties. The *amabutho* were the king's active service units and in peacetime gave service at the king's command, often as tax officials or by undertaking policing duties. When each regiment assembled to answer the king's call they were fed and quartered at the king's expense. Because it was logistically difficult to sustain such large concentrations of men for long periods, the *amabutho* were seldom mustered for more than a few weeks each year. For the most part the men lived at home with their families, fulfilling the normal duties of their ordinary civilian lives. An *amabutho*, apart from drawing young men together for military and work purposes, also served to accustom warriors to identifying the Zulu king as their leader, regardless of their origins. However, if young men came from an outlying area or had recently been absorbed into the Zulu nation, they were initially allocated menial work and were known as *amalala* (menials), *amanhlwenga* (destitutes) or *iziendane* (unusual hairstyles).

Warriors allocated to their regimental *amabutho* remained celibate until the king authorized their 'marriage'; this was another misunderstood concept that has often led to confusion. Zulu marriage has invariably been interpreted through European eyes with overtones of repressed sexuality and transposed with European values of marriage. To a Zulu, marriage denoted the most significant event of his life by giving him the right to take a number of wives; he was then free to establish his personal kraal and he could own land for his cattle and crops. King Cetshwayo controlled marriage as a means of keeping his young men under arms and out of the economic structure of Zululand. Had every warrior been permitted to establish his own kraal at will, the effect on various Zulu social processes, including production and reproduction, would have resulted in economic instability. Concomitantly, by delaying the time when Zulu women could marry, the birth rate, growth and pressure of an increasing population could be strictly controlled and maintained in line with economic production.

Every Zulu knew his or her place and their society was efficient. Those who sought to escape the rigidity, strictness and dangers of King Cetshwayo's rule had only one escape route – to flee to Natal.[7] Many of the younger Zulus who fled to Natal saw the forthcoming British invasion as a means of settling old scores and regaining lost family lands – they were quick to volunteer for the fight.

CHAPTER 3

The Zulu Military and Their Tactics

By 1878 the machine of military service in Zululand was, in effect, an integral part of everyday life in the kingdom although, unlike the British army of the time, the part-time Zulu army was neither professional nor well trained. The only military training Zulu warriors received took place during their initial induction into their age-set regiment; in all matters they relied on instructions from their *indunas* who, in turn, demanded absolute obedience from their warriors. British intelligence led Chelmsford to believe that the total strength of the Zulu army amounted to between 40,000 and 50,000 men immediately available for action. The total Zulu population in 1878 only amounted to some 350,000 people and so this figure is probably correct. At each year's *umKhosi* or 'First Fruits' ceremony, held before the king at Ulundi, young men who had attained the age of about 16 years, known as *inkwebane*, were formed into companies or *amaviyo*, which after a year's probation would be placed in an *ibutho* or regiment. This first year also symbolized the transition from boyhood to manhood as a warrior. The new *inkwebane* might either belong to another regiment with which the young one was incorporated, or be newly formed. As a rule several regiments of different ages were combined at the same *ikhanda* or barracks so that the young soldiers might have the benefit of the experience of their seniors and, when the latter died out, might take their place and maintain the name and prestige of the *ikhanda*. In this manner loyal corps were formed, occasionally some thousands strong.

The Zulu army was soundly structured and consisted of twelve such corps, each with one or more regiments. These corps necessarily contained men of all ages, some being married, others unmarried, some being old men scarcely able to walk and others mere boys. Five of these corps consisted of a single regiment while the remaining corps was composed of several regiments. Each corps or regiment possessed its own *ikhanda* and was controlled by one commander, one second in command and several junior commanders who controlled the flanks in action. The uniform of the Zulu army was clearly laid down and was different in each corps. The great distinction was between the married and unmarried regiments: the former were obliged to shave the crown of the head and to wear a head-ring made of hemp and coated with a hardened paste of gum and grease; they also carried shields with predominantly white colouring whereas the unmarried regiments wore their hair naturally and had coloured shields. By the time of the Zulu War, the total number of regiments in the Zulu army amounted to thirty-four, of whom eighteen were married and sixteen unmarried. Seven of the former were composed of men over 60 years of age, so that for practical purposes there were only twenty-seven Zulu regiments fit to take the field, amounting to some 44,000 warriors. Intelligence figures of the day break these down as 17,000 between 20 and 30 years of age, 14,500 between 30 and 40, 5,900 between 40 and 50 and 4,500 between 50 and 60.

At Ulundi the *ibutho* in residence was the uThulwana. These were the men who looked after the king and their work was rarely of a military nature; they maintained the nearby military *amakhanda* and engaged in planting, reaping and fulfilling the king's wishes. Each *amakhanda* was cared for by a skeleton staff and was only occupied when the king called up its *ibutho*. There were twenty-seven *amakhanda*, or royal homesteads, scattered about the kingdom, thirteen of them located in the region of the Mahlabatini plain, near Cetshwayo's residence at Ulundi. Ulundi itself was a huge complex of some 1,200 huts whose garrison was more or less permanently in residence.

Tactical drill was unknown to the Zulu army though they could perform a number of essential movements with some accuracy, such as forming a circle of companies or regiments. Their skirmishing skills were extremely good, and, in the coming war, would be performed under heavy fire with the utmost determination. The officers had specific duties and responsibilities according to their rank, and discipline was most rigidly enforced. Commodore Sullivan, writing in August 1878, gave an accurate account of the discipline of the Zulu army. He stated that the regiments were so well disciplined that 'the men never fell out of the ranks on the march under any pretext; they marched at the double, and were said to keep up from 50 to 60 miles daily, carrying their own provisions'.[1] It was a warning that Lord Chelmsford disregarded.

Unlike the lumbering British invasion force being assembled, the Zulu army required but little commissariat or transport. Three or four days' provisions consisting of maize or millet and a herd of cattle accompanied each regiment. The older boys followed their allocated regiment and assisted in driving the cattle; they also carried the provisions and camp equipage, which consisted of sleeping mats and blankets. They would avoid rivers that were normally impassable but, when necessary, the Zulus adopted a remarkable method to get across: they would plunge into the water in a dense mass, holding on to one another, those behind forcing the others forward, and thus they would succeed in crossing, usually with the loss of only a few of their number. When hostilities were decided upon, the king sent out messengers; travelling night and day they would order the warriors to assemble in regiments at their respective *amakhanda* where their commanding officers would be sent to receive them. When corps or regiments were assembled at the headquarters they were usually ordered to proceed to the king's royal homestead. Before marching, a circle, or *umkumbi*, was formed inside the homestead, each company together, and their officers in an inner ring with the first and second in command at the centre. The regiment then proceeded to break into companies, beginning from the left-hand side; each company formed a circle and then marched off, followed by *uDibi* boys carrying provisions, mats and food supplies. The company officers marched immediately in rear of their men, the second in command in rear of the left wing, and the commanding officer in rear of the right. This tried and tested plan was now set into operation to defend Zululand from the massing British invasion force.

By the time of the British invasion the Zulu army possessed a large number of antiquated firearms. An English trader trusted by the Zulus, John Dunn, is often blamed for this trade but he only ever obtained permits to import 250 guns for King Cetshwayo. During the 1870s as many as 20,000 guns entered southern Africa through Mozambique alone, most of them intended for the Zulu market. The majority of these firearms were obsolete military muskets, dumped on the unsophisticated 'native market'; this mass importation of firearms also contributed greatly to the destruction by Zulu hunters of remaining big game. More modern types were available, particularly the percussion Enfield, and a number of Zulu chiefs had collections of quality sporting guns. Some individuals, such as Prince Dabulamanzi and Chief Sihayo of Rorke's Drift, were recognized as good shots but most Zulus were untrained and highly inaccurate; numerous accounts of Zulu War battles note both the indiscriminate use of their firepower and their general inaccuracy.

It was a coincidence in favour of the Zulus that the British planned their invasion just as the Zulu regiments were assembling at Ulundi for the annual *umKhosi*. On arrival at the king's royal homestead, certain additional and important pre-war ceremonies took place and various medicines were administered to the warriors to enhance their fighting capacity and render them immune from British firepower. On the third day after their assembly at the king's homestead the medicine men sprinkled the warriors with magical *muti* or medicine, and after all necessary formalities were completed the warriors commenced their long march of some 70 miles towards the British border with Natal. The march was initially led by a corps specially nominated by the king, followed by the remainder of the army along the *umsila* or path beaten through the grass by the advance corps. The advancing Zulu army would have been similar to a British division advancing in line of brigade columns, each brigade in mass, each regiment in close column. The line of provision-bearers moved on the flank; the intervals between the head of columns varied, according to circumstances, from several miles to within sight of each other, and constant communication was kept up between them by runners. The march continued in this order but the baggage and provision-bearers fell in at the rear of the column on the second day and the cattle composing the commissariat were driven between them and the rearmost regiment until the force approached the advancing British force. When the latter were within striking distance the whole army formed an *umkumbi* for the purpose of enabling the commander-in-chief to address the men and to give his final orders for attack.

The battle tactic for engaging the British was proven, efficient, simple and understood by every Zulu warrior. The Zulus historically favoured a dawn attack but were prepared to fight at any time. Military operations were always controlled by senior Zulus, usually from a remote vantage point, although one of their number could be dispatched into the battle to rally or lead if an assault faltered, as happened at Isandlwana. The Zulus made great use of spies; they had an elaborate system for obtaining and transmitting intelligence and were efficient at outpost duty. They already knew exactly where the British were and were able to report their every move back to the Zulu generals. Immediately prior to an attack the Zulus would be indoctrinated by *sangomas* (diviners and medicine men) and the use of cannabis and other narcotics as stimulants was widespread.

Zulu tactics were based on the encircling movement, often wider than a mile across, which had developed over hundreds of years when hunting large herds of game. The actual Zulu battle formation resembled a crescent shape with two flanks moving to encircle the enemy. The formation was invariably known by Europeans as the 'horns of the bull' and by the Zulus as the *impondo zankomo*.

The fast-moving encircling horns consisted of the younger, fitter warriors, with the body or chest made up of the more seasoned warriors who would bear the brunt of a frontal attack. The tactic was most suc-cessful when the two horns completed the encirclement of the enemy and relied, in part, on the main body of warriors remaining out of sight until the horns met – they would then rise up and close in to slaughter the victims. A large body of troops were also kept in hand as a reserve; they were usually held with their backs to the enemy to prevent their overexcitement. The commanders and staff would assemble, where possible, on high ground between the battle and their reserves, all orders being delivered by runners. No great changes had been introduced into Zulu tactics consequent on the introduction of firearms, though in addition to firearms each man usually carried four or five spears. One short and heavy-bladed spear was used solely for stabbing and was never parted with; the others were lighter, and sometimes thrown. The men armed with firearms rarely carried a shield. Features of the attack were speed and precision; the Zulu force would approach an enemy, be it native, Boer or now the British, in huge columns that could then rapidly deploy into an encircling movement.

Once King Cetshwayo realized that the British invasion of Zululand was inevitable, he sought a decisive defeat of the invaders. Knowing the British possessed overwhelming firepower, he argued against the traditional Zulu mass frontal attack, preferring the use of untried siege tactics. He reasoned that, once trapped or starved into submission, the invaders would be forced to withdraw to Natal rather than face a humiliating defeat on the battlefield. He accordingly instructed his generals to bypass the invading columns and isolate them from their supply lines. This tactic soon proved highly effective against the Coastal Column, which the Zulus successfully besieged at Eshowe. It was very nearly successful against the Northern Column at Khambula until Colonel Buller goaded the approaching Zulu army into a premature attack on the well-prepared British position. King Cetshwayo was also a shrewd diplomat: he knew that, once the British invasion force was cut off from Natal, he could seriously embarrass Britain internationally and force Lord Chelmsford to sue for peace.

However, King Cetshwayo's generals had no intention of changing their plan. They were autonomous and either unable or unwilling to follow the king's orders. Their warriors were prepared for the final phase of the coming battle and would use Shaka's shock tactics of the mass charge and close-quarter fighting to the death.

The British commanders were aware of the principles behind Zulu tactics but they never expected the Zulus to use the tactics on a large scale. At Isandlwana, Zulu commanders were successfully able to control an extended advance across a 5 to 6 mile front to the extent that they completely encircled not only the British position but also the mountain of Isandlwana itself.

Popular myth records the Zulus moving in to attack the British position at Isandlwana in mass formation. However, the reality was an attack in open skirmishing lines although at Isandlwana these lines of warriors were up to a quarter-mile deep. Certainly, from a distance, such a large force carrying shields would have appeared very densely packed. The Zulus advanced at a steady jogging speed and would complete the final attack at a run. Once among the enemy, the short stabbing spear or assegai was most effective. The Zulus rarely used their firearms to any effect.

Many writers have credited Shaka with the development of the *impondo zankomo* but researchers are aware that the Xhosa tribes were also familiar with its effect. Certainly the technicalities were more effectively used by the Zulus who, in training, would create feints with one horn to confuse the enemy. Such a tactic succeeded brilliantly at Isandlwana; the Zulus manoeuvred and advanced the main body and left horn into full view of the British while the right horn slipped unnoticed behind Isandlwana and encircled the British position. The British were only aware of the right horn when, according to Commandant Hamilton-Browne who watched the battle 2 miles from Isandlwana, they emerged in force from behind the mountain, driving the column's bellowing and terrified cattle from the undefended wagon park straight into the unprotected rear of the British position.

After the Zulu success at Isandlwana Natal was utterly helpless to defend itself, the British invasion force was part-defeated and part-surrounded, yet King Cetshwayo failed to capitalize on his victory. Had he ordered his army into Natal, the consequences for the black and white Natal population would have been horrendous and the subsequent history of the area would have been equally difficult to imagine.

CHAPTER 4

Trade, Diamonds and War

Perhaps now there may be rest.[1]

KING CETSHWAYO

For much of the nineteenth century, British political policy in southern Africa continued to be mainly reactive, but other factors were also beginning to emerge which sharply focused British attention on the urgency of unifying the region; border disputes were a constant problem requiring supervision by British troops, immigrants from Europe were pouring into the area in increasing numbers, hugely valuable diamond reserves had been found and political and racial instability was increasing. In an attempt to bring to an end the regional rivalries and the never-ending border wars the British wanted to superimpose a single authority over the various southern African states – a policy known as Confederation. With such a controlling administration in place, a reliable and stable policy could theoretically control economic production and the resulting trade would greatly benefit Britain.

Such a unified area could then develop its own military system, albeit trained and supervised by British officers, which neatly solved the problem of Britain supplying and maintaining hugely expensive Imperial troops for distant peacekeeping. During the 1870s Confederation was becoming an increasingly important factor in British foreign policy following its successful implementation in lands as various and distant as India, Australia, the Leeward Islands and, most recently and successfully, Canada; under Confederation these areas flourished. The policy developed as a result of financially expensive lessons learned by Britain while administering her other distant colonies and lands: in southern Africa, with its diverse and mutually antagonistic populations, Confederation was considered essential.

Economically, Southern Africa had remained a commercial backwater until October 1867 when an unexpectedly large number of diamonds were discovered at the junction of the Orange and Vaal rivers, and the location was most inconvenient for Britain. Jurisdiction of the area was strongly disputed between the Boer-governed Transvaal and Orange Free State. Unhindered by any official controls, many thousands of prospectors headed for the district from all over the world and created the thriving town of Kimberley. These hardy diamond-diggers ignored any form of local administration while evidence gradually mounted of the financial potential of further valuable discoveries. In 1871 the lack of control over such great wealth and associated commercial benefits caused Britain to resolve the matter; under some protest from the Free State, British officials deftly moved the boundary and then annexed the diamond-mining area to the Crown. This annexation, so soon after the annexation of the neighbouring territory of Basutoland in 1868, undoubtedly turned many tribal leaders away from any thoughts of co-operation with the British.

After the British assumed control of the Transvaal mining area they reached an accord with the Zulu king, Mpande kaSenzangakona, father of Cetshwayo; this 1840 accord formally defined the lines of the Tugela (*uThukela* – 'river that rises with alarming suddenness') and *Mzinyathi* (Buffalo) rivers as the boundary between the two states. No such convenient physical obstacles fixed the borders between the Zulu kingdom and the Transvaal in the west, and after the 1850s and 1860s, Boer farmers had steadily encroached on Zulu-owned land in ever-increasing numbers. After the first Boers crossed the Drakensberg mountains in 1838, their settlements had continued to spread progressively towards the heartland of Zululand, itself protected by the virtually unfordable Tugela river. This barrier along the border temporarily deterred further encroachment by the Boers and certainly accorded with official British understanding of the boundary, confirmed in an earlier official dispatch from Mr (later Sir) Theophilus Shepstone that when the Boers first arrived in Natal in 1837–8,

> they found the subjects of Dingana, King of the Zulus, occupying the whole of the upper part of Tugela Valley, including the lower parts of the Mooi, Bushman's, Sunday's, and Buffalo Rivers.[2]

Throughout the whole existence of the Natal colony, King Mpande and then King Cetshwayo had made repeated representations to the government of the colony concerning successive Boer encroachments into Zulu territory. Shepstone invariably dismissed these protests on the grounds that they were 'temporizing and evasive'. Shepstone's dispatches describe the Zulu claims as 'substantially just and those for the republic [Boers] as being simply the result of an unscrupulous lust for land'.[3] Indeed, dispatch after dispatch indicates that King Cetshwayo was implicitly obeying Shepstone in refraining from hostilities and awaiting an amicable solution of the difficulties.

Shepstone's 'do nothing' policy prevailed until the Boers announced on 25 May 1875, in the name of the Boer Republic, that large areas of Zululand were their territory. Following this announcement, which seriously irritated King Cetshwayo, Boer settlers again began moving into Zululand and these new incursions were opposed by the Zulus with increasing vigour. One such area of heightened tension was an unofficial extension of the Boers' Transvaal into Zululand, which lay between the Buffalo and Blood rivers immediately north of Rorke's Drift. It was evident to all parties that relationships between the Boers and Zulus were seriously deteriorating and decisive action, beyond sabre rattling, needed to be taken. King Cetshwayo had traditionally regarded the encroaching Boers as his enemy and treated them with great suspicion and disdain, whereas he had long regarded the British as his true friends.

Boer intrusion into Zululand was perceptively described by Mr Osborne, Colonial Secretary to the Transvaal Government in 1876, who wrote, 'The Boers, as they have done in other cases, and are still doing –

encroached by degrees upon native territory.' King Cetshwayo had also alerted the British to the problem created by the Boers when he wrote:

> Now the Transvaal is English ground, I want Somtseu [Sir Theophilus Shepstone] to send the Boers away from the lower part of the Transvaal, that near my country. The Boers are a nation of liars; they are a bad people, they lie, they claim what is not theirs, and ill-use my people.[4]

The British made no reply. Then, during April 1877, a serious confrontation between the Zulus and Boers began to develop as a result of trekkers moving onto virgin land unanimously recognized as Zulu territory. Secretly supported by the Secretary for Native Affairs, Sir Theophilus Shepstone, King Cetshwayo decided to resolve the problem once and for all by massing an impressive force of over 30,000 warriors at strategic crossing points along the Boers' Transvaal border. Before the king could give the order for a full-scale Zulu attack, two events occurred in quick succession, either by coincidence or by astute British diplomatic design. Firstly, on the very same day, 12 April 1877, Shepstone was actually attending a secret meeting with the Boers, with the sole intention of persuading the Boers to surrender the Transvaal to British authority, on the logical grounds that the Transvaal government was bankrupt and the Zulus were about to attack. Agreement was swiftly reached whereupon Shepstone then and there annexed the Transvaal to the British Crown. Secondly, Sir Theophilus Shepstone immediately ordered King Cetshwayo to withdraw his army. The secretary to the annexation team, Melmoth Osborn, read the declaration to the assembled Boers. He appeared to suffer from a bout of chronic anxiety mid-proclamation; he commenced trembling and his voice failed. Shepstone's 20-year-old clerk, H. Rider Haggard, stepped forward to continue reading the script.

King Cetshwayo reluctantly complied with Shepstone's order but sent a strong letter warning him that he had intended driving the Boers 'beyond the Vaal River'. The Zulus believe to this day that Shepstone deceitfully encouraged Cetshwayo to amass his *impis* on the Transvaal border in order to coerce the Boers into submission. Likewise, the Boers accepted

Shepstone's annexation in the belief that at Shepstone's call a 'cloud of 40,000 Zulu warriors hung upon the Transvaal border'[5] threatening them in the rear.

Shepstone's motive behind this annexation may well have been to initiate Britain's policy of Confederation across southern Africa but, in pursuing this policy, Shepstone had unwittingly inherited responsibility for the rapidly developing Zulu and Boer land dispute. Prior to annexation, the British had viewed the Boers as 'foreigners'. Now that these people had involuntarily become British subjects by virtue of the annexation, the problem of the disputed territory converted itself from being an insignificant Boer–Zulu controversy into a potentially serious dispute between Britain and the Zulus. At the time King Cetshwayo welcomed British annexation of the Transvaal, as he believed it would protect Zululand from further unwelcome Boer attention, and in a note he informed Shepstone of his relief at the outcome:

> I am pleased that Somtseu has let me know that the land of the Transvaal Boers has now become part of the land of the Queen of England; perhaps now there may be rest.[6]

Later, however, King Cetshwayo would describe Shepstone – who had previously enjoyed the Zulu title 'Somtseu' or father – as a 'cheat' and a 'fraud'. As for Shepstone, he had never fully trusted the Zulus. Shepstone wrote in a letter to Lord Carnarvon, 'The sooner the root of the evil, which I consider to be the Zulu power and military organisation, is dealt with, the easier our task will be.'[7]

Mr Rider Haggard wrote that the financial effects of annexation on the Transvaalers were magical and that credit and commerce were at once restored, but only a few months later he was much more cautionary. He wrote:

> When the recollection of their difficulties had grown faint, when their debts had been paid and their enemies [Zulus] quietened, they began to think that they would like to get rid of us again, and start fresh on their own account with a clean sheet.[8]

Meanwhile, Lord Carnarvon, the Colonial Secretary in London, appointed Sir Bartle Frere as High Commissioner to South Africa and Governor of the Cape in order to accelerate the pace of Confederation. Frere, an experienced senior administrator from his time in India, soon became convinced that the independence of the Zulu kingdom posed a threat to his policies, although initially he was more concerned about the threat posed to the ports and harbours of southern Africa by the rapidly growing Russian Navy. [9] Border problems between black and white apart, the threat of violence was inherent in the policy of Confederation since many groups, both African and Boer, were opposed to British rule. In Frere's mind the Zulus posed the lesser threat so it was upon them that he focused his short-term attention. He interpreted the Zulu king's protestations concerning the 'disputed territory' as nothing more than belligerence, and came to believe that a demonstration of force against the Zulu nation would not only intimidate broader opposition to the Confederation scheme; it would also demonstrate Britain's strength. Frere's belief marked a dramatic shift in the relationship between the Zulu kingdom and the British; the first step had unwittingly been taken along the path towards open conflict between the two former friends.

Matters again came to a head during early 1878 when a number of newly arrived Boer and displaced black settlers joined those already illicitly farming a particularly sensitive Zulu area – the same area which was generally becoming known as the 'disputed territory' directly to the north of Rorke's Drift. In the British tradition of apparent compromise, Frere deferred the problem by reluctantly constituting an independent Boundary Commission to resolve this long-running boundary issue once and for all.

The original proposal for a Boundary Commission came from Sir Henry Bulwer, the Governor of Natal and a long-time friend of the Zulu people. The Commission was specifically to adjudicate on title to the disputed territory. King Cetshwayo was consulted and he agreed to abide by the Commission's decision on condition he could nominate three senior *indunas* to participate. The Commission's principal members consisted of three highly respected officials: the leader, Michael Gallwey, a barrister who had become the Attorney General of Natal in 1857 at the age of 31; Lieutenant Colonel Anthony Durnford RE who had served in South Africa for many years and who knew both the area and the Zulus thoroughly; and John Shepstone, brother and deputy of the Secretary for Native Affairs. The Boers sent Piet Uys, a farmer who had lost relatives to Dingane's *impis*; Adrian Rudolph, the Boer Landdrost of Utrecht; and Henrique Shepstone who served on his father's staff in Pretoria. The Commission sat for nearly five weeks during which time they considered voluminous verbal and written representations.[10] Gallwey utilized all his legal training to evaluate the material impartially, a task made especially difficult because several Boer documents proved to be fraudulent while a number of Zulu reports were manifestly unreliable. Gallwey concentrated the Commission's attention on two main issues: who owned the land prior to the dispute and whether any land under dispute had been properly purchased or ceded.

It has to be remembered that no boundary line had ever been agreed between the Zulus and Boers and that for many years a number of local Zulu chiefs had repeatedly implored the British Governor in Natal for advice and help in dealing with examples of Boer aggression. It had long been Boer policy – if policy it may be called – to force the Zulus gradually to edge further and further from their rich pasture lands. Hitherto, little notice had been taken of Zulu petitions. The Boundary Commission finally decided that the disputed land had always belonged to the Zulus and, furthermore, the Boer settlement of Utrecht must also be surrendered. The Commissioners eventually delivered their unexpected verdict in July 1878 to an astonished Sir Bartle Frere, who dealt with the matter by placing the document under lock and key.

While Frere was still pondering how to deal with the Commissioners' report an incident occurred on 28 July 1878, which Frere used to encourage widespread anti-Zulu sentiments. Some of the sons of a local chief, Sihayo kaXongo, crossed the river border to capture two of their father's absconding wives who had been accused of adultery. They were duly apprehended and marched back across the border, only to be clubbed to death in accordance with established Zulu tradition. The incident received officially orchestrated publicity, out of all proportion to the event, in order further to inflame white public antagonism against King Cetshwayo. Even the pro-Zulu Bulwer was forced to agree that the danger of collision with the Zulus was growing and he wrote that 'the system of government in the Zulu country is so bad that any improvement was hopeless – we should, if necessary, be justified in deposing Cetshwayo'.[11] This opinion had been reinforced by disgruntled missionaries, Norwegian, German and British, whose collective endeavours over many years to convert the Zulus had met with widespread resistance; they withdrew from Zululand and wrote copious letters to the newspapers and government in favour of war. With equal fervour Bishop Colenso argued against the missionaries' campaign for war as a prerequisite of Christianity. On 2 April 1878 Durnford wrote to his mother on this subject:

> These missionaries are at the bottom of all evil. They want war so that they might take the Zulu country, and thus give them homes in a good and pleasant land. They have not been turned out. They came of their own accord. The Zulus do not want them and I for one cannot see why we should cram these men down their throats.[12]

After hasty and delicate discussions with his senior political advisers, Frere was obliged to realize that publication of the Commission's findings could unleash powerful forces against Britain – both from neighbouring black nations who would believe their campaign against progressive European settlement was vindicated, and from furious Boers who could well retaliate by resorting to military action against British-controlled Natal. Such action could provoke additional antagonism from a number of the Boers' European allies, especially Holland and Germany. This possible complication would be most inconvenient as Britain was becoming seriously engaged in war against Afghanistan and relationships with Russia were deteriorating. Frere had not been idle since activating the Boundary Commission; he and his staff, encouraged by Shepstone in the Transvaal, had wrongly anticipated that the Commission would find for the Boers and Shepstone accordingly believed that the Zulus might retaliate against Britain with a military offensive into Natal. In consequence, plans were already well advanced for a British pre-emptive invasion of Zululand; invasion would also neutralize the dangerous findings of the Boundary Commissioners.

There were other attractive incentives for an invasion. The Zulus were blocking British progress to the north and their defeat would facilitate Confederation. It would also placate the Boers and such a display of force would certainly impress other Bantu nations who might protest against British expansion. Invasion would overturn the Zulu king by eradicating his military potential while at the same time freeing a valuable source of labour for British and Boer commercial activities. In connection with this issue, Sir Theophilus Shepstone wrote in 1878 that

> Had Cetshwayo's thirty thousand warriors been in time changed to labourers working for wages, Zululand would have been a prosperous peaceful country instead of what it is now, a source of perpetual danger to itself and its neighbours.[13]

Frere ordered his General Commanding British Forces in South Africa, Sir Frederic Thesiger (shortly to become Lord Chelmsford), to proceed to Natal in secret and prepare his forces for an immediate and brief war against the Zulus. There were also important personal considerations for both Frere and Chelmsford: success for Frere would add lustre to his already glittering career and for Chelmsford an early defeat of the Zulu army would ensure him a heroic return to England. Meanwhile, Frere gained himself more time by forwarding the Boundary Commission's findings to Sir Michael Hicks Beach, the new Colonial Secretary in London (who had succeeded Lord Carnarvon). He also requested additional Imperial troops, ostensibly to protect Natal and the Boer families still within the area. Frere knew full well that Hicks Beach's official reply would take several months to reach him and by that time the Zulus would be subjugated.

In early October there was a minor incident at one of the border crossing points. A British surveyor named Smith and a trader named

Deighton were reviewing the condition of a drift across the Tugela river near Fort Buckingham when they were accosted by some Zulus and questioned about their activities. Although they remained on the Natal side of the river, the questioning lasted for about an hour before they were released; the Zulus were on guard at the drift due to the rumours of an impending British invasion of Zululand. The matter was commented on in Smith's routine report as being of a minor nature. The incident came to the attention of Frere who virtually dismissed it out of hand, although he later included the incident in the list of grievances about King Cetshwayo that would form part of his infamous 'ultimatum'. He initially wrote:

> I concur with you in attributing no special importance to the seizure and temporary arrest of the surveyors, which was partly due to their own indiscretion, and was evidently in no way sanctioned by the Zulu authorities.[14]

On 9 October another incident occurred which precipitated action by Frere. A local chief, Mbilini, had led his warriors through the Pongola valley in the area under dispute, attacking immigrant Boers and natives and stealing herds of their cattle. Frere was already in the process of devising an ultimatum, which he and his advisers knew would be impossible for King Cetshwayo to accept. It would also negate the Boundary Commission's report and justify Frere's war against the Zulus; accordingly the raid by Mbilini formed the basis of the first item in the ultimatum. Britain effectively allied itself to the Boer cause and prepared for war against the Zulus; Frere made representations to the Boers for support and, following a meeting at Utrecht on 5 December 1878 between Colonel Wood VC and local Boers, Wood was confident of having several thousand mounted and well-armed Boers under his command. Three days later the Boers discovered that the Boundary Commission had long since found against them. Stung by the British deception, the Boers accordingly withheld their support – with the exception of isolated individuals, most notably Piet Uys, whose father and brother had earlier been killed by the Zulus.

Eventually, on 11 December 1878, Zulu representatives were summoned to the site of a shady fig tree on the Natal bank of the Tugela river to learn the result of the Boundary Commission's deliberations. The British erected a tarpaulin under the tree, laid on a roast beef lunch and even brought a photographer from Durban to record the event. John Shepstone represented the British officials, while King Cetshwayo sent three of his senior *izinduna* together with eleven chieftains and their retainers to listen to the findings. The Zulus, to whom writing was unknown, were accomplished at memorizing even lengthy speeches, which probably accounts for the number of senior Zulu representatives, who would have needed to corroborate each other when they rendered their account of the event to the king.

The findings were relayed to the Zulu officials but in heavily worded terms deliberately designed to cause confusion. The hitherto secret ultimatum was then read to the Zulus who, astonished by the about-turn, anxiously set off to report the terms of the ultimatum to King Cetshwayo. The main requirements of the ultimatum included some conditions to be fully met within twenty days, all of them impossible within the timescale: the Swazi chief, Mbilini, was required to surrender and pay a fine of 500 cattle for his previous cattle-raiding activities, as were Chief Sihayo's three sons and brother for crossing the river border into Natal and abducting and then murdering two of Sihayo's adulterous wives. A fine of 100 cattle was also to be paid for having molested the two British citizens, Deighton and Smith, at the border crossing.

Further conditions to be fully met within thirty days: King Cetshwayo was to observe his coronation 'promises' – of which he was certainly unaware. A number of prominent Zulus were to be surrendered for trial (no names were specified), summary executions were forbidden and the Zulu army was to disband along with the Zulu military system. Every Zulu was to be free to marry (a reflection of the European misunderstanding of marriage within the Zulu society), missionaries were to be readmitted to Zululand without let or hindrance and Zulus were to be permitted to attend religious classes without obstruction, a British resident official was to oversee Zulu affairs, no sentence of expulsion from Zululand could be enforced without the permission of the resident and, finally, any dispute involving a European was to be dealt with under British jurisdiction.

Even by this late stage and notwithstanding the impossible nature of the ultimatum, King Cetshwayo sent a conciliatory message to the Lieutenant Governor of Natal stating:

> Cetshwayo hereby swears, in presence of Oham, Mnyamana, Ntshingwayo and all his other chiefs, that he has no intention or wish to quarrel with the English.[15]

Again, this was ignored.

The timing of the ultimatum was unwittingly in favour of King Cetshwayo whose army was already in the process of assembling at Ulundi for the *umKhosi* ceremony. In the weeks leading up to the British invasion, the king had been fully aware that events were rapidly moving beyond his control. All along the border with Natal, Zulu women and children, often leading their cattle, could be seen moving away from the probable invasion routes and going into hiding. King Cetshwayo ordered wild animal hunts to be held along the borders of the neighbouring territories and those taking part were instructed to ensure that Shepstone's spies observed the Zulus' state of preparedness. By the time the ultimatum reached King Cetshwayo, most of the *amabutho* were already gathered at Ulundi and the ritual preparations for war began. Notwithstanding soothing reassurances from Shepstone, King Cetshwayo was not to be caught off guard; shrewdly, he decided to wait, prepare and watch. Aware of the growing consternation of his people at the menacing gathering of British troops along the Natal border, the king sent a number of *induna* emissaries to implore British restraint; but on presentation of their credentials they were arrested and imprisoned.

In the meantime the British invasion force was already gathering along the border of Zululand in total confidence that King Cetshwayo could not comply with the ultimatum. Hicks Beach's reply finally reached Frere and it was, as Frere anticipated, an indication that Hicks Beach was uninterested in southern Africa. It contained little more than a request that caution must be exercised. The reply read:

Her Majesty's Government are [sic] not prepared to comply with a request for reinforcement of troops. All the information that has hitherto reached them with respect to the position of affairs in Zululand appears to justify a confident hope that by the exercise of prudence and by meeting the Zulus in a spirit of forbearance and reasonable compromise it will be possible to avert the very serious evil of a war with Cetshwayo.[16]

Frere deliberately misconstrued Hicks Beach's reply as conferring authority to initiate a local war and, once started, he was fully aware that the British government was powerless to stop him. It took at least ten weeks for a message to travel to London and back; his exploitation of the delay, on the grounds of the tension and urgency he had created, was blatant. Without doubt there were numerous occasions when any leader other than Sir Bartle Frere could have resolved the matter peacefully, without the tragic loss of life, national honour and financial cost that war would incur.

King Cetshwayo knew exactly where the British were amassing their forces and correctly presumed that his capital, Ulundi, was their objective. Perhaps because he also knew that Lord Chelmsford was to accompany the Rorke's Drift column, the king singled it out as being the most dangerous force. Chelmsford's tactics of using three columns to advance on Ulundi was a direct copy of the Zulu *impondo zankomo* (horns of the bull) tactic and King Cetshwayo would certainly have noticed the irony. His understanding of the intricacies of the technique is perhaps one reason why the Zulu army were confident that they could defeat the British. The time for peaceful negotiation had passed; both sides, although long-standing friends, were ready for war. The first hurdle for Chelmsford's army was crossing the Buffalo river.

The first of a series of blunders was now beginning to develop. During the days following the invasion, members of the Native Border Guard – locally recruited Natal blacks under white command – learned that a large Zulu force would oppose the British invasion. By 21 January their locally gathered intelligence accurately indicated that this Zulu force was located near Isandlwana and had orders to 'cross the *Mzinyathi* [Buffalo river] into Natal during the night'. The Border Guard moved their men to meet this possible crossing and their district commandant reported the matter to Major Bengough who was with his 2nd NNC battalion at nearby Sand Spruit; Bengough passed the warning to Chelmsford, as did Mr Fannin, the Border Agent, on 20 January. The effect of these reports on Chelmsford's staff is not known; they appear to have been ignored – or forgotten. If acted upon, Fannin and Bengough's reports could have averted the approaching disaster.[17]

During the same afternoon Chief Gamdana, who had previously submitted to Chelmsford, arrived at Isandlwana camp with the news that he was expecting a Zulu *impi* that same day. He was sent away.[18]

Meanwhile, oblivious to escalating events in South Africa, Disraeli's government was wrestling with the problem of Irish Home Rule; the British Army was gearing up for war on India's North-West Frontier where the British felt vulnerable to Russia's steady absorption of the vast territories east of the Caspian Sea. Fighting had also broken out in Afghanistan during the latter part of 1878 and by early 1879 the British had occupied the capital, Kabul, and installed a puppet ruler. An uneasy peace lasted but a few months until the British Political Officer, Major Sir Louis Cavagnari, and his escort were slaughtered. It was prophetic that Cavagnari, piqued by the lack of press interest, had previously written, 'I am afraid there is no denying the fact that the British public require a blunder and a huge disaster to excite their interest.'[19] Three days later he was dead and the British public were about to have their blunder.

When confirmation was received in London, the invasion of Zululand was considered so insignificant that only one of the London newspapers bothered to send a correspondent to cover the event. Instead, all efforts were focused upon Afghanistan where, in the event, the British had a comparatively easy advance.

CHAPTER 5

The British, Invaders of Zululand

The British Government has no quarrel with the Zulu people.[1]

SIR BARTLE FRERE, HIGH COMMISSIONER,

11 JANUARY 1879

For the British troops in South Africa, life was reasonably satisfactory. The climate was good and the posting offered sufficient conflicts and skirmishes to make life interesting for the 5,000 men stationed there. The soldiers' lot was certainly better than could be expected in England.

Life was exceedingly tough throughout the British Isles of the 1870s. Many of the population were unhealthy, with a high incidence of suffering, particularly from the ravages of diseases that swept the population of the time; tuberculosis, cholera, influenza, whooping cough, scarlet fever, measles, syphilis and a variety of lesser infectious diseases were rife. The life expectancy of industrial England's labouring classes was as low as thirty-eight years, with only the well-off or the very lucky having any hope of reaching their mid-fifties. British agriculture, formerly the main rural employer, had been in decline for some decades and by the 1870s less than 15 per cent of the working population were still engaged in farming. Many young men left the countryside to seek employment in the rapidly expanding urban areas, and the 1880s witnessed a surge of emigration to the United States, Canada or Australia, not only from Britain but also Ireland where there had been the worst potato crop since the famine of 1846. It was not only agricultural workers who were finding work hard to come by. Those employed in factories, which had previously enjoyed a virtual monopoly in supplying products and materials to the rest of the world, now found that they faced increasing competition from the United States and Europe. The combination of these intensely bleak circumstances resulted in more than enough recruits for the army to make conscription unnecessary; taking the queen's shilling on enlisting was a legally binding contract between the recruit and the army.

With the increasing threat of lay-offs and lockouts, the average industrial worker felt highly insecure; unemployment was reaching terrifyingly new proportions and many workers were forced, as a last resort, to enlist in the army. Recruiting sergeants frequented the public houses and taverns where hungry and unemployed young men collected. Any recruit who was drunk at the time of his 'enlistment' could, theoretically, be released from the commitment on the immediate payment of £1, which for these young men was an improbable amount to produce on demand. Recruits were normally 'sworn in' within twenty-four hours before being medically examined and posted to a regiment or to join a draft being sent abroad. Most young men joined the army to escape unemployment, poverty and wretched squalor.

The army was still popularly regarded by the civilian population as the last resort for a desperate man and private soldiers were still looked upon as social outcasts. Giving a convicted criminal the choice of prison or the army had faded away though the option still remained for less serious offences. Because times were so hard, the unemployed and the unemployable could find security of a kind in the army. But bored youngsters, dazzled by the stories and flattery of flamboyant recruiting sergeants, soon found the reality of a home posting in the army even more restricting than their previous existence. It was something of a relief when a regiment was sent abroad to some exotic posting; it also meant escape from the grinding grimness of barrack life. A comparison of contemporary statistics reveals that in 1869 there were 12,000 recruits to the army with 3,341 desertions, or 27 per cent. In 1878 the recruits numbered 28,325 and the desertions 5,400, or 19 per cent.

The average height of an army recruit had fallen over the previous ten years to an undernourished 5ft 4in and yet, in spite of their poor physical condition, several weeks of sustained military training usually sufficed to transform the recruits into competent soldiers. Most British soldiers about to face King Cetshwayo's Zulus were resilient fellows hardened by the extremes of African weather and most were experienced veterans from six years' constant campaigning during the recent Border War. Few had any idea why they would be fighting the Zulus. They amused themselves with a variety of sports such as wrestling and spear-throwing and, in order to maintain an acceptable level of fitness, soldiers with less than fifteen years' service were expected to undertake three half-mile runs each week.

At first sight a soldier's pay appeared to be reasonable but, from the daily shilling, official deductions ensured his continued poverty. A married soldier could have maintenance deducted from his wages and paid to his wife or family though no official help, other than charity, was available to the widow of a soldier killed in action or who died of disease on campaign. It was not until after 1881 that any form of widow's benefit became payable.

The British Army of the 1870s was still absorbing the reforms implemented by Gladstone's Secretary for War, Edward Cardwell, a solicitor with no military experience. Besides such humanitarian acts as abolishing flogging during peacetime, the main reforming object was to save money. The Army Enlistment Act of 1870 shortened a soldier's active service from twelve to six years with the following six on the Reserve. For the first time in its history this gave the British Army a large, well-trained reserve and, with the short service, had the potential of attracting a better calibre of recruit. Although the number of recruits increased during the 1870s, the army's strength by 1879 was only 186,000 compared with the Prussian Army of 2.2 million.

For the British Army's privileged upper-class officer corps, Cardwell's abolition of the purchase system appeared to open the door to an unwelcome influx of non-élite officers from a more modest background. In fact the social composition of the officer class hardly altered even following the Cardwell reforms. Low pay, coupled with the disproportionately high cost of being an officer, meant those without private means could not afford to become officers – indeed, senior officers effectively subsidized the army. Also, with the establishment of the Staff College, the quality of officers from the wealthy class improved although it was not until the Great War and the decimation of the old officer class that a commission was open to all those to whom it was previously denied.

By the outbreak of the Zulu War the majority of British officers in South Africa were from the same social and educational background and had purchased their commissions prior to the Cardwell reforms. They enjoyed sports, particularly hunting, and many relished the prospect of going to Africa with the chance to hunt game and the native foe; once in South Africa emphasis was placed on fitness, loyalty, team spirit and physical bravery. On campaign there was also the opportunity to do something that would favourably catch the eye of the High Command and enhance promotion prospects. These motives prompted many officers from regiments not involved in the conflict to volunteer for any of the staff appointments available, ranging from transport and supply posts to serving with locally raised units. Officers from line regiments were generally taller and fitter than their men; they enjoyed the benefits of family wealth but, on campaign, officers were expected to display a high level of ability, loyalty and physical bravery.

The average soldier, on the other hand, had no such motivation. Initiative was not expected or encouraged by the army; just blind obedience. Those who served in the Zulu War had little or no idea of any overall plan or why they were fighting. Rumour and hearsay were rife and little or no attempt was made to keep the men accurately informed. Their needs and ambitions were more basic: keeping as dry and comfortable as conditions would allow, finding a supply of liquor, playing cat and mouse with the NCOs and generally trying to keep a low profile was a behaviour pattern familiar to British soldiers throughout history.

At the time of the Zulu War, soldiers who could write were often prolific letter-writers. An examination of their letters shows that they tended to concentrate on worrying about their families and friends at home rather than the conditions they were experiencing in Africa. Once the invasion of Zululand had begun, their life centred on staying dry and comfortable, an extremely difficult task during the heavy thunderstorms of the four-month rainy season. The older and more experienced soldiers knew how to look after themselves and their equipment; they knew to sleep among rocks rather than on damp ground to stay clean and dry, to dry out their wet kit when the sun shone and to swill out their boots daily with their own urine to fight athlete's foot. Preventative medicine as such was not knowingly practised and so dysentery, enteric fever and tuberculosis all took their relentless toll, especially when the soldiers were coughing and spitting in squalid and overcrowded conditions. The inevitable close contact with infected animals and drinking contaminated milk resulted in tuberculosis spreading rapidly among the soldiers. Enteric fever also raged, and would continue so long as the common practice continued of drawing drinking water from the same source as that frequented by local people and their animals. Sick oxen and dying Zulus tended to make for these water sources, polluting them with decomposing carcasses, but water-collecting parties ignored this fact.

Observing strict discipline and staying out of trouble were probably more important to the redcoats than the probability of disease; British soldiers quickly learned to obey every order instantly as flogging was still regularly practised. Of the 20,000 soldiers who took part in the two invasions of Zululand, 545 were flogged between 11 January and 4 July 1879; the standard punishment for insubordination or similar minor offences was twenty-five lashes; sleeping on duty or theft merited fifty lashes. It appears from their letters that soldiers mostly accepted corporal punishment, though a number described it as a sorry sight while the senior officers tended to view flogging as a necessity to maintain discipline.

Following furious protests in the British press, flogging was eventually banned at the end of 1879, even for active service offences. Colonel Bray wrote:

> The discipline of the army suffered much from the difficulty of preventing the men from buying spirits. Flogging can never be done away with in wartime in the English army unless some equally efficient punishment can be discovered.[2]

Prior to the Zulu War, communications and trade throughout Natal were so severely hampered by impassable roads, a complete lack of navigable rivers and the absence of a transport system that a government enquiry had taken place to examine the feasibility of creating a unified infrastructure. The enquiry considered developing an integrated rail and road network but due to lack of finance, the recommendations of the enquiry were never implemented. The commerce of Natal continued to depend on a network of dirt roads and inaccurate maps; and with regard to neighbouring Zululand, no reliable maps existed as much of the country remained unexplored.

One of the main reasons for failure during the earlier Crimean War was the inability of the British to supply their front-line troops. Even as late as 1878 the army still lacked an established method of supplying or transporting supplies; supplying the troops was considered by many senior officers as incidental to the overall plan. Chelmsford was more realistic and, of necessity, he devised his own unofficial procedure. Even so, it was not until the middle of 1878 that plans were well advanced for the invasion of Zululand. The invasion force would amount to an estimated total of 12,500 fighting men who would need many hundreds of wagons with thousands of oxen, mule carts, mules and horses. Chelmsford requested the imposition of martial law so that his army could commandeer all the wagons, oxen and horses needed for the invasion but the civilian Governor of Natal, Sir Henry Bulwer, refused the request.

Commissary General Strickland was duly appointed as the officer in charge of supplies. He originally had a peacetime establishment of twenty junior officers and thirty men under his command, a woefully inadequate staff for such an enormous undertaking. Chelmsford quickly realized his invasion could not take place without sufficient transport and appointed a Board, under Colonel Sir Evelyn Wood VC, to advise him. He also telegraphed the War Office for an urgent draft of experienced captains to be sent to Natal to supplement the commissariat. Then he ordered the unopened railway line that was still under construction from Durban to Pietermaritzburg, or 'Sleepy Hollow' as it was affectionately known by the British, to be made available.

While the commissariat pondered the merit of purchase as an alternative to the hire of transport, Chelmsford threw caution to the wind and ordered the purchase of 200 wagons on the open market. This sudden decision caused a dramatic increase in prices across the country and the army was soon at the mercy of speculative contractors. Chelmsford had even less luck with oxen and horses as Natal had only recently come through a two-year drought and healthy animals were already being traded at a premium. Horses in poor condition that would previously have sold for as little as £2 each were being traded for £40. Oxen could not be purchased at all but only hired at exorbitant rates as the owners realized they could levy monthly hire charges that were in excess of the animals' actual value.[3] The oxen suffered cruelly from the conditions under which they were worked, though they extracted a pyrrhic revenge when they were cooked for the troops, the beef being noted for its toughness. The cost of mounting the invasion soared by the day until an exasperated and frustrated Chelmsford took control of the commissariat and immersed himself in the task of resolving the situation. It was to his credit that, within weeks, he reversed the lack of progress and brought the profiteering back under control. Strickland's commissariat team, shortly to be reinforced by the specially drafted officers now en route from England, took over.

The Commissariat and Transport Department was still a young branch of the army, having only come into existence by royal warrant on 9 December 1875. Its officers held commissions identical to those of other army officers although their rank structure set them apart. On operations the senior officer was the commissary general; his deputy held the equivalent rank to a lieutenant colonel, a commissary to a major, a deputy commissary to a captain and an assistant commissary to a lieutenant. Sadly, other officers in the British Army looked down on their commissary brothers. Even Wolseley wrote that 'to rely upon a Commissariat officer is to be destroyed, and so it must always be until the Commissariat men are gentlemen, or at least as much gentlemen as the average British Officer'. At Rorke's Drift, Commissary officers were shortly to prove they were more than an equal match for their brother officers.

Chelmsford ordered each unit to appoint its own officers of transport. These appointments were made from within the regiments and units preparing for the invasion and their role was to co-ordinate and take responsibility for their unit's transport requirements, assisted by a sub-conductor for every ten wagons. It was an onerous task: each infantry battalion was allocated seventeen wagons, including one HQ wagon, while a battery of artillery had ten wagons and a squadron of mounted infantry had four. There was only one transport officer per invading column and he was responsible for keeping the whole column mobile.

By September Chelmsford had created an effective and efficient supply system and advanced planning for the invasion was finalized. Fate then intervened: the two-year drought suddenly came to an end with incessant torrential rain and, within a matter of days, the dusty rutted tracks of Natal had become impassable quagmires.

It soon became obvious to Chelmsford that there were simply not enough wagons available to carry the necessary stores, certainly not for five invasion columns. The list of stores was enormous and wide-ranging; it included tents, ammunition, cooking equipment, mobile hospitals and medicines, tools, spare boots and uniforms and food for the whole campaign. The regulatory ration allowance gives an indication of the logistical planning necessary just to feed the 12,500-strong invasion force. Each soldier's entitlement was a minimum of 1 pound of fresh meat, 1.5 pounds of fresh bread or its equivalent in biscuits, plus fresh vegetables and fruit or lime juice and sugar in lieu. Chelmsford instructed that a series of supply depots were to be established at intervals along each column's line of march; the column could then be 'drip-fed' on a daily basis from the nearest depot. For the Centre Column, which Chelmsford would accompany, depots were prepared and stocked with one month's supplies at Helpmekaar and Rorke's Drift. The Coastal Column's supplies were all positioned at Fort Pearson on the Natal bank of the Tugela river; thereafter they were moved across the river to Fort Tenedos. The Northern Column originally used an existing Boer laager at Utrecht as their stores depot. Later they established a forward depot at Conference Hill. By 11 January when the invasion began, Chelmsford was satisfied that he had enough stores in place to sustain his columns. Each could theoretically store fifteen days' supplies, enabling the columns to move at 10 miles per day. Chelmsford had achieved an impossible task.

The timing of Chelmsford's invasion was as unfortunate as it was deliberate. He was correctly informed that invading in early January would interfere with the Zulu harvest and demoralize the Zulu population. The recent rains would also provide natural grazing for the invasion force's numerous oxen and horses, the absence of which precluded invading during the later dry season. However, what Chelmsford did not consider relevant was intelligence that the whole of the Zulu army would be assembling before King Cetshwayo at this time; the significance of the fact that the annual 'First Fruits' ceremony at Ulundi was imminent had escaped the notice of Chelmsford's intelligence officers.

Furthermore, the rivers forming the Natal boundary with Zululand would be in full flood from heavy rain and create a natural defence for Natal against Zulu attacks and it is curious that a military commander with Chelmsford's experience would elect to invade at a time when the tracks and plains into Zululand were likely to be virtually impassable. Chelmsford soon appreciated the problem. As he wrote on 12 January, 'The country is in a terrible state from the rain, and I do not know how we shall manage to get our waggons across the valley near Sirayo's [Sihayo's] kraals.'

Unlike the Zulus, the majority of the British and Colonial officers and their troops were experienced in African warfare and it was perfectly understandable that Chelmsford anticipated a rapid defeat of the Zulu army; indeed, everyone's main fear was that the Zulus would not fight. Boer leaders, remembering their own defeats at the hands of the Zulus, had met with Chelmsford to warn that he faced a skilled and powerful adversary. Chelmsford knew that his columns would be vulnerable to sudden attacks and he accordingly ordered a high state of readiness to be observed during the advance; he even issued a memorandum to senior officers of likely Zulu ploys to ambush the unwary.[4] Following each day's march, every camp had to be laagered and alert to the possibility of a sudden attack. In planning his strategy, Chelmsford had decided to leave the reserve column, under the command of Colonel Durnford RE, at the Middle Drift. Apart from this relatively small force, the border of Natal would be virtually unprotected while the columns advanced into Zululand. He believed that by advancing on Ulundi in a three-pronged attack, they would force the Zulus to attack one or all invading columns rather than Natal; Chelmsford also reasoned that the simultaneous advance would force King Cetshwayo to commit all his *amabutho* and leave himself without reserves.

Although orders were issued by Chelmsford that no non-combatant Zulu, woman or child should be harmed, orders were nevertheless given by local commanders for every Zulu homestead and food-store in the path of the invasion force to be destroyed. This laying waste of Zulu homes and stores was intended systematically to remove supplies from any approaching Zulu force, to break the will of the Zulu people and thus provoke their army into attacking the invading column.[5] And when they attacked, they would be no match for Chelmsford's calm and experienced troops with their sophisticated firepower: well-aimed rifle volley fire supported by rockets, artillery and Gatling guns, which would, in Chelmsford's opinion, ensure the swift defeat of such an unsophisticated adversary. He accordingly gave priority to the implementation of regulations relating to the availability of ammunition. Each artillery battery of two guns carried 68 rounds together with 12 rockets with additional reserves readily available in accompanying carts and wagons. Rifle ammunition was calculated at 270 rounds per soldier, 70 in the possession of each man and 200 rounds in easily recognized colour-coded ammunition wagons. All column commanders had received written instructions that 'a commanding officer would incur a heavy responsibility should required supplies fail to arrive in time, through any want of foresight and arrangement on his part' – words that would soon haunt Chelmsford.[6]

The proposed route to be taken by the Centre Column, from Greytown to Helpmekaar and then on to the Zulu border, had already been inspected by Chelmsford during October. He noted that there were two routes from Helpmekaar, a 'good one which makes a wide detour and may be considered as two days' march distant' – this is the modern road now used by local people and battlefield visitors – 'and a bad one which takes a direct line, and could easily be accomplished in one day'. Chelmsford gave orders for the 'bad road' to be improved 'as its importance for both offence and defence, would be very great'. From his meeting with Natal blacks along the route, he became so convinced that the Zulus would shrink from his force that he also considered the establishment of camps to deal with Zulu refugees.[7]

By November the store depots along the border were stocked to the extent that supplies for the front line could begin to be forwarded to the advance supply depot once the invasion began. All ranks settled down to await the expiry of the ultimatum and, in order to retain harmony within the growing camp, commanding officers decreed that while sports should be encouraged, all games involving physical contact would temporarily be banned from Christmas Day onwards. In reporting the ban, the *Natal Witness* reporter wrote from Helpmekaar:

At sports, as is not unusual, disputes arise, and partisanship will be demonstrative; the consequences might be a quarrel, which under the present circumstances for which the forces are collected, would prove a most unhappy and untoward event. If the prohibition of sport is attributed, therefore, to severe military discipline, there is a very good reason and excuse for it.[8]

Harmony was further enhanced with the arrival of the Reverend George Smith in his new capacity of military chaplain; he was a huge and bearded man and was formerly of the local Estcourt parish. The same reporter wrote of him:

It is an impressive scene to witness 1,000 warlike men, in various uniforms, form square, and join a robed priest, standing in the centre, with a band of musicians – vocal and instrumental, in the worship of Almighty God. This is one of the greatest civilising influences which the forces could carry with them.[9]

During the week leading to the expiry of the ultimatum, Chelmsford learned that the three columns were fully equipped and ready to invade Zululand. Colonel Pearson's Coastal Column consisting of 1,800 Europeans and 2,000 auxiliaries and Colonel Wood's Northern Column with 1,700 Europeans and 300 black auxiliaries were both ready for the advance; indeed, Wood had already started his advance on 6 January, five days before the expiry of the ultimatum. The main attacking Centre Column, commanded by Colonel Glyn with 1,600 Europeans and 2,500 auxiliaries, had moved down during November from Helpmekaar to Rorke's Drift. There were two small columns held in reserve. One of these, commanded by Colonel Rowlands VC, was to stay just inside the Transvaal border. The role of this column was twofold: to be ready if called upon by Chelmsford and to keep an eye on the unsympathetic Boers who had been disillusioned since the leaking of the Border Commission's findings against them. The other reserve column, commanded by Colonel Durnford, was at Middle Drift on the Tugela river to protect the Natal border from any Zulu incursion. Theoretically Durnford had a force of 3,000 auxiliaries but his actual establishment amounted to only 500, of whom half were the élite and very loyal Edendale Contingent (known to many as the 'Natal Native Horse', a term used in the writings of Frances Colenso, daughter of the Bishop of Natal). He also had at his disposal a small rocket battery commanded by Major Russell RA.

On 10 January a general order was read to the patiently waiting troops: the Centre Column was to prepare to strike tents at 3 a.m. the following day, cross the Buffalo river and march into Zululand. At that time the camp was aroused by the trumpet calls of the different corps to feed their horses, and after a very early breakfast tents were struck; 'boot and saddle' was sounded, followed by 'prepare to mount', and then 'mount and fall in'. By 4 a.m. not a vestige of the cavalry camp could be seen; tents and baggage were all packed on wagons, and each corps was standing in line, formed ready to march. The police led off, followed by the Carrington Horse, while the volunteers brought up the rear. Once under way, the trumpet call 'trot' was sounded, and then the stillness of the moonlit scene was broken by the martial sound of cavalry on the move. As dawn approached, they reached Rorke's Drift and joined the patiently waiting columns of the 24th Regiment.

CHAPTER 6

The Five Invading Columns

It is rumoured that Cetywayo is somewhat puzzled to know what to do.[1]

LORD CHELMSFORD

There can be little doubt that Lord Chelmsford fully expected an early and easy victory over the Zulu army. His officers and most of their troops were already experienced in African warfare and his main fear was that the Zulus would not fight or that his campaign would deteriorate into a series of 'hit and run' skirmishes similar to those he had recently experienced in the Eastern Cape Colony against the amaXhosa.

The standard battle tactic employed by the British in South Africa had already proved to be completely successful. It relied on a combination of in-depth reconnaissance followed by ruthless skirmishing. In rough country, both the infantry and mounted troops would engage the enemy, the infantry by volley fire and the mounted troops by attacking them in flight. Chelmsford knew that in the unlikely event of the Zulus appearing in any number the British would form a square or entrench their position to draw the Zulus into the range of their overwhelming firepower. In Chelmsford's opinion, well-aimed rifle volley fire by calm and experienced troops supported by rockets and artillery, and, later in the campaign, Gatling guns, would ensure the swift defeat of the Zulu army.[2]

In order to ensure that the Zulu army would be brought to battle,

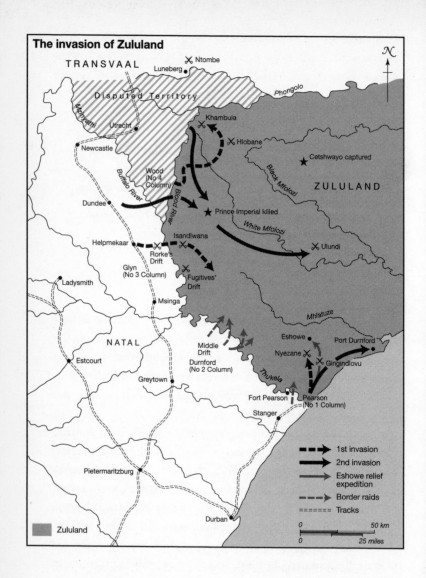

The invasion of Zululand

TRANSVAAL

Disputed Territory

Phongolo

Mzinyathi

Utrecht

Luneberg ✗ Ntombe

Newcastle

Buffalo River

Khambula ✗

✗ Hlobane

Wood
(No 4
Column)

Blood River

★ Cetshwayo captured

ZULULAND

Black Mfolozi

Dundee

★ Prince Imperial killed

White Mfolozi

Helpmekaar

Isandlwana ✗

✗ Ulundi

Rorke's
Drift ✗

Glyn
(No 3 Column)

Ladysmith

✗ Fugitives'
Drift

Msinga

Mhlatuze

NATAL

Middle
Drift

Eshowe ●   Port Durnford

Estcourt

Durnford
(No 2 Column)

Nyezane ✗   ✗ Gingindlovu

Thukela

Greytown

Fort Pearson ●   ● Pearson
(No 1 Column)

Stanger

Pietermaritzburg

Durban

1st invasion

2nd invasion

Eshowe relief
expedition

Border raids

Tracks

Zululand

0   50 km
0   25 miles

N

Chelmsford devised a three-pronged invasion that would advance on the Zulu capital, Ulundi. Each 'prong' or column was thought to be strong enough to engage and defeat the Zulu army. As already mentioned, the actual tactic was remarkably similar to the Zulu tactic of the 'horns of the bull' and the irony of its use by the British would not have escaped King Cetshwayo and his advisers.

Chelmsford originally intended that five columns would converge on Cetshwayo's capital but later modified his plan to just three, the Coastal, Centre and Northern Columns. On 8 January Chelmsford wrote:

> All the reports which reach me tend to show that the Zulus intend, if possible, to make raids into Natal when the several columns move forward. The strength of the three columns, Nos. 1, 3, and 4 is only just sufficient to enable them to advance.[3]

No. 1 Coastal Column

Chelmsford's orders to Colonel Pearson read:

> To cross the Tugela at Fort Pearson and encamp on the Zulu side; when ordered to advance, to move on to Eshowe, and there, or in its neighbourhood, to form a depot, well entrenched.[4]

In tactical terms, a Coastal Column in support of the main Centre Column was a sound move but one which overlooked the unseasonable bad weather, rugged terrain, prevalent sickness and the constant threat of an enemy whose tactical abilities and bravery were badly underestimated by senior officers.

Colonel Pearson's Coastal Column assembled at the Lower Drift of the Tugela river and was tasked with the role of marching along 37 miles of rough twisting tracks to occupy the mission station at Eshowe before the Zulus destroyed the buildings. Here the column's supply wagons were to be unloaded and returned to pick up more stores while defences were built to convert Eshowe into a fortified advanced supply depot. From Eshowe it was intended to advance on Ulundi in a converging movement with the other two columns.

No. 2 Reserve Column

Chelmsford's orders to Colonel Durnford were:

> To form a portion of No. 1 Column, but act separately, reporting to Colonel Pearson; to remain on the middle Tugela frontier until an advance is ordered, and Colonel Pearson has reached Eshowe.[5]

The Middle Drift near Fort Buckingham was one of the few places where, when the river was low, the water level dropped to a depth of some 3 feet; although this stretch of water was still about 100 yards across and fast flowing, the river could be crossed on foot with caution. The role of this Reserve Column, under the command of Colonel Anthony William Durnford RE, was to guard the drift.

Durnford was the eldest son of General E.W. Durnford, Colonel Commandant, Royal Engineers. He was born on 24 May 1830 and was educated chiefly in Germany. He entered the Royal Military Academy at Woolwich in July 1846 and obtained a commission as second lieutenant in the Royal Engineers on 27 June 1848. He then enjoyed numerous and varied postings. At the end of 1871 he embarked for South Africa; upon his arrival he was employed for a short time at Cape Town and King William's Town, and then proceeded to Natal where he formed one of the military escorts which accompanied the Minister for Native Affairs into Zululand to be present at the coronation of King Cetshwayo in August 1873. He subsequently acted as Colonial Engineer in addition to performing his own duties and under his superintendence much valuable engineering work was undertaken for the Colony.

Durnford came prominently into public notice towards the close of 1873, at the time of the Langalibalele affair, when he was the senior officer of Royal Engineers in Natal. Durnford had been sent in charge of a small group of Colonial soldiers to disarm the rebellious Zulu leader, Chief Langalibalele, who held sway in the steep foothills of the Drakensberg mountains. In bad weather Durnford's horse, Chieftain, lost its footing and fell, taking Durnford down a rocky slope. The horse rolled over

Durnford who sustained serious injuries to his shoulder, arm and two ribs. He nevertheless continued with the mission to find Langalibalele. Durnford's orders were to disarm Langalibalele's warriors without force – if possible. Durnford's small group became surrounded and, reluctant to open fire, sought to escape. The Zulus opened fire and began stabbing the riders, killing five of Durnford's men. The expedition was unsuccessful and Durnford was unjustly blamed by the civilian authorities for the loss of his men. Later, in 1878, he was one of the commissioners on the disputed Zulu boundary, whose award restored to the Zulus a considerable portion of territory.

Durnford had been pleased with his appointment to the No. 2 Column, as he wrote to his mother:

> The Governor has been pleased to express his confidence in me. I shall have some 3,000 men, infantry, cavalry and a rocket battery. So the command is at least a respectable one for a Lieutenant Colonel.[6]

While awaiting further orders, Durnford moved his main force to the small homestead at Kranskop, some 5 miles from the Middle Drift but with good access to any possible Zulu crossing points. His most recent orders were to send part of his force northwards to prevent the Zulus crossing into Natal and to be prepared to support Colonel Pearson's Coastal Column once the border was secure. The final section of the order was unclear and Durnford was about to succumb to its ambiguity. The orders gave him permission to engage the Zulus if he considered such action necessary to prevent an attack but he was then to return to the Natal side of the border; otherwise, he was to await further orders.

On 13 January Durnford received a report from Bishop Schroeder intimating that the Zulus were massing near Middle Drift prior to invading Natal. This communication seemed, at first sight, to make sense; after all, this was the very circumstance that Durnford was ordered to prevent. Durnford had not yet complied with Chelmsford's instruction to send troops towards the north; he accordingly cancelled their impending move and sent an urgent dispatch to Chelmsford informing him that he was about to engage the Zulus with his whole force at Middle Drift. Durnford ordered his men to prepare for an advance towards the river, obviously with a view to engaging the Zulus reported by Bishop Schroeder. While preparations were under way a mounted orderly arrived with an urgent dispatch from Chelmsford; its content both startled and distressed Durnford. It read:

> Unless you carry out the instructions I give you, it will be my unpleasant duty to remove you from your command and to substitute another officer for the command of No 2 Column. When a column is SEPARATELY in an enemy's country I am quite ready to give its commander every latitude and would certainly expect him to disobey any orders he might receive from me, if information which he obtained showed that it would be injurious to the interests of the column under his command. Your neglecting to obey the instructions in the present instance has no excuse. You have simply received information in a letter from Bishop Schroeder, which may or not be true and which you have no means of verifying. If movements ordered are to be delayed because reports hint at a chance of an invasion of Natal, it will be impossible for me to carry out my plan of campaign. I trust you will understand this plain speaking and will not give me any further occasion to write in a style which is distasteful to me.[7]

Durnford was certainly stung by such a severe rebuke, and Chelmsford would hold the matter against him to deadly effect in the coming weeks. On this occasion Chelmsford was right; there was no Zulu force at Middle Drift, which added to Durnford's embarrassment. The following day Durnford received fresh orders from Chelmsford to move towards Rorke's Drift; whether Chelmsford had decided to keep Durnford on a tighter rein or not is uncertain. By 19 January Durnford's force reached a point between Helpmekaar and Rorke's Drift when he received the following order:

No. 3 Column leaves tomorrow for Isandhlwana hill [sic] and from there as soon as possible to a spot about 10 miles nearer to the Qudeni forest. From that point I intend to operate against the two Matyanas [local chiefs] if they refuse to surrender. I have sent you an order to cross the river [Buffalo] at Rorke's Drift tomorrow with the force you have. I shall want you to cooperate against the Matyanas but will send you fresh instructions on this subject.

Later that day Durnford was instructed to cross the Buffalo river, await further orders and make camp on the Zulu side.

No. 3 Centre Column

Chelmsford's orders to Colonel Glyn read:

No. 3 Column to cross at Rorke's Drift when the thirty days expired; to move forward and form an advanced depot, strongly entrenched, as found advisable from the nature of the country, etc. To assist in clearing the border south-east of Rorke's Drift, and to keep up communication with the columns on left and right.[8]

The backbone of the Centre Column consisted of the two regular battalions of the 24th (2nd Warwickshire) Regiment. It was coincidental, and certainly unusual, that both battalions of this regiment were to serve alongside each other for the advance into Zululand. Both battalions were enthusiastic at the prospect of leading operations against the Zulus. The very experienced 1st Battalion had not seen home service since arriving in South Africa on 4 February 1875 after a series of Mediterranean postings. They were tough and battle-hardened after four years' active campaigning during the ninth Frontier War at the Cape. The 2nd Battalion, with twenty-four officers and 849 other ranks, had arrived in South Africa on 28 February 1878 and shortly afterwards took up their duties at King William's Town. Both battalions were then engaged in quelling small pockets of rebellion throughout the Cape area; this added experience helped to toughen the regiment in preparation for the arduous campaign looming in Natal. During the operations against the native tribes, neither battalion had sustained significant casualties. Only two officers, Captain Carrington and Lieutenant Godwin-Austen, were wounded, one man was killed and a few wounded (though from disease the loss was higher, eighteen men of the 1/24th and twenty-one of the 2/24th). Both battalions had earned much praise by their cheerfulness in facing hardships and discomforts and by their good conduct and discipline in the field. General Thesiger (later Lord Chelmsford) spoke in the highest terms of both battalions, emphasizing how well the younger soldiers, of whom the 2/24th was in large measure composed, had come through this severe ordeal of hard work in the face of difficult conditions. Likewise, the soldiers respected Chelmsford, as the *Natal Witness* reported:

> The headquarter staff camp is pitched to the right of all the others, almost in the centre as you walk from one end to the other. The Union Jack flies in front of the tent of the General, and his mule wagons are placed in position behind; otherwise there is nothing to show the difference between it and the other camps. His Excellency is much liked, and sets a good example to the men under him. He rises at daylight, and when on the march assists in striking and pitching his own tent. His manner is exceedingly affable to all, and he seems to have the happy knack of thoroughly understanding at once what is meant to be conveyed to him, although it may be wrapped up either in eloquence or long-windedness. His love of punctuality is well known through the camp, and of course leads to the same system in others.[9]

By July 1878 rumours were beginning to spread throughout Natal that King Cetshwayo was threatening to invade the province; consequently the 2nd Battalion was directed to Pietermaritzburg where its personnel assembled on 6 August. The 1st Battalion was not long in following the 2nd; it had been back at King William's Town about a month when C and D Companies, under Brevet Lieutenant Colonel Henry Pulleine, were also ordered to Pietermaritzburg. It was to be the fate of the 1st Battalion and one company of the recently arrived 2nd Battalion to face the Zulu attack at Isandlwana where almost all the men and officers involved would be killed. On the very same day, B Company of the 2nd Battalion would initially suffer the ignominy of being left behind at Rorke's Drift to guard the stores and then, within hours, find themselves facing potentially overwhelming numbers of Zulus seeking to destroy the position.

No. 4 Northern Column

Chelmsford's orders to Colonel Wood VC were:

> To advance to the Blood River. In the event of a further advance, the advance depot of this column to be near the intersection of the roads from Utrecht to Ulundi, and Rorke's Drift to Swaziland; but to delay its advance towards the Umvolosi River until the border is cleared, and to move in a southerly direction towards Colonel Glyn's column to assist it against Sirayo.[10]

Chelmsford appointed Brevet Colonel Sir Evelyn Wood VC as Column Commander for the advance across the difficult northern area of Zululand and home to the most aggressive Zulu group, the abaQulusi. Chelmsford had long since recognized in Wood the attributes he admired and would thereafter use him as a sounding board and allow him considerable autonomy. Wood was one of the most highly decorated officers of the Victorian era and his career was rich in incident and bravery. He was born on 9 February 1838 at Cressing, near Braintree, Essex, into a clerical background. In June 1857 he transferred from the Royal Navy to the army and exchanged into the 17th Lancers who were being sent to help quell the Indian Mutiny. A wealthy uncle had been persuaded to purchase his nephew promotion to lieutenant and, because he had learned to speak Hindustani, he was appointed to the post of interpreter. This led to his secondment to the 3rd Bombay Cavalry, with whom he saw repeated action. It was in 1859, with the Mutiny over, that Wood won his Victoria Cross for attacking the camp of a band of robbers who outnumbered his small force by about ten to one. He killed several, put the rest to flight and rescued two captives.

Having delivered the column to the garrison town of Pietermaritzburg, Wood and the 90th were sent north to Utrecht in the Disputed Territory on the Zululand border. Frere had initially appointed Wood as political agent for North Zululand and Swaziland to enlist support for the British invasion from the Boer population.

During the last three months of 1878 Wood was constantly on the move, visiting the small settlements, recruiting support and obtaining wagons and draught animals for the planned invasion. He later wrote:

> The incessant work, however, now began to tell on me, and my glands swelled as they had done when I was overworked in the Amatola Mountains, although for pleasure and on principle I played either lawn-tennis or polo for an hour or two every evening, the subalterns of the 90th being always available for a game.[11]

Despite ruthless and brutal raids by the abaQulusi against the Boers' black workers, led by the renegade Swazi chief Mbilini, the Boers could not bring themselves to support the hated British, whose motives they distrusted. Piet Uys was the only Boer leader to offer his services and he proved his commitment by bringing about forty of his family who acted as irregular cavalry.

Wood had the shortest distance to advance and typically entered Zululand on 6 January, four days before the ultimatum expired. Crossing the Blood river, Wood's 2,278-strong column marched 10 miles to a flat-topped hill called Bemba's Kop where he built a fortified camp. His force was made up of eight companies of the 13th and 90th Regiments, six guns of 11/7 Battery, about 200 Volunteer Cavalry and 300 natives given the rather flattering title of 'Wood's Irregulars'.

On 11 January Wood proved his fearlessness by riding south through some 50 miles of Zulu territory accompanied only by a small escort; his intention was to discuss the advance with Chelmsford whom he met at Rorke's Drift. Wood was ordered to delay his advance to allow the other two columns to catch up the extra distance. Chelmsford was so confident of success that he suggested Wood's mounted Colonials, under the command of Colonel Redvers Buller, should indulge in some cattle raiding. Ever the gentleman, Wood had warned the Zulus of his intention to invade; although the majority of Zulu warriors had since departed for Ulundi, the remaining Zulus were unprepared for the speed of Wood's advance and had not yet moved their sizeable herds to safety. Such cattle raiding was highly profitable to Buller, whose mounted troops swiftly rounded up the unprotected herds thus depriving the Zulus of their valuable cattle.[12] Wood was also orally instructed to occupy himself with the tribes to his front and left flank, mainly the fiercely independent abaQulusi Zulus. By this unfortunate change of plan the whole area, some 600 square miles to the left (north) of the advancing main Centre Column, was completely exposed; the Zulus took full advantage of this serious error by moving their main force of some 40,000 warriors and supporters across this empty area to within 5 miles of Isandlwana unseen by the Centre Column's scouts.

No. 5 Reserve Column

Chelmsford's orders to Colonel Rowlands VC were:

> To observe any Boer military activity whilst maintaining a state of readiness in northern Zululand.[13]

No. 5 Reserve Column was based at the Transvaal settlement of Utrecht under the command of Colonel Hugh Rowlands VC. Rowlands was still experiencing Chelmsford's displeasure following the unsuccessful British attempt in the preceding September and October to overcome the Pedi tribe of Chief Sekhukhune; the expedition had been controversially abandoned by Rowlands when in sight of Sekhukhune's stronghold. Chelmsford was also aware of the anti-British sentiment of the Transvaal Boers since the publication of the Boundary Commission report and, accordingly, Rowlands was instructed to await orders. The column took no part in the invasion of Zululand other than to support some local skirmishing near its posts at Derby and Luneburg. Rowlands and the bulk of his force of 1,565 officers and men remained *in situ* until Rowlands was returned to Pretoria in February 1879. At that point, the remaining troops of the No. 5 Column were attached to Wood's command.

VIEWED OVERALL, Chelmsford's main invasion force was remarkably small when the magnitude of the undertaking is considered. His force of regular troops consisted of the two battalions of the 24th; the 90th; single battalions of the 2/3rd and 1/13th; and a battalion of the 80th held in reserve at Luneburg. This force was initially divided between four columns and amounted to a total of nearly 6,000 highly professional and well-armed soldiers. In support were a similar number of native troops, known disparagingly as the 'untrained untrainables', who were divided into seven battalions and led by white officers and NCOs, not necessarily with any military training. To this force were added irregular units based on the quasi-military Natal Police together with frontier guards and local defence groups with grand names such as the Natal Hussars, Natal Carbineers and Durban Rangers.

By Christmas everything was ready for the invasion; kit was cleaned and polished, wagons were loaded and the regimental bands rehearsed the stirring themes that would spur on the columns of soldiers as they marched into Zululand. On 6 January 1879, four days before the expiry of the ultimatum, troops of Wood's Northern Column began crossing the border. Enthused with their general's optimism, the main British force crossed the Buffalo river into Zululand on 11 January; everyone's fervent hope was that the Zulus would stand and fight.

On 11 January 1879 the following notification was published in both English and Zulu.

NOTIFICATION

January 11th, 1879

The British forces are crossing into Zululand to extract from Cetewayo reparation for violations of British territory committed by the sons of Sirayo and others; and to enforce compliance with the promises, made by Cetewayo at his coronation, for the better government of his people.

The British government has no quarrel with the Zulu people. All Zulus who come in unarmed, or who lay down their arms, will be provided for till the troubles of their country are over; and will then, if they please, be allowed to return to their own land, but all who do not so submit will be dealt with as enemies.

When the war is finished, the British Government will make the best arrangements in its power for the future good government of the Zulus in their own country, in peace and quietness, and will not permit the killing and oppression they have suffered from Cetewayo to continue.

H.B.E. Frere

High Commissioner.[14]

A sequence of battles

Regardless of the validity or otherwise of the stated causes, Britain was about to engage the Zulus in a number of vicious battles; they were battles that would be fought to the bitter end with enormous losses on both sides, battles in which neither the British nor the Zulus would take prisoners.

All troops participating in the Centre Column's invasion of Zululand, apart from the 24th Regiment which had previously been stationed at King William's Town, had commenced their long and arduous march to the front from the Indian Ocean port of Durban. From Durban at the end of 1878 they set off along the dirt road to Pietermaritzburg and thence to Greytown, known to the Zulus as *Mkunkundhlovwane* or 'Little Maritzburg', and on to the Biggarsberg plateau at Helpmekaar,[15] a distance of some 120 miles. Whereas the troops marched, the many hundreds of tons of stores were moved by ox-drawn wagons along the same route to the Centre Column's main storage area which was located at Helpmekaar on the crest of a range of hills overlooking the Zulu border. For the last two years Natal had suffered from serious drought and, consequently, little thought had been given to the possibility of rain during the forthcoming invasion. The month of December saw the end of the drought and presented the troops with two extremes of African weather, baking heat followed by days of torrential rain. The roadways between the towns were nothing more than rough tracks and from the beginning of December 1878, passage and the movement of supplies were at the mercy of frequent heavy downpours that regularly made the tracks unnavigable, even though gangs of locally recruited black workers toiled to make passable the numerous bogs of slime and waterlogged dongas along the undulating track. Once the force was in Zululand, the invasion route would be even more difficult; there were no accurate maps and Chelmsford would have to rely on locally recruited guides and his reconnaissance patrols for directions and intelligence.

Before the invasion, there was little at Helpmekaar other than two rough farmers' cottages and a tiny church built in 1874 by the Vermaaks family for the Berlin missionary, the Reverend Jacob Döhne. Once they arrived, the soldiers found their destination depressing; it was remote and bleak, and any rain quickly turned the dust into heavy mud. The army commandeered the two houses and immediately constructed three zinc-sheeted sheds and a neat row of thatched huts to protect the column's perishable supplies and ammunition boxes from the heavy summer rain. A parade of white bell tents was quickly erected around the main store area and within days the camp extended for more than a mile towards the steep winding pass that descended into the valley towards the Zulu border, now only 10 miles distant, at Rorke's Drift. The centre of the temporary camp soon became a confusing mass of stores as wagons arrived and departed in a continuous flow, which, due to the summer deluges and troop movements, quickly became an unhealthy and deep quagmire of foul, clinging mud. Inevitably, one soldier after another began to suffer from dysentery. Morale among the troops slipped further when the wagons bringing their Christmas supplies became mud-bound at Umsinga, some 20 miles away, and only reached Helpmekaar the following week. However, and regardless of the varied weather of either heat or driving rain, preparations for the forthcoming invasion continued and by the beginning of January Chelmsford's force was ready to move to the Zulu border.

The spearhead of the Centre Column's invasion of Zululand, the two battalions of the 24th (2nd Warwickshire) Regiment, consisted of men who were already battle-seasoned and fresh from engagements during the recently ended Cape Frontier War. Chelmsford considered himself fortunate to have sufficient officers and men who were hardened to both battle and the climate; they were fighting fit, suntanned, most were bearded and their patched and repaired uniforms were evidence of many months of constant combat. It was unusual for both battalions of one regiment to serve together as it was War Office policy to maintain one battalion of each regiment on a home posting, partly for recruiting purposes. The 1/24th arrived at Helpmekaar just after the 2/24th who had reached Helpmekaar at the beginning of January, and on 9 January, just a few days short of the thirtieth anniversary of the 24th's unfortunate experience at the battle of Chillianwallah, the officers of both battalions, sitting on supply boxes, shared a mess dinner at which a toast was proposed, 'That we may not get into such a mess and have better luck next time.'[16]

The following day the troops marched the 12 miles from Helpmekaar and off the high escarpment by descending the winding track that led to the border with Zululand at Rorke's Drift. The whole area was a hive of activity; on arriving at Rorke's Drift they saw the Royal Engineers detachment commanded by their officer, Lieutenant Francis MacDowell, the Centre Column's only RE officer, testing the two barrel ponts that would carry them across the Buffalo river into Zululand.

Chelmsford had already visited Rorke's Drift on 4 January and was impressed with the readiness and enthusiasm of his gathering invasion force. He was looking forward to the first engagement; his intelligence officers incorrectly reported that a large force of Zulus from Chief Sihayo's nearby homestead would oppose the invasion. Such was Chelmsford's confidence that, when he was presented with three emissaries from King Cetshwayo bearing a request for an extension of the ultimatum, Chelmsford ignored them just as he had the six previous pleas from Cetshwayo. He also banned further Zulu messengers from entering British positions.

Despite the enthusiasm of the Imperial troops, there was one section that was less than happy. Rather unexpectedly, Chelmsford was faced with the unbelievable threat of mutiny by his previously loyal Colonial troops who took exception to an inadvertent snub to their commanding officer, Major Dartnell. According to paragraph 144 of the *Regulations for Field Forces in South Africa* any Colonial officer, regardless of his rank, was barred from having command over Imperial troops. Chelmsford had previously decreed that all commanders were to be Imperial officers and command of the Natal Mounted Police together with all the Natal volunteer units had been given to Brevet Major Francis Russell of the Mounted Infantry, which ignored their own experienced commandant. This ruling infuriated the Colonials who paraded at Helpmekaar to take a vote on the matter; they unanimously decided to refuse orders unless they were given by Dartnell, a highly respected officer, especially in the field of African warfare. Chelmsford wisely relented and resolved the issue by promoting Dartnell to the British rank of lieutenant colonel, and gave him authority over Russell. After a short discussion, the Colonials accepted the decision and moved down to Rorke's Drift.

The Swedish mission station, run by the Reverend Otto Witt, was situated immediately adjacent to the Buffalo river crossing of Rorke's Drift. It was sited on an elevated ledge of rock and commanded a magnificent view over the Buffalo river into Zululand. The two mission buildings consisted of the missionary's house and a small church, both made of local stone with thatched roofs. Sheltering the mission was the nearby 700ft high Oskarsberg hill, named by Witt in acknowledgement of his Swedish king. Surrounding the homestead was 3 acres of carefully cultivated land that included an orchard of grape vines, orange, apricot, apple, peach, fig, pomegranate and other fruit trees, all bordered with an assortment of lime trees and quince bushes. Between the vegetable garden and the mission was a 130ft long, 5ft high wall. Witt's home was the larger of the two buildings and was nearly 30 yards long and spacious. Witt's church was 40 yards away: small and dignified, it was used by the missionary in his daily work with the local black community. Immediately beyond the church was a small stone cattle kraal and then, below the rock terrace on which the buildings nestled, there was a similar but larger cattle kraal that could hold 100 cattle. The sole link between the mission station and the rest of Natal was a dirt track that led westwards towards the high escarpment of the Biggarsberg and thence to Helpmekaar. In the other direction, the track led to the nearby Buffalo river; it was the only safe route into Zululand for hunters and itinerant traders plying their wares among the Zulus.

On 9 January the tranquillity and beauty of Rorke's Drift was severely disturbed by the arrival of nearly 6,000 troops and all the impedimenta of Chelmsford's invasion force. Row upon row of tents were erected in neat formations on the half-mile grassy slope between the riverbank and the mission station while the Natal Native Contingent (NNC) were instructed to camp downstream of the Europeans. Notwithstanding the protestations of Otto Witt at being allowed to retain only one small room, the commissary staff commandeered his two buildings on behalf of the Crown. On the day before the invasion, Witt's twelve-roomed house was converted into a makeshift hospital to cater for the growing number of fever cases and a few soldiers with damaged limbs caused by a number of wagon-related incidents, while the church became an ammunition store. In despair at the damage caused by converting his home and church, Witt dispatched his wife and small children to stay with friends at nearby Msinga, some 10 miles south of Helpmekaar.

Due to the incessant rain, the whole area soon became a muddy quagmire strewn with effluent and rubbish, yet the soldiers' spirits remained high as the hours passed towards the expiry of the ultimatum. A few days earlier, the *Natal Witness* reported British confidence at a high level.

No attempt to cross the river will be made if opposed, except under the protection of the battery. These Zulus do not yet know what a shell is like or what effect it will have upon them. May they soon learn, and the larger the quantity that is present the better the effect will be.[17]

Chelmsford arrived at Rorke's Drift with his entourage of staff officers during the evening of 10 January, a visible sign to the awaiting troops that the invasion would take place the following morning. The excitement throughout the camp that night was so infectious that few men slept. During the night the six guns of N Battery commanded by Lieutenant Colonel Harness RA were relocated to an adjacent small rise overlooking the river in order to cover the troops while crossing. Shortly after 2 a.m. reveille was sounded and within the hour the column approached the river crossing point. One minor diversion occurred when it was discovered that a trader's supply wagon had been looted and a cursory search failed to discover the culprits or the stolen stores. By daybreak the river was covered in a heavy soaking mist; no sound could be heard and as the mist gradually lifted above the river the far bank and surrounding countryside were bathed in bright sunshine. There were no Zulus; they were already 60 miles away at Ulundi undergoing pre-war rituals in preparation for the defence of their country.

The advance guard of mounted troops cautiously rode their horses through the swirling waters of the Buffalo river using the submerged flat rocks of the original traders' crossing point. In anticipation of a Zulu attack, they spread out in a wide semicircle but all they found was three Zulu boys tending some cattle. The infantry were then slowly ferried across the river followed by the Native Contingent auxiliaries who had to be cajoled by their officers towards the fast-flowing muddy water. They began the crossing in their customary style by linking arms and entering the water in a 'V' formation, those in the front apex being pushed across by those in the rear. Once across, they pulled their colleagues over. The NNC lost several men in the crossing but as their officers did not know how many men they commanded, little concern was shown.

Within a quarter-hour the mounted patrols confirmed the absence of Zulu defenders. A new campsite was prepared on the hillside that looks back at Rorke's Drift and by noon the slow process of bringing stores and wagons across from Rorke's Drift was virtually completed. Midmorning, Chelmsford had ridden off to liaise with Colonel Wood, commander of the Northern Column. Wood was already well into Zululand about 30 miles to the north, having 'jumped the gun' by crossing into Zululand on 6 January; Chelmsford ordered him to halt his advance while the Centre and Coastal columns caught up.

CHAPTER 7

The First Invasion of Zululand, 11 January 1879

This army could not be beaten the world over.[1]

THE NATAL MERCURY

In the early hours of 11 January 1879 the Centre Column commenced the slow advance towards Ulundi; 5 miles away was a high row of steep red cliffs that formed the backdrop to the homestead of the Zulu chief Sihayo kaXongo, an anglophile who wore European clothes and had been a good friend of James 'Jem' Rorke. It was Sihayo's sons who had murdered his two adulterous wives within sight of the mission station, the act that was used by the British as one of the grounds for the invasion. Sihayo's homestead also lay directly in the path of the invading column's main supply route; accordingly Chelmsford ordered that the stronghold be neutralized. On 12 January Chelmsford and most of his Centre Column watched as the NNC, the Natal-recruited black auxiliaries of Commandant Rupert La Trobe Lonsdale, spearheaded the first attack of the invasion against Sihayo's homestead. Chelmsford commented:

> I am inclined to think that the first experience of the power of the Martini-Henrys will be such a surprise to the Zulus that they will not be formidable after the first effort.[2]

The attack was led by Lieutenant Harford, a noted entomologist and a popular young officer on loan to the NNC from the 99th Regiment. The attacking force slowly advanced towards the steep cliffs and soon came under desultory fire from a handful of Zulus left to protect the homestead. Under fire from the Zulus now sheltering in caves set deeply into the rock face, the NNC formed up and then stormed the stronghold, supported by the 2/24th. The NNC lost less than half a dozen men with a similar number wounded while the 24th sustained no casualties. The Zulus, on the other hand, lost over thirty men killed. Several of Sihayo's men, including wounded, were captured and forcibly interrogated, an unpleasant process that was to redound on the British a few days later. The captured Zulus nevertheless kept the secret that a great force of 25,000 warriors, accompanied by another 10,000 reserves and camp followers, was steadily closing with the unsuspecting British. Released the following day, the Zulus took comfort at the neighbouring village at Sotondose's Drift, soon to be known as Fugitives' Drift. Angered by the destruction of their village, the death of one of Sihayo's sons and their own brutal treatment, not to mention the theft of their 413 head of cattle, they were not well disposed to the British fugitives who were to flee through Sotondose's Drift a few days later.

The *Natal Times* on 16 January enthusiastically reported the engagement at Sihayo's homestead:

> Up to 9 o'clock last night no intimation had been received from the front of shots being fired in any quarter; but at that hour we received the following important telegram, notifying the repulse and flight of the Zulus, with great loss on their side, at the first encounter. It will be seen that the initiative in attack came from the enemy, and, as has been expected it was from Uirajo's [Sihayo's] people. We regret to see that one of Lonsdale's officers has been killed, and, we fear, two of the Natal Mounted Police; but the telegram leaves room for a probability that the latter have only been wounded. They were probably chasing the flying enemy. The prediction of those best acquainted with the Zulus, that they would never stand the fire of regular forces, has been abundantly verified.

Following the skirmish at Sihayo's homestead, the subject of Sihayo's captured Zulu cattle caused much discontent among participating column troops who were all entitled a fair share of the plunder, based on the current market price. Evidently, the 413 head of cattle captured at Sihayo's homestead and the surrounding area had been sold cheaply to contractors: cattle for the sum of £2 a head, the goats for 2s. 6d. and the sheep for 6s., and word spread quickly through the column.[3]

After destroying Sihayo's homestead, most of the invasion force moved back to their temporary camp near to Rorke's Drift; a detachment of infantry was deployed in the Batshe valley to control the forward route while the Royal Engineers repaired the track that ran through two swampy areas leading to Isandlwana. Over the next two days several local Zulus reported to Chelmsford that King Cetshwayo intended to decoy the British and then make for Natal. Chelmsford dismissed their warning and resolved to push on deeper into Zululand without delay. The *Natal Witness* reporter with the Carbineers submitted the following perceptive dispatch to his newspaper on 18 January; it was published on 23 January.

> We have already had three different patrols into the enemy's quarters.
> Rumour had it that there were thousands near to us: but, though we
> hunted up hill and down dale, 'saw we never none.' It is impossible to
> know what to believe. The Zulus must assuredly be somewhere, but
> wherever we go, we only come across deserted huts.

The battle of Isandlwana, 22 January 1879

The invading British force duly arrived at Isandlwana and there were considerable misgivings about the site on the part of the experienced colonial officers, including Major Dartnell. They were greatly concerned about the broken and wooded county to the rear of the camp, which offered ample cover for the Zulus to gather and prepare an attack completely unseen from the camp; their misgivings were ignored by Chelmsford. By 21 January some 750 tents, neatly erected according to strict military regulations, company by company, street by street, were spread out over an area nearly 1 mile square. There were tents for every purpose: medical tents, storage tents, numerous HQ and administration tents – although the majority were troop tents with either two officers or twelve men sleeping in each one. Each unit's wagons were parked behind their own regimental lines; those required for resupply were left in the adjacent wagon park ready to return to Rorke's Drift the following day. The camp location was perfect, with an ample supply of both water and wood for cooking. From a military perspective it was excellent: the position was elevated with a sheer rock face to its rear and therefore easy to defend. More importantly, it looked across the open plain towards the unseen Zulu capital at Ulundi so that any approaching Zulu force would be observed long before it could form up for an attack. Foot patrols were posted to the front of the camp while mounted patrols were detailed to ride to the surrounding hills; one patrol, accompanied by Lieutenant Milne RN, investigated the plateau that overlooked Isandlwana from the unprotected side of the camp. He later wrote that he saw a number of Zulu horsemen – which clearly alarmed him at the time. He wrote:

> We then rode to the high land to the left of our camp, the ascent very steep, but possible for horses. On reaching the summit of the highest hill, I counted fourteen Zulu horsemen watching us at the distance of about four miles; they ultimately disappeared over a slight rise. Two vedettes were stationed at the spot from where I saw these horsemen; they said they had seen these men several times during the day, and had reported the fact. We then returned to camp, the General having determined to send out a patrol in this direction the next day.[4]

On the very same day Inspector George Mansell of the Natal Mounted Police had lookouts placed along the top of the Nqutu plateau overlooking Isandlwana. Major Clery, a former professor of tactics and the senior staff officer of the 1/24th, later withdrew the lookouts on the grounds that they 'served no useful purpose'. A few hours later an officer of the Natal Mounted Police suggested to the same staff officers that the British camp might be attacked from the rear. The message was delivered to Chelmsford who retorted, 'Tell the police officer my troops will do all the attacking.'[5]

Chelmsford and his staff persistently ignored intelligence that they considered inaccurate or implausible and concentrated instead on unconfirmed reports that large numbers of Zulus were approaching from the direction of Ulundi, the Zulu capital. This was exactly what Chelmsford was hoping for, and during the afternoon of 21 January Chelmsford dispatched an experienced Colonial officer, the recently promoted Lieutenant Colonel John Dartnell, towards the distant hills of Isipezi, the site of the next British camp. He took with him a reconnaissance force consisting of sixteen companies of the NNC with most of the Natal Mounted Police and half the Natal Mounted Volunteers. Dartnell was requested to reconnoitre the area and return that evening. Meanwhile, Isandlwana camp remained unprepared for a Zulu attack even though a number of experienced Boer frontiersmen such as Gert de Jager and James Gregory had personally expressed their disquietude to Chelmsford at British indifference to the Zulus' fighting ability. As a measure of British overconfidence, some Zulus, including Chief Gamdama, were allowed into the British camp on the pretext of surrendering some obsolete firearms; having had a good look at the British position they were then allowed to depart.

Prior to the invasion Chelmsford gave his commanders specific orders requiring British positions in Zululand to be laagered or entrenched at night, yet once the invasion was under way these orders were dismissed by the staff officers as unnecessary; in effect Chelmsford neglected his own written orders to entrench or fortify the camp at Isandlwana. To be fair, he was probably swayed by the knowledge that further supplies remained to be collected the following day from the depot at Rorke's Drift. Chelmsford was also impatient to move the force just 12 miles across the plain to the next campsite at Isipezi, especially as there was no sign of the Zulus' approach. Certainly the ground at Isandlwana was rocky and hard, but a solid defensive embankment of rocks could have been effectively constructed within a few hours.[6]

During that night Chelmsford received an urgent message from

Dartnell, now bivouacked near the Hlazakazi hills, confirming that a strong Zulu force had been seen throughout the day and, more importantly, captured Zulus confirmed the imminent arrival of the Zulu army. After dark, hundreds of campfires could be seen in the hills leading off towards Ulundi. Understandably, Dartnell believed he had found the Zulu army. Chelmsford likewise presumed the main Zulu army of some 25,000 warriors had been located and at about 1.30 a.m. on 22 January he decided to split his invasion force. At 3 a.m. he set out with Colonel Glyn and a force of 2,500 men including the 2/24th Regiment and four of the six guns of the Royal Artillery to support Dartnell. The camp was to be left with two guns in case the enemy should have the temerity to attack the camp during Chelmsford's absence. As G Company of the 2/24th were still being employed on night guard duty, they remained at Isandlwana. At about the same time a message was delivered to Durnford by Lieutenant Smith-Dorrien ordering him to move forward to support Chelmsford.

Lieutenant Colonel Henry Pulleine of the 1/24th was left in command of Isandlwana camp, now manned by 1,700 men armed with Martini-Henry rifles and supported by two 7-pound artillery guns and reserves of nearly one million rounds of Martini-Henry rifle ammunition. Pulleine was 41 years old and had been in the army for over twenty years but he had never seen action. Furthermore, he had only rejoined his regiment five days earlier after holding various administrative positions in Durban and Pietermaritzburg. His orders were straightforward: to defend the camp and await orders for the move to the next site at Isipezi.

By dawn, Chelmsford and over half the strength of the Centre Column were well on their way marching towards the Hlazakazi hills where Chelmsford eagerly expected to engage the main Zulu army. Instead he was to confront an illusive enemy decoy and by 8.30 a.m. he realized that he was not about to engage anyone. He told Commandant George Hamilton-Browne of the 3rd Battalion NNC to march his battalion the 12 miles back to Isandlwana; over rough terrain and in the heat of summer, this would take at least four hours. The order Hamilton-Browne received is recorded in his book published over thirty years later:

Commandant Browne, I want you to return at once to camp [with your men] and assist Colonel Pulleine to strike camp and come on here.[7]

As dawn broke over Isandlwana, Pulleine and the men of the 1/24th had watched Chelmsford's column march out of camp. In compliance with Chelmsford's orders Pulleine dispatched the infantry to form a line extending for almost 1 mile approximately 1,000 yards to the left front of the camp. Further positions were taken up at dawn by several companies of the NNC; these covered the base and shoulder of the nearby Nqutu plateau overlooking the north of the camp.

At 7 a.m. a number of disquieting events began with a report from the plateau that confirmed a large force of Zulus advancing towards the camp. The men on outpost duty had seen large numbers of armed Zulus approaching and of special concern to Pulleine was a report of a concentration of Zulus 'in the broad valley before them. There were very many of them and they appeared to be moving in the direction of the camp'.

In response to the reports coming in, Pulleine ordered the buglers to sound 'stand to'; breakfast was abandoned and the British enthusiastically prepared for action. No Zulus appeared; the troops were stood down but almost immediately a returning patrol reported large bodies of Zulus moving north-west towards Chelmsford's position. The confusion in camp was reflected in the final diary entry of Lieutenant Pope – the diary was later discovered on the battlefield. He wrote:

Alarm. 3 Columns Zulus and mounted men on hill E. Turn Out. 7,000 (!!!) more E.N.E., 4,000 of whom went round Lion's Kop. Durnford, Basutos, arrive and pursue. Rocket Battery. Zulus retire everywhere. Men fall out for Dinners.[8]

Small groups of Zulus appeared along the edge of the plateau and within minutes the distant sound of firing was heard but due to the echoing among the hills it was impossible to pinpoint its exact position. Larger groups of Zulus then appeared on the plateau and the bemused British soldiers were again 'stood to'. Pulleine knew the Zulus should not be on the plateau to his left – they were supposed to be to his front being engaged by Chelmsford's attacking force, and he dithered. Unbeknown to Pulleine, the Zulus overlooking the camp were the commanders completing their pre-battle reconnaissance.

At about 10.30 a.m. Lieutenant Colonel Durnford arrived from Rorke's Drift with 500 mounted men of the No. 2 Reserve Column. Durnford's orders from Chelmsford, received only that morning, were vague:

> You are to march to this camp at once with all the force you have with you of No. 2 Column. Major Bengough's battalion is to move to Rorke's Drift as ordered yesterday. 2/24th, Artillery and mounted men with the General and Colonel Glyn move off at once to attack a Zulu force about 10 miles distant.[9]

When questioned later, Clery stated that his order to Durnford was very specific. He claimed he ordered Durnford, on Chelmsford's behalf, to 'take command of it', referring to the Isandlwana camp. As can be seen from the actual order, only discovered a hundred years later, Durnford was the commander of No. 2 Column and was never ordered to take command of the Centre Column camp at Isandlwana.

Durnford apprised himself of the puzzling situation and was discussing the various sightings of the Zulus with Pulleine just as one of Chelmsford's staff officers, Captain Shepstone of the NNH, arrived to report that Zulus had been sighted some 3 miles away on the plateau. Trooper Barker was one of the mounted scouts on the plateau and he later wrote:

> Shortly afterwards, numbers of Zulus being seen on all the hills to the left and front, Trooper Swift and another were sent back to report. The Zulus then remained on the hills, and about two hundred of them advanced to within three hundred yards of us, but on our advancing they retired out of sight, and a few of us went up to this hill where the Zulus had disappeared, and on a farther hill, at about six hundred yards distance, we saw a large

army sitting down. We returned to Lieutenant Scott, who was then about three miles from camp, and reported what we had seen. Hawkins and I were then sent back to camp to report a large army to the left front of the camp. On our way back we noticed the Zulus advancing slowly, and when about a mile and a half from the camp we met the rocket battery, who enquired the enemy's whereabouts. We advised the officer to proceed to where Lieutenant Scott was stationed, but he asked if he could get up a hill to his left. We informed him that the Zulus were advancing towards that hill, and most probably would be seen on it within half an hour. The officer decided to proceed up this hill, and the battery was, half an hour afterwards, cut up to a man, just as they arrived, I believe, on the top of the hill in question. (We, the videttes, were at the time in a donga firing at the Zulus, and witnessed the cutting up of this battery without their having time to fire a single shot.) Hawkins and I reported to an officer, staff, I believe, about the advance of the Zulus, and as we left camp to return to Lieutenant Scott, another Carbineer, I am not sure of his name, galloped in and reported Zulus in every direction advancing. He was then sent on to the General with some report, and was never seen again alive by any in camp, although he is reported to have given a dispatch to the General, who sent him back to camp, at which the poor fellow never arrived.[10]

To these experienced officers who had served in the previous Cape wars, large forces of warriors were not necessarily considered to be dangerous. Pulleine was undoubtedly thankful for Durnford's presence and calm analysis; he gave the order to 'stand down' and turned his attention to the more routine task of moving the camp. Durnford was senior in service to Pulleine and much has revolved upon this seniority, the presumption being that command of the camp devolved upon Durnford, thus relieving Pulleine of overall responsibility. Pulleine may well have wished this to happen but as Commander of the No. 2 Reserve Column, Durnford was independent and no orders were ever given to merge the two columns.

Durnford was, however, forced to acknowledge that a significant enemy force was deploying along the plateau, possibly to drive a wedge between the Isandlwana camp and Chelmsford's vulnerable force now 12 miles away towards Ulundi. At about 11.30 a.m. Durnford departed to join Chelmsford but before doing so he sent two of his mounted troops, under the command of Lieutenants Raw and Roberts, onto the plateau to obtain a factual report of Zulu movements. This small force would shortly collide with the advancing Zulu army.

Durnford had hardly departed when heavy firing was heard coming from the plateau; two companies of the 24th commanded by Lieutenants Cavaye and Mostyn and a company of the NNC were firing down at a large body of Zulus which was moving off and away from the plateau towards the undefended rear of the British camp, ignoring the British. The intention of this large body of Zulus, the right horn, was to seize the track back to Rorke's Drift and deny the British any possibility of retreat or escape.

In readiness to defend the camp, the remaining companies of the 24th were extended 800 yards to the left and front of the north-facing position in order to cover the plateau and the plain towards Ulundi. The soldiers were positioned 3 yards apart in a double line. Men of the NNC also formed a section of the line, with the two 7 pound guns of the Royal Artillery between them and the Imperial troops. The garrison troops were elated; the Zulus were about to attack and they, not Chelmsford's force, would have all the glory. In every previous battle fought by the 24th Regiment in Africa the attacking warriors fled when volley firing commenced. The British, though, had never fought the Zulus.

In the midst of the uncertainty, one of Chelmsford's staff officers, Captain Alan Gardner, arrived at Pulleine's tent with orders from Chelmsford to transfer the camp to the area beyond Mangeni waterfall, Chelmsford's current position. The note arrived just as the Zulus began to advance on the camp. However, Pulleine could neither see nor communicate with his front line because his headquarters tent was located on the far side of camp. He had not realized that, in order to cover the extensive dead ground to their front, his front-line officers had advanced their troops

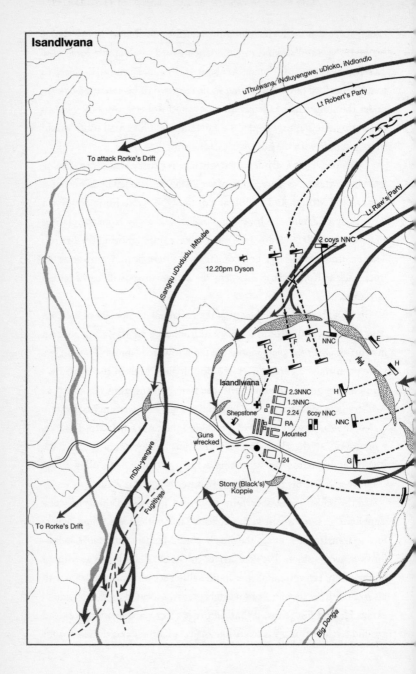

Isandlwana

uThulwana, iNdluyengwe, uDloko, iNdlondlo

Lt Robert's Party

To attack Rorke's Drift

Lt Raw's Party

iSangqu uDududu, iMbube

12.20pm Dyson

F   A

2 coys NNC

C   F   A   NNC

E

H

H

Isandlwana

Shepstone

2.3NNC
1.3NNC
2.24
RA

6coy NNC

NNC

H

Guns
wrecked

Mounted

1.24

G

mDlu-yengwe

Stony (Black's)
Koppie

Fugitives

To Rorke's Drift

Big Donga

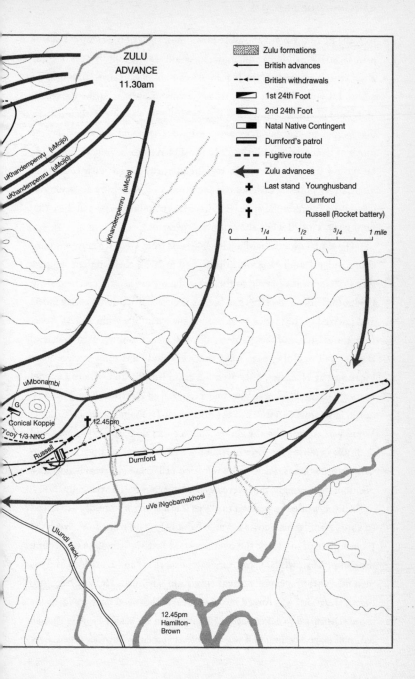

ZULU
ADVANCE
11.30am

Zulu formations
British advances
British withdrawals
1st 24th Foot
2nd 24th Foot
Natal Native Contingent
Durnford's patrol
Fugitive route
Zulu advances
Last stand   Younghusband
               Durnford
               Russell (Rocket battery)

0   ¼   ½   ¾   1 mile

uKhandempemru (uMcijo)

uKhandempemru (uMcijo)

uMbonambi

G

Conical Koppie

'coy 1/3 NNC

† 12.45pm

Russell

Durnford

uVe iNgobamakhosi

Ulundi track

12.45pm
Hamilton-
Brown

127

over the lip of the plain and were now out of sight of the camp.[11] Pulleine now faced a bewildering dilemma; he could see the rapidly approaching Zulu army sweeping off the Nqutu plateau but not his own front line. To add to his woes, his last order from Chelmsford was to strike the camp, and half Pulleine's men were still occupied with packing. Pulleine knew that by initiating further defensive precautions he would seriously delay the move of the camp, and if the Zulu force proved to be only skirmishers, he would incur the derision of Chelmsford. Faced with too many alternatives Pulleine ordered the camp garrison to deploy according to Chelmsford's orders; he appears to have taken no further part in the battle until he was killed when the camp was overrun.

The actual orders that Pulleine inherited from Glyn when he assumed command at Isandlwana were discovered in 2001; their content suggests that Pulleine was obeying to the letter the orders he had received from Chelmsford. Identical orders had been issued to all five column commanders and referred to the tactics to be used in the event of a Zulu attack. Apart from the existence of these orders, identical tactics to those used to defend Isandlwana had also been used that very same morning at two other locations: at Nyezane, only 50 miles from Isandlwana, where Colonel Pearson's Coastal Column came under a sustained Zulu attack; and likewise during a skirmish 40 miles to the north near Hlobane, in which Colonel Wood was engaged by the Zulus. Pulleine had no battle experience and faithfully deployed his force in front of the Isandlwana camp according to Chelmsford's orders. Such tactics were doomed to fail in a weakly defended position; interestingly, they were never used again against the Zulus.

All the while the massed ranks of Zulu warriors rapidly advanced towards Isandlwana across a 5 mile front before pouring down from the Nqutu plateau to attack the overextended British firing line protecting the camp. Meanwhile, some 3 miles out on the plain, Durnford and his men met with the rapidly advancing Zulu left horn. Heavily outnumbered, Durnford was forced into a tactical withdrawal back towards the camp. Durnford's rocket battery, commanded by Major Francis Russell RA, had lagged behind and was completely taken by surprise when, over the brow of the plateau, the Zulus suddenly appeared less than 200 yards away; the battery managed to fire one ineffectual rocket before being overrun by the leading ranks of warriors. Retreating, Durnford gathered up the battery's three shocked survivors and continued back towards the camp, now less than a mile distant.

At the same time, Captain Reginald Younghusband's E Company was sent out from the camp to climb the spur to the plateau to support the retreat of Cavaye and Mostyn's men, who were now in danger of being overrun; Cavaye and Mostyn retreated under fire but only one company reached the camp – which company it was remains unclear. Their withdrawal now left Younghusband's men isolated on the spur. The NNC on the line were ill equipped with only one rifle per ten men; seeing the Zulus rapidly advancing upon them, they knew they faced certain death if they stayed so they fled across the camp and into rocky terrain towards Natal.

With the camp now surrounded by the two Zulu horns, the central body of the main Zulu force consisting of some 15,000 warriors came into view. They descended from the plateau and rapidly advanced upon the overextended line of British infantry. The two guns of the Royal Artillery, directed by Major Stuart Smith and Lieutenant Curling, began firing and several rounds of their case shot (shrapnel) scored direct hits on the advancing warriors before the Zulu front line swept over and surrounded the British guns. Curling's gun was on the left of the front line when his detachment was suddenly silenced; hotly pursued by the closing Zulus, Curling's men clung to the guns as they retreated back towards camp in search of another firing position. Being mounted, Curling was able to lead the way through the battle. His letters home confirm that many of Pulleine's men were not deployed on the front line as historians had previously believed but were still engaged in packing the camp as the Zulus attacked. He wrote:

At 7.30 I got the message to turn out at once and we got ready in about 10 minutes forming up by the 1/24th on their parade ground. The companies were very weak, no more than 50 in each and there were only 6 of them in all. We congratulated ourselves on the chance of our being attacked and hoped that our small numbers might induce the Zulus to come on, I suppose that not more than half the men left in the camp took part in its defence as it was not considered necessary and they were left in as cooks etc.[12]

At this early stage of the battle, the three *amabutho* making up the main body, the uNokhenke, uKhandempemvu and uMbonambi, all suffered serious losses from the defenders' sustained rifle fire. The officers and NCOs in the centre of the British front line calmly controlled their men's volley fire to the extent that the main Zulu attack faltered, which encouraged the soldiers to laugh and joke about the drubbing they were giving the Zulus. Captain Edward Essex, one of the five Imperial officers to survive, later wrote:

> I was surprised how relaxed the men in the ranks were despite the climactic tension of the battle. Loading as fast as they could and firing into the dense black masses that pressed in on them, the men were laughing and chatting, and obviously thought they were giving the Zulus an awful hammering.[13]

At the centre of the British front line the men's spirits were momentarily high but on the left of the line the soldiers, like the artillery, were being overwhelmed. On the right of the line Durnford's men had been forced to withdraw to a dried-up watercourse less than a mile from the camp. A party of colonial riders sped to Durnford's assistance but the position quickly became untenable; Durnford's men became seriously outnumbered as the Zulus' left horn began outflanking them. Within minutes Durnford realized his men were running out of ammunition and sent several riders back to the camp with urgent requests for replenishments, but they were unable to find their allocated supplies. As ammunition supplies were not forthcoming Durnford requested a volunteer to warn Pulleine of his predicament; there were no volunteers, which left Durnford with no option but to give the order to withdraw back to the main camp.

G Company 2/24th under command of their monocled officer, Lieutenant Charles Pope, were now occupying the extreme right end of the British line. Pope saw that Durnford's men were in danger of being engulfed by the Zulus' flanking advance so he ordered his company to move towards Durnford's position. However, as they left the extreme right of the British line Durnford simultaneously ordered his men to retreat. Being mounted, Durnford's force quickly vacated their position, leaving G Company fatally exposed. Pope's company was swiftly overwhelmed by the charging mass of several thousand Zulus; not a single soldier survived.

Meanwhile the main Zulu attack in front of the camp had stalled. The Zulu commanders on the overlooking heights of the iNyoni cliffs dispatched Chief Mkosana of the uKhandempemvu to restart the attack. Under his direction the uKhandempemvu resumed their advance. Chief Mkosana was then shot dead but without his brave intervention, the Zulus could have lost the battle. Instead, they charged the thin line of British infantry. In an instant the Zulu masses closed with the entire British position; even sustained volley fire proved ineffective against such numbers. The Zulu left and right horns now joined up behind the British camp and then charged into the surviving soldiers from their undefended rear. Survivors from the centre companies in the line had fought their way back through the main camp to the wagon park where they tried to form a defensive square. At the same time Captain Younghusband's E Company was steadily forced back along the base of the cliff wall of Isandlwana until the thirty or so survivors reached a small plateau overlooking the bloody struggle in the wagon park. Having been furthest from the main Zulu attack, Younghusband had managed to maintain good order and discipline until the Zulus were about to overwhelm them. One Zulu later reported:

> The soldiers gave a shout and charged down upon us. There was an induna in front of the soldiers with a long flashing sword, which he whirled round his head as he ran. They killed themselves by running down.[14]

In less than one hour, the battle of Isandlwana was over. The Zulu attack had been brilliantly and courageously executed across many miles of rugged and difficult terrain; the British were powerless to engage the sheer number of Zulus and the challenge they posed. The officers in charge of the two 7 pound guns that day were Major Smith and Lieutenant Curling, both riding fine artillery horses. Smith was killed in the latter stage of his flight from Isandlwana while Curling, the only officer to have continuously engaged the Zulus until the British line broke under the force of the Zulu attack, survived to tell a remarkable tale. He wrote to his mother:

> We trotted off to the camp thinking to take up another position there but found it was in possession of the enemy who were killing the men as they ran out of their tents. We went right through them and out the other side losing nearly all our gunners in doing so and one or two of the sergeants. The road to Rorke's Drift that we hoped to retreat by was full of the enemy so no way being open we followed a crowd of natives and camp followers who were running down a ravine. The Zulus were all among them stabbing men as they ran … and finally the guns got stuck and could go no further. In a moment the Zulus closed in and the drivers who now alone remained were pulled off their horses and killed.[15]

Having successfully manoeuvred their right horn behind Isandlwana, the Zulus emerged in force from behind the mountain, driving the column's bellowing and terrified cattle through the wagon park and into the undefended rear of the British position. Very quickly, the camp transformed itself from a scene of peaceful activity to a nightmare of gunfire, noise, terror, confusion and bloody slaughter everywhere. The pandemonium was further exaggerated by the lack of visibility, a vital component usually overlooked by authors and historians. According to Lieutenant Wilkinson, a veteran of several Zulu War battles, 'independent firing means, in firing for twenty seconds, firing at nothing; and only helped our daring opponents to get close up under cover of our smoke'.[16] Isandlwana sits in a wide bowl ringed by hills which, on a hot day, can be airless and so still that volley fire would soon have created a thick hanging smokescreen between the British line and the advancing Zulus. It could also account for the relatively few Zulu casualties, not only at Isandlwana but also at other Zulu War battles through to the final battle at Ulundi.

In order to avoid this problem, contemporary army instruction manuals recommended firing volleys by sections: 'In firing volleys by sections it is well to commence from the section on the leeward flank, in order that the smoke may not inconvenience the remainder.' [17] Private George Mossop perceptively wrote of volley fire:

> We were armed with Martini-Henry rifles charged with black powder, and each shot belched out a cloud of smoke; it became so dense that we were almost choked by it – and simply fired blindly into it. There was one continuous roar from cannon, rifles and the voices of men on both sides shouting. The smoke blotted out all view. It made every man feel that all he could do was to shoot immediately in front of him – and not concern himself with what was taking place elsewhere. [18]

The British line at Isandlwana may well have fought and then withdrawn back to the camp in a fog of their own gunsmoke – only to encounter the massive Zulu right horn as its 4,000 warriors charged through the unprotected camp and into the rear of the retreating British troops.

As the Zulus smashed their way into the camp, panic quickly spread among the camp's followers and within moments calm British discipline descended into serious rout; it was every man for himself amidst the fury and carnage of the Zulu attack. Surviving soldiers tried to rally by forming defensive groups but with the British force so outnumbered, it was remarkable that anyone could escape back to the safety of Natal, although of the estimated sixty Europeans who did escape Isandlwana and lived to tell the tale, the majority were camp followers who departed before the battle was under way, or were Colonials who were mounted and could outrun the Zulus. Several groups of red-coated soldiers valiantly fought their way out of the camp but all were soon overwhelmed; their graves can still be seen along the trail that had earlier been taken by the camp fugitives.

Of the escaping British officers, only Lieutenant Curling RA and four mounted transport officers, Captains Essex and Gardner together with Lieutenants Cochrane and Smith-Dorrien, would see the end of the day. Apart from Curling who alone survived the front line, these officers had all been engaged on duties within the camp before they made good their escape. Curling later wrote:

> They behaved splendidly in this fight. They were all killed in the ranks as they stood. Not a single man escaped from those companies that were placed to defend the camp. Indeed, they were completely cut off from any retreat and could not do as we did, gallop through the Zulus. When last I saw them, they were retreating steadily but I believe a rush was made and they were all killed in a few minutes.[19]

Beneath Isandlwana 52 officers, 810 white troops and 500 supporting black troops of the British column now lay dead among a probable 3,000 Zulu fatalities. At night, the hills around Isandlwana echoed with the baying of packs of dogs whose owners lay slain on the battlefield. Spaniels, pointers and mastiffs all packed together and, when tired of rotting human flesh, would hunt whatever they could, including sheep and cattle.[20]

In the early 1900s it was realized that a partial eclipse had occurred across southern Africa as the battle of Isandlwana drew to its bloody close. Although it featured in contemporary calendars, no mention of the event was made at the time by any of the British military in Zululand; it must therefore be presumed that the eclipse was not perceptible to the naked eye at the time.

Three months would elapse before the British could return to bury their dead.

CHAPTER 8

An Appalling Disaster

Never has such a disaster happened to the English Army.[1]
TROOPER RICHARD STEVENS

In the dying camp there was no one to give orders and no one to rally the men not that anyone could have been heard over the tumult and confusion of such terrible slaughter. Many of the camp civilians took the opportunity to flee for their lives and, finding the road back to Rorke's Drift blocked by the closing Zulus, they fled through the gap made when a section of the iNgobamakhosi detached themselves from the closing left horn to chase the NNC who were also trying to flee across the rough, boulder-strewn terrain. This temporary gap enabled the last few escaping whites to follow through, only for most to run into the Zulus who killed them; only a few riders would escape to reach the river 6 miles away. It was through this gap that Lieutenant Curling and Major Smith rode alongside the two artillery guns, only to see them being driven out of control down the steep slope behind the camp where the guns overturned amidst the Zulus. Curling and Smith rode on; Smith was caught and killed near the Buffalo river but Curling managed to reach the river and safety.

Only those whites on horseback had any chance of reaching the river and with little doubt many of the survivors, with the exception of Curling and two 24th Regimental officers, Lieutenants Coghill and Melvill, left Isandlwana before the main battle got under way. The majority of the survivors were also wearing blue jackets, including Coghill. The 24th's officers had a choice of regimental jackets to wear in the field so there is no special significance in Coghill's jacket being blue, other than the fact that it may have saved his life on the ride along the Fugitives' Trail. King Cetshwayo had ordered the Zulus to concentrate on red-jacketed soldiers in the mistaken belief that only they were the Imperial troops.[2]

The surviving disciplined troops, those under Durnford and some of the 24th Regiment, probably no more than 200 men in all, made a hopeless but gallant stand in the area of Isandlwana wagon park. Durnford and his men were forced into a back-to-back struggle next to Black's Koppie; all died making their final stand. The 24th similarly fought against over-whelming odds; the 24th then tried to effect a fighting retreat following the earlier fugitives; a few individuals managed to get as far as a mile to the rocky ledges overlooking the Manzimyama stream but all were cut down and died in the attempt. An unknown number of other fugitives were killed in the Buffalo river under the hail of Zulu gunfire or spears. Curling later wrote to his mother:

> I saw several wounded men during the retreat, all crying out for help, as they knew a terrible fate was in store for them. Smith-Dorrien, a young fellow in the 95th Regiment, I saw dismount and try to help one. His horse was killed in a minute by a shot and he had to run for his life, only escaping by a miracle.[3]

Lieutenant William Cochrane was also in the camp when it was overrun by the Zulus; he echoed the desperate attempts to escape when he wrote to his family:

> I made in the direction which I had seen taken by the mounted men, guns and Royal Artillery, and natives on foot. I was cut off by the enemy, who had now reached the line of retreat; but with a good horse, hard riding, and good luck, I managed to reach the Buffalo River. The Zulus seemed

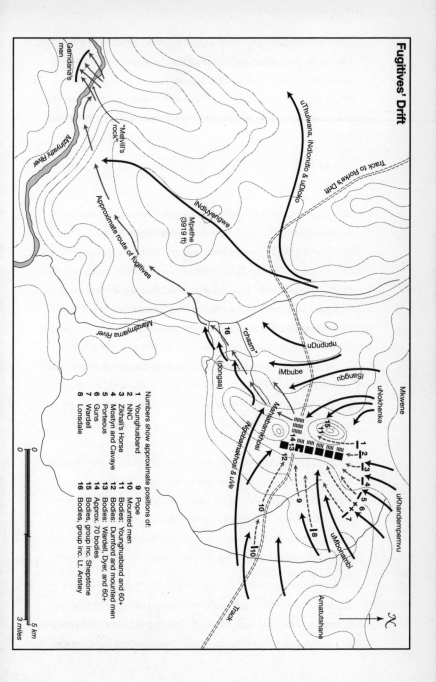

Fugitives' Drift

Gamdana's men

Mzinyathi River

uThulwana, iNdlondlo & uDloko

"Melvill's rock"

iNdluyengwe

Mpethe (3919 ft)

Approximate route of fugitives

Track to Rorke's Drift

Manzimnyama River

"chasm"

(dongas)

"Nyobamakhosi" & uVe

Malabamkhosi

16

uDududu

iMbube

iSanqgu

uNokhenke

14 13

15 11

12

Mkwene

uNokhenke

uKhandempemvu

uMbonambi

1 2

3 4

5 6 7

9

8

10

10

Amatutshane

uMbonambi

Track

Numbers show approximate positions of:

1	Younghusband	9	Pope
2	NNC	10	Mounted men
3	Zikhali's Horse	11	Bodies: Younghusband and 60+
4	Mostyn and Cavaye	12	Bodies: Durnford and mounted men
5	Porteous	13	Bodies: Wardell, Dyer, and 60+
6	Guns	14	Approx. 70 bodies
7	Wardell	15	Bodies, group inc. Shepstone
8	Lonsdale	16	Bodies, group inc. Lt. Anstey

0   1   2   3 miles
0   5 km

N

perfectly fearless; they followed alongside, having desperate fighting with those retreating, mostly our natives on foot. On several occasions they were quite close to me, but I was fortunate enough to escape, while others dropped at my side. They fired at us the whole way from the camp to the river, but having mounted the bank on the opposite side we were safe.[4]

Private Barker survived the day and his account reveals the horror and terror of his escape:

Up to this time I had never thought of disaster, but only that we were retiring on a point to rally; but the defeat was only too palpable, and we had to spur and hurry on our jaded horses over the most awful country I had ever ridden. Riderless and wounded horses were galloping past and tumbling down precipices and gullies. Here I heard for the first and only time the awful scream of a terrified or mad horse. He was a black horse with the saddle turned round, and as he passed us and went crash against a mounted man in front of us, rolling over the krantz, this awful scream was heard. Zulus seemed to be behind, before, and on each side of us, and as we hurried on we had to leave poor fugitives crying and begging us not to leave them. Many were shot as we rode past them, but we met no Carbineers or volunteers whom we knew until we neared Fugitives' Drift, when we caught up C. Raw, and well it was for us two, as his men, mounted Basutos, were already on the Natal side of the river, and had it not been for these Basutos I doubt if a single white man would have escaped by Fugitives' Drift, as they kept the Zulus in check while the few escaped. As we ascended the hill on the Natal side the firing of the Zulus was very good, and I saw a contingent native drop just in front of us and shortly after we passed another who had been shot. The Zulus would then be about nine hundred yards off.[5]

As the fleeing NNC reached the riverbank the pursuing Zulus caught them. Because the river was in flood, and few blacks could swim, they tried to make a stand against the Zulus but were quickly overwhelmed and killed. It was through the midst of this slaughter and chaos that the last of the escapers, including Coghill, Melvill and Curling, were able to reach the river. An unknown number of other fugitives were killed in the river under the hail of Zulu gunfire and spears.

For those who made it to the opposite bank, there was yet more danger to overcome. As mentioned earlier, following the initial British attack on Sihayo's homestead, a number of surviving Zulus were detained for questioning, invariably a rough and brutal process. These captives were released during the following day or so and a number of them took refuge with relatives living in the vicinity of Fugitives' Drift on the Natal bank of the Buffalo river, then known as Sotondose's Drift. These natives, resentful of the British action and grieving for their chief's son and friends killed in the attack, were not necessarily well disposed towards the British. As the few British survivors from Isandlwana crossed the river, these very same natives observed them; the time for revenge had arrived. Local Zulu folklore holds that Coghill and Melvill were both killed by these previously friendly local natives and not by Cetshwayo's Zulus. One member of Chelmsford's staff actually wrote that 'some of them [survivors] got right down to the river six miles off and were killed by a lot of scoundrels whom the General had taken prisoner a few days before'. This fact was kept secret at the time, although it was well known to Chelmsford's staff.

Having crossed the river, Curling and the other European survivors made their way to the deserted camp at Helpmekaar where they arrived during the early evening. Another survivor, Captain Essex, had the presence of mind to send a note to the garrison at Rorke's Drift warning them of the defeat at Isandlwana.

The morning of 22 January began frustratingly for Chelmsford's force; after the long march from camp his four companies of the 2/24th found themselves chasing elusive groups of Zulus around the hills beyond Mangeni. As the morning wore on disquieting messages began to reach Chelmsford's staff officers that there might be a problem at Isandlwana camp. As early as 9.30 a.m. a message was received from Pulleine that the Zulus were advancing towards the camp. A junior staff officer,

Lieutenant Berkley Milne RN, was dispatched to a nearby hilltop with his telescope; he saw nothing untoward. Chelmsford then set off to scout the area between Magogo hill and the Mangeni waterfall. Accompanied only by a small escort, he did not think it prudent to inform his staff officers of his whereabouts and when subsequent messages arrived from Isandlwana, Chelmsford could not be found until 12.30 p.m. Distant firing could now be heard from the direction of Isandlwana. Chelmsford and his staff rode to the top of a nearby hill and observed the camp through field glasses. Nothing untoward could be seen, partly because of the thick heat haze and partly because the battle at the camp was taking place in a long valley. Chelmsford assumed that any Zulus there had long been rebuffed but he nevertheless decided to ride back towards the camp, leaving Glyn to concentrate the force and organize the new campsite near Mangeni, a location considered by Chelmsford to be ideal as a bivouac site for the night.

Colonel Arthur Harness RA was with the guns that accompanied Chelmsford's force and, during the morning, he heard gunfire from the camp and realized the probability that Isandlwana was under a serious attack. He spontaneously ordered those under his command to march back to the camp. His force had only travelled a mile and a half when a message from Chelmsford ordered Harness to 'about turn' to the new campsite. Meanwhile Lieutenant Colonel Russell, who had been leading a party of mounted troops, arrived on the scene and informed Chelmsford that Durnford was also engaging the Zulus. An uneasy Chelmsford and his staff set off towards the camp to ascertain the situation. After a few miles they came across Commandant George Hamilton-Browne's battalion observing the camp, and Chelmsford reordered Hamilton-Browne to advance just as Commandant Rupert Lonsdale arrived to report that the camp had been taken. Lonsdale had ridden back to the camp having suffered from a fall and sunstroke; as he approached the camp in a dazed state he suddenly realized the camp had been taken. Only 200 yards from the camp he turned and, riding for his life, escaped back across the plain towards Chelmsford's force. The Zulus would not have bothered with

Lonsdale, having already begun their retreat from the battlefield; having got their victory, there was a very strong imperative for them to leave the scene as soon as possible, as they needed to perform the rites of purification after shedding blood. This reason why the Zulus would retreat without further resistance after a battle was never understood by the British, who nevertheless turned it to their advantage to rout and attack retreating Zulus in the aftermath of subsequent battles.

It took Chelmsford until 6.30 p.m. to muster his remaining force just 3 miles from Isandlwana. The sun had set and under the cover of darkness the cautious troops advanced towards the silent camp; the artillery fired several rounds of shrapnel to dislodge any remaining Zulus before the exhausted column reoccupied the body-strewn position at about 9 p.m. The Zulus had long since departed and there was no sign of life from the 1,350 men left there that morning although, it being dark, no one looked. In fact, several survivors of the NNC feigned death through the night lest they should be found by the soldiers and taken for Zulus, as the soldiers had earlier been seen to bayonet some drunken Zulus who had taken refuge under a wagon.

As Chelmsford struggled to come to terms with the situation his attention was drawn to the distant fire that lit the sky over the British camp 10 miles distant at Rorke's Drift, and other fires could be seen towards the Helpmekaar hills.[6] Chelmsford's weary force was too exhausted to march any further and was ordered to settle down in a position of all-round defence and to expect an attack at any moment. As dawn broke, Chelmsford's force silently marched away from Isandlwana towards Rorke's Drift where B Company 2/24th was stationed. The Zulus at Rorke's Drift had probably intended to make one last attack on the outpost at dawn but, in sheer disbelief, saw Chelmsford's column advancing out of the mist. This caused them much confusion, as they believed the whole of Chelmsford's force had been destroyed.

A few days after the battle, it was discovered that two mounted officers of the 24th Regiment, Lieutenants Coghill and Melvill, had not only escaped from the camp but had reached Natal on horseback before being killed. Contrary to mythological explanations, nothing is known concerning their escape from Isandlwana camp while their regiment's soldiers were still fighting for their lives, and the matter was to become the subject of much speculation, debate and harsh criticism from Chelmsford's successor, Sir Garnet Wolseley. Only three Victoria Crosses were awarded for the battle of Isandlwana; curiously, each recipient had fled the battlefield. Private Samuel Wassall's VC for his bravery at the Buffalo river was presented to him in 1879; Lieutenants Coghill and Melvill were honoured posthumously, nearly thirty years later. The eminent British historian of the time, Sir Reginald Coupland, wrote of Coghill and Melvill that these two officers

> had charged themselves with saving the colours of the 24th and then, after their six-mile flight on horseback across impossibly rocky terrain, they reached the river together and plunged straight into it.[7]

It is highly probable that Coupland had studied and then relied on the original report written by Lieutenant Colonel Glyn, now isolated at Rorke's Drift, in his capacity as the officer commanding the No. 3 Column. (Coupland even copied Glyn's incorrect spelling of Melvill's name as 'Melville'.) This highly emotive but fascinating report, the earliest record relating to the fate of these two officers, was written by Glyn after the enquiry into the disaster of Isandlwana and, no doubt, after much anguish and personal reflection on his part. At the time of the Zulu attack at Isandlwana, Glyn was 12 miles away with Chelmsford at Mangeni; his report therefore is based on a combination of his imagination, speculation and hearsay. It is Glyn's personal and emotional attempt at vindication of his officers' actions at Isandlwana; the official history of the 24th Regiment, similarly based on hearsay and possibly Glyn's report, records the event with soothing Victorian eloquence:

> On the fateful 22nd January 1879, when it was evident that all was lost in Isandhlwana camp, Lieutenant and Adjutant Melvill, 1st battalion 24th, received special orders from Lieutenant Colonel Pulleine, to endeavour to

save the colour.'You, as senior subaltern', that officer is reported to have said, 'will take the colour, and make your way from here'. Accompanied by Lt. A.J.A. Coghill, 1st Battalion 24th, who was orderly officer to Colonel Glyn, but had remained in camp on account of a severe injury to his knee, Melvill rode off with the colour, taking the same direction as the other fugitives. Both officers reached the Buffalo [river] although, owing to the badness of the track, the Zulus kept up with them and continued throwing their spears at them. The river was in flood, and at any other time would have been considered impassable.

They plunged their horses in, but whilst Coghill got across and reached the opposite bank, Melvill, encumbered by the colour, got separated from his horse and was washed against a large rock in mid-stream, to which Lieutenant Higginson, of the Native Contingent, who afterwards escaped, was clinging. Melvill called to him to lay hold of the colour, which Higginson did, but so strong was the current that both men were washed away. Coghill, still on his horse and in comparative safety, at once rode back into the stream to their aid. The Zulus by this time had gathered thick on the bank of the river and opened fire, making a special target of Melvill, who wore his red patrol jacket. Coghill's horse was killed and his rider cast adrift in the stream. Notwithstanding the exertions made to save it, the colour had to be abandoned, and the two officers themselves only succeeded in reaching the opposite bank with great difficulty, and in a most exhausted state. Those only who know the precipitous character of the Natal side at the spot, can fully realise how great must have been the sufferings of both in climbing it, especially of Coghill with his wounded knee. They appear to have kept together, and to have got to within twenty yards of the summit when they were overtaken by their foes and fell. On 3rd February, a search party found the bodies of Melvill and Coghill covered with assegai wounds and with several dead Zulus around them. Next day the flood, having subsided, the Colour, on its pole, was recovered further downstream. For their gallantry in the saving of the Colour, Lieutenants Melvill and Coghill were later each awarded a posthumous Victoria Cross.[8]

Higginson wrote in his statement that he had left Coghill and Melvill after the three of them had safely reached the Natal bank; he went on to relate how he, being the fittest, then left the two exhausted British officers in order to find some horses and, on reaching a vantage point, he looked back and saw the bodies of Coghill and Melvill surrounded by Zulus. Unable to help them, he then rode off to Helpmekaar. However, the reality of Higginson's escape was very different; two troopers, Barker and Tarboton, under covering fire by Lieutenants Raw and Henderson from the Natal bank, had managed to swim with their horses across the flooded Buffalo river to safety. The officers then rode up the steep Natal side of the river gorge closely followed by Troopers Barker and Tarboton; on looking back towards the river the two troopers saw a distant figure scrambling on foot towards them. Tarboton rode on to join Raw's group while Barker rode back down the hill to assist the scrambling escapee; this fugitive turned out to be none other than Higginson. Barker gallantly surrendered his mount to the exhausted officer but implored him to wait at the top of the hill. With Zulus closing in around them, Higginson rode away leaving Barker to struggle alone to the summit only to find that Higginson had galloped off. The exhausted Barker was forced to run for his life; he was pursued for another 2 miles before the pursuing group gave up the chase.

Meanwhile, Higginson had come across Lieutenants Raw and Henderson who, together with some Basuto scouts and Tarboton, had waited on the Helpmekaar track for Barker to rejoin them. Tarboton immediately recognized Barker's horse, which Higginson insisted he had found at the Buffalo river; under duress, Higginson relinquished the horse in exchange for a spare Basuto pony. Higginson was sent off alone towards Helpmekaar to make his report while Raw's group backtracked towards the escarpment overlooking the river until they came upon the exhausted Barker still running for his life. Within a few days, the truth of Higginson's escape from the scene became well known and, now with a black eye, he quietly disappeared into obscurity. Higginson received no recognition for his endeavours to save either the two officers or the Colour; he was a Colonial officer, his story was not corroborated and there was the unmentionable matter of the horse stolen from Barker.

Higginson's embellished report soon reached Glyn at Rorke's Drift. Basing his impressions on the report, Glyn realized that Melvill had reached the river with the Colour, lost it midstream and then, having been saved by Coghill, lost his own life trying to save Coghill. There is little doubt that Melvill could have escaped on foot with Higginson but chose instead to assist Coghill. Glyn dispatched a search party to the river where the bodies of Coghill and Melvill were found the following day and their bodies were buried where they had fallen. It later occurred to Glyn that the Colour could still be in the vicinity of the bodies and on 3 February he dispatched a party to search the river bank. Lieutenant Harford and Captain Harber soon discovered the Colour case and further down the river found the Colour pole protruding out of the water. Captain Harber waded into the river and pulled the pole, still attached to the Colour, out of the water. As he recovered the Colour, the gold-embroidered centre scroll fell back into the water and was lost. In a moving ceremony back at Rorke's Drift, the Colour was restored to Colonel Glyn, the officer to whom it had originally been presented in June 1866.

Chelmsford was understandably cautious before making any official comment concerning the circumstances and deaths of Coghill and Melvill. He was already aware that an unacceptable number of officers had escaped from both Rorke's Drift and Isandlwana, including Lieutenants Avery and Holcroft who were part of Major Dartnell's force sent to scout ahead at Isandlwana and Lieutenant Adendorff who departed from Isandlwana where he was on picket duty.[9] On 14 May 1879 Lord Chelmsford wrote to the War Office:

It is most probable that Melvill lost his life endeavouring to save Coghill rather than vice versa. He [Coghill] could hardly walk and any exertion such as walking or riding would have been likely to render him almost helpless. He could not have assisted, therefore, in saving the colours of the 1st 24th, and as I have already said I fear he was a drag on poor Melvill. As regards the latter [Melvill] I am again puzzled how to reply to your question. I feel sure that Melvill left camp with the colours under orders received. He was too good a soldier to have left without. In being ordered to leave, however, he no doubt was given the best chance of saving his life which must have been lost had he remained in camp. His ride was not more daring than that of those who escaped. The question, therefore, remains had he succeeded in saving the colours and his own life, would he have been considered to deserve the Victoria Cross?[10]

The new British Military Commander, Sir Garnet Wolseley, was to write even more strongly on the issue:

I am sorry that both of these officers were not killed with their men at Isandlwana instead of where they were. I don't like the idea of officers escaping on horseback when their men on foot are killed. Heroes have been made of men like Melvill and Coghill, who, taking advantage of their having horses, bolted from the scene of the action to save their lives, it is monstrous making heroes of those who saved or attempted to save their lives by bolting or of those who, shut up in buildings at Rorke's Drift, could not bolt, and fought like rats for their lives which they could not otherwise save.[11]

With regard to Coghill and Melvill, it is interesting that no specific recommendation was submitted from Glyn, the commander in the field, and although his emotive dispatch praised their conduct he made no suggestion of any award. The Duke of Cambridge intimated to the Secretary of State for War that the terms of the dispatch merited the issue of a memorandum to the effect that they would have been recommended to the queen for the award of the Victoria Cross had they survived. Exactly the same situation applied to the recommendation made by the Indian Government on 15 May 1879 for the Victoria Cross to be awarded to Lieutenant Walter Hamilton for his action at Futtehabad in India. As with other attempts to bend the rules, the Indian application failed, as did the case for Coghill and Melvill.

There can be no doubt that Melvill richly deserved his award on at least two counts, firstly for denying the Colour to the enemy and secondly for remaining to assist the injured Coghill into Natal. The case of Coghill is only marginally less clear although, sadly, the awkward question concerning the authority for his flight from the battlefield remains unanswered. He probably left Isandlwana, under orders and early in the battle, to summon help from the reserves he fully expected to be at nearby Rorke's Drift or even closer to Isandlwana. He also surrendered his only chance of escape by plunging back into the river, under heavy enemy fire, to assist Melvill and Higginson who were floundering midstream.

On 19 May 1879 the Prime Minister notified Melvill's wife, Sara, that Queen Victoria had awarded her a pension of £100 a year 'in recognition of the heroic conduct of your late husband in saving the Colours of the 24th Regt. on the field of Isandlana' [sic]. Melvill's father received a letter from Major General Dillon, War Office, dated 21 April 1879 which included the following line:

> It is gratifying to His Royal Highness to inform you that, if your son had survived his noble effort, it was Her Majesty's intention to confer upon him the Victoria Cross, and a notification to that effect will be made in the London Gazette.[12]

In 1907 the rules were altered to allow for the award of a posthumous Victoria Cross; perhaps the continuous pressure on King Edward VII from Coghill's father, Sir Jocelyn Coghill, and Sara Melvill, influenced the change. On 15 January 1907 the *London Gazette* published the names of a number of families who were to receive a posthumous Victoria Cross, the list including the names of Melvill and Coghill, Melvill for attempting to save the colour, Coghill for attempting to save Melvill and the Colour. Sadly, Sir Jocelyn Coghill died just before the awards were announced.

Private 427 Samuel Wassall of the 80th Regiment of Foot (Staffordshire Volunteers) earned the only instantaneous Isandlwana Victoria Cross. When the camp at Isandlwana was taken by the enemy, Private Wassall retreated towards the Buffalo river, in which he saw a comrade, Private

Westwood, struggling and apparently drowning. He rode to the bank, dismounted, leaving his horse on the Zulu side, rescued the man from the stream and again mounted his horse, dragging Private Westwood across the river under a heavy shower of bullets.

After his escape from Isandlwana, Wassall was unofficially attached to the Northern Column under Colonel Wood VC. Westwood was still recovering in hospital at Helpmekaar from his near drowning when he overheard two officers discussing an unrecorded event of 'unparalleled bravery' by an unknown soldier in the river. Weakly, Westwood managed to provide the required information but it took the army several weeks to trace Wassall. In the meantime Wassall had also fought with Colonel Buller at Hlobane, the second major British disaster of the war; Wassall uniquely survived both. In the *London Gazette* dated 17 June 1879 the War Office gave notice:

> That the Queen has been graciously pleased to signify Her intention to confer the decoration of the Victoria Cross on the under mentioned Officers and soldier of Her Majesty's Army, whose claims have been submitted for Her Majesty's approval, for their gallant conduct during the recent operations in South Africa, as recorded against their names.

One of these was Samuel Wassall of the 80th Regiment of Foot. On 11 September 1879 Samuel Wassall, along with Robert Jones of the 24th Regiment (for his part in the defence of Rorke's Drift), were presented with their Victoria Crosses by Sir Garnet Wolseley GCMG, KCB. Wassall was 22 years and 9 months old. His VC was the first awarded during the Zulu War; he was also granted a pension of £10 per annum for life.[13]

The incident of Higginson and Barker resurfaced at Pietermaritzburg on 17 December 1881. Sir Evelyn Wood was visiting Trooper Barker's regiment, the Natal Carbineers, to distribute campaign medals. At the medal parade in the town's market square, Wood concluded his speech with the following words:

I have only now heard of a gallant act performed by a straggler [Barker]
whose late arrival [at Helpmekaar] is well explained by his having, during
the retreat, given up his horse to an officer who was exhausted. Into this
matter it will be my pleasure to enquire more.

Wood wrote to the War Office and recommended Trooper Barker for the
Victoria Cross. The War Office duly replied on 10 March 1882:

Major General Sir Evelyn Wood VC.

Sir,
I am directed by the Field Marshal Commanding in Chief to acknowledge
your letter of 6th instant, and to acquaint you in reply, that statements re
Trooper Barker, Natal Carbineers, at the battle of Isandhlwana, on 22nd
January, 1879, have carefully been considered. His Royal Highness desires
me to state that, while trooper Barker's conduct on the occasion referred
to is deserving of every commendation, there does not appear to be
sufficient ground, according to the terms of the statute, for recommend-
ing him for the distinction of the Victoria Cross.[14]

CHAPTER 9

Rorke's Drift, 22–23 January 1879

This showed what a few men could do if they only had pluck.[1]

GUNNER HOWARD

The camp at Rorke's Drift mission station was situated half a mile from the Buffalo river, Natal's border with Zululand. Its commanding officer was Major Spalding of the 104th Regiment, Chelmsford's deputy assistant adjutant and quartermaster general who enjoyed overall responsibility for the small garrison together with communications and supplies to and from the front line. During the previous two weeks the area between the mission station and the river had been home to over 6,000 troops; now it lay silent, guarded by a token force supplied by B Company of the 2/24th (2nd Warwickshire) Regiment. The detachment consisted of just 100 men to guard the advancing column's reserve of stores and the hospital. Lieutenant Gonville Bromhead, a 35-year-old officer from a distinguished military family, commanded B Company. Bromhead has been popularly credited with poor mental acuity and little enthusiasm for anything of a military nature. This was undoubtedly the belief of his superior officers but he was popular with his men. He was an accomplished boxer and wrestler and a top-scoring regimental cricketer, although he suffered from deafness which caused him embarrassment on parade when he misheard orders. Bromhead's senior NCO was 24-year-old Colour Sergeant Bourne, only

5ft 3in tall, who had originally joined the army under-aged as a 16-year-old. His father had initially tried to purchase his release due to his age and lack of stature but as he was doing so well his service continued.[2] Bourne found success in the army and his three promotions to lance sergeant, sergeant and his present rank had all been made within the last year; furthermore, he had taken command in action on several occasions during the recent Cape Frontier wars.

Bromhead was not the only officer at the mission station. Lieutenant Smith-Dorrien was in charge of a small wagon repair unit; the hospital building was commanded by Surgeon Reynolds who cared for the fifteen or so hospital bed patients suffering from a variety of illnesses and a similar number of walking wounded with minor injuries. The Reverend George Smith was also at Rorke's Drift, having been left behind by the advancing column. The boxes of stores were organized by three hard-working officers of the Commissariat. Their senior officer was Assistant Commissary Walter Dunne who was supported by Acting Assistant Commissary Dalton, a very experienced officer with over twenty years' previous service with the 85th Regiment, from which he had retired as a sergeant before moving to South Africa. Dalton's deputy was 21-year-old Acting Storekeeper Louis Byrne, a civilian from Pietermaritzburg who had joined the Commissariat at Dalton's request. Due to their lower status in the army, these three officers lived and dined separately from Bromhead and the other officers. Bromhead may have been aware that another officer, 33-year-old Lieutenant John Rouse Merriott Chard of the Royal Engineers, had arrived the day before in answer to Chelmsford's request for an additional detachment of engineers, although most of Chard's men remained sick at Durban suffering the after-effects of smallpox vaccinations.

On his arrival Chard reported directly to the engineers' tents by the river where his fellow officer, Lieutenant MacDowell, and his engineers had their camp. He was disappointed to find that MacDowell and his men were now at Isandlwana helping with road repairs. Chard decided to remain at the drift and await orders. The following day he made contact with Spalding who instructed him to plan a redoubt overlooking the river and to supervise its construction as soon as further reinforcements of the 24th, still at Helpmekaar, arrived to undertake the work. Like the Commissariat officers and Captain George Stevenson, a Colonial officer of the Natal Native Contingent who commanded some 300 natives, Chard was not considered to be a 'proper' officer. All knew their place and each busied himself with his own responsibilities.

The next day, 20 January, Chard was content to tinker with the ponts but soon there was nothing for him to do. During the evening of 21 January an ambiguous order arrived from the Centre Column ordering the engineers to Isandlwana: 'The party of R.E. now at Rorke's Drift are to move at once to join the Column under the charge of the NCO.' Clearly irritated that he was not mentioned in the order, Chard sought out Major Spalding to clarify his role and responsibilities. Not knowing what to do with him, Spalding suggested that Chard should ride to Isandlwana the following morning to discuss the matter with MacDowell, or with the column commander's staff.

For those who remained at Rorke's Drift, including Lieutenant Bromhead and the eighty-five members of B Company of the 2/24th, there was little to do other than to recover from the long marches of the previous weeks. The men's favourite haunt was the cooking area where they could lounge about. When it rained hard they retired to their tents, which were pitched in two neat rows between the church and the small cattle kraal. Only the surgeon and his small team were fully occupied, caring for the growing number of hospital patients, who were suffering the effects of fever, trench foot, lumbago and rheumatism; there were also several patients who had been injured in wagon accidents. The senior ranking patient, Sergeant Maxfield, was given Otto Witt's bed as he was delirious with fever while the remaining patients were on straw beds laid on wooden pallets propped up on bricks. Two men from the NNC were suffering from wounds sustained from the engagement at Sihayo's homestead; Corporal Schiess, a Swiss national, had a bullet wound to his foot and Corporal Meyer was suffering from a leg injury. One of Sihayo's Zulus had been shot through the leg and he was isolated from the other hospital patients. All were in the care of Surgeon Reynolds and his three orderlies from the Army Hospital Corps. On loan as cook to the surgeon was Private Henry Hook, the B Company cook, a 29-year-old teetotaller from Gloucestershire.

Unlike previous days, the morning of 22 January was unusually hot. A section of eight men were detailed to guard the ponts while the remainder busied themselves with their own affairs. Camped next to the river to the right of the old drift was Captain Stevenson's NNC Company who lazed in the sun, as did their officer and six white NCOs. In the absence of any wagons to load, the Commissaries also enjoyed a peaceful morning.

After sunrise, Chard dispatched his small detachment consisting of Corporal Gamble and Sappers Cuthbert, MacLaren, Wheatley and Robson and all their stores, to Isandlwana. Chard rode on ahead of his men and on arriving at Isandlwana he found the main camp in a state of some confusion. Chelmsford was well on his way to Mangeni with half the force to support Major Dartnell who believed he had discovered the advancing Zulu army. The camp forward line was now manned by the 1/24th who were almost out of sight a half-mile from the camp. Chard learned that Zulus had been seen gathering about 2 miles distant on the Nqutu plateau which overlooked the British position, yet those left in camp were busy preparing to take down tents while the remainder – clerks, cooks and bakers, bandsmen, farriers and other camp staff – pursued their normal duties. All were indifferent to the Zulus observing them from the plateau. Chard went to the officers' mess for breakfast and then sought out the headquarters staff to find out what his orders were. He was disappointed to find that no orders had been issued for him so it was suggested that he should return to Rorke's Drift to supervise the ponts and keep the road between Rorke's Drift and Isandlwana in good working order. Hearing some excited voices, he investigated and saw a much larger group of Zulus obviously observing the camp defences from the Nqutu plateau. Using his binoculars, he saw a number of Zulus move off to the west, perhaps, thought Chard, towards Rorke's Drift. Chard decided to return to the drift and 1 mile from the camp he met Colonel Durnford's column advancing towards Isandlwana accompanied by his own engineers; following a brief discussion with Durnford, Chard continued to Rorke's Drift.

Chard was aware that Rainforth's Company of the 24th were supposed to be coming from Helpmekaar to assume responsibility for the ponts but they were now several days overdue. On his return he discussed the matter with Spalding. Spalding was clearly irritated by the situation as he had already sent two written orders to Helpmekaar and could not understand Rainforth's non-arrival. Spalding decided to ride to Helpmekaar to clarify matters; as he was about to depart, he asked, 'Which of you is senior, you or Bromhead?' Chard did not know so Spalding returned to his tent and examined his copy of the Army List. He told Chard, 'I see you are senior, so you will be in charge, although, of course, nothing will happen, and I shall be back again this evening, early.' Spalding departed Rorke's Drift at 2 p.m. and with his departure he abandoned his chance of glory;[3] Chard returned to his riverside tent for a late lunch with Commissary Dunne without informing Bromhead that the Zulus might be approaching. He decided to spend the afternoon writing letters.

It is unclear why neither Chard nor Spalding informed Bromhead, the commander of the only fighting troops at Rorke's Drift, that he had seen Zulus heading in their direction. Chard may not have understood Zulu tactics but it meant that Bromhead and his men were oblivious of approaching danger. Meanwhile the Swedish missionary Otto Witt, the Reverend George Smith, Surgeon Reynolds and Private Wall of the 24th took some horses and rode to the Oskarsberg summit behind the mission station where they had a panoramic view across the Buffalo river into Zululand and beyond to Isandlwana. From the summit they heard the distant rumble of artillery fire from Isandlwana; they strained their eyes to see the 10 miles to Isandlwana and even used a telescope that the Reverend George Smith had brought with him, but could see nothing out of the ordinary. At the same time, the muffled sound of gunfire was also heard by those at Rorke's Drift, but not by the semi-deaf Bromhead. Because Chard's campsite was in a depression by the river and out of sight of Isandlwana the sound of gunfire was muted; Chard remained unaware of unfurling events.

Then, from their vantage point, Witt's group saw three distant columns of natives approaching the Buffalo river from the direction of Isandlwana. Smith's first impression was that these were detachments of the NNC returning to Rorke's Drift. It was not until half an hour later that he realized that there were two warriors on white horses leading an obvious *impi* of Zulus. The group also noticed scouting patrols of Zulus who appeared to be searching in wide sweeps and firing into the bush. In stunned horror they watched the advancing Zulus until Surgeon Reynolds saw some European riders approaching the mission station from the direction of the river; thinking that they might need medical attention, he set off down the hillside, quickly followed by the others. All four were now in no doubt that a large Zulu force had somehow bypassed Chelmsford's main column and was heading for Rorke's Drift. The Zulus were led by Prince Dabulamanzi, a half-brother of King Cetshwayo, and included the uThulwana, iNdlondlo and uDloko *ibutho*; they crossed the Buffalo river 4 miles below Rorke's Drift and once across they divided into raiding parties. One group advanced along the Natal bank and onto the plateau behind Rorke's Drift where they rested and took snuff. Prince Ndabuko kaMpande, the king's younger brother, had urged his uMbonambi warriors to join Dabulamanzi's warriors crossing into Natal – but because of their casualties they declined and returned to plunder Isandlwana.

Whether or not King Cetshwayo had told his generals to stay out of Natal is open to conjecture. Addressing his assembled army only days earlier, he had ordered his army to drive the British back to the Drakensberg. Certainly on 21 January the Native Border Guard protecting Natal's border along the Buffalo river had heard that a large Zulu force was gathering at Mangeni, only a dozen miles from the camp at Isandlwana, prior to crossing into Natal. The NBG's district commandant informed Major Bengough (Durnford's second in command) who gave orders to prepare for the attack. Bengough sent an urgent message to Chelmsford warning him of the Zulus' possible intention; the message was not acted upon.[4]

Even if the order to stay out of Natal had existed, only three hours earlier the Zulus had attacked Isandlwana in disregard of the king's instructions not to attack the British when encamped; crossing the border into Natal was no worse, especially if serious damage could be caused and Natal cattle looted. To the commander of the marauding Zulus, Prince Dabulamanzi, the prestige from invading Natal and engaging in serious plunder and 'spear washing' would offset the ignominy of having led the non-participating reserve force at Isandlwana; since the time of Shaka, warriors returning from battle with unblooded spears were viewed as cowards. By killing any Natal farmers they came across between the Buffalo river and Helpmekaar, and by burning farms and plundering cattle, they could still retire back to Zululand with honour vindicated.

It must be unequivocally stated that attacking Rorke's Drift was incidental to Prince Dabulamanzi's plan to engage in some casual looting. The garrison was not even an objective; it just happened to be located in the area about to be plundered. Indeed, Prince Dabulamanzi may not have known of the close proximity of the mission station or of the presence of Bromhead's B Company when his force crossed into Natal since, once across the Buffalo river, the Zulus split into several raiding parties. Some headed off to plunder and burn farms and *imizi* in the area towards Helpmekaar; one of these *impis* encountered Major Spalding, forcing him to abandon his relief march to Rorke's Drift and return to Helpmekaar. Some Zulu raiders moved south and then inland while others followed the river northwards towards Rorke's Drift where they came across a recently abandoned farm belonging to a white farmer, Edward Woodroffe, which they burned to the ground. It was only then that the first small group of Zulus approached the mission station and discovered that the buildings were manned by troops. As a result of the ensuing action the mockery that Dabulamanzi's warriors were subjected to on returning home was severe, as it was popularly said that 'You marched off, you went to dig little bits with your assegais out of the house of Jim, that had never done you any harm.'[5]

Meanwhile, and just as the breathless Witt and his party arrived back at the mission station, Chard was enjoying his afternoon rest a half-mile away on the river bank. At 3.30 p.m. he noticed two horsemen, Lieutenants Vane and Adendorff of the NNH, galloping towards the drift from the direction of Isandlwana; they plunged their horses into the river shouting to Chard that the Zulus were approaching. There can be little doubt that Chard was bemused by the news, but before he had time to react, another messenger arrived from Bromhead requesting that Chard should strike his tents, inspan his wagon, load his tools and report immediately to the post. A rider from the Edendale Contingent had just delivered a note to Bromhead, written by Captain Essex who had survived Isandlwana, reporting the loss of the British camp to the Zulus. Chard dispatched Vane and Adendorff to Bromhead with his reply that he would return to the post once he had collected his working party. As Adendorff rode off, he called back to Chard that he would stay on and fight.

Having ordered his men to collect a water cart filled with river water, Chard set off on the half-mile ride to the post. At the mission station, Lieutenants Vane and Adendorff reported to Bromhead and strongly suggested that the garrison should move out with all speed before the Zulus arrived. Vane was ordered by Bromhead to ride on to Helpmekaar to warn the garrison; meanwhile, the dreadful news from Isandlwana had been reconfirmed by three more survivors from the battle, including Private Frederick Evans 2/24th on loan to the Mounted Infantry. Having made their reports, they too made off at the gallop towards Helpmekaar.

Bromhead's initial thought was to withdraw back to Helpmekaar; he ordered all tents to be struck and the two available wagons to be made ready to convey the hospital patients away from danger. However, Commissary Dalton intervened to point out the serious implications of the news and suggested that trying to outrun the Zulus over a distance of 12 miles of open country with a slow-moving convoy was doomed to failure. The climb to the ridge that led to Helpmekaar was long, steep and winding, and they would be vulnerable to attack. Without doubt it was Dalton's advice that convinced Bromhead to stay and fight; Dalton was an experienced campaigner and Bromhead heeded his suggestion that the only course of action was to fortify the post and defend it. Furthermore, Bromhead hoped that Major Spalding would return at any moment with Rainforth's company. Dalton may well have anticipated such an attack; during his earlier army service he had attended at least two field defence courses and may well have recognized that the post was undefended, something that neither Spalding nor Bromhead had realized. Many contemporary accounts and letters written by private soldiers acknowledge Dalton's leadership and calm professionalism; the soldiers would certainly have been aware that he had served as a sergeant during the ninth Frontier War. It was undoubtedly with Bromhead's approval that Dalton controlled events at this early stage.[6]

After consulting with Dalton, Bromhead gave orders for a 4ft high wall of mealie sacks and boxes to be built around the perimeter of the storehouse and between the two buildings. There were piles of commissariat stores and a large number of 200 pound mealie sacks plus stacks of hundredweight biscuit and meat boxes; B Company's men and some 300 black auxiliaries from Captain Stevenson's NNC provided more than sufficient manpower to complete the work quickly. Along the front of the buildings was a 60 yard long 5ft drop off the ledge overlooking the Helpmekaar road, the orchard and Witt's garden. Below the ledge and in front of Witt's two buildings was a substantial garden wall so no further significant defences were considered necessary along the entire front of the position.[7]

Witt and his party returned from the Oskarsberg shouting out the news of the approaching Zulus. Witt lost his composure when he saw his two buildings being fortified as part of the barricade; he became, in the words of Surgeon Reynolds, 'excitable, and in broken English, demanded an explanation', which was not forthcoming. Witt suddenly remembered his family, remounted his horse and rode off in a cloud of dust towards Helpmekaar.[8] The Reverend George Smith sought to follow Witt but his horse and black groom had long since departed for Helpmekaar, so Smith had no option but to remain with B Company.

As Witt rode out of the post, Chard arrived. Under Dalton's direction the barricading was nearing completion and the two buildings were in the process of being loopholed for the defenders to fire through. Meanwhile, amidst the flurry of intense activity, the hospital sick and wounded were being transferred to the wagons; there was a short period of indecision before the process was reversed and all were returned to the hospital. Once it was decided to make a stand at the hospital, Dalton instructed that the external doors of the building were to be barricaded and its walls loopholed. It is a testament to Dalton's great experience that Chard and Bromhead both deferred to him despite the fact that, as a mere Commissary officer, he was both socially and militarily inferior.

By about 4 p.m. the two main buildings, the storehouse and the hospital, were linked by the perimeter wall which faced the Oskarsberg, and this wall was strengthened by incorporating the two wagons that would have taken the sick and wounded to Helpmekaar. Colour Sergeant Bourne was now instructed to take a small skirmishing party to a point east of the Oskarsberg where he could observe the approach of the Zulus; he was ordered to delay the Zulu advance while defensive preparations continued at the post.

At some point, and despite his promise to Chard at the river that he would stay and fight, Adendorff quietly slipped away. He had already survived the British disaster at Isandlwana, and as he knew that Rorke's Drift was about to be attacked by the same Zulus, his departure is understandable. Chard wrote in both of his official reports that Adendorff 'stayed to assist in the defence' but there is insufficient evidence from contemporary reports to indicate that he remained. Even his departure from Isandlwana was suspect; Adendorff initially reported to Chard that he had fled Isandlwana by the 'Rorke's Drift road' but the Zulus had blocked the road well before their attack on Isandlwana. Vane met Adendorff only at the river crossing and it has to be presumed that he fled Isandlwana before the battle began. When Chard claimed later that Adendorff stayed and helped at Rorke's Drift he probably confused him with Corporal Attwood of the Army Service Corps.[9]

Chard's sappers had obviously not taken the threat of a Zulu attack seriously and had not yet arrived back at the post; Chard returned to the river to urge them on and had to forcefully decline an offer from Sergeant Milne to defend the ponts. Lieutenant Henderson and his troop of mounted NNH then arrived at the drift and informed Chard that they had escaped from Isandlwana. Henderson bravely agreed to cover the ponts and engage the Zulus to give those at the post warning of the Zulus' approach from the drift; Chard then returned to the mission station. Meanwhile Bromhead dispatched a rider with a hurriedly scribbled note to the garrison at Helpmekaar which reads simply, 'Sir, Intelligence has just reached camp that the camp at Isandula Hill is taken by the enemy.'[10]

The first rank of Zulu skirmishers arrived at the drift and were promptly engaged by Henderson's NNH. Outnumbered, the NNH withdrew, bypassed the mission station and headed off towards Helpmekaar. Lieutenant Henderson shouted his apologies towards the post whereupon Stevenson's NNC, already greatly agitated by the prospect of facing the Zulus in overwhelming numbers, jumped over the barricades and ran after the fleeing riders, hotly followed by their white NCOs and Captain Stevenson. The mass defection of the untrained NNC was probably a blessing but for Stevenson and the NCOs to follow was not acceptable to the Imperial troops who stayed behind. They fired a volley after the deserters and Corporal Anderson fell dead.[11] No one remembered who gave the order to fire and the matter was forgotten. With only minutes to go before the Zulus arrived, Chard gave orders for a dividing wall to be built across the position. Instead of abandoning the isolated hospital and moving the sick into the newly created smaller compound, he decided to defend the whole of the original perimeter.

The first group of marauding Zulus to approach Rorke's Drift did so cautiously from a distance of about half a mile. The Zulu scouts had reported back to Prince Dabulamanzi that the British position was weakly defended; it was an unexpected prize with piles of stores, food and soldiers' rifles. Prince Dabulamanzi ordered the attack to begin and the advancing Zulus spread out into their 'horns' battle formation. As the Zulus advanced, they pushed Bourne's skirmishers back to the post; Bourne later wrote, 'I was instructed ... to take out and command a line of skirmishers ... and about 4.30 the enemy came in sight round the hill to our south and driving in my thin red line of skirmishers, made a rush at our south wall'.[12]

On his return, Bourne supervised the opening of additional ammunition boxes and a supply system was arranged to ensure that every defender had a ready store of cartridges. Everyone could hear the approaching sound of gunfire coming from behind the Oskarsberg as the Zulus fired randomly into the rocks and bushes as they advanced. The work to defend the outpost was as complete as it could be and Commissary Dalton with the Reverend George Smith joined Bourne in opening ammunition boxes and distributing rounds to the soldiers along the defensive wall. Chard placed Sergeant Windridge in charge of the Commissariat store along with several casks of medicinal rum – both knew the soldiers' proclivity for drink in times of crisis. The attack on Rorke's Drift was about to begin.

Meanwhile, Bromhead had directed six soldiers of B Company to take up defensive positions in the hospital rooms that Dalton had carefully prepared with loopholes. Those nominated were Privates Joseph Williams, John Williams (real name Fielding), Robert Jones and William Jones, Henry Hook and Thomas Cole. Those patients who were mobile were quickly issued with rifles and Gunner Howard and Privates Adams, Horrigan and Waters were nominated to look after the patients. Each defender was provided with a haversack full of ammunition, then all the doors and windows were sealed tightly with sacks and boxes. None of the defenders apparently noticed that they were now effectively trapped inside their allotted rooms.

Private Hitch had been detailed to act as lookout from the roof of the commissariat store; he was positioning himself on the thatched roof when, at about 4.30 p.m., he shouted a warning as the first thirty or so Zulus

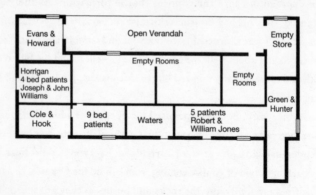

came into sight. They were the iNdluyengwe scouts whose main force was making its way along the Buffalo river towards Rorke's Drift looking for plunder opportunities. The scouts waited until another 500 or 600 warriors arrived; the Zulus then adopted the classic 'horns' attack formation to surround the post. Once in position, the Zulus advanced at a run towards the outpost's south wall between the hospital and storeroom. The defenders opened fire at a distance of between 300 and 400 yards and a scattering of warriors fell. The Zulus ran with their shields held away from their bodies in the anticipation that the soldiers would fire at the steadily held shields and not the darting bodies holding them and, by using this tactic, many Zulus got to within 50 yards of the outpost. However, once they had recovered from the initial shock that they were under attack, the defenders' fire began to improve and soon the British volleys forced the Zulus to retreat behind the numerous boulders that littered the lower slope of the Oskarsberg. The warriors then retreated and awaited Dabulamanzi's main marauding force while others took refuge behind the 5ft high garden wall facing the ledge in front of the mission station. Meanwhile, any Zulu who showed himself immediately came under heavy crossfire from the two buildings.

As more Zulus arrived at the post they spread out behind the garden wall to reinforce those in the orchard; they then charged at the rocky

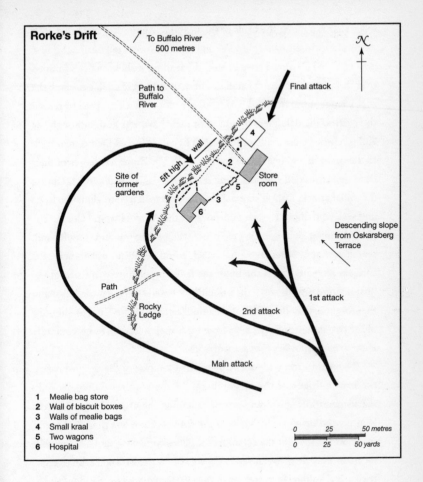

Rorke's Drift

To Buffalo River
500 metres

Path to
Buffalo
River

Final attack

𝒩

wall

5ft high

Site of
former
gardens

4

1

2

Store
room

5

3

6

Descending slope
from Oskarsberg
Terrace

1st attack

Path

Rocky
Ledge

2nd attack

Main attack

1 Mealie bag store
2 Wall of biscuit boxes
3 Walls of mealie bags
4 Small kraal
5 Two wagons
6 Hospital

0   25   50 metres
0   25   50 yards

163

ledge that ran along the front of the hospital. Again they were met with devastating close-range volley fire and many warriors fell during this first concentrated charge. Those behind the leading Zulu casualties jumped over them but this bravery had little effect, as they were unable to climb the rocky ledge, now smeared with slippery blood. With no time to reload their rifles, the defenders fought with their bayonets and, although the Zulus relished close combat, the British bayonets forced their retreat back to the orchard and behind the garden wall. The Zulus left scores of their dead and wounded warriors lying several deep against the ledge. During the initial attack, Dalton shot a Zulu who had managed to climb the ledge and was who about to stab a corporal of the Army Hospital Corps. The overwhelming Zulu numbers were increasing as the minutes went by and, realizing that another ferocious attack could occur at any moment, the soldiers retreated from the lip of the ledge immediately in front of the hospital and withdrew to the biscuit box barrier between the ledge and the storehouse. In the midst of the initial attack Private Dunbar shot one of the two mounted Zulu chiefs from his horse; according to his comrades Dunbar later shot another six warriors.

The main Zulu body then appeared at the rear of the outpost across the lower slopes of the Oskarsberg. As the soldiers watched, Zulu marksmen took up sniping positions among the Oskarsberg caves and commenced firing at the backs of the soldiers from less than 300 yards' range; fortunately for the defenders the Zulus were poor shots. Meanwhile the main Zulu force assembled in the area of the garden and began creeping forward through the rough bush that grew right up to the front of the rock ledge. Although Dalton had given orders for the garden wall and bush to be cleared, there had been insufficient time to carry out his orders. Consequently the British defended their side of the garden wall, the Zulus the other. The British defenders now feared the Zulus would rush their position but the Zulus were not organized and their mounted chief, Prince Dabulamanzi, seemed unable to co-ordinate their attacks even though his force was assembled less than 100 yards from the front of the hospital. Dabulamanzi had earlier seen his *induna* shot from his horse and he was undoubtedly encouraged to remain out of sight of the defenders. Darkness would fall within the hour and the few uncoordinated rushes by the Zulus were beaten back by the British, who had not yet incurred any serious casualties.

As darkness fell, and under cover of the bushes and long grass, the Zulus began moving to the far side of the post and along the mealie bag walls on either side of the hospital, and were able to get to within 5 yards of the hospital without being seen. From this point, in parties of fifteen to twenty, they repeatedly attacked the end room of the hospital. They made these attacks in the most deliberate manner, advancing after the manner of their dancing, with a prancing step and high action. Each attacking group of Zulus faced the impact of close-range volleys and those who survived could only run onto the line of blood-covered bayonets, yet they appeared to care little about their inevitable slaughter.[13]

Such close combat was new to the British soldiers whose previous experience was limited to volley fire – now, bemused by the combination of gunfire and screaming Zulus, and with their vision clouded by the acrid smoke from their own volley fire, they were fighting for their lives. Through the smoke and noise of battle Chard, Bromhead and Dalton managed to keep control over the outpost and when a gap appeared, one or other of these officers would step forward and join the fight. For the next few hours this pattern of assault continued, with each wave of Zulus being forced to retreat. Meanwhile the Zulu casualties were steadily increasing while the Zulu marksmen on the higher Oskarsberg terraces kept up their sporadic but ineffective rifle fire into the British post; a number of the Zulu marksmen had Martini-Henry rifles captured earlier at Isandlwana.[14]

Then Dalton was shot at close range through his shoulder; he calmly handed his rifle to Chard before collapsing. Surgeon Reynolds quickly pulled him from the firing line to dress the wound. Within a matter of minutes, Dalton was back on his feet encouraging the defenders and, where necessary, giving orders. Surgeon Reynolds, separated from the hospital and his patients, also actively assisted with the defence; he repeatedly carried ammunition along the line, a Zulu bullet once striking his helmet as he did so. Corporal Schiess of the NNC, a Swiss national, had been hospitalized with a gunshot wound to his foot following the attack against Sihayo's homestead; he joined the defensive line at the front of the outpost and fought alongside his British colleagues. He observed a Zulu who had hidden himself on the far side of the mealie bag wall and who was taking shots at the defenders. Without a thought for his safety, Schiess went to the barrier only to find himself looking down the barrel of a Zulu rifle. The Zulu fired and the round missed Schiess but pierced his soft hat; Schiess bayoneted the warrior, reloaded his rifle and shot a second, only to be attacked by a third warrior whom he bayoneted off the wall. Schiess later received the Victoria Cross for his bravery. Another hospital patient, Corporal Scammell of the NNC, had joined the line only to be shot in the back by a Zulu sniper firing from the Oskarsberg. As Scammell fell wounded he was attended to by Acting Commissariat Officer Byrne who opened his water bottle. As he bent down to give Scammell a drink, Byrne was shot dead by a Zulu sniper and fell on top of Scammell. The corporal pulled himself free of Byrne's body and, seeing Chard with Dalton's empty rifle, crawled over to Chard and gave him the rounds in his pouch before reporting to Surgeon Reynolds.

One determined Zulu rush caused Chard and Bromhead to join a threatened group of half a dozen men but they were still too few so, during a short lull, Chard gave the order to abandon the outer position and to withdraw to within the inner wall of boxes between the rock ledge and the storehouse. The British move now halved the size of the area to be defended but left the hospital and its six able-bodied men and patients surrounded by Zulus. Chard's men were beginning to suffer serious casualties and apart from two fatalities, Byrne and Private Cole, four were seriously wounded – Corporal Allen and Privates Chick, Fagan and Scanlon. Now concentrated in the small entrenchment, Chard could no longer communicate with those trapped in the hospital some 40 yards away.

The side and far end of the hospital facing the Oskarsberg could no longer be protected by the defenders' covering fire and the Zulus quickly massed along these two unprotected sides of the building to attack the barricaded doors and windows by grabbing the soldiers' rifles as they fired through the loopholes. To make matters worse for those inside, the hospital now caught fire. It is possible that some Zulus threw spears with tufts of burning grass onto the thatched roof. It is more likely that the fire was started from within the building when a paraffin lamp broke during the fighting. Due to the heavy rains of the previous weeks, the thatch was still sodden and when the roof did eventually catch fire, it was slow to burn.

According to Private Hook in his account of the action, the defenders of the hospital were now caught 'like rats in a trap'. He was defending a corner room with Private Cole when the pressing Zulus began clawing and battering at the barricaded doors. The claustrophobic Cole opened the door and in a wild panic fled outside, only to be shot to death by the massing Zulus. Another patient, Private Beckett, escaped in the same direction; he was wounded by a number of spear thrusts but in the darkness he managed to hide himself in the scrub near the garden, only to be found dying the following morning. Now alone, Hook used his bayonet to cut and hack his way through to the adjacent room where three more defenders, Privates John and Joseph Williams and Horrigan, together with their four patients, were trapped. The Zulus were about to break through and the smouldering thatch was filling the room with choking smoke. Hook took it upon himself to keep the Zulus at bay with his bayonet while John Williams smashed a hole into the next room; the intention was to reach the far end of the building before the Zulus got to them. They cut their way through and managed to pull three sick men after them before the Zulus broke the wall down and killed the remaining patients, including the wounded Zulu prisoner from the attack on Sihayo's stronghold.

Hook was firing and wielding his bayonet by the hole as his colleagues broke through the next wall into the adjacent room where they found Private Waters who, when the time came to crawl through into the final room, hid instead in a wardrobe where he remained undetected by the Zulus until he was able to rejoin his comrades as dawn broke. Private Connolly had suffered a broken leg and while he was being dragged through the hole, his leg was inadvertently reinjured, causing him to scream pitifully. Hook guarded the hole for another fifteen minutes before the final wall could be breached; the Zulus repeatedly tried to get through the hole but were met by Hook's bayonet; each time the Zulus would pull the twitching victim back only to enable another warrior to receive the same treatment.

The Zulus were unable to breach the hole guarded by Hook and the roof fire had not yet reached their end of the building, but there was no door out and the only possible exit point was a window high up in the wall. It overlooked the space between the hospital and Chard's position 40 yards away but the window was too small to get a man through. Quickly they smashed the frame out. At Chard's position the light of the hospital flames illuminated the defenders who were now lowering the hospital survivors to the ground. The Zulus were only yards away as Chard called for two volunteers to run across the no-man's-land and bring the casualties to safety. Private Hitch and Corporal Allen immediately volunteered. Hitch had already been shot through his shoulder and Allen through his arm; notwithstanding their serious injuries, the two raced to and from the hospital – each man carrying a patient – as Chard ordered covering fire.

Trooper Hunter of the Natal Mounted Police escaped from the hospital and as he crawled towards safety a Zulu leaped over the barricade and killed him before the defenders' eyes; the Zulu was then shot dead by a furious British volley. Sergeant Maxfield was on the verge of leaving the hospital but, being delirious, he refused to co-operate until properly dressed and fought repeated attempts to save him. The far end of the burning hospital then collapsed, which gave Gunner Howard the opportunity to escape; he dashed for cover and lay in the darkness – surviving to tell the tale. Private Adams stayed behind and died. Commissary Dunne later wrote 'overhead, the small birds disturbed by the turmoil and smoke flew hither and thither confusedly'. The terrifying ordeal in the darkness,

Rorke's Drift hospital at time of attack

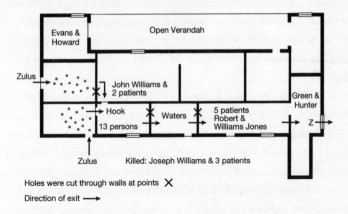

Holes were cut through walls at points ✗

Direction of exit ⟶

thick smoke and deafening noise of the hospital battle had lasted over two hours. The thatched roof of the hospital was now well ablaze, which illuminated the attacking Zulus.

For Chard and his men the final desperate fight for survival now began. The other Zulu skirmishers who had been burning local farms had been drawn back to Rorke's Drift by the flames and sounds of constant firing. They now joined Prince Dabulamanzi's force and in the light from the burning hospital the Zulus increased their pressure all round. Fortunately for the British, the Zulus had not yet realized that the fire illuminated their massing ranks and made them easy targets for Chard's marksmen.

Then Prince Dabulamanzi changed tactics; he ordered the firing of the storehouse's thatched roof. As soon as Chard realized that the Zulus were making a determined effort to do this, presumably to force out the defenders, he ordered Commissary Dunne to construct a redoubt from two huge piles of mealie bags that had been previously stacked at the front of the store. Chard knew that if the storehouse fell, the Zulus would

169

be able to surround the defenders at a distance of less than 20 yards. Dunne, a quiet young man, directed this work without thought for his personal safety; he stood on the mound of sacks and encouraged half a dozen weary soldiers to construct the final redoubt. In so doing he attracted steady fire from the Zulus on all sides but he remained unscathed throughout.

Suddenly a shout rang out from a soldier pointing towards the Helpmekaar road. The word quickly spread that marching redcoats were approaching from the direction of Helpmekaar, although when everyone peered into the growing darkness no sign of help could be seen. Believing relief was at hand, some of the men cheered, which confused the Zulus; they withdrew to safety to await events and for ten minutes little was heard other than more rounds being issued to the defenders. But no relieving troops came and then the Zulus regrouped ready for the next assault. Chard wrote of this incident:

Second withdrawal 7 p.m.

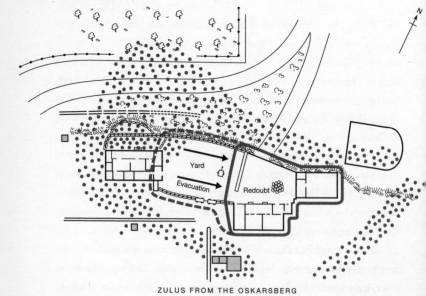

ZULUS FROM THE OSKARSBERG

It is very strange that this report should have arisen amongst us, for the two companies 24th Regiment from Helpmekaar did come down to the foot of the hill, but not, I believe, in sight of us. They marched back to Helpmekaar on the report of Rorke's Drift having fallen.[15]

Major Spalding, the officer commanding Rorke's Drift, had ridden to Helpmekaar that same afternoon to speed up the overdue reinforcements. At about 3.30 p.m. he encountered the two relieving companies of the 24th marching to Rorke's Drift and accompanied them back to the top of the steep pass. He then went on ahead accompanied by Mr Dickson of the local Buffalo Guard. As they descended the pass, they saw the first black auxiliary fugitives from Rorke's Drift; puzzled, they continued on until they met the first fugitives from the Mounted Infantry. There was no doubting their story; Isandlwana had fallen to the Zulus and Rorke's Drift was now suffering the same fate, though Spalding rode on until he gained a low crest where he could see the mission station in flames. He and Dickson then saw a large group of Zulu skirmishers approaching them; the Zulus came to within 100 yards while forming their traditional attack formation. Realizing their predicament, Spalding and Dickson rapidly retreated back to the column to learn that other Zulu raiding parties were approaching the pass to Helpmekaar. Spalding ordered the column to 'about turn' and the two companies, along with all their wagons, began the ascent of the pass. All safely reached Helpmekaar at about 9 p.m. where they built a defensive laager using the wagons and all available stores. There can be little doubt that the defenders at Rorke's Drift, even in the failing light, had seen the marching column when it was less than 3 miles from Rorke's Drift; the relieving force certainly saw the burning mission station. Spalding later attempted to justify his actions and though Chelmsford backed him up, he was removed to an inconspicuous desk job.[16]

With no hope of relief, the British now retreated behind the barrier protecting the remaining building, the storehouse. Corporal Attwood defended a window in the building throughout the action and was kept busy shooting at the warriors as they attempted to fire the thatch above him. He held his position until the end of the battle and the Zulus failed to fire the roof. The pressure of hand-to-hand fighting continued until the defenders holding the outer wall of the cattle kraal were forced to retire, first to an intermediate wall that divided the kraal and then finally behind the wall which actually joined onto the storehouse. This was to be the final British position; there was nowhere else to go.

Dunne completed the conversion of the two large pyramids of bagged maize into an oblong redoubt. The wounded were then placed inside the new position and Chard detailed marksmen to occupy the upper rampart. With an elevated field of fire illuminated by the dying glow of the burning hospital the marksmen poured several volleys into the massed Zulu ranks now pressing up against the final wall of boxes and mealie bags. As the night wore on, the glow from the hospital fire began to dwindle and, as it did, the Zulus' enthusiasm for close combat waned. After midnight the

Final assault

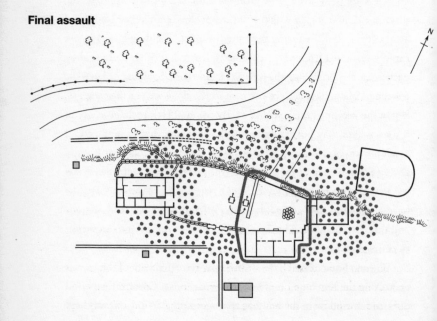

battle had degenerated into a series of isolated attacks that enabled the British to anticipate more accurately the direction of each attack. The defenders had been without water for over eight hours and all were suffering from thirst so regardless of darting warriors, Chard led an almost suicidal bayonet charge over the wall to reach the water cart that he had brought from the river and which had been abandoned halfway between the two buildings. Curiously, the Zulus had ignored it, even though they were also desperate for water. The cart was brought back to the wall but was too heavy to lift over – so Chard improvised with a leather hose and drained the water through a hole in the wall into an assortment of containers.

By midnight Prince Dabulamanzi was in serious trouble; his men had suffered enormous casualties with nothing to show for their bravery and efforts. Their attacks had become unenthusiastic and sporadic in sympathy with the final flickering from the remains of the burning hospital, which died out at about 4 a.m. Thereafter there were no more Zulu attacks, only an 'exchange of salutations' according to a Zulu warrior, Munyu, who was present.[17]

Chard ordered his battle-weary men to remain at their posts and at 5 a.m. dawn came. Apart from the dead and wounded, the Zulu force had vanished. Just after 7 a.m. the Zulus reappeared on the western slope of the Oskarsberg but Prince Dabulamanzi's men were exhausted. They collected themselves together before heading back towards the drift and Zululand. Chard later wrote that he was glad to seize an opportunity to wash his face in a muddy puddle, in company with Private Bush, a hospital defender whose face was covered with blood from a wound in the nose caused by the bullet which had killed Private Cole.

Many of the dead Zulus were locked in strange contorted positions by rigor mortis and some were horrifically disfigured by Martini-Henry bullet wounds. The numerous dead were ignored as the soldiers were too exhausted or caring for their own wounded; all were suffering from bruising and burns caused by firing their Martini-Henry rifles for hours on end. Commandant Hamilton-Browne wrote that the dead Zulus lay in piles, in some places as high as the top of the parapet. Pools of congealed and smeared blood bore witness to the death throes of both British and Zulu warriors and the whole area was littered with spears, empty ammunition boxes, torn cartridge packets and clusters of spent ammunition cases. Trampled maize from the damaged sacks lay thickly along the walls, and the remnants of red jackets lay in the dust, having been used by the soldiers for binding their red-hot rifle barrels to save their hands from burns as they fired. The nauseating smell of roasted human flesh emanating from the burnt-out hospital pervaded the area and on examining the ruined building the defenders discovered the charred bodies of Sergeant Maxfield and the other patients alongside a number of Zulus who had died within its walls. Fourteen dead Zulus lay outside the room that Joseph Williams had defended; his speared body showed that he had fought bravely to the end.

Colour Sergeant Bourne then remembered the casks of rum that had been guarded throughout the battle; he recovered them intact and began issuing the spirit among the defenders. Private Hook, a known teetotaller, joined the queue with the comment, 'I feel I want something after all that'; he then returned to his campfire where he was making tea. An undamaged bottle of beer, discovered in the wreckage of one of the wagons, was handed to Chard and Bromhead who shared it in celebration. Neither could have anticipated the future impact of the battle they had just fought.

Chard sent out a patrol to flush out any hidden Zulu marksmen; all round the British outpost lay dead Zulu warriors, with more human remains still visible in the smouldering hospital building. Unnoticed by the defenders, a warrior walked straight into the British position and, being unarmed, was not fired upon. When challenged he claimed to be a member of the NNC. Daniels the pontman started interrogating the man by waving a sword at him but Chard took pity on the terrified prisoner and, believing his innocence, sent him to the officer commanding at Help-mekaar with a situation report and a request for assistance. Chard's wagon driver had panicked when the Zulus first arrived and had climbed the slope of the Oskarsberg before secreting himself in the back of a cave, only to be unknowingly joined by Zulu marksmen who then spent several hours firing into the British position. Terrified into silence, he remained undetected and left his hiding place when the Zulus departed. Not being totally sure what the Zulus were doing, Chard initiated further patrols around the mission station and set the weary soldiers to repair their defences. They strengthened and raised the walls. Some considered removing the thatch from the roof of the commissariat store to prevent another fire but instead decided to collect the arms and ammunition from the numerous dead Zulus. The soldiers contemplated the dead, sometimes five deep; the dying and wounded Zulus were given the *coup de grâce* by bayonet to put them out of their misery; there was no malice on the part of the soldiers and except for taking occasional Zulus for questioning, taking prisoners had never been British Army policy in South Africa.

The defeated Zulus assembled on the far bank of the Buffalo river. It was at this stage that the defenders first noticed the distant but slowly approaching column led by Lord Chelmsford; until that point the defenders presumed that the whole column had been defeated. The column was approaching the drift from the direction of Sihayo's stronghold and, not wishing to engage the British, the departing Zulus followed the river bank to avoid conflict. It is uncertain whether the Zulus knew that Chelmsford and a portion of his force had survived; local myth suggests the Zulus genuinely believed that Chelmsford's force had all died at Isandlwana. Chelmsford's direct approach certainly confused the retreating warriors and the two groups passed each other at a safe distance, neither side wanting a fight. Chelmsford's force had but twenty rounds of ammunition per man and it was as well that the Zulus were equally exhausted because as the departing Zulus closed with Chelmsford's approaching column some of the 3rd NNC panicked and began firing at the Zulus; a young Zulu retaliated by singly charging at the British column, only to be shot at close range. Both sides ignored the incident and order was quickly restored.

Some ten minutes later the first troop of mounted men, commanded by Major Cecil Russell and Lieutenant Walsh, crossed the drift and galloped up to the battered remains of the mission station. They were relieved to find the outpost still in British hands; as they crossed the river they had seen the rising smoke from other smouldering homesteads and farms towards Helpmekaar and feared that the garrison had suffered the same fate. Lord Chelmsford, with his full complement of staff officers, arrived half an hour later. When Lieutenant Milne, the Royal Navy staff officer to Lord Chelmsford, arrived at Rorke's Drift at about 9.30 a.m. he noted that 'the occupants received the General with three cheers. Then was seen the gallant defence made by the small garrison of 80 men'.

Chelmsford and his staff were shocked by the sight that greeted them. Hundreds of bodies lay around the mission station and the hospital building was still smouldering. After the tragedy of Isandlwana, he was relieved to see that the garrison had survived, and now made it his business to find out what had happened. A few defenders who had displayed exceptional bravery were interviewed by Chelmsford himself. Private Hook was still making tea when he was called forward by Lieutenant Bromhead, to which he replied, 'Wait till I get a coat on.' 'Come as you are' was the retort, so Hook 'went into the midst of the officers and Lord Chelmsford asked me all about the defence of the hospital as I was the last to leave the building. An officer took down all our names and wrote down what we had done.' Chelmsford then addressed the assembled defenders and thanked them for their endeavours. Gunner Howard recalled Chelmsford's words in a letter home: 'The general said we were a brave little garrison, and this showed what a few men could do if they only had pluck.'[18]

With Chelmsford's men swelling its numbers, the garrison at Rorke's Drift had now increased to over 700 men. The arrivals included the surviving companies of the 2/24th and sixteen companies of the NNC. The mounted troops and the Royal Artillery horses under the command of Colonel Harness were ordered to ride on to Helpmekaar where the air was believed to be healthier for the horses; the Royal Artillery guns and men remained at Rorke's Drift as part of the garrison.[19]

While the officers supervised the tasks of clearing and protecting the area the Commissariat officers checked their stores so that hot food and tea could be prepared for the ravenous column. A makeshift barrier was erected along the front of the outpost from blocks of stone that were prised from the burnt-out hospital and from the nearby garden wall that had afforded such protection to the Zulus during the fighting.

As Chelmsford and his staff rode out of Rorke's Drift he left behind a very subdued Colonel Glyn of the 24th Regiment in command. Chelmsford now knew he faced reporting to his government and the world that he had lost not only the battle of Isandlwana but also most of a famous British regiment. At this point it is unlikely that Chelmsford had realized his good fortune in splitting his force; had he not done so, it is probable that the Zulus would have attacked the sleeping Isandlwana camp either before dawn on 22 January or when it was strung out on the move to Mangeni. It would be a few more days before he realized that his decision had saved half the Centre Column and he had a magnificent victory to report at Rorke's Drift; he was able to write:

> The defeat of the Zulus at this post, and the very heavy loss suffered by them, has, to a great extent, neutralised the effect of the disaster at Isandhlwana, and no doubt saved Natal from a serious invasion.[20]

Even when news of Isandlwana and Rorke's Drift reached King Cetshwayo, he was not initially apprised of the situation with any accuracy. Prince Dabulamanzi claimed that his attack on the mission station had been a success although he had sustained casualties. Cetshwayo had to wait for some two weeks before he learned the full extent of Zulu losses. He gave two orders: firstly for the two artillery guns to be brought to Ulundi along with any rifles and ammunition that could be recovered from Isandlwana; secondly that the Zulu army should reassemble at Ulundi. When Cetshwayo realized the extent of Zulu losses, he stated:

> They say that we suffered this heavy loss from a small force, the [British army] is still there and we are not able to cope with it.[21]

CHAPTER 10

Post-battle: A Deep Sigh of Relief

It was indeed God's mercy that saved us.[1]

CAPTAIN TONGUE, 24TH REGIMENT

The surviving Rorke's Drift defenders were utterly exhausted; all they wanted was some water to drink, and to sleep. Their red jackets were now unrecognizable through being used to bind red-hot Martini-Henry rifles during the heavy fighting and no replacement uniforms were to be found in the piles of stores. Sleep was not yet possible; the wounded needed caring for, the mission station was in chaos and the Zulus might return. Once they had been supplied with hot tea and some biscuits, the soldiers set about trying to get warm; there was no alternative but to begin making rough jackets from the heavy and abundant mealie sacks that had served them so well in the defence; they simply cut holes in the sacks for their heads and arms. With no money and no new uniforms available they continued to wear such makeshift clothing for many weeks. It took a question in Parliament before one flannel shirt and a pair of trousers, but not jackets, could be issued to the defenders 'cost free' as compensation for uniforms damaged during the fighting. The *Referee*, an English newspaper, published an amusing ditty to publicize the soldiers' plight and to embarrass the government, after which a replacement uniform was authorized (see Appendix C).

Within a matter of hours of the engagement an inventory of the remaining ammunition revealed that only seventy rounds per man remained. Author Donald Morris stated that the 104 British combatants had fired 20,000 rounds of Martini-Henry ammunition in the space of twelve hours.[2] This roughly equates with twenty rounds per man per combat hour – yet the 300 Zulu casualties indicate that it took roughly sixty rounds to kill one Zulu in a close-range battle. Were the British poor marksmen, was the figure of 20,000 rounds correct or were there other factors? This question becomes even more interesting in view of the lack of archaeological evidence concerning the few finds of empty ammunition cases or of fired rounds ever found on the battlefield.[3] Commandant Hamilton-Browne, commander of the Natal Native Contingent, clearly believed that the British bayonet had been more effective than the Martini-Henry rifle. He wrote, 'The dead Zulus lay in piles, in some places as high as the top of the parapet. Some killed by bullets and the wounds, at that short range, were ghastly but very many were killed by the bayonet.'[4]

No one knows whether the figure of 20,000 rounds for B Company serving in a reserve capacity is correct. It was certainly the allocation of ammunition to each infantry company. It is possible the defenders were short of ammunition before the battle began, resulting in their having to rely on their bayonets to drive the Zulus from the defensive positions. No examination was conducted to establish the individual causes of death among the Zulu attackers so the reason for the apparent ineffectiveness of the Martini-Henry rifle at Rorke's Drift remains unclear. While some of the fighting took place in darkness, defenders' reports confirm that the burning hospital illuminated the attacking Zulus.

Commandant Hamilton-Browne, the commander of the NNC who had accompanied Chelmsford during the previous two days, was ordered to remain at Rorke's Drift with his black troops. He later recalled some of the events that then occurred when he wrote:

> Well we went into the laager. No one seemed to know what to do and certainly no one tried to do anything. I spoke to several of the seniors and suggested that the thatch should be taken off the store and more

loopholes made, also that the stacks of forage should be removed, but until I came to Colonel Harness, R.A., no one would pay the least attention. He at once saw things in the same light as I did and said, 'I will send my gunners to remove the thatch if you will get the forage away.' This we did and in a short time the place was secure from fire.

No sooner had I seen my part of this work done than I began to feel as if I was rather hollow and I rejoined Lonsdale and Harford. Rations had been served out and we had bully beef, biscuit, tea and sugar in plenty but no cups, plates, knives, forks or spoons – not even a pot or kettle to boil water in. However we made shift to eat the bully and biscuits with our fingers, then boiled water in the empty bully tins, added tea and sugar and drank it with gusto.

Well Lonsdale and myself went round to the front and there saw what a tremendous effort must have been made by both sides.

The attack must have been well pushed home and both sides deserve the greatest credit. The hospital was still smouldering and the stench from the burning flesh of the dead inside was very bad; it was much worse however when we came to clear the debris away two days afterwards. Some of our sick and wounded had been burned inside of the hospital and a number of Zulus had been also killed inside of the building itself.

In front of the hospital lay a large number of Zulus also a few of our men, who had been patients, and who when the hospital had been set on fire had, in trying to escape, rushed out among the enemy and had been killed, their bodies being also ripped and much mutilated.

A few dead horses lay about, either killed by the assegai or by the bullets of the defenders, and I wondered why they had not been driven away before the fighting began.

One thing I noticed and that was the extraordinary way in which the majority of the Zulus lay. I had been over a good many battlefields and seen very many men who had been killed in action but I had never seen men lie in this position. They seemed to have dropped on their elbows and knees and remained like that with their knees drawn up to their chins.

One huge fellow who must have been, in life, quite 7 feet high lay on his back with his heels on the top of the parapet and his head nearly touching the ground, the rest of his body supported by a heap of his dead comrades.[5]

Every member of the replenished Rorke's Drift garrison was seriously fatigued, either having survived the Rorke's Drift fighting or being from Chelmsford's weary column. All were exhausted, hungry and undoubtedly anxious lest the Zulus should return in force. There was little order or control; ammunition reserves were low and a fresh Zulu attack could come at any moment. There was a general atmosphere of fear about the garrison, and since not all troops could fit inside the relative security of the laager, shamefully, the black troops of the NNC were ordered to remain outside. Hamilton-Browne described what happened:

The evening grew on and Lonsdale went into the laager for orders. He returned and told us that the white troops were to hold the laager and that we were to remain outside. This was as absurd as it was shameful; not only were our white officers and non-coms to meet, unprotected by the laager, the first rush of the Zulus, in case of an attack, but we should have been swept away by the fire of our own friends inside it.

We were also to find the outlying pickets and the advanced sentries. Our natives, with the exception of the Zulus, were quite useless for this service. In fact they had all taken refuge in the caves and among the rocks of the mountain, and sternly refused to come out. And now there was a row. Of course the roster was lost and I regret to say that the officers and the non-coms, furious at what they considered their unfair treatment, refused to turn out. Lonsdale, Cooper and myself talked it over with them and at last we said we would take the outlying picket ourselves. Harford at once chipped in, so three commandants and a staff officer formed the most dangerous picket that night.

Quin, my servant, swore that I should not go on picket while he was to the fore and Captains Duncombe, Develin and Hayes volunteered for the other picket. Of course when we were moving off everyone wanted to come

181

and the cuss words and recriminations flew like hail. We quieted them down. We took one picket, Captain Duncombe and three other officers formed the other; there was not much choice between them. In-lying pickets were told off and as soon as it was dark we took our posts, extending the Zulus in a chain between them. The night was very dark but passed off quietly although there was a false alarm at the laager, and most of our white men who had remained there got inside. I don't blame them. What was the use of staying outside to be shot down by their own friends?[6]

The command structure under Glyn now failed and strangely nothing more is heard of Chard or Bromhead. The troops' morale sank proportionately, the sickly smell of burnt bodies hung over the camp and the knowledge that reserves of ammunition were critically low did not help matters. In reality, there was no prospect of fresh supplies as the ammunition for Rorke's Drift had been buried near Helpmekaar when the officer in charge of the supply wagon heard the news from Isandlwana. Two days later a patrol was sent to recover it but the incessant rain had washed away any traces of the cache; the ammunition was never found. Later that day the British reluctantly set about burying the putrefying Zulu dead. Their own black troops refused to handle the bodies due to *umnyama*, the belief that the spirits of the dead would attach themselves to anyone touching the bodies. They were persuaded to dig the deep pits while the 24th Regiment collected the Zulu bodies by dragging them with makeshift ropes to the freshly dug graves. The NNC then collected brushwood and trees from the nearby orchards for funeral pyres. When the resulting blazes subsided, the remains were covered with spoil previously dug from the pits; the whole macabre process took several days to complete.

Later a rumour spread around the post that several hundred Zulus, either wounded or in hiding, had been found and killed by British soldiers at two separate but nearby locations, both less than a mile from the outpost. When the British patrols discovered Zulus hiding they killed them with their bayonets or the Zulus' own spears in order to conserve their depleted ammunition supply. Commandant Hamilton-Browne wrote of one incident that occurred that same day:

> During the afternoon it was discovered that a large number of wounded and worn-out Zulus had taken refuge or hidden in the mealie fields near the laager. My two companies of Zulus with some of my non-coms and a few of the 24th quickly drew these fields and killed them with bayonet, butt and assegai. It was beastly but there was nothing else to do. War is war and savage war is the worst of the lot. Moreover our men were worked up to a pitch of fury by the sights they had seen in the morning and the mutilated bodies of the poor fellows laying in front of the burned hospital.[7]

Lieutenant Smith-Dorrien, who had escaped from Isandlwana to Helpmekaar, later wrote concerning two gallows he had constructed at Rorke's Drift prior to the battle. These gallows were originally intended to stretch leather *riems* for the ox wagons but were then put to a more conventional use. Smith-Dorrien wrote:

> The next day [23rd January] I rode down to Rorke's Drift, some twelve miles, to resume charge of my depot. There was the improvised little fort, built up mostly of mealy-sacks and biscuit-boxes and other stores which had so gallantly been defended by Chard, Bromhead, and their men, and Parson Smith, and all around lay dead Zulus, between three and four hundred; and there was my wagon, some 200 yards away, riddled and looted; and there was the riems gallows I had erected the previous morning. Dead animals and cattle everywhere – such a scene of devastation! To my young mind it was impossible that order could ever be restored, but I set to work, and next day, whilst sitting in my wagon, I saw two Zulus hanging on my gallows and was accused by the Brigade Major, Clery (afterwards General Sir Francis Clery) of having given the order. I was exonerated, however, when it was found that it was a case of lynch law performed by incensed men, who were bitter at the loss of their comrades. Other incidents of the same sort occurred in the next few days before law and order were re-established.[8]

Later that same day Lieutenant Curling RA returned to Rorke's Drift, and that night he wrote:

> The farmhouse at Rorke's Drift was a sad sight. There were dead bodies of Zulus all round it, in some places so thick that you could hardly walk without treading on them. The roof had been taken off the house as it was liable to be burnt and the wounded were lying out in the open. A spy was hanging on one of the trees in the garden and the whole place was one mass of men. Nothing will now be done until strong reinforcements arrive and we shall have much bloodshed before it is all over.[9]

Private Ashton of B Company found an uninjured Zulu warrior and took him prisoner. That evening, Bromhead learned that the Zulu had been hanged by mistake after Ashton had asked Bromhead what to do with the prisoner. Bromhead had replied, 'Get the hell out of here with him.' Ashton had misinterpreted the oath as an instruction and executed the hapless Zulu.[10]

The necessity of killing seriously injured Zulus on the field was reciprocated by the Zulus who killed any British soldiers left wounded at Isandlwana; it was a fate well understood by both sides. Regrettably, the British action of killing fleeing Zulus or those who had gone into hiding well away from the post was to be more disturbing, even in the climate of such total warfare. Comment on the Zulus' fate was deliberately omitted from official reports to prevent such detail being published. Such merciless mopping-up operations were, nevertheless, deemed necessary and were repeated as a matter of military policy after each of the remaining battles of the Zulu War, especially after the British victories at Gingindlovu, Khambula and Ulundi. The total number of Zulu dead from Rorke's Drift will never be known. The most likely figure of Zulu casualties would tally at about 300 with probably another 300 or more being accounted for during the subsequent securing of the surrounding area. By comparison, British casualties were comparatively light with fifteen men killed and one officer and nine men wounded, two mortally. The indiscriminate and wholesale killing of Zulu survivors in hiding or fleeing from the battlefield was later to cause the military authorities much embarrassment.

During the week following the battle, only five Zulus were taken prisoner and brought back to the post; four were later released unharmed. The fate of the fifth Zulu was sealed when he was brought to Hamilton-Browne's position for questioning. In his memoirs Hamilton-Browne related what happened:

> He [Glyn] ordered me to return to the prisoner, question him and then to report anything I might find out. This I did but of course could get nothing out of him, though he owned up readily he was a spy and that he wore the piece of red stuff round his head as a disguise. I was turning round to return to the O.C. when I struck my shin, which I had badly bruised a few days before, against the boom of the wagon. The pain was atrocious and I had just let go my first blessing when the Sergeant-Major, a huge Irishman, not seeing my accident, asked, 'What will we do with the spoy, sor?' 'Oh, hang the bally spy,' I tripped out and limped away, rubbing my injured shin and blessing spies, wagons and everything that came in my way. On my reporting to the O.C. that I could get no information, but that the man owned up to being a spy, he ordered the Camp Adjutant to summon a drumhead courts-martial to try him. Paper, pens and ink were found with difficulty; true, there was no drum but a rum keg did as well.
>
> The officers, warned, assembled and the Sergeant Major being sent for was ordered to march up the prisoner.
>
> He stared open-mouthed for a few seconds, then blurted out, 'Plaze, sor, I can't shure he's hung, sor.' 'Hung!' exclaimed the O.C., who was standing within earshot. 'Who ordered him to be hung?' 'Commandant Browne, sor,' replied the Sergeant Major. 'I ordered him to be hung?' I ejaculated. 'What do you mean?' 'Sure, sor, when I asked you at the guard wagon what was to be done with the spoy did you not say, sor, "Oh, hang the spoy," and there he is,' pointing to the slaughter poles, and sure enough there he was. There was no help for it. It was clear enough the prisoner could not be tried after he was hung, so the court was dismissed and there was no one to blame but my poor shin.[11]

Chard wrote, albeit cautiously, of events at Rorke's Drift on the 23rd:

On the day following, we buried 351 bodies of the enemy in graves not far from the Commissariat Buildings – many bodies were since discovered and buried, and when I was sick at Ladysmith one of our Sergeants, who came down there invalided from Rorke's Drift, where he had been employed in the construction of Fort Melvill, told me that many Zulu bodies were found in the caves and among the rocks, a long distance from the Mission house, when getting stone for that fort. As, in my report, I underestimated the number we killed, so I believe I also underestimated the number of the enemy that attacked us, and from what I have since learnt I believe the Zulus must have numbered at least 4,000.[12]

Frances Colenso, the daughter of the Bishop of Natal, was an ardent campaigner for fair play and she strongly expressed her views on matters at Rorke's Drift. Following representations made to her by sources she never revealed, presumably witnesses, a number of instances of mal-treatment were given limited publicity; no official denials of her allegations were made. She wrote:

The general and his staff hurried on to Pietermaritzburg via Helpmekaar while the garrison at Rorke's Drift was left in utter confusion – as testified by many present at the time. No one appeared responsible for anything that might happen, and the result was one disgraceful to our English name, and to all concerned. A few Zulu prisoners had been taken by our troops – some the day before, others previous to the disaster at Isandl-wana, and these prisoners were put to death in cold blood at Rorke's Drift. It was intended to set them free, and they were told to run for their lives, but they were shot down and killed, within sight and sound of the whole force. An eye witness, an officer, described the affair to the present writer, saying that the men he saw killed numbered 'not more than seven nor less than five'. He said he was standing, with others, in the camp, and hearing shots close behind him, he turned, and saw the prisoners in question in the act of falling beneath the shots and stabs of a party of

our own men. The latter, were, indeed, men belonging to the Natal
Contingent, but they were supposed to be under white control, and
should not have been able to obtain possession of the prisoners under
any circumstances.[13]

Meanwhile, not knowing where the Zulu force was, Colonel Glyn
ordered regular mounted patrols to scour the surrounding countryside.
These patrols ranged far and wide and wreaked havoc on Zulu villages.
Hamilton-Browne wrote:

By this time myself and my boys had made ourselves decidedly
unpopular on the other side of the river. No decent kraal could retire at
rest and be sure they would awake in the morning to find themselves
alive in their huts and cattle intact.[14]

Bulwer, the Lieutenant Governor of Natal, expressed his views against
such cross-border raids. He believed that the indiscriminate burning of
empty homesteads would be counter-productive and wrote, 'This action
could hardly be attended with much advantage to us, it would invite retaliation.' The Border Police commander, Major Dartnell, was also concerned
to the point that he cautioned against further cross-border raids on the
grounds that they were provocative. He also forbade his men to cross the
river unless they were part of a large raiding party sanctioned by the
military authorities.

The deteriorating conditions at Rorke's Drift drove the men's morale
deeper yet there was little Glyn and his staff officers could do to ease the
suffering. The situation led Major Clery to comment on the conditions
when he wrote home on 4 February:

We have lost simply everything we had, except what we stood in –
tent, clothing, cooking things, everything in fact – so that when we
got anything to eat, we had nothing to cook it in, and when we got
something to drink we had nothing to drink it out of.

My present abode consists of a tarpaulin held up by some sticks and
this I share with Col. Glyn and the other staff officers. We have a little straw

to lie on, but as this is the rainy season and as the rain here comes down in torrents, our straw gets very soaky at times. The ground is too hard for lying on, so one wakes in the morning very tender about one's bones.

At first it was very hard on the men for they used to get wet through and had no change; indeed, for that matter there is very little in the way of change for any of us yet, but fortunately the Buffalo River lies close by, so by spending some time every day therein, and utilizing the powerful rays of this tropical sun for the things we hang out to dry, we are holding on till we get some things from Pietermaritzburg.[15]

To make matters even worse the largest force of men, the black troops of the NNC, collectively mutinied. The overall treatment received by these black troops had been appalling. During the Zulus' successful decoy of 22 January, they had been left without food for two days and the events of that day had destroyed any confidence they might have had in Chelmsford's ability to defeat the Zulus. As they returned through Isandlwana, they had witnessed the awful consequences of the Zulu victory; at Rorke's Drift they had been virtually ignored except to act as a buffer in the event of a Zulu attack. Disillusioned and demoralized, they now threatened to leave.

Hamilton-Browne pondered the situation; they were, after all, his men. He called for Umvubie, the *induna* of his small band of friendly Zulus, and through him addressed the NNC. He told them that they were not cowards like the other NNC and he requested them to stay. Umvubie had a better idea; he and his men were quite ready to attack the 1,200 non-Zulu blacks to prevent them leaving. Hamilton-Browne dissuaded them from this course of action and, after further discussion with his white officers, it was agreed that all the black troops should be disbanded. Perhaps wisely, Glyn allowed them to depart once they had been disarmed, though they spread alarming stories of an immediate Zulu invasion of Natal that severely frightened everyone along their various routes home. Hamilton-Browne wrote:

Umvubie paused for a minute to beg my permission to be allowed to kill only a few of the Natal Kafirs, who he was sure had annoyed me very much. Alas! I could not grant his modest request. The other natives had fallen in and gathered round me in a ring. I told them in a few plain words what I thought of them. I told them that the Great White Queen would send them women's aprons when she heard of their cowardice and that they had better go home and dig in the fields with their wives. This is the greatest insult you can offer a warrior and they hung their heads in shame.

But when I told them to go, and advised them to go to a country even hotter than Natal, they waited not for pay or rations but those who had guns threw them down and the whole of them breaking ranks bolted each man for his own home. The Zulus (friendlies) forming themselves into solid rings, marched past our group of officers, raising their shields in the air, in salute, and rattled their assegais against them; then breaking into a war-song marched proudly away, every one of them a man and a warrior. So exited the rank and file of the 3rd NNC.[16]

On 24 January Glyn sent a pitiful note to Chelmsford; it reads:

My Dear General,
The whole of the native contingent walked off this morning. Their rifles were taken from them; all the hospital bearers then went, and now the native pioneers are going. I am now left without any natives. What is to be done with Lonsdale and his Europeans? I shall, of course, keep them until I hear from you.[17]

Three days later Lord Chelmsford forwarded the letter to Sir Henry Bartle Frere along with a note saying:

Unless these men are at once ordered back to their regiments, or punished for refusing to go, the most serious consequences will ensue. I myself by speaking to Major Bengough's battalion have, I hear, prevented them deserting.[18]

The Resident Magistrate at Estcourt, Pieter Paterson, was tasked with conducting an enquiry into events and his detailed report, efficiently submitted on 4 February, was based on his examination of the NNC *indunas*. The Parliamentary Papers record the correspondence:

Some of the men examined say that they understood they would be wanted again in two months, others say they did not hear anything about their being called out again. No officers accompanied them out of the camp. The men complain: –

First. Of the insufficiency of food, they say that only a quarter of a beast was issued daily for 100 men, and a small pannikin of meal each, and that instead of the insides of the cattle killed for them being given to them, the butchers sold them on their own account.

Secondly. That when they captured cattle and asked for some to kill and eat, according to their custom, they were refused and had no food given them, and when they surprised the enemy's people cooking and captured their food, they were not allowed to eat it, but it was restored to the enemy.

Thirdly. That they had no food at all for three days at the time of the General's advance against Matyane and the capture of the head-quarters camp.

Fourthly. That very many of their men were flogged for making water within certain forbidden bounds and for washing themselves in certain streams, although they never heard any orders that they were not to do so; the floggings ranging from 6 to 20 lashes.

Fifthly. That they could not understand their officers, many of them could not speak any native language, and the others only the Amapondo dialect, and if they (the men) spoke when they received any order they did not understand, their officers said they were impatient.

Sixthly. That they were drilled continually, and that the old men were tired and incapable of understanding the drill, and if they made mistakes their officers struck them.

Seventhly. That when out in the field their men were always divided into small companies and scattered in various directions, and could at any time have been destroyed by the enemy, being thus divided and dispersed.

Eighthly. That their system of fighting was ignored, and whatever they said regarding the Zulu movements in warfare were disregarded, and they were told to shut their mouths.

Ninthly. That the Zulus would fire at them as long as their ammunition lasted and then hide, and the Contingent men were ordered not to kill them, but take them alive, and when men in caves fired at them they were not allowed to go in and kill them, but were ordered to make prisoners of them.

Tenthly. That whilst the Zulus spared no one, they were not allowed to kill different tribes.

The foregoing is the substance of the statement made to me by the indunas of the different tribes.

The Chiefs and indunas are unanimous in expressing their very strong desire to be allowed to fight tribally and in their own way and under their own indunas, with white leaders whom they know and who can speak their language.

If the natives are to be employed again in military service, I would strongly urge a favourable consideration of the foregoing wish of the native tribes to be allowed to fight in their own fashion; employed thus, under white leaders who understand them, they will doubtless render valuable service; if again called out and placed under the late organisation, they will be discontented, and may become insubordinate and a source of danger rather than of strength.[19]

Lord Chelmsford read the report and promptly wrote to Sir Bartle Frere:

February 22, 1879

The complaints made by the natives lately belonging to the contingent attached to No. 3 Column, and the reasons given for their dispersing and going to their homes, have no doubt a sub-structure of truth, but I do not believe that there was any serious cause for dissatisfaction up to the day of the Isandula misfortune, except that the natives were not supplied with food on the 21st, consequent upon their not returning to camp as originally intended.

There were, I believe, in every company officers or non-commissioned officers who were capable of making themselves understood. The men were arranged by companies tribally, and had their own indunas; several Chiefs also accompany them.

There was so much hesitation and delay on the part of the Natal Government in calling out or even in giving permission for the calling out of the 6,000 natives asked for, that it was impossible to make as good arrangement for their organisation as I should have wished. Natal could not supply the requisite number of Europeans, and I was obliged therefore to indent upon the Cape Colony.

Whilst fully recognising the necessity of having an interpreter in each company, capable of explaining the orders of the commander or the wishes of the men, I entirely dissent from the axiom which it is apparently the endeavour to lay down, that those officers who cannot speak the Zulu language are not only of no use with natives but absolutely an encumbrance.

If all the qualities required for a company leader are to be found in addition to that of speaking Zulu, there can be no question that he is the right man, but if an officer is selected purely for his linguistic knowledge, without reference to the other necessary qualities, then he can only turn out a failure.

Colonel Evelyn Wood has just had to get rid of men of the latter stamp, and has substituted British officers in their place (who are quite innocent of Zulu), with the most satisfactory results.

As the High Commissioner points out, natives when brought together under whatever conditions must have some recognised and workable organisation, and must be subdivided into recognised units corresponding to regiments or companies.

(Signed) CHELMSFORD

Lieutenant General Governor [20]

Without doubt the serious problems following the battle of Rorke's Drift can be attributed to the lack of control by Colonel Glyn, now the

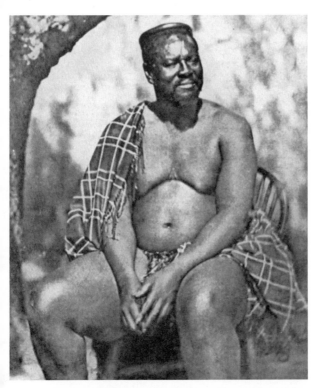

LEFT King Cetshwayo (Anglo Zulu War Historical Society)

BELOW Prince Dabulamanzi, King Cetshwayo's half brother, at Cetshwayo's coronation (Killie Campbell Africana Library)

TOP A typical Zulu homestead *c.*1880 (Cambridge University Library)

ABOVE Chief Ngoza in war dress (Killie Campbell Africana Library)

OPPOSITE PAGE

TOP Cetshwayo's chief residence (*London Graphic*)

ABOVE Chief Ntshingwayo, who directed the Zulu army at
Isandlwana and Khambula (Killie Campbell Africana Library)

TOP LEFT Sir Bartle Frere (Ron Sheeley collection)

TOP RIGHT Theophilus Shepstone (Killie Campbell Africana Library)

ABOVE The ultimatum being read to the Zulus, 11 December 1878 (AZWHS)

OPPOSITE PAGE

TOP The battle of Blood River (AZWHS)

BELOW Piet Uys and his four sons, Boers who fought with the British (National Army Museum)

TOP LEFT Lieutenant Colonel Anthony Durnford (Private Collection)

TOP RIGHT Lord Chelmsford (Brian Best collection)

ABOVE Recovering the wagons from the shattered campsite at Isandlwana (Private Collection)

The retreat of the fugitives across the
Buffalo River (*Illustrated London News*)

ABOVE LEFT James Langley Dalton (*Illustrated London News*)

ABOVE RIGHT Lieutenant Curling, one of the few survivors of Isandlwana (AZWHS)

LEFT Contemporary engraving of the defence of Rorke's Drift (*London Graphic*)

OPPOSITE PAGE

TOP LEFT & RIGHT John Chard and Gonville Bromhead, who held the garrison at Rorke's Drift and were subsequently awarded VCs (Ron Sheeley collection)

TOP LEFT Colonel Charles Knight Pearson, who led the Coastal (no.1) Column into Zululand (National Army Museum)

TOP RIGHT Contemporary lantern slide – Colonel Pearson sets light to a Zulu village (Mary Evans)

ABOVE Fort Eshowe (AZWHS)

OPPOSITE PAGE

TOP Contemporary engraving of the final repulse of the Zulus at Gingindlovu (Mary Evans)

BELOW Zulu remains at the battlefield of Gingindlovu (National Army Museum)

ABOVE The battle of Ntombe River (*Illustrated London News*)

TOP LEFT Colonel Sir Evelyn Wood, VC, whose Northern Column led the British invasion (Popperfoto)

TOP RIGHT Napoleon Eugène Louis Jean Joseph Buonapart, the French Prince Imperial, a few weeks before he was killed by a party of Zulus (Killie Campbell African Library)

BELOW Gatling gun in Zululand, 1879 (National Army Museum)

Lord Chelmsford directing fire at the battle of
Ulundi, 4 July 1879 (*Illustrated London News*)

TOP The surrender of Zulu chiefs to Sir Garnet
Wolseley (Mary Evans)

ABOVE King Cetshwayo, in Capetown at the
beginning of his exile (National Army
Museum)

commanding officer of Rorke's Drift. In a complete state of shock at the loss of his regiment, fellow officers and men, he and his senior officers were left unsupported and isolated in the midst of chaos, fear of attack and despondency. There were no armed Zulus within 10 miles of Rorke's Drift yet Glyn believed the Zulu army would attack at any time; he ordered the perimeter around the camp to be rebuilt and made everyone move inside during the hours of darkness. The unremitting rain ensured that conditions remained desperate and to make matters worse, urgent supplies had to be hauled from Helpmekaar along the execrably waterlogged tracks and the interior of the fort became boggy from the trampling of so many boots. In due course the repair and reconstruction of the defences around the mission station and the construction of the outpost cemetery gradually brought some order back to the garrison. On 25 January all the able-bodied men were put to work repairing the storeroom and enough stones were collected from the nearby rock terraces to rebuild the fortification around the post's perimeter. This work was undertaken by Lieutenant Porter and his 5th Company of Royal Engineers who rebuilt a loopholed barricade round the entire post. A 7 pound gun was placed at each corner – the same guns that had accompanied Chelmsford to Mangeni and which had shelled Isandlwana camp on their return. The newly constructed position was named Fort Bromhead. Immediately outside the barricade were the graves of the men killed during the Zulu attack. Initially, rough wooden crosses were placed over the graves; these were afterwards replaced by a neat stone monument with an inscription by the 24th Regiment. Being a civilian, Acting Storekeeper Byrne was buried outside the cemetery; the location of his grave remains unknown.

Without tents, blankets or change of clothing, the heavy rain began seriously to affect the men. In recognition of B Company's bravery, they were privileged to have sole use of a tarpaulin and the rafter section in the ruins of Witt's wrecked house. It was a meagre covering and gave this select group some shelter from the rain; the remaining men slept out in the open with nothing more than a soaking blanket or greatcoat for their protection. The whole garrison was crammed into the small walled area between sunset and sunrise, which was churned into an unhealthy, foul-smelling mess so that fatigue parties were employed for the best part of the day in removing the liquid mud from within the perimeter. Rotting stores, appalling weather and poor sanitation, together with the monotonous uncertainty, rapidly took their toll and disease soon broke out among the men, including Chard. All medical supplies had been destroyed when the Zulus set fire to the hospital and there was nothing with which to ameliorate the suffering of the sick. Glyn suffered alongside his men; seriously depressed by events, he took little interest in the misery around him. During the day it was possible for Glyn to observe the distant battlefield of Isandlwana where vultures wheeled overhead for weeks on end and the ground was white with his soldiers' bleaching bones. Captain Parke Jones of the Royal Engineers felt little sympathy for Glyn when he wrote: 'Col. Glyn our chief does nothing and is effete'.[21] A perceptive comment about the conditions was made by Lieutenant Harford, when he wrote:

> This terrible state of things, living in slush, caused a lot of sickness from fever and dysentery that carried off a large number of men and one or two of the officers. Notwithstanding this, and the knowledge that the fort was overcrowded, Colonel Glyn declined to have any tents pitched outside to relieve matters, being afraid that the Zulus might sweep down on the place again, no one but the officers and NCOs of the Contingent were allowed outside the fort.[22]

On 4 February a patrol led by Major Black discovered the bodies of Coghill and Melvill on the Natal bank of the Buffalo river just 5 miles from Rorke's Drift. The lost Queen's Colour was also discovered in the river some half-mile downstream, events which improved morale throughout the garrison. A cairn of stones was piled on the bodies and the colour was brought back to Rorke's Drift. Glyn was moved to tears when he received the colour and learned of the fate of his favourite young officers. Two months later he wrote a moving letter to his young daughter following the discovery of the colour:

Yesterday I went down to where poor Melvill and Coghill's remains were lying to erect the cross Sir Bartle Frere and staff sent. I had two strong coffins made and exhumed the bodies, rolled them up in blankets, put them into the coffins and buried them just under the rock on which the cross is placed. Henry D [Degacher] took a sketch that he is going to finish off at once and have photographed. I got from Melvill's pockets a white silk pocket handkerchief, ten shillings and six pence in silver, a little dog whistle and his gold watch and chain which I shall carefully keep until I hear from Mrs Melvill what she wishes done with them. The water when he was in the river has got into the watch – and discoloured the face – it stopped at ten minutes past two p.m. which must have been about the time they crossed the Buffalo.[23]

By the end of February conditions had become so bad at Rorke's Drift that a new fort, initially named 'Fort Revenge', but renamed Fort Melvill (as Chelmsford thought the original name too provocative), was built 800 yards away on an adjacent hillock overlooking the pont river crossing. Rorke's Drift was abandoned and demolished, the stonework being removed for the construction of Fort Melvill. The *Illustrated London News* commented:

Fort Melvill, named after the late Lt. Melvill, is an oblong fort with flanking towers, built partly in masonry, partly with dry wall, loopholed through-out, and surrounded by a ditch, with an obstacle formed of aloes planted on the glacis. It is constructed on a height 150 yards from, and overlook-ing and commanding, the ponts by which the invading army crossed on January 11th last. Lieutenant da Costa Porter, RE, has superintended its erection; and manned with 200 Europeans, it may be considered impregnable against any number of Zulus. A large stone store, roofed with galvanised iron, has been built inside, to hold commissariat supplies.

Once the garrison was removed to Fort Melvill, the grim conditions soon returned as the men were still tightly confined at night. This stubborn attitude of Glyn ensured that sickness and disease continued to spread unchecked. During the short period of occupancy of Fort Melvill no fewer than twelve men died.[24]

For the dishevelled and fatigued survivors from Isandlwana, Help-mekaar offered little consolation; the lively depot they had left just a fortnight earlier had been transformed into an unfortified, barren and sodden area consisting of three corrugated store sheds and a few decrepit tents belonging to a section of infantry that had been left behind as guards. On arriving from Isandlwana, Captain Essex took command and prepared its defence with the few tools that he had at his disposal. A small laager was constructed around the main zinc shed utilizing the three remaining wagons and infilling the gaps with sacks of mealies. Some forty-eight people, including volunteers, camp followers and three farmers with their families, swelled the small number but there were just twenty-eight rifles to defend Helpmekaar from the attack that was fully expected (but which never came). The fatigued Colonial volunteers had little enthusiasm for the fight and began to take their horses and drift away. When Essex realized that his force was melting away he threatened to shoot all the horses to stop further desertions.

At its best, Helpmekaar is a high, open, windswept and desolate location on the edge of the Biggarsberg range of hills. In 1879 it was described by Major Harness RA as being like the bottom of the sea with grass on it; with the passage of time it has not changed. Never a popular place with British soldiers, its reputation was about to get much worse, especially among the sick and wounded. In the days that followed, over 1,000 men arrived at Helpmekaar; all were suffering various ailments and now they were exposed to cold and rain, some sleeping on wet mealie bags, others on the waterlogged ground saturated with the overflow from the latrines. At night there were constant alarms to play on everyone's nerves. Bilious, remittent and enteric disease struck; the first to succumb were the young and weak men already suffering fever, diarrhoea and dysentery.

The more seriously wounded from Rorke's Drift were accommodated in one end of a corrugated zinc shed. This was one of several filled with commissariat stores, chiefly bags of maize that had been repeatedly soaked by heavy rains during their transportation from Pietermaritzburg; tons of damp bagged maize were now decomposing and giving off the most offensive smell. For the seriously sick and wounded the only bedding, until replacement stores arrived from Pietermaritzburg, consisted of heavy square biscuit boxes arranged along the inside of the building with empty sacks laid over them. The station's medical stores were non-existent; such stores had been sent to the column's hospital at Rorke's Drift where they had been destroyed in the fire. Fortunately the doctor at Helpmekaar, Surgeon Blair-Brown, had one small personal medical kit that contained a mixture of pills, powders, bandages and a tourniquet; unfortunately the labels of the pills and medication had been washed off in a storm and the doctor relied on his intuition and luck when dispensing to the patients. With the decline in morale and general health, the doctor was kept very busy; 646 soldiers reported sick or sought treatment during their first week at Helpmekaar. Surgeon Blair-Brown wisely took control of a crate containing bottles of brandy and port wine; this form of medication proved very popular and efficacious in treating most conditions.

Lieutenant Curling RA was among those who escaped from Isandl-wana and after reaching Helpmekaar wrote to his mother mentioning that life at Helpmekaar was bleak. 'We have 30 sick and wounded men inside and several typhoid patients who however are left in a tent outside where of course they will at once be killed if we are attacked.' In the aftermath of Isandlwana there was a climate of paranoia about any native caught near either Rorke's Drift or Helpmekaar; indeed, the gulf of cultural misunderstanding was so wide that, after Isandlwana, any Zulu who fell into British hands was doomed. Surgeon Reynolds wrote in his diary that a Zulu prisoner was tried by court martial and found to be a spy; 'he was shot by 10 Basutos. He jumped into his grave to try & escape the bullets, but without avail'.[25]

On a visit to Rorke's Drift Curling had seen a Zulu hanging from a tree and several natives met a similar fate at Helpmekaar, even though they were probably entirely innocent. On 2 February Curling wrote:

What is going to happen to us, no one knows. We have made a strong entrenchment and are pretty safe even should we be attacked. The only thing we are afraid of is sickness. There are 50 sick and wounded already who are jammed up at night in the fort. The smell is terrible, 800 men cooped up in so small a place. Food, fortunately, is plentiful and we have a three months supply. All spys [sic] taken now are shot: we have disposed of three or four already. Formerly, they were allowed anywhere and our disaster is to a great extent due to their accurate information of the General's movements. What excitement this will cause in England and what indignation.[26]

Curling was right about the shock and outrage with which the news of the disaster was received in Britain, though the suggestion that a Zulu spy network was behind Chelmsford's defeat was indicative of the wild rumours circulating around the British camps.

Little that was positive could be said concerning Major Spalding. One rumour focused upon his departure from Rorke's Drift and suggestions abounded that he deserted his command prior to the Zulu attack. Chard had certainly informed Spalding that the Zulus were possibly approaching the position and if Spalding had felt the need to hurry up the reserves, any one of the several underemployed officers or NCOs could have been sent the short distance to Helpmekaar with the task. Furthermore, having collected the two companies, Spalding reached a point less than 3 miles from the beleaguered mission station and could have pressed on to relieve the post. Inexplicably, no official questions were asked of Spalding although Major Clery came straight to the point in one of his letters home. He wrote from Helpmekaar on 13 April, 'Spalding is utterly worthless, so that the General was – as regards an opinion on any subject – practically without an adjutant or quarter-master.' Spalding pre-empted any criticism by submitting an explanatory report to Chelmsford detailing his actions on the day. If Spalding had remained at his post he would, as the commanding officer, have certainly been awarded the Victoria Cross. It was inevitable that rumours of Spalding deserting his men would spread and reach Chelmsford, who intervened on Spalding's behalf. He wrote a memo to the adjutant general which exonerated Spalding; Chelmsford believed that Spalding was acting correctly when he left Rorke's Drift to chase up the overdue replacements.

For the shocked survivors from Chelmsford's column who managed to reach Helpmekaar, the fear of another Zulu attack remained. Consequently, Captain Walter Parke Jones RE and his able subordinate Lieutenant da Costa Porter commenced the construction of a substantial entrenchment. Jones described the fort's location as 'vile'; its position had been determined by Chelmsford who insisted that its construction should focus on defending the existing iron storehouses. Jones thought the position was totally unsuitable; the ground was waterlogged and following one particularly heavy downpour, the surrounding ditch was filled with water to a depth of 6ft. And when it rained, the fort quickly became a swamp. As at Rorke's Drift, there were no tents and the whole garrison was shut in every night and marched out for ablutions an hour before daybreak under a police escort. When supplies arrived from Pietermaritzburg some tents were erected outside the fortifications but, due to the close proximity of fit and sick men, such accommodation was moved on 31 March to a new location 500 yards away and a wagon laager was built to house the hospital tents. Much discomfort arose and, with few stores and constantly driving rain, life at Helpmekaar was physically and mentally exhausting. Washing facilities were limited to one bathe per week in a nearby stream and men and officers had to let their beards grow. Improvisation and invention flourished and rubbish heaps were scoured for empty tins that could be used to fashion knives, forks and combs.

As soon as the people of Ladysmith learned of the plight of their Natal Mounted Police at Helpmekaar, they sent a wagonload of useful articles. They dispatched food, clothing and washing equipment for the Colonial troops, most of whom were recruited locally. There was no such comfort for the Imperial troops who would have to wait until March before they were resupplied. The personal equipment that previously belonged to the officers and men killed at Isandlwana, including the possessions of Major Stuart Smith, were auctioned and fetched high prices.

By the beginning of February most of the Helpmekaar force succumbed to the conditions and became stricken with enteric fever or typhoid. The medical officers were mystified by the speed with which diseases spread and it was believed, mistakenly, that the sodden and rotting mealie bags were responsible. Captain Walter Parke Jones wrote, 'I cannot account for it all as the place used to be so healthy. Of course being crowded together in a fort with rotten meal and other stores and difficulties about sanitary arrangements has something to do with the question.' Although it was usual for more men to die through sickness when campaigning than to be killed fighting, the rate of sickness was so severe that the Army Intelligence Branch at the War Office voiced its own opinion as to the cause:

Immediately after Isandhlwana this important place strategically was secured for defence by extemporizing with sacks of mealies to build revetments. The garrison of 1,000 Europeans and Natives were crowded together without tents or shelter except for a few tarpaulins, exposed to cold and rain. Some slept on wet mealie bags, others on the damp ground, disturbed by frequent alarms and subjected to noxious exhalation. The military authorities were informed of the danger from decomposing grain and mealies, and of the unsanitary conditions, but failed to take action, because it was considered vital for the military position. Thus men soon succumbed to the malaise, lost their appetite and the young men especially were attacked by fever, diarrhoea and dysentery.[27]

The feelings of the troops are well represented by a piece of graffiti scratched on the sign over the store at Helpmekaar:

When war is on and danger nigh
God and the soldier is all the cry
But when war is over and all things righted
God is forgot and the soldier slighted

It is well known that the disaster of Isandlwana, combined with the appalling conditions, inactivity, boredom and ill-founded rumours, culminated in psychological disturbances through all ranks. Isandlwana haunted all those who survived or witnessed the aftermath of 22 January. A number of officers were equally affected while the men became lethargic and sullen. At Rorke's Drift Glyn was dysfunctional due to depression. At Helpmekaar Colonel Harness, his friend Colonel Cecil Russell and Lieutenant Curling lost interest in their commands, though Curling could blame fever for his bout of apathy. The collapse of Russell had more serious consequences as he was responsible for mounted patrols that were sporadic and ill planned, which allowed the Zulus to roam at will. Among the troops, speculation on the progress of the war and possible future tactics occupied much time at Helpmekaar.

It took several weeks, an improvement in the weather and the news of a new military commander before morale began to improve. Even then conditions remained far from satisfactory. A letter dated March 5 from an unnamed Colonial soldier to his family was reported in the *Natal Witness*; it reads:

> Here we are, Foot, Artillery, Engineers, Police, and Carbineers (about 500 strong), living in tents during the day, and turning into the fort at night. With the exception of a stink of rotten mealies, and the rain continually swilling through and through, the fort is not so bad, being so strong and well built that the men here now could hold it against the whole of the Zulu army. It is not healthy though, for the hospitals are always full, and we have had eight or ten deaths here. Hay of the Carbineers died last night; one of the N.M.P. shot himself last week, and several Engineers have died. What with guards, vedettes, &c., the duties are very heavy.

By March Chelmsford's preparations for the second invasion of Zululand were well under way, although he would avoid marching his rejuvenated army past Isandlwana which was still strewn with the debris of the wrecked camp and, worse, unburied bodies of the 24th Regiment. This change of plan accordingly reduced the strategic importance of the

Helpmekaar garrison whose role was transferred to Dundee, 20 miles to the north. By the middle of April only two companies of the 1/24th remained at Helpmekaar before they also joined the new advance into Zululand. Helpmekaar then became a shell with a small guard to watch over several sheds of unwanted supplies; these were eventually sold off at a public auction on 25 October and the garrison then closed. Helpmekaar was later reopened as a military garrison during both the Boer War and the Zulu uprising of 1906.

After the glowing reports of victory at Rorke's Drift came the recognition and awards for bravery. Victoria Crosses were awarded to the six soldiers named in Bromhead's report, and also to Lieutenants Bromhead and Chard but only after Lord Chelmsford secretly added the officers' names to the list. This was an unprecedented breach of military protocol, which was further disregarded by the War Office as neither of the two officers responsible for these recommendations was ever consulted, namely Chard, as the senior officer during the battle, and Glyn as the overall commander of those involved. Yet Glyn had not seen fit to recommend them and in accordance with established military protocol, any recommendation beyond being 'mentioned in despatches' should have come from Glyn as the commanding officer of Rorke's Drift. A member of the royal household, Lieutenant Colonel Pickard, mentioned this in a letter to Sir Evelyn Wood (commander of the Northern Column in Zululand) after Chard had been to Balmoral to meet Queen Victoria. Pickard wrote on the matter:

> It seemed odd to me that he [Chard] was not consulted on the distribution of the VCs. But it is only one of the things that 'no fellow can understand'. He is not a genius, and not quick, but a quiet plodding, dogged sort of fellow who will hold his own in most situations in which, as an English officer, his lot may be cast.[28]

It is probable that, to those who were serving in South Africa at the time, the award of so many medals seemed an indication of the perceived propaganda value of the successful defence rather than a measure of the enormous bravery of those involved. As author Ian Knight wrote, 'by elevating Rorke's Drift to the level of a major strategic victory the more damaging significance of Isandlwana was obscured'.[29] This was certainly the opinion of Lord Wolseley, the new Commander-in-Chief and General Officer Commanding South Africa. Wolseley was not shy of speaking his mind and his observation concerning the award of VCs for Rorke's Drift is typical:

> It is monstrous making heroes of those who saved or attempted to save their lives by bolting or of those who, shut up in buildings at Rorke's Drift, could not bolt, and fought like rats for their lives which they could not otherwise save.[30]

The announcement of the awards was also significant, coinciding as it did with the second invasion of Zululand. Morale among the second invasion force was fragile, especially among the many troops fresh and inexperienced from England – all were daunted by the Zulus' reputation. The prospect of meeting the victorious Zulu army was mainly responsible and the widespread publicity of the award of an unprecedented number of Victoria Crosses was important to help boost the troops' morale. The awards were also extremely popular with the British press and public and in a short time the War Office was considering further awards. In March questions were asked in Parliament as to why the ordinary soldiers at Rorke's Drift had not been nominated or considered for their acknowledged acts of bravery. Some boldly challenged the involvement of Queen Victoria and her uncle, HRH the Duke of Cambridge, in his capacity as Commander-in-Chief of the Army. It was not long before further difficult questions were asked; on 27 March 1879 an MP, Mr Osborn Morgan, asked Colonel Stanley as Secretary of State for War why no awards had been conferred upon NCOs and private soldiers. The reply given was that such awards took a considerable time to process – but that the matter was under consideration. The press noticed that the only nominations to date were for members of the 24th Regiment, which prompted another MP, Doctor Ward, to ask on 8 May why Surgeon Reynolds had been overlooked for an award. The Secretary of State for War gave a defensive reply by stating that it was premature for him to consider what awards or honours should be given; he then added that Surgeon Reynolds had already been promoted fourteen months in advance of his seniority and had passed over the heads of sixty-four other medical officers. Nevertheless, the first to benefit from such serious lobbying was Surgeon Reynolds; in addition to his promotion to surgeon major being backdated to the date of the battle, his name was subsequently added to the medal list on 17 June 1879.

On 16 June Mr Stacpoole MP succeeded in embarrassing the government by asking whether it was true that, in recognition of the gallantry of the NCOs and privates at Rorke's Drift, they had been awarded one free flannel shirt and one pair of trousers. Colonel Stanley, stung by the innuendo, replied that such an order had been given to compensate the soldiers for damage to their uniforms and added, 'Whether regard was had for gallantry or not I cannot say.'

Dalton's role at Rorke's Drift was also being questioned in both England and South Africa. Dalton was undoubtedly responsible for many aspects of the successful defence; rumours that he had previously gained a military qualification in field fortifications were confirmed which prompted fresh questions both in Parliament and from the Duke of Cambridge. The matter was referred on to Lord Wolseley. By now Wolseley was becoming uneasy about the award of certain medals and wrote:

I presented Major Chard RE with his Victoria Cross: a more uninteresting or more stupid looking fellow I never saw. Wood tells me he is a most useless officer, fit for nothing. I hear in the camp also that the man who worked hardest at Rorke's Drift Post was the Commissariat Officer who has not been rewarded at all.[31]

The matter was directed to Chard for his comment on the actions of both Dalton and Dunne but, rather surprisingly, he merely acknowledged their actions and avoided making any recommendation. But the story only grew, supported by Dunne's and Dalton's commissary general, Sir

Edward Strickland, who was convinced that the actions of his officers in the defence of Rorke's Drift had been deliberately overlooked. Within the week the correspondence concerning the matter was placed before the Duke of Cambridge. His decision, released on 18 October, was brief, final and, worse, inequitable.

> We are giving the VC very freely I think, but probably Mr Dalton had as good a claim as the others who have got the Cross for Rorke's Drift Defence. I don't think there is a case for Mr. Dunne.[32]

Dalton was awarded the Victoria Cross in November 1879; it was presented by Major General H.H. Clifford during a parade at Fort Napier. Quite perversely, Dunne received nothing. Nevertheless, Dunne fared pretty well knowing that he had been recommended for the VC. He was involved in the first Boer War in 1880–81 and was present at the battle of Tel-el-Kebir, when the British defeated the Egyptian army. He transferred to the newly formed Army Service Corps as a lieutenant colonel, was awarded a CB and retired as a full colonel.

When it was realized that another body of men, the Colonial forces, had been omitted from the medal list the reports were re-examined and on 29 November Corporal Schiess NNC was gazetted as a recipient of the Victoria Cross for his actions during the battle. When he received his medal from Lord Wolseley on 3 February 1880 Wolseley expressed the wish that Schiess might live long to wear the decoration. Sadly he was to die a pauper only three years later.

The time-span of medal awards extended well into the following year and, apart from the politicking and scheming, each award was given the highest level of publicity by the press, for which the government was equally grateful. Even so, there were dissenters. The *Broad Arrow* of 23 August 1879 wrote:

> It must be confessed that the military authorities in Pall Mall have shown lavish prodigality in the distribution of the Victoria Cross, which would probably startle their contemporaries in Berlin [a reference to the

profusion of Iron Cross awards]. We say there is a chance of the Victoria
Cross being cheapened by a too friendly eagerness in Pall Mall to
recognise acts of equivocal valour.

It is a myth that the Reverend George Smith was offered the choice
of a Victoria Cross or an army chaplaincy; he received the chaplaincy but
there is no evidence or recommendation to substantiate the story that he
ever had a choice.

Gonville Bromhead received his Victoria Cross from Wolseley, a man
who had let it be known that he thought the awards for the defence of
Rorke's Drift were 'monstrous'. When Bromhead returned to England,
he was invited with Chard to dine with the queen at Balmoral. Unfortunately he had gone fishing in Ireland and did not receive his invitation
until the date had passed. Despite sending his apologies, he was never
invited to Balmoral again. Bromhead was promoted to captain and brevet
major and served in the East Indies and in the Burma campaign of 1886.
He attained the rank of major in 1883 and was serving with the battalion
in India when he was struck down by typhoid and died on 9 February
1891. Bromhead's medal is currently owned by his descendants and is
held at the Regimental Museum, Brecon.

John Chard received a hero's welcome when he arrived at Portsmouth.
The Duke of Cambridge, who brought the invitation to dine with the
queen, personally greeted him. In contrast to some of his critical superiors,
Victoria was taken by Chard's unassuming manner and the modest way in
which he related events. She was most impressed by the battle, asking for
photo portraits of the Victoria Cross recipients and commissioning Lady
Butler to paint a picture of Rorke's Drift.

Chard continued to enjoy the royal favour and rose in rank to colonel.
He was posted abroad several times but never saw action again. In 1896
he was diagnosed as having cancer of the tongue and he was forced to
retire. Queen Victoria was kept informed of his condition, which deteriorated and led to his death in November 1897.

CHAPTER 11

Enquiry and Cover-Up

I regret to have to report a very disastrous engagement. [1]

LORD CHELMSFORD

Within days of the two battles Chelmsford and his staff began casting about for a scapegoat on whom they could put the blame for Isandlwana. They settled on Colonel Durnford, the senior officer at the battle who had died with his men, and set about preparing a number of damning official memoranda. Lord Chelmsford's Order Book dated Wednesday 22 January 1879 states, 'Camp entered. No wagon laager appears to have been made. Poor Durnford's misfortune is incomprehensible.' Major Francis Grenfell, one of Lord Chelmsford's staff, wrote in a letter to his father, 'The loss of the camp was due to [the] officer commanding, not Colonel Pulleine, but Colonel Durnford of the Engineers who took command after the action had begun and who disregarded the orders left by the General.' Sir Bartle Frere's communication to the colonial secretary in London dated 27 January was equally harsh: 'In disregard of Lord Chelmsford's instructions, the troops left to guard the camp were taken away from the defensive position they were in at the camp, with the shelter which the wagons, parked [laagered] would have afforded', and a few days later he added, 'It is only justice to the General to note that his orders were clearly not obeyed on that terrible day at Isandlwana Camp.' [2]

Chelmsford convened a Court of Enquiry at Helpmekaar that commenced on 27 January 1879, just 10 miles from Rorke's Drift. The court president was Colonel Hassard with Lieutenant Colonel Law RA and Lieutenant Colonel Harness RA as court members. Harness was a crucial witness to events but he was tactically barred from giving evidence to the enquiry by Chelmsford, who insisted on his inclusion as a court member. Colonel Glyn, another vital witness, was not called to give evidence before the court. The enquiry was tasked merely to 'enquire into the loss of the camp'. Those officers and men who had escaped from Isandlwana had been required to tender brief written statements though the court considered only those of Major Clery and Colonel Crealock, Captains Essex and Gardner, Lieutenants Cochrane, Curling and Smith-Dorrien and NNC Captain Nourse. It was subsequently argued, within the army and the press, both in the UK and South Africa, that insufficient evidence was considered in order to divert the blame away from Chelmsford and that the final line of the report indicated the defensive nature of the enquiry:

> The duty of the Court was to sift the evidence and record what was of value: if it was simply to take down a mass of statements the court might as well have been composed of three subalterns or three clerks.[3]

In reality the report served no real purpose apart from whitewashing the defeat at Isandlwana and giving Chelmsford time to prepare his explanatory speech before he returned to England to present his case before Parliament. Meanwhile Chelmsford's staff were busy; official blame for the British defeat was about to be irretrievably laid upon the NNC and Durnford. At the enquiry, Colonel Crealock gave false evidence by stating that he had ordered Durnford, on behalf of Chelmsford, to take command of the camp; this false witness neatly exonerated Chelmsford. With regard to the NNC, the court heard confusing evidence as to their actions on the battlefield, yet it judged the issue on the evidence of Captain Essex who clearly recorded that he did not know their location. The court resolutely declined to listen to several surviving NNC officers who did know.

Chelmsford's staff successfully implicated Durnford in the defeat. He was not from an infantry regiment of the line and he was dead, which made him the perfect scapegoat. The court accepted Crealock's false evidence that Durnford had been in charge, knew that there had been a defeat, and after noting Durnford's various 'deficiencies' the deputy adjutant general, Colonel Bellairs, forwarded its findings to Chelmsford with the following condemnatory observation:

> From the statements made to the Court, it may be gathered that the cause of the reverse suffered at Isandhlwana was that Col. Durnford, as senior officer, overruled the orders which Lt. Col. Pulleine had received to defend the camp, and directed that the troops should be moved into the open, in support of the Native Contingent which he had brought up and which was engaging the enemy.[4]

Also effectively silenced were the five surviving officers, who were in an obvious predicament; their own departure from the Isandlwana battlefield could still be the subject of some uncomfortable consequences and they all knew that Colonel Glyn had been ignominiously relieved of his column duties and transferred to the command of the outpost at Rorke's Drift, effectively isolating him from the enquiry and its aftermath. Lieutenant Curling nevertheless gave damning evidence of the chaos and confusion at Isandlwana, both before and during the battle, in his private letters. On April 28 he wrote to his mother from the Victoria Club at Pietermaritzburg:

> I see they have published the proceedings of the Court of Inquiry: when we were examined we had no idea this would be done and took no trouble to make a readable statement, at least only one or two did so.[5]

The *Natal Witness* astutely observed on 29 May that:

> It is notorious that certain members of Lord Chelmsford's staff ... came down to 'Maritzburg after the disaster, prepared to make Colonel

Durnford bear the whole responsibility, and that it was upon their
representations that the High Commissioner's telegram about 'poor
Durnford's misfortune' was sent.

Not content with damning Durnford, Chelmsford's staff then turned
their malevolent attention to Colonel Glyn, Chelmsford's second in
command, now isolated from any news at Rorke's Drift and suffering
from depression. Glyn was sent a number of official memoranda requiring
him to account for his interpretation of orders relating to the camp at
Isandlwana but, recognizing the developing entrapment, he returned the
memoranda unanswered, but with the comment, 'Odd the general asking
me to tell him what he knows more than I do.' Glyn maintained his dignity
and position by stating that it was his duty to obey his commander's
orders. Thereafter Glyn remained silent on the matter but Mrs Glyn was
highly indignant at the treatment of her husband; she robustly defended
him in the coming months, forcing Chelmsford's staff to retreat in the
face of her fearless defence, and little was said beyond this point.

Chelmsford's staff now faced the task of finding an acceptable explanation of their unexpected defeat. The initial explanation they produced
was brilliantly simple, logical and, yet again, neatly blamed the officers
who fell on the battlefield rather than those who placed them there. They
reasoned that the soldiers on the line had run out of ammunition and
therefore the disaster was not of Chelmsford's making. Certainly
Durnford's men had experienced an earlier ammunition supply failure
when they attempted to obtain supplies from Chelmsford's quartermaster
– only to be ordered to find their own ammunition wagon, which could not
be found. When the scene of the disaster was later visited, it was discovered that the Zulus had taken all the Martini-Henry rifles from the dead
along with the ammunition that had remained on the ammunition carts.
Most of the boxes had been smashed open and ransacked by the Zulus
immediately following the battle and it was conveniently presumed by
Chelmsford's staff officers that this was evidence of frantic British attempts
to obtain further supplies rather than of the reality of victorious Zulus

helping themselves; and so the myth was born that the British line had been overrun because the soldiers had run out of ammunition. Other Zulus had removed the remaining ammunition from the pouches of dead soldiers; when the British subsequently buried the bodies they noticed the empty pouches, which supported the explanation that the soldiers had exhausted their available ammunition supply before being overwhelmed. Most accounts of the battle have perpetuated the myth, which still persists in uninformed circles, and so the blame was continuously deflected from those in command.

Curiously, these accounts have overlooked the numerous survivors' reports that confirm that extra ammunition was steadily moved out to the line both before and during the Zulu attack. Private Wilson wrote that before the battle 'ammunition was beginning to be brought down to the companies'. Captain Essex confirmed that the quartermaster issuing ammunition to the line was actually shot dead early in the battle before it had been loaded onto a cart, but also stated that he later saw the same cart deliver ammunition to the line. Zulu accounts over the years confirm that the last survivors were still firing furiously until their ammunition became exhausted, then all perished. Perhaps the inadvertent progenitor of the myth was General Sir Horace Smith-Dorrien who wrote of an ammunition box difficulty nearly fifty years after the event, having clearly forgotten that a few days after the disaster he wrote, 'I was out with the front companies of the 24th handing them spare ammunition'.[6] The myth grew to make an inexplicable defeat explicable; it also denied the enormous bravery and skill of both the Zulus and the British and while only Curling lived to tell the tale from the firing line, several accounts survive from Zulu warriors interviewed after the battle.

> They threw down their guns, when the ammunition was done, and then commenced with their pistols, which they fired as long as their ammunition lasted; and then they formed a line, shoulder to shoulder, and back to back, and fought with their knives.[7]

Some covered their faces with their hands, not wishing to see death. Some ran around. Some entered into their tents. Others were indignant; although badly wounded they died where they stood, at their post.[8]

One specific report clearly related to Durnford's last stand. Mehlo-kazulu, one of Chief Sihayo's sons, was present when Durnford and his men died and gave a detailed statement of events when he was later interviewed at Pietermaritzburg:

When we closed in we came onto a mixed party of men who had evidently been stopped by the end of our horn. They made a desperate resistance, some firing with pistols and others with swords. I repeatedly heard the word 'fire' but we proved too many for them, and killed them where they stood. When all was over I had a look at these men, and saw an officer with his arm in a sling and with a big moustache, surrounded by Carbineers, soldiers and other men I did not know.[9]

On 19 August 1880 Chelmsford completed his attack against Durnford's reputation in his speech to the House of Lords. Chelmsford stated that 'In the final analysis, it was Durnford's disregard of orders that had brought about its destruction.'[10] Most historical accounts relating to Durnford's actions at Isandlwana are, at best, uncertain of his orders, or the exact sequence of events, or they suppose that Durnford failed to assume command of the camp from the subordinate Pulleine and irresponsibly took his men off towards Chelmsford. Typical is the account of Major the Hon. Gerald French DSO who wrote in support of Chelmsford:

As to Lord Chelmsford's orders to Colonels Pulleine and Durnford before leaving the camp on the morning of January 22nd, the evidence adduced before the Court of Inquiry conclusively proved that the former was directed to *defend the camp*, whilst the latter was to move up from Rorke's Drift and *take command of it* on his arrival. Colonel Durnford would consequently, on assuming command, take over and *'be subject to the orders given to Colonel Pulleine by Lord Chelmsford'*. [Original italics][11]

Durnford's character was ruined beyond redemption. Notwithstanding the decision of the court to vindicate Chelmsford, it is relevant to raise the question: who actually had command at Isandlwana? The answer has to be Pulleine. Chelmsford never intended the two columns to merge and it is inconceivable that he would not have referred to such an important policy change in his orders. It was later 'leaked' by Chelmsford's staff that Durnford and Pulleine had hotly discussed the issue of taking Imperial troops from the camp to deter the Zulu advance, but Lieutenant Cochrane, who was present, denied that this was so. It seems more likely that Durnford wished to strengthen the weak position to the north of the camp but at the same time also protect the rear of his mounted men as he moved towards Chelmsford's location at Mangeni. Pulleine's concern was apparently shared by some of the camp's officers who felt that the removal of such a large part of the camp's force did not accord with Chelmsford's orders. Durnford's two reconnaissance troops were still out on the Nqutu plateau, and without their reports neither Durnford nor Pulleine knew what the Zulus were intending. Cochrane recalled that Lieutenant Melvill, the adjutant of the 1/24th, approached Durnford and said:

> 'Colonel, I really do not think Colonel Pulleine would be doing right to send any men out of camp when his orders are to defend the camp.' Durnford replied: 'Very well, it does not much matter. We will not take them.'[12]

Following Durnford's departure to intercept the advancing Zulus, two companies of the 1/24th had been marched from the camp to the spur leading to the Nqutu plateau. The suggestion may originally have been Durnford's but Pulleine had clearly thought it necessary. One of the two companies so dispatched was quickly overrun by the advancing Zulus; the other just made it back to the camp before it too was annihilated. The whole question of Durnford's orders has previously hinged upon the supposition that Durnford received specific orders from Chelmsford to take charge of the camp. Following Isandlwana, Chelmsford reproduced from memory his recollection of this particular order for his official report and expediently backdated it to 19 January; he knew that the original order had

213

never been found and no one challenged his account. The replacement version of the order, using Chelmsford's remembered words, reads:

Head Quarter Camp
Rorke's Drift, Zululand

19 January 1879

No 3 Column moves tomorrow to Insalwana Hill and from there, as soon as possible to a spot about 10 miles nearer to the Indeni Forest.

From that point I intend to operate against the two Matyanas if they refuse to surrender.

One is in the stronghold on or near the Mhlazakazi Mountain; the other is in the Indeni Forest. Bengough ought to be ready to cross the Buffalo R. at the Gates of Natal in three days time, and ought to show himself there as soon as possible.

I have sent you an order to cross the river at Rorke's Drift tomorrow with the force you have at Vermaaks.

I shall want you to operate against the Matyanas, but will send you fresh instructions on this subject.

We shall be about 8 miles from Rorke's Drift tomorrow.

In 1885, in an unusual twist of fate, the commanding officer of the Royal Engineers in Natal, Colonel Luard, heard rumours of a 'cover-up'. This related to the surreptitious removal of Chelmsford's written orders to Durnford from his (Durnford's) body by the then Captain Shepstone of Chelmsford's staff. Luard cautiously advertised his fears in the *Natal Witness* newspaper and on 25 June 1885 he received the following significant reply:

P.M.B. 25 June 85 ORIGINAL TEXT
F. Pearse & Co
14 Cole St.

E.D. Natal Witness Office
Dear Sir

Referring to yr. Advertisement wh. Appeared a few weeks ago in the Natal Witness respecting relics of the late Colonel Durnford. I write to inform you that I have in my possession a document which was picked up by my brother A. Pearse late trooper in the Natal Carbineers. It appears to be the instructions issued by Lord Chelmsford to the late Colonel on taking the field.

I have written to my brother to ascertain whether he is willing to part with it in the event of your wishing to have it in your possession.

Yours truly

(signed) F. Pearse

These original orders were discovered on or near Durnford's body by Trooper Pearse who was searching for another brother, also a trooper and presumed killed. The papers were in a poor condition, having been subjected to several months of weathering; at the time of their discovery some parts were so fragile that they could not easily be unfolded or read. The details on the envelope and the location when found were clearly sufficient for Pearse to realize that the envelope contained Chelmsford's instructions to Durnford. They were possibly kept as a battlefield keepsake but in consequence of the advertisement, Pearse forwarded the papers to the editor of the *Natal Witness* who promptly delivered them to Luard.

The discovery of Chelmsford's original orders to Durnford provoked Luard to write to Sir Andrew Clarke, Head of the Corps of Royal Engineers, with a plea to reopen the enquiry. This was duly approved although the Acting High Commissioner in South Africa was quick to see the implications for Chelmsford and wrote to Luard before the court convened at the end of April 1886, 'I have taken measures to limit proceedings and to prevent, I trust, the possibility of other names, distinguished or otherwise, being dragged into it'.[14] Shepstone, now a successful lawyer, agreed to attend a new Court of Enquiry.

To Luard's surprise, those in authority maintained the conspiracy against Durnford and, worse, certain important witnesses who could have given evidence were refused leave from the army and the civil authorities. The enquiry was strictly limited to the investigation of whether or not papers had been removed from Durnford's body. Without being able to refer to relevant evidence, or call vital witnesses, Luard's case crumbled. The conspirators' 'cover-up' succeeded, Shepstone was cleared and Luard was obliged to apologize to Shepstone. And there the matter rested – for the time being.

At a date unknown, the envelope and orders were forwarded to the Royal Engineers Museum at Chatham where they lay, presumably unread, until discovered in 1990 by two researchers, Jackson and Whybra, who painstakingly analysed the orders. The orders are in two parts; the first relevant part was Chelmsford's original order, genuinely dated 19 January 1879, and it is on this order that Durnford must have based so much of his decision-making when he arrived at Isandlwana. The original text is reproduced below and the order leaves little doubt what was in Chelmsford's mind when he wrote it. The order differs considerably from Chelmsford's later recollection, printed above.

NB Where a word or words are unreadable, a possible interpretation is included in **bold**.

Lieut. **Colonel Durnford** R.E

Camp Helpmakaar

1. You are requested to move the troops under your immediate command viz.: mounted men, rocket battery and Sikeli's men to Rourke's Drift tomorrow **the** 20th inst.; and to encamp on the left bank of the Buffalo (in Zulul**and**).

2. No. 3 Column moves tomorrow to the Isandhlana Hill.

3. Major Bengough with his battalion Native Contingent at Sand Spruit is

to hold himself in readiness to cross the Buffalo at the shortest possible notice to operate against the chief Matyana &c. His wagons will cross at Rourke's Drift.

4. Information is requested as to the ford where the above battalion can best cross, so as to co-operate with No. 3 Column in clearing the country occupied by the chief Matyana.

By Order, H. Spalding. Major DAAG

Camp, Rourke's Drift 19.1.79

This penultimate order to Durnford, signed and sent by Crealock, preceded the final order that was received by Durnford at Rorke's Drift on 22 January. Durnford was clearly ordered to 'co-operate with No. 3 Centre Column in clearing the country occupied by the chief Matyana'; likewise, he was never ordered to take command of the temporary camp at Isandlwana. In essence, Durnford did exactly as he was ordered. Because the final order is so ambiguous, it is reproduced exactly:

You are to march to this camp at once with all the force you have with you of No. 2 Column.

Major Bengough's battalion is to move to Rorke's Drift as ordered yesterday. 2nd 24th, Artillery and mounted men with the General and Colonel Glyn move off at once to attack a Zulu force about 10 miles distant.[15]

In 2001 yet another set of Chelmsford's orders came to light; they had also been recovered as a souvenir from the battlefield and had since been held in private ownership without their significance being noted. The orders were addressed to the officer in command at Helpmekaar and the hypothesis has to be that they were Glyn's original orders. With minor exceptions, these recently discovered orders match those of Durnford. At last there is additional evidence to prove that both Pulleine and Durnford totally obeyed Chelmsford's orders. It is also evident that, after Isandlwana, Chelmsford's original orders to Durnford and received by him on the day of battle were later ambiguously reworded by Crealock to vindicate Chelmsford and his staff – a deliberate action to incriminate Durnford.

One must presume, therefore, that Chelmsford's staff believed that the actual orders had been destroyed on the battlefield; indeed, until recently there was no indication that these orders even existed.

Early on the morning of 22 January 1879, the same day as Isandlwana, Pearson's column was attacked near the Nyezane river. Pearson arranged his troop dispositions according to Chelmsford's instructions to all column commanders, i.e. the same instructions as issued to Durnford and Glyn (and inherited by Pulleine).

Although separated by 50 miles, the respective troop deployments by Pulleine and Pearson on 22 January correspond exactly to both known sets of Chelmsford's orders. It is unlikely to have been a coincidence as within hours Colonel Wood's Northern Column dispersed a strong force of Zulus near Hlobane mountain 40 miles to the north of Isandlwana; Wood also used identical tactics in accordance with the orders.

In 1998 a further remarkable set of documents was discovered; three bundles of faded letters were about to be discarded when it was realized they related to the Zulu War. They were the letters of Lieutenant Curling RA, the only surviving British officer who fought and witnessed events on the British front line at Isandlwana. His letters provide a fascinating insight into what really happened at Isandlwana as well as casting some doubt on the previously accepted theories of the RA guns' final position after the British defeat. The crux of the difference between Curling's eye-witness version and that previously guessed by modern historians is that Curling saw the horses and limbers overturn beside Black's Koppie whereas the historians consistently maintained that the guns ran along the ravine for some 400 yards and then stuck.

Curling also wrote a report for the Court of Enquiry though it is not surprising that the enquiry members ignored his evidence; his account confirmed Pulleine's inability, probably as a result of his lack of fighting experience, both to prepare for the Zulu attack and then to take appropriate measures to counter it. On 28 April Curling wrote to his mother from the Victoria Club, Pietermaritzburg:

I am sorry to say our column is still to be commanded by the General [Lord Chelmsford]. I feel these disasters have quite upset his judgement or rather that of his staff and one does not feel half so comfortable under his command as with a man like Col. Wood. Our column is likely to be the one that will have all the fighting.[16]

Indeed, Chelmsford formally sought to be returned to the UK on the grounds of ill health. On 9 February 1879 he wrote:

In June last I mentioned privately to His Royal Highness The Duke of Cambridge, Commander in Chief, that the strain of prolonged anxiety and exertion, physical and mental was even then telling on me – What I felt then, I feel still more now.[17]

The *Standard* quipped:

No such appeal to the Authorities of England for dismissal from a position to which Lord Chelmsford felt himself unequal had ever before been addressed to them by a General in the field commanding Her Majesty's troops.[18]

He was not replaced until after the battle of Ulundi on 4 July 1879.

Matters were no less complicated following the battle for Rorke's Drift. Before Chelmsford departed from Helpmekaar, he not only gave specific instructions for a formal enquiry to be conducted into the Isandlwana defeat, but also ordered a further report concerning the victory at Rorke's Drift. Chelmsford's own correspondence reveals that he was most anxious to receive the account, although it is not known who ordered the report or who was to write it. As early as 28 January Chelmsford wrote to Glyn:

I hope you are sending me in a report of the defence of Rorke's Drift post and also the names etc of the killed during that gallant fight.[19]

A further request from Chelmsford's staff officer reached Glyn on 31 January; it is ambiguous as it relates to 'reports', indicating that Chelmsford was expecting at least two reports, presumably concerning Isandl-wana and Rorke's Drift. He wrote:

> Your immediate attention is called to the fact that no reports have been received from you regarding the entrenchment of your column or of the occurrences of the 22nd instant; neither has any return of casualties been made.[20]

Back at Rorke's Drift, the soldiers would have normally occupied themselves with writing letters home but all available paper had been burnt in the fire or destroyed during the fighting. When Commandant Hamilton-Browne sought to arrange a field court martial for a captured Zulu spy he had great difficulty finding paper or pens to record the pro-ceedings. All of a sudden, paper had become a very rare commodity; one soldier, Private Robert Head, was so desperate to write a letter to his brother with the news that he was still alive that he paid one shilling, a day's pay, for a scrap of paper burnt on two edges. This scrap of a letter survived – but the true identity of the soldier remains unknown as there was no Private Robert Head recorded either in the 24th Regimental records or on the list of Rorke's Drift defenders. Presumably he wrote home using his correct name but at the time of his enlistment used a false name.

Lieutenant George Stanhope Banister of the 2/24th, having accom-panied Chelmsford during the previous four days, was unexpectedly appointed as assistant garrison adjutant at Rorke's Drift. Because the Zulus had destroyed the officers' tents, there was no writing paper; Banister wrote a brief note to his father dated 27 January 1879: 'No paper or pens or in fact any single thing. I have managed to get some foolscap in my extra capacity as Garrison Adjutant.' No camp orders could be issued until 28 January, six days after the battle, when a limited official supply arrived from Helpmekaar. The soldiers had to make do with scraps; one soldier, Private John Bainbridge, even sent a note to his family in England with a request for writing paper – on the grounds that there was 'none to be had within 200 miles of here'. Lieutenant Curling, who was a compulsive letter writer, could not find any writing paper; he bemoaned his plight but was thankful to have been the sole survivor from the British front line. He eventually managed to write home and stated:

> One ought not to think of anything after having had such a wonderful escape. As to clothing, blankets etc., there have been sales of all the kits belonging to the officers who were killed and I have been able to get the most necessary things one requires. This paper I am writing on belonged to one of the poor fellows in the 24th.[21]

Notwithstanding that there was no shelter from the incessant heavy rain and the camp was wallowing in mire and chaos, within two days of the battle Chard ostensibly managed to obtain a sufficient supply of clean, undamaged paper in order to secretly prepare and submit a perfectly sequential report of the battle. Though not noted either for report-writing skills or for eloquence, he carefully composed a neatly written account of the battle that was complete in extraordinary detail. The report included accurate and precise timings, and locations and names of the thirteen different units represented, as well as listing all the names and units of those who were killed or injured or who might receive acknowledgement for their outstanding courage during the battle. Yet there is no record of any participant in the battle having assisted Chard with his meticulous report. It is also a mystery how Chard was able to recall accurately the names of all the participants, bearing in mind that prior to the battle he had not met anyone at the post other than Bromhead; and how he was also able to prepare accurate drawings of the hospital building after it had been destroyed by fire. Bromhead was subsequently requested to write an account but he repeatedly avoided the issue until 15 February when he wrote a brief report outlining the bravery of certain participants in the battle. There is no evidence that anyone present during the battle assisted Chard or Bromhead in the preparation of their reports, and none of the purported 'original' Chard reports bears his signature. Colour Sergeant Bourne left no contemporary account. Both before and after the battle of Rorke's Drift, Chard's reputation was linked with slothfulness. The mystery of Chard's report deepens because this truly masterful and perceptive account of the battle was written under extraordinarily difficult circumstances. Curiously, if Chard made any notes in the preparation of the report, they have never been seen; when, over twelve months later, he was asked to rewrite the account for Queen Victoria, he reported that he had lost his original notes.

On 3 February Glyn received a further curt note from Chelmsford marked 'Private' reminding Glyn that Chelmsford was still waiting for the Rorke's Drift report; Glyn ignored the communication, knowing that Chard's report would soon reach Chelmsford. When it arrived, Chelmsford immediately forwarded the report to the Secretary of State for War. Chelmsford knew that the victory at Rorke's Drift could deflect those who would soon seek to humiliate him for the appalling loss of men and the longer-term implications of a highly trained British force being defeated by a native army. It would not have escaped Chelmsford that an inglorious defeat could be offset by a glorious victory. And so it was. Chelmsford also had influential friends and before Parliament could act to censure him for his unauthorized invasion of Zululand, Queen Victoria pre-empted any criticism by ordering a congratulatory message to be sent to him via the Secretary of State for War:

> The Queen has graciously desired me to say she sympathises most sincerely with you in the dreadful loss which has deprived her of so many gallant officers and men and that Her Majesty places entire confidence in you and in her troops to maintain our honour and our good name.[22]

This was followed by a further message from the Field Marshal His Royal Highness the Duke of Cambridge, Commander-in-Chief of the British Army. His telegram reads:

> Have heard, by telegraph, of events occurred. Grieved for 24th and others who have fallen victims. Fullest confidence in regiment, and am satisfied that you have done and will continue to do everything that is right. Strong reinforcements of all arms ordered to embark at once, February 13th.[23]

Chelmsford's use of the 'Chard report' was skilful; it was initially hailed throughout the British and Colonial press as evidence of Britain's strength in adversity while both Chard and Bromhead were fêted in the newspapers and popular weekly journals as heroes – as indeed they were. Yet the event was viewed differently among their fellow officers; resentment and incredulity for their unexpected status as popular heroes began to grow and Curling and others were soon annoyed by the intensity of fame being attached to the two officers. Curling wrote:

It is very amusing to read the accounts of Chard and Bromhead. They are about the most commonplace men in the British Army. Chard is a most insignificant man in appearance and is only about 5 feet 2 or 3 in height. Bromhead is a stupid old fellow, as deaf as a post. Is it not curious how some men are forced into notoriety?[24]

On 15 February a report now known as the 'Bromhead Report' was submitted to Glyn concerning the bravery of certain soldiers of the 24th during the Rorke's Drift skirmish. This report, signed by Bromhead in his capacity as commander of B Company, was submitted to Colonel Glyn more than two weeks after the defence of Rorke's Drift. The identity of the author of this report is unknown although the report is signed by Bromhead. The report recorded the names of the six men belonging to B Company who specially distinguished themselves during the attack. It was to this report that Lord Chelmsford added the names of Lieutenants Bromhead and Chard, a highly irregular action, as Chelmsford should have discussed any recommendation for awards with Glyn. Apart from the above 'Bromhead Report' and his note warning those at Helpmekaar, only two other letters are known to have been written by Bromhead during this period. The first was to Lieutenant Godwin-Austen of the 2/24th on 19 February; Godwin-Austen had been with Chelmsford on 22 and 23 January. The style and syntax in the official Bromhead Report differ significantly from those used in the two letters – which suggests that Bromhead was not the willing author of the report. (Both letters are reproduced as Appendix F.)

CHAPTER 12

The Coastal (No.1) Column

*The column marched only 17 miles in four days – hardly a
lightning campaign.*[1]

CAPTAIN WYNNE RE

But for the brilliant Zulu victory at Isandlwana and the remarkable
heroism of the Rorke's Drift defenders, the achievements of the Coastal
Column would have ranked among the finest deeds recorded in British
military history. However, because Colonel Pearson's victory at Nyezane
occurred on the same date as Isandlwana and Rorke's Drift, the battle of
Nyezane and the subsequent Zulu siege of Eshowe were both overlooked
and then largely forgotten, and in many accounts of the Zulu War neither
receives much more than a footnote entry.

Colonel Charles Knight Pearson was 45 years old. He was highly
regarded for being a well-balanced officer with sound experience on active
service with the 3rd Regiment, the Buffs, from which he had resigned in
order to obtain a more prestigious appointment on Chelmsford's staff.
He was a veteran campaigner whose regiment had already served in South
Africa for three years and Chelmsford was aware of Pearson's deep-seated
affinity with the Buffs, which may explain the agreeable appointment to
Pearson of command of the Coastal Column – thus reuniting him with
his regiment.

The starting point for the Coastal Column was the very strong fortification of Fort Pearson, named in his honour. This was purpose-built on the Natal bank of the 200 yard wide Tugela river which separated Natal and Zululand. It overlooked the Lower Drift all the way to the Indian Ocean shimmering in the distance. Its hilltop position on the bluff gave it a commanding view to the sea and across the Tugela river, giving the British a clear view for several miles into Zululand. Like the depot at Helpmekaar, its sole purpose was to keep its advancing column well supplied. Pearson's orders were to move his column the 35 miles from Fort Pearson to Eshowe to occupy and convert the small Norwegian mission station into a fortified advanced supply depot. Mission stations were conveniently situated at strategic crossing border points so it was no coincidence that both the Centre and the Coastal columns planned to use missions as their forward bases. Once the depot was established, the column's supply wagons were to return to Fort Pearson to collect additional stores before Pearson could advance on the Zulu capital at Ulundi, ideally at the same rate of advance as the Centre and Northern columns.

The Coastal Column's infantry was composed of the Buffs and the less experienced 99th Regiment, while the column's heavy firepower came from the Royal Artillery and the Naval Landing Brigade which each supplied two 7 pound guns and a rocket battery. The 136-strong blue-jackets from HMS *Active* and HMS *Tenedos* provided a further two rocket tubes and were supported by the American-built Gatling gun, about to be used in action by the British for the first time.[2] With the column was a force of about 2,000 black retainers of the NNC. These locally recruited auxiliaries were poorly trained, ill equipped and not expected to fight; their role was to scout, and disperse the beaten foe. The Royal Engineers supplied eighty-five sappers, and the 312-strong squadron of horsemen was made up from the Mounted Infantry as well as from local units such as the Natal Hussars, Victoria Mounted Rifles, Alexander Mounted Rifles and the Durban Mounted Rifles, making the total number of fighting men in excess of 4,000. In addition, 620 civilians were employed to drive the 384 ox-wagons. All in all it was a formidable force, but it constituted a logistical nightmare.

Having assembled his force, Pearson's first task was to cross the Tugela river, now dangerously swollen by the first of the inevitable summer storms, and establish a base on the far bank. This enormous task was unopposed by the Zulus and successfully accomplished in just five days by the use of a large pont constructed by the carpenters from HMS *Active*. Seaman Martin of that ship's crew had the sad distinction of becoming the first casualty of the Zulu War when he fell into the fast-flowing, crocodile-infested river and was lost. Having crossed the Tugela, Pearson immediately constructed a fortified camp that was named Fort Tenedos.

Strategically the concept of a Coastal Column in support of the main Centre Column was logical, but it overlooked some important factors. It was the beginning of the rainy season and the task of moving several thousand men and heavily laden wagons over 37 miles of rugged terrain, following nothing more than a rough, twisting track, proved extremely difficult. Furthermore, debilitating sickness had begun to spread among the men and there was the constant threat of an enemy whose tactical aptitude and enthusiasm for battle were unknown qualities. So far the few Zulus seen had kept their distance, content to observe and report back to King Cetshwayo. Leaving a garrison of sailors, two companies of the 99th and some NNC to guard Fort Pearson, Colonel Pearson and two columns set off on 19 January across enemy country towards the abandoned Norwegian mission station at Eshowe. Because of the heavy rains, long stretches of the track quickly became treacherously boggy and the many dongas and rivers crossing the route were swollen with deep rushing water. Progress was slow but steady; the most difficult part was manoeuvring the heavily laden wagons through stretches of deep mud and across the many flooded watercourses, which necessitated the Native Pioneers digging away the steep banks to create crossing points. Soaked to the skin and exhausted from each day's toil, the men endured miserable nights in their leaky tents. When on night guard the inexperienced and nervous recruits of the 99th further tried their comrades' patience with regular false alarms. Notwithstanding Chelmsford's orders, no attempt was ever made to laager the wagons and, with the two columns stretched out for several miles along the track, they were highly vulnerable to Zulu attack. In fact, a Zulu *impi* numbering some 3,500 warriors had already been detached from Cetshwayo's main army at Ulundi and was steadily marching to intercept Pearson's straggling column.

Then, on 21 January, Pearson received information that between 4,000 and 5,000 warriors were assembling close to his proposed route to Eshowe at the royal Gingindlovu *ikhanda*. In order to verify this information Pearson detached two companies of the Buffs with most of the Naval Brigade, his artillery, some mounted men and two companies of NNC. It was certainly good luck for this strung-out British reconnaissance force that the report was inaccurate, otherwise they might have been annihilated. The *ikhanda* was deserted; pausing only for some target practice on the deserted huts, the detachment returned to the main column.

Unseen by Pearson's men the destructive activities of the column had been observed at a distance by the approaching Zulu scouts, which forced their leader, Chief Godide kaNdlela, to hasten his plan to attack the column. After dark, the Zulu force assembled at the smouldering homestead and then followed the detachment's trail until they approached the sleeping British camp. Fortune again favoured the British; the gathering Zulus surrounded Pearson's camp but did not attack, being uncertain of Pearson's exact position. During the night the Zulus were joined by increasing numbers of local warriors until their force totalled more than 6,000. Under the cover of darkness they silently moved across the valley to the nearby Wombane hill, a location that held special significance for the Zulus, having been the setting of an earlier Zulu success against a Boer commando. The hill crest overlooks the Nyezane river and at first light the Zulu scouts were able to assess the main advancing British column as it began crossing the river in the valley below them. The dawn discovery of heavily trampled grass around the camp alerted Pearson and his column to their narrow escape and the proximity of a large force of Zulus. Chief Godide kaNdlela now commanded 6,000 Zulus from the uDlambedlu, izinGulube and umXhapho regiments and an unknown number of local irregular Zulu units.

Opposing him was Colonel Pearson's force, which amounted to a total of 2,782 men of whom 1,660 were black auxiliaries. Pearson's column ponderously set off at 7 a.m. with its advance scouts following the existing traders' track which led towards a plateau between two low hills, the final approach to Eshowe.

Wombane Hill, only 3 miles from Eshowe, dominated the front and right of the infrequently used traders' track now being followed by Pearson's column and looked down on the river crossing less than a mile distant. On the left of the track and nearing the summit was an abandoned *umuzi*. The location boded well for the Zulus who began to assemble out of sight of the unsuspecting British – now highly vulnerable as they prepared for the river crossing.

The shallow Nyezane river was to be Pearson's first obstacle of the day; he sent his mounted scouts ahead and their officer, Captain Barrow, reported that a flat plateau just beyond the far bank would make a suitable place to halt the wagons for breakfast. The track from the river followed a low ridge that ran up the middle of a valley; on either side were gullies thickly filled with tall reeds and long grass. Despite having reservations about halting in an area surrounded by thick undergrowth, Pearson decided to accept Barrow's suggestion and ordered the first wagons across the river.

It was difficult and overgrown terrain that confronted Pearson as he joined Barrow to discuss the next stage of the advance; meanwhile the laborious task of bringing the wagons across the Nyezane river was well under way. The day was already stiflingly hot and some of the troops took the opportunity to bathe in the river as the first wagons passed them by before halting at the open area below the centre spur. Shortly after 8 a.m. one of the vedettes reported to Barrow that a small party of Zulus had been seen gathering on Wombane; it was clear to Barrow that the column was being observed so he passed this information on to Pearson who immediately ordered the NNC forward to engage the Zulus. Led by Captain Hart, the NNC advanced up the track and along the centre spur, which prematurely sprang the Zulu trap. A small party of Zulus was then seen moving on the skyline above, melting into the bush and then reappearing on the lower slopes of Wombane to the right of the British.[3]

Hart led his NNC up the slope with the intention of clearing the hill of Zulus. They left the track and crossed through the thick undergrowth in the ravine before emerging onto the lower reaches of Wombane hill. The NNC officers in question, of German extraction, had all been locally recruited and few had any military training; they had no knowledge of their troops' language and during their advance confusion inevitably ensued. The leading NNC skirmishers quickly became aware that Zulus were hiding in the long grass ahead and tried to warn their officers. In turn, the officers could not understand their men's reluctance to advance and tried to urge them on. At the sight of a party of Zulus moving towards them the NNC panicked, probably because they possessed only ten rifles between them, and ran back down the slope towards the protection of the ravine. At the same time hundreds of Zulus emerged from behind the crest of the hill and fired a number of ragged volleys towards the column before charging down in pursuit of the retreating NNC. Several white officers and NCOs were either overconfident or rooted to the spot with fear; they appeared to try to hold their ground for a moment but were quickly overrun and killed. Hart sped after the fleeing NCOs and managed to get back to safety.

Meanwhile the sudden sounds of gunfire and shouting alerted the remainder of the troops still crossing the river and those at the wagon park. The bathers hastily dressed and rushed forward towards the centre spur. Sapper Cullern later wrote:

> I am thankful to say I escaped. We expect another battle in a few days. We were taken by surprise in the bush.[4]

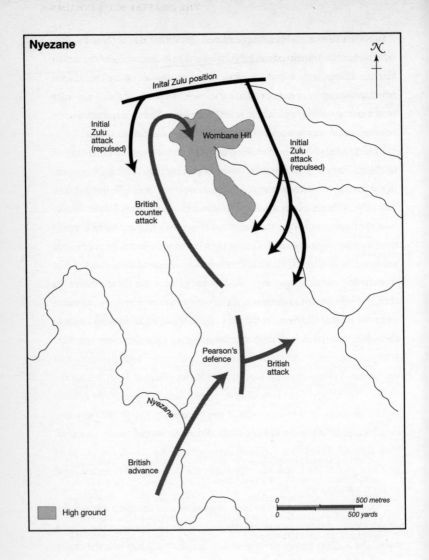

Nyezane

Inital Zulu position

Initial Zulu attack (repulsed)

Wombane Hill

Initial Zulu attack (repulsed)

British counter attack

Pearson's defence

British attack

Nyezane

British advance

High ground

0 — 500 metres
0 — 500 yards

N

The Zulu charge was the premature attack by their left horn: they were supposed to be part of a carefully planned ambush, but the centre and right horn were not yet in position to pose an effective threat. The Mounted Volunteers quickly formed a firing line to the right of the track and fired into the approaching left flank of the Zulu horn as they tried to work their way towards the wagons. In the confusion, Hart's NNC started to emerge from the undergrowth of the ravine only to be met by undisciplined friendly fire until they were identified.

Pearson could see he was in a highly vulnerable position. His wagons were strung out for over a mile and the river was dividing his command. Initially he was in no position to form an effective defence and his only course of action was to rush as many reinforcements forward as possible. Fortunately he already had his artillery with him together with the gun and the men of the Naval Brigade plus two companies of the Buffs. As they were getting into position, the men of the Royal Engineers, who had been working at the river crossing, joined the Mounted Volunteers along the firing line and helped keep the Zulus at bay. One Zulu later stated:

> The whites shot us down in numbers, in some places our dead and wounded covered the ground, we lost heavily, especially from the small guns, many of our men were drowned in the Nyezane River.[5]

Another recalled the difficulties experienced by the Zulus:

> We went forward packed close together like a lot of bees. We were still far away from them when the white men began to throw their bullets at us, but we could not shoot at them because our rifles would not shoot so far … the battle was so fierce that we had to wipe the blood and brains of the killed and wounded from our heads, faces, arms, legs and shields after the fighting.[6]

Pearson was now able to order a defensive deployment by his column – and he did so in full accordance with Chelmsford's written orders for engaging Zulu forces. Indeed, identical orders were being followed by Colonel Pulleine at Isandlwana that very same morning less than 100 miles away. The Zulus responded by advancing towards Pearson's column, leaving the British officers in no doubt that they were about to come under a serious attack. Pearson quickly deployed two companies of the Buffs and part of the Naval Brigade along with two guns and a rocket tube from the Royal Artillery. Still further down the track were the Mounted Infantry and Volunteer troopers; when they heard the firing they ran forward and formed a skirmish line to the right of Pearson's headquarters and started to fire steadily into the mass of Zulus who were now streaming down Wombane hill with the intention of surrounding those wagons that had managed to cross the river.

Pearson placed himself on the knoll, now accompanied by the artillery and the Buffs, and gave orders for both the Queen's and regimental colours to be unfurled. The Zulus to the right of his position were difficult to see as they advanced through the long grass. To make things worse, other groups of Zulus began to appear and also put down heavy long-range fire into the gathering British defenders. One casualty was Colonel Pearson's favourite horse, which was badly wounded, necessitating its destruction. Pearson's casualties were mounting and, in response, several officers directed a series of carefully aimed volleys into the Zulu sharpshooters who were causing the most damage.

The Zulu centre and right horn then advanced into the attack but Pearson had prejudged their intention and already manoeuvred his force to counter them. Earlier that morning Midshipman Coker and his Gatling gun team had been with the assembled wagons servicing the weapon. On hearing the firing they had hurriedly completed their work and ran with the Gatling to a prominent knoll. From here they put down a devastating rate of fire among the Zulus. The warriors began to panic and retreated once more, suffering further heavy casualties as they withdrew. On seeing the Zulus' disarray, Pearson audaciously gave the order to advance. There was a race between the Buffs and sailors to close with the Zulus but their combined advance slowed towards the top of the rise as the assembling Zulus made a determined stand. Led by Commander Campbell, the sailors made a wild cutlass charge and the Zulus finally broke and fled in disarray.

Groups of Zulus were seen to take refuge in the undergrowth but well-placed artillery shells rapidly forced them into the open and onto the spears of the pursuing NNC.

The battle lasted less than ninety minutes and another potential disaster for the British became a remarkable victory. Pearson's men had behaved admirably under fire but he was undoubtedly lucky. If the Zulu attack had been co-ordinated against the strung-out column, especially while it was crossing the river, the outcome for Pearson's whole column could have been disastrous. By the end of the battle the British had lost twelve men killed and some twenty wounded, two of whom later died of their wounds. The Zulus suffered in excess of 500 killed and many hundreds wounded. Indeed, the condition of the wounded shocked many soldiers. One wrote:

> It was pitiful to see the fellows lying with fearful wounds. They were very quiet, and seemed to bear pain well, no groaning or crying out … one of them had crawled at least a quarter of a mile with a broken leg. One poor fellow was in an ant bear hole about 70 yards from the vedettes in front of them, and they did not see him for a long time until he called out – asking them to find him.[7]

The battle was, in the words of Colour Sergeant Burnett of the 99th, 'terribly earnest work, and not at all child's play'.[8] During the aftermath of the battle the British assisted the Zulu wounded but such humanitarianism ceased when the slaughter and mutilations of Isandlwana became known to the troops. In later actions of the Zulu War few wounded were spared – by either side. During questioning of the wounded Zulus Pearson learned that the Zulu plan to attack the column had been pre-empted due to the early attack by the NNC; he was also left in little doubt that an even greater Zulu force was gathering to oppose him.

The column's dead were carefully buried in a single grave. The column's padre, the Reverend Mr Robertson, formerly of Eshowe, led the burial service and, without further delay, the march was resumed towards Eshowe. Pearson did not want the Zulus to believe that they had slowed his advance and he also needed to be clear of the very rough bush country along the Nyezane river to lessen the possibility of a further Zulu ambush. The Zulu dead were left to the circling vultures and scavenging wild animals. The day had been unbearably hot and after a further arduous march onto high ground Pearson called an early halt for the night.

At 3 a.m. on the following morning the column resumed the march; only 2 miles remained and the column reached Eshowe without further incident at 10 a.m. on 24 January. The Reverend Mr Robertson's first point of call was to his wife's grave in the mission cemetery.

The defence and relief of Eshowe

The abandoned mission station occupied conveniently high ground and the first troops to arrive discovered that it was in good condition. The station consisted of a corrugated iron-roofed steepled church, three other mud-built structures and a nearby garden filled with orange trees. It covered an area of just 120 yards by 80 yards, sloping west to east, and there was a good supply of water from two nearby streams. In addition there were three more buildings standing a short distance away. The senior Royal Engineer present, Captain Warren Wynne, had reservations that some marginally higher ground within sniping range overlooked the mission. Furthermore, a deep ravine filled with impenetrable undergrowth and home to a colony of puff adders came right up to the perimeter and could conceal a Zulu assault.

Pearson's view of Eshowe was summed up in his first report to Chelmsford. He wrote, 'It is the ugliest bit of ground for a camp or a defensible post I have seen. However the buildings, which have all been left – are good for stores that it would be a pity to abandon it for another site.' [9]

As soon as camp was made, work started on making the area defensible. Pearson ordered an earthwork to be built around the mission site and trenches to be dug. The fruit trees were cut down and the offending undergrowth was soon cleared to give unrestricted fields of fire. The already weary men then toiled on through the stifling heat of the afternoon until all stores were unloaded and placed in the outlying buildings. The next day, 25 January, forty-eight of the empty wagons were escorted back to Fort Pearson to collect more stores. They passed another convoy en route to Eshowe and the first rumours began to spread that all was not well with the Centre Column. Some even reported hearing a rumour that Colonel Durnford and his NNC had been annihilated.

Like Isandlwana, Eshowe was intended to be little more than a staging post on the line of advance and Pearson did not expect to remain there long. Nevertheless, the following day his Zulu-speaking Colonial mounted pickets heard Zulus in the surrounding countryside calling to one another across the hilltops that they had won a great victory. The next day a runner from Fort Pearson brought the first of a series of confusing messages, which confirmed that the Centre Column had been defeated. Pearson and his column were shocked by the incoming news; it seemed inconceivable that the Zulus, primarily armed with spears, could overcome an army equipped with sophisticated modern weapons. Furthermore, Pearson's force all knew that they were a long way from the safety of the Natal border; they were also surrounded and vulnerable and possessed limited supplies.

Without volunteering any opinion or advice, Chelmsford formally withdrew his earlier orders to Pearson and replaced them with the option of remaining at Eshowe or retreating back to Fort Tenedos. Pearson took the unusual step of calling his officers together to decide whether to retreat or stay. Having finally fortified Eshowe, he was reluctant to withdraw. If the Zulu army was heading for Eshowe, any slow-moving column returning to Fort Pearson would seriously risk being overwhelmed. The officers were divided; some felt that they should try to reach Natal where they could assist in its defence against the anticipated Zulu counter-invasion, while others sought to stay in order to force the local Zulus to maintain a siege rather than allowing them to intimidate. Captain Wynne of the Royal Engineers put forward a robust case for remaining at Eshowe. He argued that a retreating column would be highly vulnerable to attack and that a strong garrison at Eshowe would require a large force of Zulus

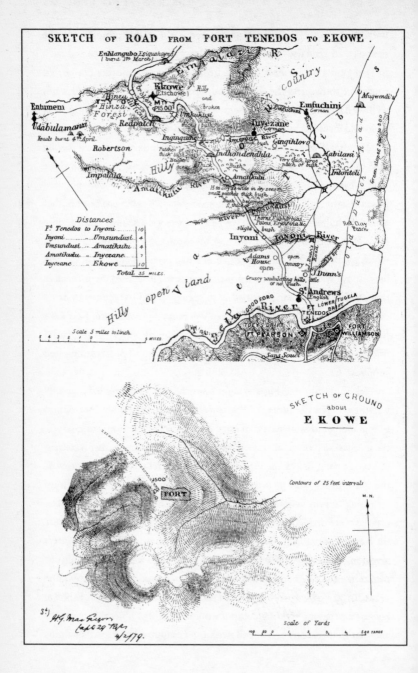

SKETCH OF ROAD FROM FORT TENEDOS TO EKOWE.

Enhlangubo Esiquakayna
(burnt 1st March)

Umlaloar R.

Ekowe
(Etschowe)
MT
1500

Enhlangubo

country

Emfuchini
German

Mugwendi's

Hinza
Hinza
Forest

Entumeni

Umkukusi

Tuyezane
German

Udabulamanzi

Redpatch

Injingana

Inyezane River

Gingihlovo

Mabilani

Kraals burnt 4th April

Robertson

Indhondenhla

Intonteli

Impalala

Patches of
thick bush
(burnt)

Green slopes zoo to 300

Dutch Road

Amatikulu River

Amatikulu

Very thick open
patch of bush

15 to 20½ miles in dry season,
small patches thick bush.
Bush becomes
thicker

Distances

Ft Tenedos to Inyoni		10
Inyoni ... Umsundusi		4
Umsundusi ... Amatikulu		4
Amatikulu ... Inyezane		7
Inyezane ... Ekowe		10
	Total	35 MILES.

Inyoni

Inyoni River

Palms Euphorbias
Palms Erythrina &c.

slight
bush

Adams
House

open
country

J Dunn's

Grassy undulating hills, little
or no bush

St Andrews
English

FT LOWER TUGELA
TENEDOS DRIFT

GOOD FORD

Tugela River

FT PEARSON

FORT
WILLIAMSON

Hilly

open land

Red Clay
Patch

Scale 5 miles to 1 inch.

5 4 3 2 1 0   5 MILES

Sans Souci

SKETCH OF GROUND
about
EKOWE

1500

FORT

Contours of 25 feet intervals

M. N.

St H.G. MacGregor
Capt 29 Regt
4/2/79.

Scale of Yards

100 50 0   1   2   3   4   500 YARDS

236

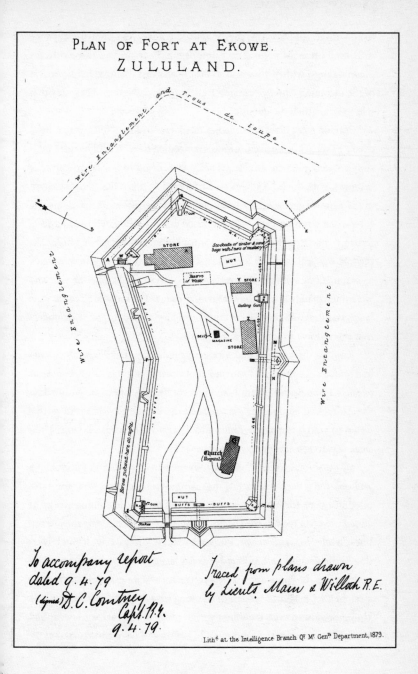

PLAN OF FORT AT EKOWE.
ZULULAND.

Wire Entanglement and Trous de loupe

Wire Entanglement

Wire Entanglement

STORE

Stockade of timber & sand bags with 3 tiers of musketry

HUT

Reserve of Water

Y STORE

Gatling Gun

BELL

MAGAZINE

STORE

Church (Hospital)

HUT

BUFFS — BUFFS

GUN

GUN

Horses picketed here at night

BUFFS

To accompany report
dated 9.4.79
(signed) D. C. Courtney
Capt. R.E.
9.4.79

Traced from plans drawn
by Lieuts. Main & Willock R.E.

Lith^d at the Intelligence Branch Q^r Mr Gen^th Department, 1879.

237

to contain it. Additionally, they would be ready to continue the advance to Ulundi once the second invasion began. Pearson and those officers present agreed with Wynne and so the die was cast. Boosted by the arrival of the incoming convoy bringing fresh supplies, all hands worked with a will to strengthen the defences.

Pearson recognized that the mounted men and the NNC were unnecessary in such a defensive position and feeding them would be difficult if supplies were interrupted. He accordingly ordered Major Barrow to take his force, with the NNC, back to Fort Tenedos; this reduced the strength of the Eshowe garrison to 1,460 combatants and about 335 civilians. He forwarded a full report of his proposed activities to Chelmsford and in return requested a full tactical appraisal of events along the border. As the fort was still cramped for space, some 1,000 oxen were also sent back to Natal, along with their drivers; many oxen strayed along the way and were immediately lost to the shadowing Zulus. The remaining cattle were laagered alongside the entrenchment until it dawned upon the defenders that this made a noisome health hazard.

King Cetshwayo was understandably indignant that Pearson's column had settled at Eshowe, and responded by ordering the local Zulu regiments to encircle the British position and prevent their withdrawal. Within days the Zulus had completely surrounded the British position and settled down to watch the proceedings and listen to the bands playing. Their siege was to last seventy-two days.

By the second week of February Wynne had loopholed all the buildings and ordered a deep ditch to be dug around the perimeter with the earth piled inside to form a defensive rampart. During the coming weeks he added traverses to stop the possibility of Zulu rifle fire raking the interior lines, while 'trous-de-loup', known by the soldiers as 'wolf-pits', were dug in the ground with pointed stakes placed in the bottom; these were built across the three approaches to the fort. Wire entanglements were stretched from stakes hidden in the long grass so that any Zulu attack would be slowed once it entered within range of the garrison's weapons. Firing platforms for the cannon and Gatling gun were constructed at the angles of the ramparts while drawbridges were built at the two gates. All in all, the fort at Eshowe became an impressive-looking fortress and was the most sophisticated of the ninety-nine British earthwork forts built during the entire war.

After working in the oppressive heat of the day the men then had to sleep wherever they could, usually in the open, as there was no room to erect their tents within the encampment. The lucky ones slept under the wagons. Due to the presence of the Zulus around the fort, disturbing false alarms were a nightly feature; and large bodies of Zulus were regularly seen, although none actually approached the fort. On one occasion, troops opened fire on figures seen moving near the lines, only to discover at dawn that they had riddled their own laundry hung out to dry. However, the Zulus were not completely inactive during this time; some evenings they ventured close to the camp in order to move the range marker posts under cover of darkness, and they also removed posts marking a new roadway under construction from the fort. Wynne and his sappers resolved this particular irritation by mining the posts with explosives. Pickets and vedettes were regularly detailed to keep the Zulus away from the immediate area around the fort; these were dangerous assignments as the Zulus would regularly fire on such patrols. Private Kent of the 99th, attached to the Mounted Infantry, was killed when Zulus hiding in long grass attacked a patrol and a Corporal Carson was also shot at; he returned wounded to the fort but lived to tell the tale.

The stifling hot weather eventually broke and heavy tropical rain added to the soldiers' miseries. Everyone was constantly drenched and with no available shelter, sickness quickly spread among the men. The garrison had sufficient food and plenty of ammunition but it lacked adequate medical supplies and on 1 February the first man died of fever. The heavy rains turned the area within the entrenchment into a quagmire of effluent-polluted mud that added to the garrison's growing discomfort. It was too late for a withdrawal back to the Lower Drift; instead, nearly 1,800 men were now effectively under siege with no immediate prospect of receiving supplies or reinforcements. In response, Pearson ordered the commissariat to put the garrison on three-quarter rations.

Aware of the danger of disease spreading through the overcrowded garrison, Pearson took steps to prevent the camp's fresh water supply from becoming polluted and orders were given to site and rotate the latrine area downhill away from the camp. Despite these precautions, the overwhelming stench of the camp and the nearby cattle laager became increasingly offensive, attracting huge clouds of flies that infested the garrison's food supplies. The men's general health continued to deteriorate to the extent that, by the end of February, the majority of soldiers were suffering from serious stomach disorders and seven men had died, including one who committed suicide by drowning. The casualties were all buried on a grassy slope nearby. Surgeon Norbury of HMS *Active* complained that the health of the garrison was at risk from the men's habit, against orders, of filling their water bottles from a stream that drained through the cemetery – but despite his complaints the practice continued. As well as coping with disease, few in the garrison escaped the infectious 'Natal sores'. With few efficacious medicines, treatment was limited to bandages and an unidentified powder. Captain Pelley Clark described the suffering:

> There were few in the fort that did not appear with a piece of rag round one of their fingers, or their noses enveloped in cotton wool, with some white powder on it, giving them a most unearthly appearance.[10]

The garrison was completely isolated and totally unaware of events in the outside world; not knowing whether the war was being won or lost, the men were prey to every type of rumour and imagining. In the hope of maintaining morale, Pearson had the regimental bands of the 3rd and 99th perform regularly and this did much to lift the men's spirits. Although the hills near Eshowe had a direct line of sight across the 25 miles to the Tugela river and Fort Pearson, Chelmsford had not thought that heliographs would be of use in South Africa. As a result, the only reliable means of communication between Eshowe and the outside world was unavailable. A system of sending messages using black volunteer runners was tried but most were caught and killed by the Zulus. As the siege progressed Wynne made various attempts to build a semaphore, most of which were frustrated by the weather. These included a large paper screen, which was blown down by a sudden storm. He then constructed a hot-air balloon, also made of paper, which the wind blew in the wrong direction. Various attempts were made to improvise a signalling system from items found around the mission site and after six weeks of siege, Wynne succeeded in making a heliograph, using a carefully positioned piece of lead piping taken from the church roof and an officer's shaving mirror.

As the weeks went by, healthy food became scarce. Captain Wynne wrote to his wife about the rations:

> We chew the generally very tough, much stewed ox, with, as a rule, about a tablespoon of preserved carrots, sometimes some large haricot beans. These, and biscuit, is our daily food at breakfast, lunch and dinner: in fact every meal the same, except that we have coffee at breakfast and tea at dinner. I really do not mind it, but most fellows get very tired of it, and complain of insufficiency.[11]

To supplement the men's reduced rations Pearson encouraged foraging patrols to plunder local deserted Zulu homesteads in the hope of finding additional food. Although the garrison's meagre rations held out until Eshowe was relieved, plundered vegetables and fruit from such homesteads were enthusiastically collected and there was even greater excitement when a wagonload of consumables was discovered, having been left behind by the Volunteers. Pearson decided that these goods should be auctioned; all went for high prices, especially several jars of pickles.

Meanwhile Chelmsford and his staff were busy with preparations for the second invasion of Zululand. However, before these could be finalized, the relief of Eshowe was essential. The political embarrassment of having such a large military force besieged by the Zulus was a constant burden and Chelmsford's plan depended on having Pearson's wagons and men for the new force. By focusing British attention on extricating Pearson's column, Chelmsford successfully ameliorated the ongoing storm that had broken over him following the disaster at Isandlwana, and the relief column's ultimate success undoubtedly helped to restore his reputation and personal confidence.

At the beginning of February the first flashed messages from the border were received at Eshowe but relief was not imminent. It was generally acknowledged by all at Eshowe that until Chelmsford received additional troops from Britain, he was powerless to offer any hope to the beleaguered garrison. Pending the arrival of these reinforcements at Durban and the long march to Eshowe, the garrison had to fend for itself. When news eventually came that a relief column was being assembled spirits rose at Eshowe, only to be dashed again by the realization that the late summer rainstorms would seriously hinder any relief column. Pearson also learned that the Zulus were gathering along Chelmsford's route to Eshowe but he was powerless to intervene. To maintain morale, Pearson detailed several mounted forays against nearby homesteads; one such homestead belonged to Prince Dabulamanzi but this action merely provoked the Zulus into harassing Pearson's patrols with greater determination.

During early March Chelmsford built up a strong enough force to attempt Pearson's relief. He had 400 men from HMS *Shah*, and 200 from HMS *Boadicea* with two Gatling guns. Beside the Buffs and 99th left at the Lower Drift by Pearson, the infantry comprised the newly arrived 57th, 91st Highlanders and 60th Rifles. The NNC and Major Barrow's mounted troops made up the balance of the relieving column. The total strength was 3,390 whites and 2,280 blacks, well exceeding the number flashed to Pearson. It was Chelmsford's intention that the column would be commanded by Major General Henry Crealock, but as Crealock did not reach Natal in time, Chelmsford took personal command on 23 March.

The battle of Gingindlovu

Chelmsford wrote to Wood who was holding the northern part of Zululand and asked him to undertake a major offensive action that would be sufficient to divert Zulu forces away from his attempt to relieve Eshowe in the south. The resulting action was doomed to failure as, unbeknown to the British, the main Zulu force was already approaching Wood's position.

The relief column eventually crossed into Zululand on 29 March and was ferried by ponts across the Tugela river; it began its advance further to the east than the obviously difficult route originally taken by Pearson. Chelmsford was now more cautious; he selected open country where he could laager his wagons and entrench his column each night. The relief column travelled light; no tents or baggage were allowed even though it was known that the column would suffer from the heavy rain and intolerable heat that marked late summer in Zululand. Chelmsford's scouts reported back to him that the Zulus were gathering in considerable numbers near Gingindlovu to oppose his relief column; their force consisted of the Zulus who had so successfully besieged Eshowe, reinforced by regiments from Ulundi under the command of chiefs Somopho kaZikhala and Phalane kaMdinwa.

Chelmsford's new-found caution made him choose more open country where he could laager his wagons and entrench each night. He further ordered that open ammunition boxes were to be readily available on the wagons. Once he had reached Eshowe, Chelmsford intended to relieve the garrison and replace them with fresh troops and supplies.

The progress of the column was slowed by torrential rain that appeared each evening, swelling the rivers and streams and turning the track into a morass. Due to the adverse weather, their early attempts at laagering were chaotic and officers and men alike had to sleep on the ground totally unprotected from the regular downpours. Experienced men like John Dunn despaired of the British ever defeating the Zulus. By the third evening a simpler system had been devised so that each laager would be a square 130 yards each side, made up of thirty wagons butted together, and all the livestock placed within. At each night's stop the troops dug a shelter trench 15 yards in front of the laager's sides and sited the artillery and Gatling guns at each corner.

On the evening of 1 April Chelmsford's rain-soaked column formed a square laager on the top of a low rise leading from the southern bank of the Nyezane river. It was close to the ruins of kwaGingindlovu, the Zulu homestead that Pearson had attacked on the way to Eshowe, and within sight of Pearson's earlier battle of Nyezane on 22 January. Knowing that a force of Zulus had detached from those surrounding Eshowe and was fast approaching, and having learned his lesson at Isandlwana, Chelmsford ordered the column's wagons to be parked in a tight square with a trench dug around the outside of the wagons. The earth from the trench was then stacked to form a solid rampart which the men lined with the wagons behind them; all the column's animals were brought into the square at dusk in anticipation of a Zulu attack. Chelmsford and his column were ready.

As dawn broke over the Nyezane valley, the scene was partially obscured by a hanging mist that evidenced the heavy rain during the night. Then, through the gaps in the mist, several large columns of Zulus could be seen advancing towards the camp from the direction of the river. In preparation for their attack the advancing Zulus had already formed into their 'horns' battle formation. Chief Somopho was in command of the Zulus, with Prince Dabulamanzi, Chiefs Masegwane and Mbilwane and *induna* Sigcwelegcwele leading approximately 12,000 warriors from the uThulwana, uMbonambi, uMcijo, iNgobamakhosi and the uVe regiments plus an unknown number of local irregular Zulu units.

Chelmsford's men were urgently roused and all rushed to man the barricades. They patiently held their fire until the first Zulus reached the 400 yard marker posts; the battle was opened at 6.10 a.m. by a siting burst from a Gatling gun followed by a number of well-aimed volleys which cut through the advancing Zulus. In the still of the early morning, the British were enveloped in their own dense powder smoke and were forced to cease firing until the light breeze cleared their view.

Undeterred, the Zulus sought to surround the British and steadily advanced through the tall grass. The first Zulu attack, on the north front of the square, came so close to the British position that one young Zulu

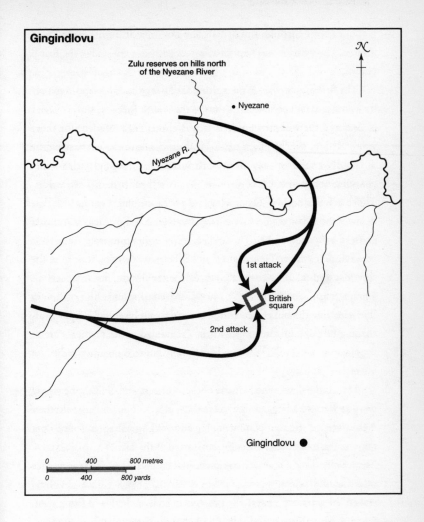

Gingindlovu

Zulu reserves on hills north
of the Nyezane River

• Nyezane

Nyezane R.

1st attack

British
square

2nd attack

Gingindlovu ●

0   400   800 metres

0   400   800 yards

N

warrior broke through the British line and was promptly seized by a marine. The warrior was kept as a mascot and later enlisted in the Royal Navy.

The first assault was on the north side of the position, defended mainly by young and inexperienced recruits of the 3/60th Rifles who were about to undergo their baptism of fire. It was a terrifying moment for these young soldiers who had been regaled with gruesome stories of the slaughter at Isandlwana; now they were confronted by a seemingly irresistible charging horde of fearless warriors. Many either froze or fired wildly. Those officers and NCOs on elevated positions and wagons saw that many of the young soldiers were firing too high and the order was quickly given to lower rifle sights. The soldiers were further unnerved when their commanding officer, Lieutenant Colonel Francis Northey, was hit in the shoulder and taken to the ambulance. The wound did not look serious when it was dressed, but as Northey prepared to resume his position in the firing line the bullet penetrated an artery and he collapsed, haemorrhaging through his dressing. Northey remained under medical care at the laager at Gingindlovu where he painfully lingered on until he died on 6 April.

Due to the determined efforts of their officers and NCOs, the young recruits were steadied enough to repel the attack. The officers held their men's rates of fire to a commendable and well-aimed seven rounds per minute; the more experienced marines fired at the higher rate of sixteen. Meanwhile the Zulu centre commenced its attack against the west face of the square, which was manned by the 99th. Their well-aimed volleys stalled the warriors' charge. During this furious exchange of firing Lieutenant George Johnson, who had fought at the earlier battle of Nyezane, was shot dead.

The Zulu right horn then attacked the south wall occupied by the new recruits of the 91st Highlanders, who were much steadier than their counterparts of the 60th and beat off the attack. The remnants of this attack moved round to launch a final assault on the east side of the laager, which was defended by the older and more experienced men of the 57th, whose steady firing prevented any warrior getting close. Because the main Zulu force was advancing through very long grass, those defenders with rifles had a better field of fire from atop the wagons and inflicted many casualties. As the Zulu attack appeared to falter, Chelmsford prematurely ordered Barrow's mounted troops out of the laager to drive off the warriors, only to recall them hastily when he saw they were in danger of being surrounded.

As the shrapnel from the 7-pounders continued to take its toll the Zulus' assault on the square ceased. Unable to break through the British defences, the Zulus lost their momentum and began to retreat to the comparative safety of the long grass and some nearby clumps of palm bushes. The officers then directed their men's fire into the groups of hiding Zulus; this had the effect of killing a large number, forcing the survivors to flee back towards the river crossing and Wombane hill from where the Zulu reserves were observing the battle. The final shots were fired at 7.15 a.m. just as the Zulu reserves on Wombane, seeing their force beaten, also withdrew.

Finally, after an hour's fighting, Chelmsford reordered Major Barrow to take his mounted men and drive the remaining Zulus further away from the laager. They were followed into the fray by the riders of the Natal Carbineers who rode out with alacrity, cutting down exhausted and wounded warriors without mercy. The NNC were ordered to follow suit to seek out and deal with any Zulus attempting to hide. This was a task they relished with brutal enthusiasm, killing every Zulu they could find.

Over 500 Zulu bodies lay around the laager, including one Zulu wearing an officer's sword belt taken from Isandlwana, and many more bodies could be seen along their line of retreat. The Zulus lost more than 1,100 killed or seriously wounded; as many died in the post-battle mopping-up as were killed during the actual assault against the British position. The ruthless pursuit and killing of fleeing and wounded Zulus had first been witnessed at Rorke's Drift. The post-battle operation at Gingindlovu was identical and was to give rise to many uncomfortable questions about Chelmsford towards the end of the war.

Although the enemy were in retreat, they were still capable of putting up a spirited and deadly resistance. Finally they were thoroughly dispersed and the task of totting up the casualty lists began. The British had lost two officers and nine men killed and four officers and fifty men wounded. The rest of the day was spent burying the dead and reducing the size of the laager. Chelmsford decided to leave a reduced laager and press on to Eshowe with a flying column.

Meanwhile in Eshowe, those with telescopes and binoculars had keenly followed the battle. Pearson ordered congratulations to be flashed to Chelmsford and the garrison awaited impatiently to be relieved. Chelmsford's men finally reached Eshowe after a tough 15 mile march. When Chelmsford set out to relieve the Eshowe garrison, he had fully intended to replace the defenders with fresh troops and supplies in preparation for the onward march to Ulundi. After the battle of Gingindlovu he changed his mind and decided that Eshowe was too exposed to hold. Accordingly, he proceeded to Eshowe with a smaller, fast-moving column, leaving the remainder of the relief column at the Gingindlovu laager. Chelmsford and his reduced force arrived at Eshowe early that evening and were enthusiastically welcomed by the besieged garrison; following the initial euphoria of seeing new faces and catching up with news, the defenders were aghast to learn that Chelmsford had decided to abandon the fort instead of replacing it with a fresh garrison. During that evening feelings ran high as many of the defenders believed their heroic efforts, together with their considerable personal suffering and loss of colleagues, had all been in vain. To the open disgust of many in the garrison, they were ordered to destroy the fort and then withdraw. The following day Pearson's men began their retreat back towards Fort Pearson while Chelmsford took Major Barrow and a mounted detachment to destroy Prince Dabulamanzi's empty homestead, already ravaged by Pearson's patrols, before joining Pearson's retreating column. They failed to surprise the Zulu chief who retreated to some nearby heights from where he watched his homestead put to the torch.

Collecting the rest of his men, Chelmsford abandoned Eshowe and marched after Pearson's column. As soon as it was deemed safe, the ever-watchful Zulus entered the deserted mission and burned it to the ground. Catching up with Pearson, Chelmsford ordered him to head back by the most direct route to the Lower Drift, which he subsequently reached on 7 April. Chelmsford marched his column back to his old laager at Gingindlovu where the stench from the many Zulu dead drove him to remove to a fresh site nearby, which he felt could be supplied comfortably from Fort Tenedos. Chelmsford's column reached the border soon after Pearson had arrived.

Chelmsford acknowledged that, of all the different terrains that were fought over in Zululand, the coastal area was the most difficult. He was generous in his praise for the tenacious Colonel Pearson and his men and well pleased with the outcome of the two battles which had dealt the Zulus a severe blow. The human cost of holding Eshowe was evidenced by twenty-eight crosses in the cemetery below the mission and hundreds of sick, some 200 of whom were so ill that they were ferried to the hospital at Fort Pearson; one of them was Captain Wynne whose energy and skill had turned the mission into an impregnable fortress.

Colonel Pearson was also beginning to suffer from typhoid; nevertheless he was appointed a brigade commander for the new invasion. He never fully recovered from his illness and, instead of leading part of the new invasion, was invalided home. For leading the Coastal Column for the initial invasion, he was made Companion of the Bath. No awards for bravery were made or personal reputations enhanced and the participants had to be content with the campaign medal as the sole reward for their exceptional endurance.

It was following the battle of Gingindlovu that several British officers first examined the layout of Zulu casualties. They were curious concerning the defeat at Isandlwana, as previously everyone believed Martini-Henry rifles would produce effective volley fire at a range of up to 600 yards and should have been more than sufficient to repel any Zulu attack, regardless of its size. Although the opening Martini-Henry volleys at Gingindlovu had been fired at a range of 400 yards, few Zulu bodies were found beyond 200 yards. The efficacy of the rifle was never in doubt but the wisdom of opening fire beyond 200 yards began to be questioned by the British front-line officers.

Chelmsford was also forced to realize certain realities; he had achieved nothing since the original invasion of Zululand on 11 January. Worse still, the border between Natal and Zululand was effectively undefended; superior Zulu forces and tactics had destroyed his Centre Column and the Northern Column under Wood was effectively locked in at Khambula. He now faced restarting the campaign. Fresh troops, new columns and different tactics would all be necessary before the reinvasion of Zululand could begin. The task of facing the now triumphant Zulus was daunting, yet, unbeknown to Chelmsford, the tip-over point to British success was rapidly approaching.

CHAPTER 13

The Northern Column

The ground was strewn with bodies.

NATAL MERCURY, 12 APRIL 1879

Towards the latter part of January 1879 the Centre and Coastal columns had advanced through Zululand towards their new camps at Isandlwana and Eshowe; meanwhile, the Northern Column of Chelmsford's combined pincer movement was making good progress advancing from the north towards Ulundi. With his distinctive enthusiasm for independent action, the Northern Column commander, Brevet Colonel Henry Evelyn Wood VC, had advanced his column into Zululand on 7 January, four days before the ultimatum expired. Wood was a remarkable leader; his father, Sir John Page Wood, had been chaplain and private secretary to Queen Caroline and his maternal grandfather was an admiral. Not surprisingly, Wood passed his Royal Navy entrance examination at the first attempt and entered the service. At the age of 14 he joined HMS *Queen*; two years later he was promoted midshipman. In 1854 HMS *Queen* was part of the fleet that bombarded Sebastopol when the navy was called upon to send ashore a twenty-one gun battery to shell the Russian defences; Captain Peel, son of the former prime minister, Sir Robert Peel, commanded the battery. Wood was appointed ADC to Peel who mentioned Wood's daring exploits in several of his dispatches. On 18 June the British made a suicidal assault on the heavily defended Russian stronghold, the Redan. The 17-year-old Wood carried a scaling ladder and although twice wounded by grapeshot, he was the only one to reach the Redan and was recommended for a Victoria Cross – but was turned down. Instead, he was awarded the Légion d'Honneur and the Order of the Medijidie.

Sent back to England to recover from his injuries and clearly excited by fighting on land, Wood resigned his naval commission and applied to join the army. His outstanding service at Sebastopol gained him a cornetcy without purchase in the 13th Light Dragoons and he was immediately posted back to the Crimea. Within days of his arrival Wood contracted both typhoid and pneumonia and for the next five months he was hospitalized at Scutari. This was the beginning of his lifelong encounter with sickness and accidents, and during the next fifty years Wood would suffer deafness, dysentery, eye problems, malaria, neuralgia, sunstroke, toothache and, to crown it all, ingrown toenails. He was further wounded by gunshot during the Ashanti War. He also received severe facial injuries when a giraffe, which he attempted to ride, trod on him; he was scratched by a tiger, and broke his nose and collarbone when his horse threw him against a tree while fox-hunting. At the age of 50, while attempting to ride a bicycle, he collided with a Hackney cab horse; the horse bit him and scarred him for the rest of his life.

By June 1857 Wood had learned sufficient Hindustani for him to be appointed interpreter to the 3rd Bombay Cavalry, with whom he saw much action in India. In 1859, with the Mutiny now over, Wood won his Victoria Cross when he led an attack into the camp of a rebel band that had taken a number of European hostages. His small force was heavily outnumbered but Wood personally killed several rebels, put the rest to flight and heroically rescued the captives. He then returned to England and entered Staff College from which he graduated in 1864. Wood became one of the original members of the 'Wolseley Gang' and in 1873, when Wolseley was made commander of the British force sent to subdue the West African Ashanti tribe, he chose Wood to be his transport officer and to raise a locally recruited black auxiliary regiment. The campaign was successful and both Wolseley and Wood found fame as the result of their exploits, Wood being made Companion of the Bath and breveted full colonel.

Wood was sent to South Africa in early 1878 as Colonel of the 90th Perthshire Volunteer Regiment and with his regiment he marched many hundreds of miles between postings and became campaign-hardened. The British commander in South Africa, General Thesiger, came to rely on the opinion of the experienced Wood and the two became friends and confidants. Having pacified the Transkei, Thesiger (soon to become Lord Chelmsford) and the High Commissioner, Sir Bartle Frere, now turned their attention to the invasion of Zululand. Wood persuaded Thesiger that the field force, called the Natal Column, should march to Natal rather than attempt the difficult sea journey. Wood marched the column 500 miles over rough terrain and crossed thirty-seven rivers before they reached Pietermaritzburg. In his biography Wood wrote of service in South Africa in glowing terms:

> It was a healthy climate, for, with proper sanitary arrangements and the absence of public-houses, the young soldiers improved out of recognition.

Artillery subaltern Lieutenant Henry Curling wrote with cautious admiration:

> Col. Wood who commands the column is the most energetic, plucky man I ever met, in fact his energy almost amounts to a mania as he wears himself out and everybody under him. He is so plucky that he imagines that everyone is like him and would lead us into trouble if there is any serious fighting.[1]

Wood and the 90th were then sent north to Utrecht, which was situated in the disputed territory on the Zululand border. Sir Bartle Frere appointed Wood as his political agent for Northern Zululand and Swaziland and gave him the delicate task of enlisting Boer support for the British cause. Despite serious raids by the local Zulus led by the rebel Swazi, Prince Mbilini, the Boers declined to ally themselves with the

British, having recently learned that they were to lose part of their territory to the Zulus under the terms of the British border initiative, the Boundary Commission. As mentioned earlier, only one Boer leader, Piet Uys, offered his services along with about thirty-five male family members who acted as irregular cavalry with Wood's Northern Column.

The starting point for the 2,500 strong Northern Column was the Boer hamlet of Utrecht. Having crossed the Blood river into Zululand on 7 January, the column then marched 10 relatively easy miles to a flat-topped hill called Bemba's Kop where Wood built a fortified camp. His force was made up of eight companies of the 13th and 90th Regiments, six guns of 11/7 Battery, about 200 volunteer cavalry and 300 black auxiliaries who were given the rather flattering title of 'Wood's Irregulars'. The local Zulu chief, Tinta, duly tendered his submission and was conducted under a strong escort into camp, together with his people and his herds.

On the night of 20 January, accompanied by Buller's mounted troops, Wood led a force into the nearby Zunguin mountains where they captured several herds of Zulu cattle and successfully skirmished with a sizeable force of about 1,000 warriors. When Wood's force reached the eastern end of Zunguin they observed an estimated 4,000 warriors drilling in the shade of the adjacent Hlobane mountain; being heavily outnumbered Wood broke off his action, and during their return to camp the following evening the distant sound of guns to the south could be heard. This later proved to be Chelmsford's 7-pounders firing at the wrecked Isandlwana camp when Chelmsford's men returned, having earlier been decoyed out of camp by the Zulus. The following morning Wood received confirmatory news from Captain Gardner, an Isandlwana survivor, of Chelmsford's crushing defeat. With the news came the realization for Wood of the serious implications of Chelmsford's defeat for his own force. Accordingly Wood withdrew his Northern Column from their temporary camp at Tinta's Kop to a safer hilltop location known as Khambula, which Wood immediately fortified. The new position was located 20 miles east of Utrecht.

After relieving the garrison at Rorke's Drift, Lord Chelmsford withdrew back to Pietermaritzburg. Having reported his defeat to Sir

Bartle Frere, he turned his attention to defending the unprotected colony of Natal from the threat of a Zulu attack. Anxiety among both the black and the white Natal population was high and Chelmsford was obliged to seek the support of the local press to prevent the panic from spreading. The Natal blacks feared Zulu revenge for siding with the British while the white population believed that their self-embellished pre-war prophecies were about to be realized. Durban, Greytown, Pietermaritzburg and Stanger were all placed on the defensive while the two supply depots of the surviving Centre Column at Helpmekaar and Rorke's Drift were strongly fortified to discourage a Zulu incursion at those main border crossing points. Chelmsford had no military option other than to temporarily suspend the invasion of Zululand pending the arrival of reinforcements from England and, to keep his remaining troops safe, he ordered a general withdrawal of Centre and Coastal Column troops out of Zululand. Although it was completely at his mercy, King Cetshwayo never attacked Natal; he realized that by defending Zululand while remaining within his border, he had secured the moral high ground.

Wood's Northern Column was unaffected by the Centre Column's withdrawal to Natal and Chelmsford readily appreciated that he needed Wood to harass the northern Zulu tribes, particularly the aggressive abaQulusi tribe, and to discourage them from bolstering King Cetshwayo's main army or, alternatively, moving south nearer to Natal. The abaQulusi were not strictly within the Zulu military system – they were descendants from a separate group originally formed by King Shaka – but nevertheless operated as an independent army across northern Zululand and were extremely loyal to King Cetshwayo. They dominated a large part of the territory through which Chelmsford's second invasion force would need to pass; their stronghold was a 4 mile long almost unclimbable flat-topped mountain known as Hlobane.

To comply with Chelmsford's wish, Wood ordered Colonel Buller, the commander of his irregular mounted men (all local volunteer horsemen except for a few Imperial officers) to conduct a number of harrying reconnaissances along the proposed route. On 1 February Buller attacked and destroyed an important Zulu homestead situated 30 miles east of the British camp at Khambula towards the further end of the Hlobane range of hills; the homestead was a traditional rallying point of the northern Zulus and hitherto regarded as impregnable. Buller's mounted force captured some 300 head of cattle and destroyed the homestead's 250 huts; a number of Zulus were killed in the raid without any losses to Buller. Shortly afterwards Prince Mbilini kaMswati, a pro-Zulu prince of Swazi origin, and Manyanyoba, another chief of the Ntombe valley district, led marauding parties of Zulus into the neighbourhood of Luneburg, now abandoned by the white farmers, and commenced an appalling massacre of the local tribesmen who had previously worked for white farmers. Their wives and children were especially brutalized, being killed either with spears or by being burnt alive in their huts. On 13 February Buller led a force to undertake retaliatory measures and succeeded in driving Mbilini and Manyanyoba's men back into the nearby hills. Buller divided his force with half assaulting the ridges while the remainder attacked along the river valley. Five of the strongholds were successfully stormed; thirty-four Zulus were slain and a herd of 400 cattle was captured. Buller lost two auxiliaries in the action and returned to Luneburg that evening, intending to mount a second attack the following day.

Colonel Rowlands VC, commander of the reserve No. 5 Column, was coincidentally moving a strong force to attack the same stronghold, having failed to persuade the Swazis to co-operate with the British. On the same day Rowlands marched part of his column from Luneburg towards Derby followed by the remainder of his column under Major Tucker. The next day Captain Harvey, Tucker's staff officer, took a patrol across the Pongola river and engaged a force of Zulus who had been harassing the line of communications between Luneburg and the camp at Khambula. Because the route between Luneburg and Derby passed only 4 miles from the stronghold of Prince Mbilini, a friend and ally of King Cetshwayo, the area remained open to such attacks, so much so that on 12 March a valuable British supply column was successfully attacked by the Zulus and plundered while crossing the Ntombe river.

The battle of Ntombe River (Meyer's Drift)

No particular precautions appear to have been taken.

SURVIVOR'S REPORT[2]

Hitherto the area along the Transvaal border to the north of Hlobane had not caused Chelmsford any real concern. Following Colonel Hugh Rowlands's timid advance against the hostile Sekhukhune in 1878, and in consequence having lost Chelmsford's confidence, Rowlands was moved to Pretoria to watch over the disgruntled Boers' increasing militancy. His No. 5 Reserve Column had been relegated from an invasion force to one holding the northern border between Zululand and the Transvaal settlement at Derby. Gradually Rowlands's command was stripped down as men were transferred to No. 4 Northern Column at Khambula hill under the command of Colonel Wood. The last regiment to be transferred was the 80th (South Staffordshire) Regiment under the command of Major Charles Tucker; this move commenced in mid February. By March the 80th had moved to their new post at Luneburg where Tucker was in command of five companies of the 80th Regiment so that all that remained to be transported from Derby was stores and ammunition. The route crossed the Ntombe river only 4½ miles from Tucker's base at Luneburg but it was within sight of the mountainous stronghold of Mbilini. Due to the proximity of the Zulus, who were well known for their raiding abilities, these convoys required strong escorts and so Tucker's companies were rotated to march to meet the wagons and to bring them safely to the hamlet.

On 1 March Captain Anderson's D Company marched from Luneburg and linked up with a floundering twenty-strong wagon train bringing the garrison urgently needed supplies, a rocket battery and 90,000 rounds of Martini-Henry ammunition. Progress was painfully slow as the torrential rain had not let up for days, making the track virtually impassable. The wagons had to be manhandled most of the way and continually sank to their axles in thick mud, and after four days of toil the men were exhausted. Anderson then received an ambiguous message from Tucker, which he interpreted as a recall to Luneburg; he gratefully took his men, leaving the floundering convoy all but unprotected. A small force of Mbilini's warriors had been shadowing the convoy and when they realized that there was no escort they seized their chance and raided the wagon train. They ignored the wagoners and made off with a small amount of stores and some oxen.

When Anderson arrived back at Luneburg without the wagons Tucker was horrified and immediately ordered out a fresh company of 106 men under Captain David Moriarty to escort them to safety. When the relief reached the Ntombe river, Moriarty found that the wagoners had succeeded in bringing just two wagons to the south bank; meanwhile they had attempted to recover the remaining wagons but their efforts had been overwhelmed by the impossible conditions. The heavy rain had also caused the river to flood beyond its normal 30 yard width and to a depth of over 5ft; this forced Moriarty to leave thirty-five men under the command of Lieutenant Lindop on the south bank to recover the two wagons while the remaining soldiers were ferried across the river on an improvised raft. Moriarty took this force and after two days of backbreaking work the remaining wagons were recovered to the north bank. By 11 March the river was still in flood and totally impassable, but Lindop's men had managed to bring another two wagons across the river to the south bank during a temporary drop in the river's water level. Just as Moriarty's force returned with the remaining seventeen wagons the river burst its banks, preventing them from crossing until the water level subsided; accordingly, Moriarty ordered the wagons to be laagered in a 'V' formation, with the two legs reaching the water's edge.

During the afternoon Major Tucker, accompanied by Lieutenant Henry Harward, Sergeant Anthony Booth and thirty-two soldiers, arrived at the river crossing to assess the situation. Tucker found a bedraggled company of utterly exhausted men and their convoy of wagons virtually trapped by the high water on the northern bank; he realized they had laboured in continuous rain for four days without cooked food and he could do little to ease their predicament. He made suggestions for the wagons to be laagered correctly, although he noticed that there were growing gaps between the wagons and the river where the water level had begun to recede. Although the men were exhausted and highly vulnerable to attack, Tucker may have presumed that, as they were only 4 miles from their destination, the danger from attack was minimal. Instead of assuming command, he ordered Moriarty to remain in command but relieved Lieutenant Lindop and his men with Harward's force; Tucker then returned to Luneburg.

Using an improvised raft, Harward and his men crossed the river to help Moriarty secure the camp. Some cattle had wandered off so Harward took a small search party and traced the cattle in the nearby foothills, killing a number of Zulus responsible for the loss. By the end of the day the wagons on the south bank were guarded by Harward, Sergeant Booth and thirty-four men. There were still seventeen wagons on the north bank; all were arranged in a defensive 'V' formation, under the guard of the remaining seventy-one men under Moriarty.

All settled down for the evening and began to have dinner. Sergeant Booth was in the laager when one of the European drivers drew his attention to an unknown black man eating corn and talking with some of the wagon auxiliaries. The driver expressed the opinion that this stranger was none other than Prince Mbilini, whose stronghold was only 3 miles away. Booth reported this suspicion to Moriarty who assured him that the locals were friendly. Moriarty added, 'You're as bad as your pals said of you; you would shoot your own brother.'[3] Booth was later to write that he was not reassured and believed that, Mbilini or otherwise, the stranger was there to spy out the defences.

Sergeant Anthony Booth was an experienced 33-year-old NCO. Born in 1846 in a village near Nottingham, he enlisted in the 80th in 1864 at the age of 18. During his army career he had several promotions and demotions. He had served abroad since 1872 and was entitled to the Indian Service Medal bar 'Perak'. Due to his length of service and experience he had been appointed quartermaster sergeant for this wagon detail, and he had spent much of the afternoon butchering two cattle to feed the men during the following days.[4]

The interior of the wagon laager covered little more than half an acre and was filled with the soldiers' tents and oxen. Moriarty gave instructions for just two sentries and even felt safe enough to pitch his tent outside the noisome confines of the laager. Following the evening meal, Harward was sent back across the river to his own command. Moriarty's exhausted men were grateful to have the shelter of their tents for the first time in days and retired early. On the other side of the river, Harward's camp was fast asleep when, at about 4 a.m., Harward was awakened by the sound of a distant shot. Noticing that the sentries could not be seen and no one on the north bank had stirred, he ordered Booth to alert the north bank. Booth eventually managed to spread the warning but it had little effect and the camp continued to sleep.

Mbilini's visit had disturbed Booth and he later wrote that he began to feel increasingly uneasy. He dressed quickly and, taking his rifle and ammunition pouch, climbed into one of the wagons for a smoke. Booth had every reason to feel uneasy for, unbeknown to the sleeping soldiers, Mbilini had mustered a force of about 1,000 warriors that was nearly upon the camp, having silently advanced under cover of the early morning mist. The Zulus were expecting little resistance and carried only their stabbing spears and knobkerries; they had left their shields behind though a few were armed with pillaged Martini-Henry rifles.

About 4.45 a.m. another shot was heard, causing Booth to jump from the wagon just as the Zulus emerged from the mist. Now less than 50 yards from the British position, they fired a ragged volley into Moriarty's tents and then charged; within seconds they were overwhelming the sleeping camp. Moriarty dashed from his tent firing his revolver; he killed three warriors before an assegai finished him and with that he and most of his men died. Bemused and naked soldiers struggled from their tents only to be clubbed or stabbed to death in the nightmare of frightened cattle and terrified men. Some managed to plunge naked into the river and several managed to reach the south bank, now manned by Lieutenant

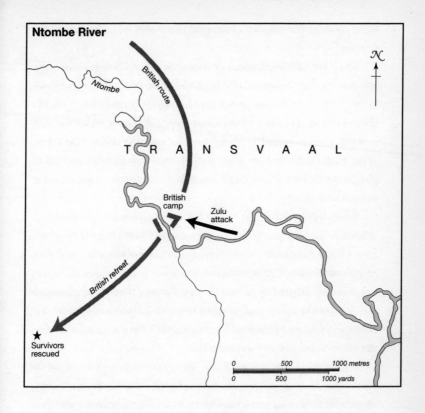

Ntombe River

Ntombe

British route

T R A N S V A A L

British camp

Zulu attack

British retreat

★ Survivors rescued

N

| 0 | 500 | 1000 metres |
| 0 | 500 | 1000 yards |

Harward and a few men who attempted to cover their escape with steady rifle fire.

Booth rallied the remainder of the command and they commenced a sustained fire into the mass of Zulus on the far bank. Booth lost his helmet in the jostling and confusion but kept his men in a tight formation. He noticed that he was next to Lieutenant Harward's horse, which was tied to the wagon. Harward appeared from his tent and shouted out, 'Fire away, lads, I'll be ready in a minute!' He then mounted his unsaddled pony and rode off towards Luneburg, followed by an undisciplined surge of most of his men.

Booth later recalled that he was left with only eight of his company. While he and his small group kept up a steady rate of fire some of the men who had crossed the river managed to arm themselves and then grabbed whatever clothing was available. Booth realized his position was hopeless and, assisted by Lance Corporal Burgess, formed the remaining men into a tight square and prepared to retreat back towards Luneburg. Booth was later complimented for choosing to form a square rather than the more commonly used extended line.

Fortunately for Booth, the Zulus were more intent on plundering the two wagons than on pursuing his men, although the Zulus made a number of concerted efforts to overwhelm the small square. Booth controlled their rate of fire while keeping the square moving towards a deserted farmhouse that Booth had seen some 2 miles off. Apart from four men who panicked and fled the group, and who were promptly run down and killed by the Zulus, Booth managed to bring his remaining men to the protection of the building.

Meanwhile Lieutenant Harward had galloped the short distance to Luneburg where he arrived at 6.30 a.m. He roused Major Tucker and blurted out the news. 'The camp is in the hands of the enemy; they are all slaughtered, and I have galloped in for my life.' According to witnesses, Harward then fell onto the bed in a dead faint. Once revived, he managed to give more detail and then added that there could be no survivors. Tucker immediately ordered 150 men to turn out and quick-marched them towards the Drift. Tucker left on horseback accompanied by several of his officers; within minutes they came upon Sergeant Booth's party at the farmhouse, causing the attacking Zulus to flee. In typical style, Booth volunteered to accompany Tucker's command back to the river but his offer was declined – Booth had done enough.

As Tucker's men reached the rise overlooking the river they saw hundreds of Zulus moving away from the camp towards their nearby stronghold, most laden with plunder. On riding into the wrecked camp they discovered all their colleagues were dead, naked and mostly disembowelled. The Zulus had killed all the dogs, scattered mealies and flour and shredded the tents; all 300 camp cattle had been driven off. When the marching relief arrived, Tucker set them to work collecting the mutilated bodies, ferrying them across the river and burying them on the slope above the crossing. Being officers, the bodies of Captain Moriarty and a 28-year-old civilian doctor named William Cobbin were taken back to Luneburg for individual burial.

In the aftermath of the disaster at Isandlwana there was a considerable amount of covering up and Ntombe was no different. To conceal the embarrassment of his actions, Lieutenant Harward's report stated that

> The enemy were now assegaing our men in the water, and also ascending the banks of the river close to us; for fear therefore, of my men being stabbed under the wagons, and to enable them to retire before their ammunition should be exhausted, I ordered them to retire steadily, and only just in time to avoid a rush of Zulus to our late position. The Zulus came on in dense masses and fell upon our men, who being already broken gave way, and a hand-to-hand fight ensued. I endeavoured to rally my men, but they were too much scattered, and finding re-formation impossible, I mounted my horse and galloped into Luneburg at utmost speed, and reported all that had taken place.[5]

Likewise, Major Tucker made no mention in his report that he felt the camp had been inadequately laagered. Instead he praised Harward's efforts in giving covering fire to enable some men to escape across the river. These two reports were the basis of Lord Chelmsford's report to the War Office, which was not received in London until 21 April. Up to this point the circumstances surrounding Harward's desertion of his men were contained within the regiment. The final death toll was put at seventy-nine. As Colour Sergeant Henry Fredericks had been killed in the incident Booth was promoted to Colour Sergeant to replace him.

Over the next few weeks the regiment moved to Utrecht and joined Wood's column in its advance on Ulundi. Significantly, Lieutenant Harward was left behind. At Ulundi the 80th formed part of the massive square that finally broke the Zulu fighting spirit, and during the engagement the regiment sustained two dead and five wounded. Amazingly, and despite seeing much action throughout a long military career, the only injury Booth ever sustained was when a stray bullet struck his mess tin, Booth receiving some metal splinters in his face.

At the end of the year, long after the war was over, the regiment was stationed at Pretoria and it was from here, on 20 December, that three survivors of the Ntombe engagement wrote to General Sir Garnet Wolseley to set the record straight and 'to be of service to Colour Sergeant Booth'. There was a great deal of anger throughout the regiment that had built up over the months. Tucker was asked why he had not previously recommended his sergeant for a medal. To defuse the situation, the newly promoted Lieutenant Colonel Tucker belatedly recommended Booth for the Distinguished Conduct Medal. Wolseley began to ask embarrassing questions and Tucker finally had to explain that the facts would have revealed the 'far different conduct of Lieutenant Harward'. On 26 December the whole regiment was paraded prior to leaving for England. Wolseley took the salute and, in a most unusual ceremony, presented Colour Sergeant Booth with a revolver, holster, belt and a knife, which were all donated by European settlers. On the same day, Wolseley forwarded his personal recommendation that Booth should be awarded the Victoria Cross. This was an exceptional gesture as Wolseley had been highly critical of the number of VC awards during the campaign.

The 80th then began their long march to Durban, which they reached on 3 April. Meanwhile, on 14 February, as a result of Wolseley's investigations, Lieutenant Harward was arrested and taken to Pietermaritzburg, where he was charged with two offences. The first of these was 'having misbehaved before the enemy, in shamefully abandoning a party of the Regiment under his command when attacked by the enemy, and in riding off at speed from his men'. Secondly, he was charged with 'conduct to the prejudice of good order and military discipline in having at the place and time mentioned in the first charge, neglected to take proper precautions for the safety of a party of a Regiment under his command when attacked'.

The court martial was held at Fort Napier in Pietermaritzburg and was in session from 20 to 27 February. Harward's defence was that he had only joined the convoy escort the night before and could not form a proper laager with just two wagons. When his command began to disintegrate, he had decided to ride to get help. Much to the surprise of many and the fury of Wolseley, the court acquitted Harward of all charges and he was allowed to return to his regiment; he then resigned his commission and left the army.

Wolseley could not alter the verdict but he refused to confirm the court's findings, adding his own view:

> Had I released this officer without making any remarks upon the verdict in question, it would have been a tacit acknowledgement that I had concurred in what appears to me a monstrous theory, viz. that a Regimental Officer who is the only Officer present with a party of men actually and seriously engaged with the enemy, can, under any pretext whatever, be justified in deserting them, and by so doing, abandoning them to their fate. The more helpless a position in which an officer finds his men, the more it is his bounden duty to stay and share their fortune, whether good or ill. It is because the British officer has always done so that he possesses the influence he does in the ranks of our army. The soldier has learned to feel, that come what may, he can in the direst moment of danger look with implicit faith to his officer, knowing he will never desert him under any possible circumstances.[6]

When the findings and Wolseley's comments reached the Duke of Cambridge, Commander-in-Chief of the British Army, he instructed them to be read out as a general order to every regiment throughout the British Empire. In most instances, Harward's name has been expunged from his regiment's records. Harward's abandoning of his men was an action that occurred all too often during the Zulu War; this caused dismay to leaders like Wolseley, Wood and Buller and may well explain the strength of comment following Harward's court martial.

With his army career in tatters, Harward had little option but to resign his commission, which he did on arriving at King's Town on 11 May 1880.

On 26 June 1880 Colour Sergeant Booth was summoned from his station in Ireland to Windsor Castle where the queen presented him with the Victoria Cross.[7]

Booth's conduct and that of another 80th man, Private Samuel Wassall, who won the only Isandlwana Victoria Cross at Fugitives' Drift, gave the regiment justifiable pride in what had been a less than glorious campaign.

Through his misplaced confidence and casual approach to defending the camp, Captain Moriarty was held to be to blame for the poorly arranged laager notwithstanding that he had lost his life. His superior, Major Tucker, was deemed at fault for not insisting on the wagons being pushed together when he had voiced his reservations about the laager. Tucker's subsequent deception to cover up a fellow officer's cowardice at the expense of recognizing Sergeant Booth caused intense comment and resentment within the regiment. Tucker's role in this matter does not seem to have affected his career for he retired a major general and remained Colonel of the South Staffordshire Regiment (the amalgamation of the 80th and 38th Regiments) until he died in 1935 at the age of 97.

Hlobane, 28 March 1879

The disaster which befell us was caused mostly by the careless manner of our Commanding Officers.

SERGEANT MAJOR CHEFFINS [8]

Lord Chelmsford's plan for a second invasion of Zululand was well advanced but he was deeply concerned that the belligerent abaQulusi Zulus, who occupied the Hlobane hills and territory immediately to the north of the proposed invasion route, could cause him two serious difficulties. Firstly, they could move south in support of King Cetshwayo's main army and hinder Chelmsford's relief of the besieged column at Eshowe. Secondly, they could menace and sit across his second invasion route and supply line. Either possibility constituted an unacceptable risk for Chelmsford. Wood appreciated the serious danger posed by the abaQulusi but was uncertain how to neutralize such a powerful force ensconced only 25 miles from his Khambula base.

On 20 March he received an order from Chelmsford to 'demonstrate' against the abaQulusi, which in turn would theoretically draw Zulu forces away from southern Zululand and enable Chelmsford's relief column to lift the siege of Pearson's camp at Eshowe. Wood saw the logic of the order and Chelmsford's instruction provided him with the ideal opportunity; he accordingly made preparations to send a strong force to attack the Hlobane stronghold during the night of 27 March. His overall plan was to rout the Zulus there and seize their cattle; a successful action would wrong-foot the abaQulusi as well as deprive any approaching Zulu army of essential food supplies. He proposed to mount a night attack against the Hlobane hills with two independent columns of mounted Colonial troops and black auxiliaries, a force of 1,300 led by Lieutenant Colonels Buller and Russell.

The flat top of Hlobane is nearly 4 miles long and 1½ miles wide; it is generally 1,000ft above the surrounding plain and, apart from two or three precipitous pathways, a skirt of vertical cliffs protects the virtually inaccessible mountain. The link between the upper level of Hlobane and its lower level, Ntendeka, was little more than an illusion; at best it was an extremely steep, boulder-strewn knife edge. The location had never been visited by a European and its precipitous descent would severely test Buller and his men.

The operation was ill conceived; even though the defeat at Isandl-wana was still fresh in his mind, Wood had not subjected Hlobane to any form of reconnaissance other than a cursory appraisal some two weeks earlier. The routes up and down the mountain were based on Wood's distant viewing and although he had roughly guessed their location, the exact routes to the top of Hlobane were unknown to the British. Wood's fatal presumption was that the connecting ridge between the two levels of Hlobane and Ntendeka presented an easy passage; it would prove to be a graveyard for many of Buller's men. The plan was for the two groups to attack the mountain after dark – Buller's from the east to take the higher plateau of Hlobane and then seize Zulu cattle, while Russell's force simultaneously attacked from the west along Ntendeka. Wood believed the final stage of the plan was equally easy to execute – Russell would meet up with Buller and their combined force would drive the captured cattle back to Khambula.

Buller's force consisted of about 400 mounted men, all local volunteer horsemen except for a few Imperial officers, and 280 black auxiliaries. Russell's group was made up of approximately 200 mounted troops and 440 black auxiliaries, including 200 Zulu warriors who had defected to the British along with their leader, Prince Hamu, a half-brother of King Cetshwayo. Both groups left Khambula just after dawn on the 27th. They had been issued with extra rations and, unusually, twice the amount of ammunition normally carried on such a raid.

At noon Buller's men unsaddled for an hour to take lunch and then moved off to the south of Hlobane. Their presence was clearly seen by the abaQulusi on Hlobane who lit a row of signal fires, although the sig-nificance of the fires was not realized by Buller who proceeded for several miles beyond Hlobane before making camp. The intention was to give the abaQulusi the impression that the real target of his column was the

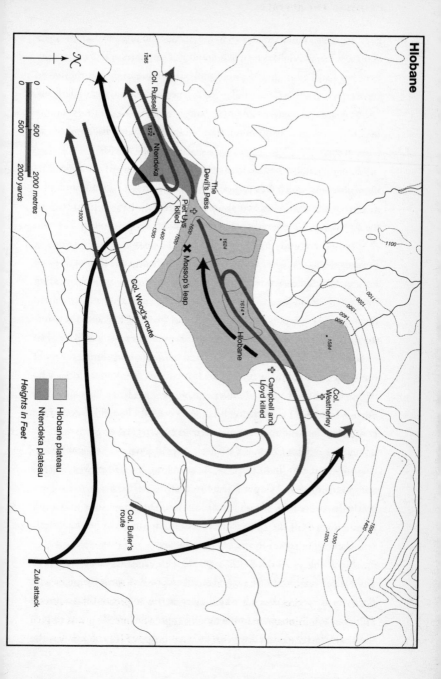

Hlobane

Col. Russell

Ntendeka

The Devil's Pass

Piet Uys killed

✕ Mb333's leap

Col. Wood's route

Col. Weatherley

Campbell and Lloyd killed

Col. Buller's route

Zulu attack

Heights in Feet

Hlobane plateau

Ntendeka plateau

Zulu army, its location unknown to the British who presumed it was on its way from Ulundi. Buller's men lit a number of campfires and after dark the fires were stoked to give the abaQulusi the impression that they were staying put. At about 8 p.m. Buller led his men under the cover of darkness back towards the eastern end of Hlobane where they began the laborious task of following a cattle track that led in the general direction of the plateau top.

In reality, Buller had no idea of the close proximity of the approaching Zulu army which was camped only 5 miles from Hlobane and now alerted by the abaQulusi signal fires. Had Buller's force looked back in the direction of Ulundi rather than concentrating on the route up Hlobane they would certainly have seen signs of the distant Zulus advancing towards them. Likewise, Buller's colonial scouts proved incompetent and for a crucial few hours seriously neglected their duty by concentrating their attention on their own welfare rather than observing events behind them. His black scouts had seen the Zulus' fires but had kept the information to themselves, knowing their words were never heeded. Even when a scouting patrol accidentally discovered the Zulu army during the night the British failed to make use of the information. The Border Horse, who were supposed to be part of Buller's group, had left Khambula later than intended and had inadvertently become mixed with Russell's force. In the confusion, they and their commander, an experienced ex-cavalry officer named Lieutenant Colonel Weatherley, spent most of the night unsuccessfully trying to find Buller. While searching for Buller, Weatherley's second in command Captain Dennison and a party of scouts inadvertently discovered the encamped Zulu army. They crept to within a few hundred yards of the Zulu force to assess the situation before quietly withdrawing to report the fact to Weatherley.

Meanwhile, Colonel Wood, together with Captain Ronald Campbell and his personal staff officers and small escort, had spent the night with Russell's force. As dawn broke they rode out to watch the action on Hlobane, totally unaware of the rapidly approaching Zulu army – which they incorrectly assumed was on its way to oppose Pearson 100 miles away at Eshowe. While riding beneath the towering cliffs at the eastern end of Hlobane they unexpectedly met up with Weatherley and his Border Horse, who were fully aware of the approaching Zulus but uncertain where they should report for the impending clash. At this point a most interesting exchange took place. Weatherley told Wood about the strong Zulu force, still unseen from Hlobane due to the undulating terrain, but now rapidly closing with Wood's force. Indignantly Wood replied, 'Nonsense, I have had my men out yesterday, there is no Zulu *impi* about.' Dennison was Weatherley's deputy and he replied, 'I saw them, I was in fact almost within touching distance of them and judged them to be a strong force.' Wood retorted, 'Can't be, Dennison, you are mistaken.'[9] Confused by Wood's assertion, Weatherley seems to have accepted it; he gathered his riders and they commenced the climb with the intention of joining Buller for his attack across Hlobane.

Wood conveniently omitted referring to this conversation in his memoirs but he did remember that, just as the two groups parted, they were fired upon by Zulu marksmen hiding in a cave near the top of the cattle track that led onto the flat top of Hlobane. Both groups took cover to assess the situation. Wood later pointedly wrote that he, with his staff, pushed through Weatherley's sheltering men directly towards the enemy, leaving most of the Border Horse 200 yards behind. Within moments a Zulu marksman killed Mr Llewellyn Lloyd, Wood's political officer, the son of a retired British general and a member of the Natal Legislative Assembly. According to Wood, Campbell impetuously ran forward and brought back Lloyd's body to a stone cattle kraal where Wood and his staff were sheltering.

Wood alleges that he then told Campbell to order the Border Horse forward, but Weatherley's men, also under heavy fire from the unseen Zulu snipers, apparently declined to advance as they considered the Zulu position impregnable. Wood later claimed that three of his staff then attacked the snipers' position after his request for assistance to Weatherley was refused – although this version is strongly disputed by the few Border Horse survivors. In any event, Campbell approached the snipers only to be shot dead as he entered their cave. Captain the Hon Ronald Campbell, Coldstream Guards, was only 30 years old and the second son of the Earl of Cawdor. After quickly burying Campbell and Lloyd, Wood and his remaining escort rode off to Khambula, narrowly escaping the advancing Zulu army; unaccountably, Wood then disappeared for some eight hours before he returned to Khambula. Weatherley and his Border Horse reached the top of Hlobane and set off to find Buller.

During the previous night, the abaQulusi on Hlobane had seen Russell's column heading towards the western end of the mountain and correctly anticipated that their stronghold was to be attacked from both ends. Knowing that the main Zulu army was approaching, the abaQulusi prepared for the attack with confidence, building stone barriers at each end of Hlobane. Buller's attack against Hlobane, undertaken in a violent thunderstorm under the cover of darkness, was virtually unopposed; some shots were fired and several boulders were rolled down on the advancing force as they struggled up the steep cattle track, and a number of casualties were sustained. Once on top, Buller left A Company at the head of the path as a rearguard. The abaQulusi had disappeared into a number of underground caves, enabling the British to loot their cattle as they headed towards the far end of the plateau to meet up with Russell. Unbeknown to Buller, Russell had arrived at the bottom of the precipitous face known as 'Devil's Pass' and found his route to the higher plateau of Hlobane virtually inaccessible due to its steepness. He dispatched a messenger to climb up the rocky face to find Buller and advise him not to attempt the route.

Meanwhile, the abaQulusi warriors hiding in Hlobane's caves could clearly see the main Zulu army now less than a mile distant and steadily closing. They left their caves and were joined by some 2,000 reinforcements that had climbed onto Hlobane from the adjoining Ityentika plateau to the east; combined into a sizeable force, they prepared to attack Buller's men who were now retreating before them with the Zulu cattle. At the far end of the plateau Buller's black auxiliaries began forcing the looted cattle down the Devil's Pass to the lower plateau with the intention of driving them back to Khambula. It was several minutes before Buller became aware of the main Zulu army now approaching Hlobane; his first reaction was to rush the remaining unmounted black irregulars down the precipitous face so that they could escape back to Khambula. He then detailed Captain Barton to take thirty riders from the Frontier Light Horse to quickly recover the body of Lieutenant Williams, killed in the ascent of Hlobane; he was then to find Weatherley and warn him to retreat off Hlobane and retire back to Khambula. As Buller's remaining force converged towards the top of the Devil's Pass, the emboldened and reinforced abaQulusi advanced upon them.

The abaQulusi had already routed A Troop who had been left defending the original ascent route; the survivors fled towards Buller's men who were now being driven towards the western end of Hlobane. It was during the growing chaos that Buller first became aware of the enormity of the danger being created by the main Zulu army moving to encircle Hlobane. He sent two troopers in hot pursuit of Barton with an order for Barton to retreat 'by the right of the mountain'. Barton was still unaware of the encircling Zulu army when, several hundred yards ahead of him, he saw Weatherley and his force reach the summit rim of Hlobane; at that very moment the two troopers arrived with Buller's message and Barton presumed from the new order that because he was now facing east, he should continue as previously ordered by Buller. Barton's misinterpretation of Buller's ambiguous message was about to have disastrous consequences.

Barton and his burial party rushed to join Weatherley's force assembling at the top of the cattle track which had earlier brought Buller's force to the top of Hlobane. Having been rebutted by Wood, and concentrating their attention on the steep climb in front of them, no one in Weatherley's force had noticed the rapidly closing Zulu army now less than a mile from the beginning of the cattle track. Barton blurted out the awful news and in the minutes that Weatherley, Barton and their men had left to live, they rapidly descended by the same track in the mistaken belief that they could escape back to Khambula if they complied with Buller's last order.

Once off Hlobane they realized their predicament; they had inadvertently ridden towards the main Zulu army who were now less than a quarter of a mile away and rapidly closing. They about-turned to discover that the abaQulusi had come up behind them and they were now surrounded, but they successfully charged through the abaQulusi and rode with all speed towards the nearby saddle between Hlobane and Ityentika Nek in the mistaken belief that they could ride across the saddle and descend to safety down the far side. It was not to be. The Zulus knew that the saddle ended abruptly at the head of a 400ft precipice to the valley below. The Zulus rushed at Weatherley's trapped force, now in a state of panic, and drove them to the very edge of the cliff that ran along the northern side of Hlobane. In the fierce fighting that ensued, Weatherley, his son and sixty-six men were killed.

The terror of the bloody rout and slaughter caused some men and horses to jump off the cliff. Captains Dennison and Barton somehow managed to lead their horses down the almost sheer scree, followed by a handful of men and some riderless horses, but few made it to the foot of the slope. Those who avoided the pursuing Zulus, including Dennison, then set off towards the camp at Khambula. Barton lost his horse in the descent but, having found a loose but winded horse, followed the other fugitives; he quickly caught up with Lieutenant Poole of the Border Horse who had also climbed down the cliff and was now running for his life. Barton collected up the exhausted Poole behind him but the pair were seen to be in difficulty by a group of fleet-of-foot Zulus who gave close chase; a grim pursuit ensued over the next hour but on their weakening horse the outcome was inevitable. The Zulus overhauled and killed the pair 8 miles from Hlobane, on the bank of the Manzana river. The following year a Zulu who claimed to have killed Barton escorted Wood to the scene. The two bodies were found and buried on the river bank; numerous attempts have since been made to find the graves but the location has not been traced.

Meanwhile on Hlobane, both Buller and Russell's columns simultaneously experienced a state of confused alarm; with the Zulus bearing down on them, both could clearly see that they were on the verge of being surrounded by an overpowering force. At this point Russell received an ambiguous message from Wood which would save Russell's life and those of his men. Unsure whether Buller and Russell had seen the approaching Zulus, Wood tried to warn his two commanders and sent a written order to Russell mistakenly ordering him to move immediately to Zunguin Nek 5 miles from the scene. The message read, 'Below the Inhlobane. 10.30 A.M. 28/3/79 There is a large army coming this way from the south. Get into position on Zunguin Nek. E.W.' Wood had intended that Russell should remain on Ntendeka to support Buller down the Devil's Pass, but had confused his locations. Russell did not hesitate for a moment: he and his men departed as fast as they could ride – controversially abandoning Buller and his men to the encircling Zulus.

So steep was the descent down the Devil's Pass that many of Buller's men and horses fell to their deaths; for the survivors, their ordeal was to become even more serious as the Zulus from the main force now reached the lower reaches of the pass and began closing in on both sides of the fleeing men. The Zulus began firing at point-blank range into the desperate soldiers while others darted among them, stabbing and spearing them to death. Trooper Patterson had managed to lead his horse safely down the pass and had just mounted up when he was speared from his horse and left defenceless. As the Zulus closed to kill the injured rider, Trooper Whitecross drove them off by using his rifle as a club. Patterson was hauled to safety and both troopers lived to tell the tale. As more survivors reached the bottom of the pass, the remaining Zulus closed with them. In the midst of the life-and-death struggle, a young trooper of the Frontier Light Horse, 16-year-old George Mossop, had earlier abandoned his horse on the upper plateau of Hlobane and scrambled down the steep face to join his colleagues fighting at the bottom of the pass. Buller shouted at the youth to recover his horse, knowing that without a mount the young trooper would be lost. Mossop dashed through the fighting back up to the top of the Devil's Pass. He later wrote of the fight:

Zulus, crawling over the huge rocks on either side, were jabbing at the men and horses. Some of the men were shooting, and some were using clubbed rifles and fighting their way down. Owing to the rocks on either side the Zulus could not charge. The intervening space was almost filled with dead horses and dead men, white and black.[10]

On regaining the plateau Mossop saw his horse, Warrior, some 40 yards away near the cliff edge. He ran to the horse, only to find himself being encircled by Zulus and with only one other unhorsed trooper for company. The two men moved towards the sheer cliff edge. In terror at what was about to befall him, the other trooper shot himself:

… placing the muzzle of his carbine in his mouth he pulled the trigger. A lot of brains and other stuff splashed on my neck.[11]

Mossop was now trapped. The only alternative to imminent death at the hands of the Zulus now stared him in the face; with seconds to spare he jumped off the cliff with his horse. Both bounced down the cliff face and finally fell into a clump of trees and boulders. Miraculously both Mossop and his horse survived the jump, although Mossop saw that Warrior was bleeding profusely from injuries sustained in the fall; thankfully the area was free of Zulus so Mossop adjusted the saddle to staunch the horse's blood before mounting up. By evading the Zulus, who were intent on dealing with Buller's men higher up, both Mossop and Warrior were able to escape from Hlobane and the pair reached the safety of Khambula later that day. Mossop nursed his dying horse through the night but Warrior died as dawn broke.

At the base of the pass there was little that Buller or his surviving officers could do other than hold their men together and pour rapid fire into the attacking Zulus. Buller and Major Knox-Leet repeatedly rode back into the fighting to rescue men whose horses had been killed or to help men in danger of being isolated by the Zulus. Lieutenant Metcalfe Smith later wrote:

I was on foot, my horse having been shot. When we got down a little way a
great many Zulus rushed after us, and were catching us up very quickly.
The side of the mountain was dreadfully steep and rugged and there was
no pathway at all. They were firing and throwing their assegais at us while
they rushed upon us.[12]

With hundreds of Zulus converging on the Devil's Pass the fighting was
soon over and only those riders who had reached the lower plateau with
their horses had any chance of getting away; those on foot soon fell. The
harrowing experience continued for the mounted survivors who were chased
for several miles by the jubilant Zulus. It was a long and frightening trek for
those fleeing for their lives as any horse unable to maintain the pace during
the first few miles was quickly overhauled and its rider slain. Buller arrived
back at Khambula after sunset, to learn that several of his men whom he
had seen escaping were still missing. Typical of Buller, he took a fresh horse
and went in search of his men; they all returned safely just before midnight.

By attacking Hlobane at all, Wood and Buller had embarked upon a
suicidal expedition. All the lessons from the recent disaster at Isandlwana
were disregarded; the reconnaissance was scant and the scouting equally
negligent. No one taking part in the attack knew the layout of Hlobane
and, as at Isandlwana, the scouts failed to detect a Zulu army camped
only 5 miles distant. Even when Weatherley informed Wood of the
proximity of the Zulus, Wood scornfully dismissed his timely warning.
Collectively Wood and Buller provoked the second greatest disaster of
the war, yet the news and implications of the defeat at Hlobane were successfully screened by the British victory at Khambula the following day, just
as the successful defence at Rorke's Drift screened Isandlwana.

Wood and his escort survived to tell the tale. They managed to remain
ahead of the encircling Zulus and escaped back to Khambula. Wood's
movements for the remainder of the day have never been satisfactorily
explained. He arrived back at Khambula after nightfall.

When the exhausted Dennison reached the safety of Khambula he
saw to his men's welfare before allowing himself to be cared for by the
mess staff. At dawn the following day he went to Weatherley's tent with the

intention of preparing a casualty list, just as Buller arrived to congratulate him on his survival. In their conversation Buller observed that it had been unfortunate that the presence of the Zulu army had been unknown. Dennison retorted that it had been known and furthermore, he had personally reported the army's presence to Wood. Clearly taken aback by Dennison's allegation Buller commented, 'I believe you, Dennison, what a sad mistake, but say nothing for the present and lie low.' It is evident that Wood tried to hide the debacle of Hlobane behind his victory at Khambula; nothing was officially said that could have alerted the British press to the disaster and for several weeks the tale of Hlobane went untold. Even Chelmsford was uncertain what had happened and in a dispatch to the Secretary of State for War he wrote that he had 'not observed in Col. Wood's despatch any reference to the reason why he considered it desirable to attack [Hlobane] on the 28th'. But the majority of the Hlobane casualties were Colonials and with the inevitability that accompanies cover-ups, the story of the disaster was soon taken up by the Natal press; Wood and Buller came in for ferocious criticism but the press had little influence on the matter and Wood calmly rode the storm by blending the two battles into the successful account of his great victory at Khambula.[13]

Buller reported to Wood that there were too many instances of bravery at Hlobane to mention particular cases or individuals. Wood thought otherwise and in due course he made a number of recommendations; both Buller and Major Knox-Leet were awarded the Victoria Cross, though Knox-Leet uniquely applied for the medal,[14] and Corporal Vinnicombe was awarded the Distinguished Conduct Medal. Following pressure from Wood, two further VCs were awarded three years later to Lieutenant Lysons and Private Fowler, as were awards of the DCM to Privates Walkinshaw and Power, and Trooper Brown. It was previously thought that Lieutenant Browne, on loan to Buller from the 1/24th Regiment, had received a VC for bravery at Hlobane but it is now known that Browne's VC was awarded for his bravery at Khambula the following day. The debate arose because the inscription on the VC has Khambula's date juxtaposed with 'Inhlobana'.

Khambula, 29 March 1879

I must tell you of our glorious victory at Khambula Hill.

PRIVATE JOHN SNOOK [15]

By the following afternoon the British troops remaining in the Khambula camp began to hear rumours of the unbelievable disaster that had befallen Buller's force. Until this point, the prevailing atmosphere throughout the camp was one of absolute confidence; rumours had long since been circulating that the Zulu army might seek to attack the Northern Column and the men enthusiastically welcomed the prospect of avenging Isandlwana. That afternoon the Hlobane survivors began arriving back at Khambula camp in their ones and twos; many were wounded, all were deeply shocked. These were men who had earlier set out with boundless confidence to attack the Zulu stronghold. Now the full extent of their loss was abundantly clear:

> [T]he men [came] into camp in twos and threes, without coats, rifles, and ammunition belts, having thrown them away to lighten themselves for running, when their horses were shot or lost. Then there were two on a horse, and then perhaps you would see an officer come in mounted behind a trooper, glad to get in anyhow. Now and again, as the men came into camp, you would hear someone ask where was so-and-so, and the answer would be 'Left behind','He's gone'. [16]

With such a large Zulu force now so close to Khambula, Wood correctly expected that an attack on his position was imminent and that evening everyone in camp completed their preparations for the expected battle. All knew that the Zulu army would heavily outnumber them.

For the attack against the Northern Column, King Cetshwayo again gave command to Ntshingwayo kaMahole, the victor of Isandlwana; he was supported by Chief Mnyamana kaNgqengelele of the Buthelezi. The brutal lesson learned by the Zulus at Rorke's Drift had convinced King Cetshwayo that the British force should not be attacked in an entrenched position; rather, they should be attacked on the move or between camps.

King Cetshwayo was also aware that his warriors were supremely confident and would relish the opportunity of attacking the British and perchance forcing the invaders to retreat back to Natal. He accordingly warned his warriors, 'Do not put your faces into the lair of the wild beasts for you are sure to get clawed.'[17]

The British position at Khambula was positioned on the highest point of a long ridge that itself was overlooked by a far range of surrounding hills, known locally as Nqaba kaHawana (Hawana's place of refuge). It was an ideal position to defend as it dominated the immediate and lower surrounding area for more than half a mile. Only 3 miles from the camp was a forested area with abundant wood for campfires, and a number of freshwater springs around the camp led into streams that formed the headwaters of the White Mfolozi river. A rocky cliff protected the camp to the south and the flat terrace leading from the camp to the cliff was used as a cattle pen. The main headquarters of the camp was built on a small knoll or natural rise in the ridge, which was fortified with an earthwork redoubt. Immediately next to the redoubt was the main camp area which consisted of two strongly entrenched wagon laagers.

The unexpected defeat at Hlobane had seriously affected the morale of Wood's Boer volunteers and many of the black auxiliaries thought better of staying and deserted during the night. The British element of Wood's force were unaffected by Hlobane and continued to look forward to the possibility of a major battle; the 90th Light Infantry and seven companies of the 13th Light Infantry were supported by a total of six 7 pound guns, two rocket troughs, and over 500 mounted men; a combined force of 2,086 well-trained troops. Two guns were placed in the redoubt itself; the remainder were located on the high ground between the redoubt and the camp from where they could cover any Zulu advance.

Hardly slowing for the battle at Hlobane, the Zulu army continued its march towards Khambula and spent the night 10 miles from the British position along the banks of the White Mfolozi river. Early the following morning they began their advance towards Khambula in five well-spaced-out columns. Towards midday the whole Zulu army stopped to undergo

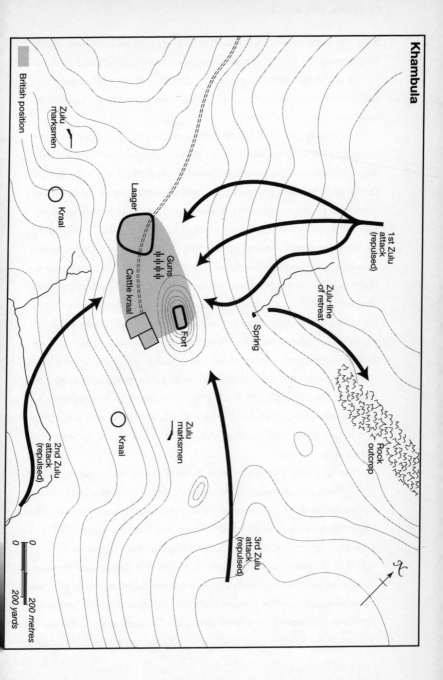

Khambula

British position

Zulu marksmen

Kraal

Laager

Guns

Cattle kraal

Fort

1st Zulu attack (repulsed)

Zulu line of retreat

Spring

Rock outcrop

2nd Zulu attack (repulsed)

Kraal

Zulu marksmen

3rd Zulu attack (repulsed)

0   200 metres
0   200 yards

281

their pre-battle purification rituals followed by an address from Chief Mnyamana; he gave a timely reminder to the regiments that King Cetshwayo's order was not to attack the British in an entrenched position; they were to seize the camp cattle which would lure the soldiers away from their wagons and tents.

The British prepared for the forthcoming battle by taking an early lunch and striking the camp tents. Wood expressed his concern that the Zulus might bypass Khambula and instead attack the unprotected European settlement at Utrecht but, by early afternoon, it was obvious to all that Khambula was the Zulus' objective. As at Isandlwana, the Zulus were advancing on a front estimated by Wood to be 10 miles wide and they maintained the formation until it divided into the classical 'horns' formation. The right horn, consisting of the uVe and iNgobamakhosi regiments, moved towards the north of the camp; the left horn, the uKhandempemvu, uMbonambi and uNokhenke regiments, were advancing from the south; and the main chest of the Zulu army slowed to take up position about 1 mile west of the redoubt. It is still a mystery why the Zulu commanders permitted the attack to take place against such a strongly fortified British position; this flew in the face of the king's orders and it must be presumed that the enthusiasm of the mass of warriors overruled the orders of the commanders. It is also possible that the Zulus interpreted the tents in the camp being collapsed as an indication that the British were about to abandon their position.[18]

The right horn approached from the north across open ground well out of rifle range and swung round towards the British position. To the south the left horn ran into unexpected difficulties: their approach to the camp followed the course of a stream, which was wet and marshy. Within moments the leading warriors became bogged down in knee-deep mud and their advance stalled less than a mile from the camp. Chief Ntshingwayo's intention was for both horns to join up on the ridge level with the camp and, with the British surrounded, attack simultaneously – but each horn was still out of sight from the other. The right horn to the north presumed the left horn had made matching progress and by 1.30 p.m.

the right horn had advanced to within 800 yards of the British position where they paused to regroup. From his scouts' reports, Wood perceptively assessed that the left horn was bogged down; making a brave tactical decision to provoke the right horn into attacking before the left horn could emerge from the marsh, he ordered Buller to take about 100 of his mounted men to fire point-blank volleys into the packed ranks of the waiting uVe and iNgobamakhosi. Notwithstanding the appalling disaster of the previous day, these riders were well practised in the tactic of provocation and rode out to within 100 yards of the Zulus. Buller's men calmly dismounted and fired several fast and deadly volleys into the packed ranks of chanting and stamping warriors; this action was too much for the Zulus who immediately charged the horsemen.

The riders hurriedly retreated back towards the camp hotly pursued by the Zulus; unfortunately several riders had earlier failed to notice a small spring and their retreat took them through boggy ground, slowing their retreat. With the Zulus upon them, two men were pulled from their horses and killed. Another rider, Trooper Petersen of the Frontier Light, also got into difficulties and his plight was seen by Lieutenant Colonel Russell, who had so rapidly fled Hlobane the previous day. Russell bravely went to Petersen's aid but found himself in a similar predicament. Several of the Natal Native Horse, including the young Trooper Mossop, rushed to assist the trapped Petersen while Lieutenant Browne of the 24th Regiment went to Russell's aid; all had a miraculous escape and reached the camp just as the artillery began firing case shot over their heads. Browne was later awarded the Victoria Cross, the only VC of the day, and Troop Sergeant Major Learda of the NNH received the DCM. Wood disliked Russell, especially after his underhand retreat from Hlobane, and so Russell's bravery went unrecognized.

With shouts of 'we are the boys from Isandlwana!'[19] the right horn charged towards the camp and into a firestorm from the artillery and a rapid series of violent close-range volleys. Some Zulus even managed to reach the outer line of wagons but eventually they were forced into an urgent retreat. Many British soldiers were forced to admire the Zulus' bravery; one wrote, 'I never saw anything like it, nothing frightened them, and when any of their numbers were shot down, others took their places.'[20] The Zulus made several gallant attempts to breach the British line; each attack was driven back by further close-range volleys, causing great loss to the Zulus. About a half-mile to the north of the camp was a rocky dip in the ground; the attacking Zulus withdrew to the protection of this cover and apart from a desultory and inaccurate fire, they took no further part in the battle.

The Zulu left horn were still largely unaware of the course of the raging battle and by the time they had cleared the marsh, the right horn were in full retreat. A brief lull ensued in the British position, which allowed Wood to turn his attention, and that of the 7 pound guns, in the anticipated direction of the approaching left horn that was now clambering up the ridge towards the British. The attacking Zulus began to mass within 100 yards of the camp's cattle laager. While they prepared for their first attack, unexpected rifle fire began to hit the main British position from the east where Zulu snipers at the front of the main Zulu force commenced fire; simultaneous sniper fire came from the camp's old rubbish and dung dumps some 300 yards to the west. The recent rains had caused a tall crop of mealies and grass to sprout around the dumps, which provided the Zulu snipers with relatively close cover. It was soon apparent to the soldiers under fire that the Zulus were in possession of numerous Martini-Henry rifles taken from Isandlwana. One British observer recalled, 'The bullets whizzed across the camp like a perfect hailstorm.'[21] Their accuracy left much to be desired but the fire was a serious irritation to the British defenders. At this point some of the uNokhenke broke through the camp's outer defence, which resulted in a brief hand-to-hand skirmish involving Captain Cox's company; in the desperate fray Cox was shot in the leg and Colour Sergeant Fricker received a serious head wound. Private Grosvenor helped Fricker away only to be fatally speared himself by a Zulu. Wood ordered a series of volleys into the advancing Zulus, which steadily drove them back from the close proximity of the camp.

The chest, consisting of the uThulwana, iNdlondlo, iNdluyengwe, uDloko, iMbube, iSangqu and uDududu regiments, now mounted its first attack. The warriors initially advanced in good order but soon took serious casualties from the sustained volleys of rifle fire and, like the right horn, they too fell back.

The calm control that now pervaded the British camp was in stark contrast to the extensive confusion among the Zulus; Wood noticed several *indunas* attempting to encourage the Zulus back into the fray. It is believed that it was at this point Wood took his orderly's rifle from him and shot two of the Zulu commanders, causing the remainder to take cover. Wood then turned his attention to the Zulus still hiding behind the cattle laager and ordered Major Robert Hackett to take two companies of the 90th and, with fixed bayonets, drive the Zulus from the shelter. Hackett's men fired several volleys and advanced behind their bayonets towards the Zulus; sporadic fire from the Zulus struck a number of the soldiers and a sniper's bullet struck Hackett in the head. The bullet passed right through his head directly behind his eyes. (Later that night Hackett called for a candle as he found the night 'uncommonly dark'; the wound rendered him blind for the rest of his life.) His subaltern, Lieutenant Bright, was hit in the thigh by a bullet that smashed one leg and lodged in the other. The British retired to the camp, taking with them their two seriously wounded officers.

The uVe and iNgobamakhosi made one final determined attack towards the redoubt but, once again, they were beaten off and sustained further serious casualties. The whole Zulu attack was now stalled; the main force made no attempt to advance on the British camp and the only fire still affecting Wood's men was coming from Zulu marksmen firing from the rubbish dumps. Buller took charge: he ordered his men to fire directly into the rubbish heaps, a tactic so successful that after the battle over fifty Zulu bodies were recovered from the dumps.

The 90th recaptured the cattle laager at bayonet point and from this moment the willingness of the Zulus to mount further attacks dissipated. The Zulus were exhausted and by late afternoon it was evident to Wood that they were on the verge of effecting a mass withdrawal. Wood seized the opportunity to turn it into a rout; he ordered the guns to fire canister shot into the retreating Zulus and unleashed his several hundred mounted irregular troops to harass their withdrawal.

Among the riders were a number who had survived Hlobane the day before. The event was still very raw in their memories and all had lost friends, so they saw this as their chance to exact revenge. They were led out by Commandant Cecil D'Arcy of the Frontier Light Horse who spurred his men on with a chilling cry: 'No quarter, boys, and remember yesterday.' The fleeing Zulus were easily run down and were mercilessly slaughtered in their tens and twenties. Private John Snook created something of a stir at home when a letter he wrote to his parents was published in the British press; it included the chilling words:

> I can tell you some murdering went on. Every Zulu caught was killed; the killing went on until darkness fell; only then did the slaughter cease.[22]

Wood lost eighteen NCOs and men killed, with eight officers and fifty-seven NCOs and men wounded of whom three would die of their injuries, including Lieutenant Bright. The surgeon attending Bright had failed to notice that the round had also passed through his other leg, causing him to bleed to death. Major Hackett survived and was returned to his home in Ireland where his brother nursed him into old age.

It is probable that over 500 Zulus were killed in the immediate area around the camp but it is even more likely that twice as many again were slain along their line of retreat. The dead around the camp were transported by wagons and buried well beyond the camp area. The close-range rifle and cannon fire had horribly mutilated many Zulu bodies and the results of the action distressed many soldiers in the burial parties. According to a journalist who was present at the battle,

> The ground was strewn with bodies, most of the bullets taking effect on their heads and blowing their brains out. After the battle terminated I took a walk for a distance of a mile to the old camping ground near the hill, and the trenches were full of killed from the shells bursting. It was the

most ghastly sight ever seen; on some bodies the entrails were torn out by the shells. Several were shot in the act of throwing their assegais and firing their rifles, and retained those same positions when shot. The frightful appearance of those killed would make the most hard-hearted man's blood creep.[23]

I confess that I do not think that a braver lot of men than our enemies in point of disregard for life, and for their bravery under fire, could be found anywhere. We were all employed burying the dead yesterday, and we had not finished by dark, pits being made three-quarters of a mile from camp, and the dead taken in carts. A more horrible sight than the enemy's dead, where they felt the effects of shellfire, I never saw. Bodies lying cut in halves, heads taken off, and other features in connection with the dead made a sight more ghastly than I ever thought of.[24]

Wood and Buller realized that the battle had been decisive; they had the victory they desperately needed to obscure the awful loss at Hlobane just twenty-four hours earlier.

CHAPTER 14

The Second Invasion, 31 May – 4 July 1879

Too many cooks spoil the pudding.[1]

LIEUTENANT CURLING RA

Following the battle of Khambula the Zulu capacity to mount a serious offensive against the British was broken. At the opposite end of the country, the Zulus had also been defeated at Gingindlovu and their total casualties since Isandlwana now numbered over 5,000 dead with countless numbers wounded. All the strategic advantages that King Cetshwayo had won at Isandlwana were irretrievably lost and the tide of war turned decisively against him. The king desperately tried to reopen diplomatic contacts with the British in a final attempt to discover what terms they would accept for peace, but both Chelmsford and Sir Bartle Frere needed a decisive military victory to avenge Isandlwana.

With his campaign in tatters after the shattering defeat at Isandlwana, Chelmsford was determined to defeat Cetshwayo without risking another humiliation. To this end he began to assemble the largest field force that Britain had sent against an enemy since the Crimean War. A total of 23,500 men were to be pitted against the remnants of the once invincible Zulu army, whose numbers had dwindled to below a demoralized 20,000. This time Chelmsford was not taking any chances.

There was an impression among the soldiers scattered along the Natal border that very little was being done during the aftermath of Isandlwana. In fact, five days after the battle Chelmsford had sent a telegram to the War Office requesting immediate reinforcements, specifying at least three infantry and two cavalry regiments and another company of engineers. He followed this telegram with a report to the Duke of Cambridge, indicating his temporary depression by requesting a successor for both himself and Sir Bartle Frere:

Might I suggest to Your Royal Highness the advisability of sending out a Major General who will be competent to succeed me not only as Commanding the Forces, but also as Lt. Governor & High Commissioner should anything happen to Sir B. Frere.[2]

Once he had recovered his composure and become focused on the second invasion, he appears to have completely forgotten the report. Conversely Sir Garnet Wolseley recognized the career opportunity and, eager for a field command, volunteered his services within days of learning of the Isandlwana defeat. The result of Chelmsford's hasty missive was that reinforcements were rushed to South Africa and General Sir Garnet Wolseley was appointed to take over from both Chelmsford and Frere but, due to the slowness of communications and transport, the new commander could not arrive for some time yet.

For the second invasion Chelmsford planned on making a two-pronged attack using two divisions. The first division would advance along the coast using troops already in place from Pearson's original Coastal Column and supplemented by the re-equipped Eshowe relief column. It was under the command of Major General H.H. Crealock. Chelmsford's main fighting force, designated the Second Division, would advance from the north-west along the intended route of the previous Centre Column but avoiding the battlefield of Isandlwana, where the dead still lay unburied. The Second Division consisted largely of inexperienced troops fresh out from England and was commanded by the recently arrived Crimean veteran Major General Newdigate. Like Glyn before him, Newdigate was to have little or no responsibility as the column would be accompanied by Chelmsford and his staff. His command was composed of men of the 2/21st, 1/24th, 58th and 94th regiments and was supported by artillery, engineers and colonial volunteers. Just before the invasion, Newdigate met with a riding accident but gamely insisted on retaining command. With his leg encased in plaster and in obvious pain, Newdigate was lifted on and off his saddle during the month-long advance and was even able to participate in the battle of Ulundi.

The one force that had been lacking during the first invasion was cavalry; accordingly, a new cavalry division was formed consisting of the 1st (King's) Dragoon Guards and the 17th Lancers, commanded by Major General Marshall – according to one witness they were all dressed in 'booted overalls and gold lace all complete like a lot of damned tenors in an opera'.[3] The fourth general sent by the Duke of Cambridge to assist Chelmsford was Major General the Honourable Sir Henry Clifford VC, who was appointed Inspector General of Line Communication and Base. He was resentful that his authority ended at the Zululand border and became a thorn in Chelmsford's side with his tactlessness and constant criticism. Conversely, ever mindful of Colonel Wood's unflinching support and willingness to take risks in the face of overwhelming odds, Chelmsford promoted Wood to the local rank of brigadier general and his column was redesignated the Flying Column. Wood was given full command of the Flying Column and ordered to advance in tandem with the Second Division to Ulundi.

The presence of so many generals in support of Chelmsford provoked cynical comment from many officers. Lieutenant Curling RA wrote home:

> Col. Wood's Column marches a few miles ahead of us. It is a pity we are not organised like him but we consist of Generals with large staffs; too many cooks spoil the pudding and we have no less than five generals (including two Brigadiers) with us.[4]

Curling's commanding officer, Lieutenant Colonel Harness, also commented on the top-heavy nature of the staff:

> There is a tremendous staff: all Lord Chelmsford's and General Newdigate's. Indeed the whole thing has taken such large proportions that it makes one rather sad and wish for the old days when two or at most three tents formed the headquarters camp; now it is as large as a regiment.[5]

The second invasion commenced on 31 May. So far Chelmsford had little more than a series of serious setbacks to show for all his efforts and Zululand was still unconquered. On 1 June a further unimaginable disaster beset Chelmsford when the Zulus killed the 22-year-old Louis Napoleon, Prince Imperial of France, an exile to England and recently appointed to Chelmsford's staff as a civilian observer. The South African correspondent of Le Figaro, Paul Deléage, neatly summed up this curious appointment:

> After all, what's the Prince supposed to be doing in this row? He'll get no credit from us, and I can't see what good it's to do him in his own country, unless he goes back a cripple – and even then![6]

But who was this enigmatic young prince who considered himself to be next in line to the title of Napoleon, and what was he doing in Africa supporting a British invasion of Zululand? His pedigree was not quite as French as France might have expected, for his family line reveals him to be half British.[7] The prince had attended the Military Academy at Woolwich where he ensured that every physical feat was carried to excess; he was immediately noted for his extravagance and white-hot enthusiasm. Louis had passed out seventh but, being French, he was not permitted to take a commission in the British Army.

When the Zulu War first broke out, not even the prince had thought it worth going to. It was hardly a war; it was merely a skirmish against black warriors and nothing more than a punitive expedition. Then came the slaughter at Isandlwana and the affair grew 'serious' overnight. Since so many of his comrades were going to the war the prince worked on Sir

Lintorn Simmons, Governor of the Royal Military Academy at Woolwich, for permission to join them. He badgered his mother, the Empress Eugénie, to such a point that she actually visited the War Office in secret to plead his cause. With Queen Victoria's tacit approval, the decision he desperately wanted then arrived; the prince would leave for Zululand 'in the capacity of a spectator'.

The young prince quickly frustrated those charged with his care. Even when attached to Lord Chelmsford's staff, he soon exasperated his senior officers, including Colonel Buller. He displayed a penchant for over-enthusiastically giving chase to lone Zulus without authority, putting his own life, and that of others, at unnecessary risk; accordingly he was confined to camp. On the morning of 1 June, he had persuaded his super-visory officer, Major Harrison, to overlook the restriction on his movement and allow him to accompany a small sketching party.

Accompanied by Lieutenant Carey and an escort of six members of Bettington's Horse, the prince set out from Chelmsford's headquarters to sketch the territory through which Chelmsford's second invasion would pass. The route had previously been declared free of Zulus by a cavalry patrol and the party was accompanied by a friendly Zulu scout, a normal procedure for a routine sketching mission. The party had intended to meet six mounted BaSotho troopers to bolster their force but the two groups missed each other and the prince's party continued into Zululand. At about midday the group paused on a hill overlooking the valley of the Tshotshozi river. From here they spotted an apparently deserted Zulu homestead near the river and rode down with the intention of examining the Zulu huts and making coffee. The small cluster of huts was surrounded on three sides by a fully grown mealie plantation. The question of command now arose. Carey spoke French and was used to the prince's company, and though Carey was the only officer in the party it appears that he allowed the prince to exercise a token command. Carey would have appreciated the prince's importance and the prince would doubtless have enjoyed the unofficial privilege of giving certain routine commands.

Having checked that the Zulu homestead was abandoned, the party off-saddled; coffee was brewed and the men relaxed while the prince and Carey chatted. The safety of the group was left to the scout who was instructed to watch the surrounding area. Even though the reinvasion was well under way, Carey would certainly have known that the Zulus employed a system of fast-moving scouting parties to relay intelligence back to the Zulu commanders. One such group, from a combination of the iNgobamakhosi, uMbonambi and uNokhenke regiments that coincidentally included one of the king's personal attendants, Mnukwa, was in the area and decided to investigate the resting British patrol. The Zulus had first seen the prince's party from a distance and, using the cover of the ground, successfully drew near to the resting soldiers. The Zulus were able to use the protection of the head-high mealie crop to close in. At this point the scout reported to Carey that he had seen faces in the mealies; unperturbed by the information, Carey allowed the prince to give the order for the horses to be gathered together and saddled. This took a few minutes and it appears that no one thought the scout's information warranted any immediate action. Once the horses were saddled the prince gave the order to mount. At this critical moment the Zulus fired a close-range volley at the mounting soldiers and then charged among them; the patrol was put to flight and in the confusion every man sought to protect himself as best he could. Amazingly the Zulus' volley missed the soldiers, but Trooper Rogers's horse had taken fright, leaving the trooper helpless. The Zulus fell upon him; they chased him through the huts and killed him. Trooper Abel was equally unlucky; he was spurring his horse away when a bullet struck his spine; he fell from his horse to share the same fate as Rogers. The black scout darted away on foot but was quickly caught and killed.

As the Zulus opened fire on the patrol the prince tried to mount his horse, but something was seriously wrong; he had always been regarded as one of Europe's pre-eminent horsemen but earlier that day he had been seen experiencing difficulties mounting his horse. Sir William Beresford had witnessed the first occasion and initially commented that the prince's horse was too high for him, but then suggested that the difficulties were solely due to the tight trousers favoured by the prince. Only a few hours later the prince failed to perform this routine but now life-saving action. With the remainder of Carey's party mounted and galloping out of danger the prince desperately tried vaulting into the saddle but instead of grasping the saddle, he grabbed the flimsy holster strap, which gave way under the strain. He fell heavily to the ground. Dazed, he managed to regain his feet as the Zulus closed around him. He ran towards a dried river bed and turned to face the Zulus; he drew his revolver and fired several shots before a spear struck him in the thigh. The prince withdrew the spear to use it as a weapon but the Zulus quickly overwhelmed him before spearing him to death. The Zulus may have realized that they had killed an officer as several warriors took the opportunity to blood their spear blades in the prince's body; the seventeen stab wounds subsequently gave rise to the myth that in death, the prince had bravely 'faced his foe', just as he had prophesied.

In the ensuing panic Carey and the surviving troopers rode for their lives, only reining in about a half-mile from the scene. There was little Carey could do; to return would mean certain death and without a doubt the prince was already dead. He decided to report the awful loss of the prince to Chelmsford and set off for camp, only to meet up with Buller who was also returning from a patrol. Carey blurted out what had happened to an incredulous Buller who ferociously responded with the words, 'You deserve to be shot, and I hope you will be. I could shoot you myself.' Buller was later to ameliorate his views; he knew Carey had a sound military reputation whereas the prince had wilfully disobeyed his orders on several occasions.

The death of the Prince Imperial came as a severe shock to Chelmsford and the whole invasion force was stunned; the immeasurable shock waves reverberated through both the British and French nations and across the British Empire; the news even overshadowed Chelmsford's earlier disaster at Isandlwana. Charles Norris-Newman, the noted war correspondent for the *London Standard*, wrote at the time:

But various causes, his rank and misfortunes, his connection with the British army, the actual incidents of the fatality arising out of the duties of the expedition, and lastly, the subsequent proceedings in connection with the inquiry by court martial, all combined to invest it with a special pathos and interest, almost world-wide.[8]

Nevertheless, fearing that the British soldiers would be less than respectful to a Frenchman, not to say the grandson of Napoleon Bonaparte, the black-bordered special order specifically laid out how the troops were to behave and not display any disrespect or anti-French sentiment.

The senior military establishment immediately went on the defensive but this time the lowly culprit was obvious; the junior officer in charge of the patrol, the French-speaking and experienced Lieutenant Jahleel Carey of the 98th Regiment, had inexplicably abandoned the prince to a small force of Zulus. His court martial was quickly arranged. Others, though, knew of the prince's blatant irresponsibility and realized that he alone was responsible for his own demise. When the details surrounding the incident became known, Carey's brother officers softened their views. After all, the significance of the incident arose only because one of the casualties was the Prince Imperial; had this aristocratic tourist not been present, or not exercised command of the patrol, or if Troopers Abel and Rogers had been the only casualties, the minor rout of an insignificant sketching party would quickly have been forgotten. As far as Chelmsford was concerned the Zululand campaign had already witnessed, on several notable occasions, the unpleasant spectacle of officers abandoning their men to the enemy. At Isandlwana two colonial officers, Lieutenants Avery and Holcroft, both disappeared from the battlefield; they were followed by Lieutenant Adendorff whose mysterious disappearance at both Isandlwana and Rorke's Drift preceded that of Lieutenants Coghill and Melvill, who both departed from Isandlwana under unverified circumstances. Rorke's Drift had been abandoned by Major Spalding and had then seen Captain Stevenson, his NCOs and the NNC abandon the mission station just as the Zulus were about to attack. The case of Ntombe Drift, where

Lieutenant Harward deserted his men during a Zulu attack, had yet to come to official notice. Meanwhile an example was needed to bring home the message that officers must remain with their men, and Carey was the perfect scapegoat.

Carey's case was unique because the man he deserted was a member of the French aristocracy who had been specially authorized to join Chelmsford's force by none other than Queen Victoria. It is unlikely that more than a few of the rank and file even knew of the prince's attachment to the army while he was still alive yet Archibald Forbes summed up the common reaction of indignation and sentiment when he wrote, 'throughout the force there was a thrill of sorrow for the poor gallant lad, a burning sense of shame that he should have been so miserably left to his fate, and a deep sympathy for the forlorn widow in England'.[9]

In due course Carey was found guilty by court martial on a charge of misbehaviour before the enemy, and was sent home to be sentenced. The findings were forwarded to London for confirmation but the Judge Advocate General, J.C. O'Dowd, was unable to ratify the decision, as the proceedings had been rushed – the officers of the court martial had not been sworn in according to military regulations. He also questioned the assertion that Carey had been in charge of the patrol. Meanwhile the British press had learned more about Chelmsford's blunders and his staff's quest for scapegoats to take the blame; now the death of the Prince Imperial bore too many similarities as, yet again, a junior officer was to take the blame for the faulty decisions of senior officers. The British press protectively gathered around Carey who duly became a *cause célèbre*. When he arrived at Southampton, still under arrest, the mayor, the city council and a large crowd spurred on by a brass band met his ship to express their support. It is possible that such a public display of public opinion persuaded the Judge Advocate General to look at Carey's case with greater care. Following a request from the Prince Imperial's mother, the Empress Eugénie, Queen Victoria intervened.

Within weeks, the decision of the court martial was refused ratification and its verdict was annulled. Carey returned to full duty with his regiment.

There is no evidence that he was treated by his fellow officers other than with respect and proper courtesy. He died in 1883 of peritonitis while still serving in India and many historians have written that Carey died after being kicked by his horse; there is no contemporary evidence to support this myth.

In the military context, the prince's death amounted to little more than a scandal; it was an insignificant incident and had no bearing on the conduct or outcome of the campaign. The prince's body was returned to England for burial, firstly at Chislehurst and then later at Farnborough Abbey in Hampshire.

The advance on Ulundi

By March a constant flow of greatly needed supplies and reinforcements had arrived in Durban; these enabled Chelmsford to regain his enthusiasm for the campaign. Once he had recovered his composure and become involved in the second invasion, he appears to have completely forgotten the letter he wrote on 1 February to the Duke of Cambridge requesting a replacement. For his part, Garnet Wolseley, eager for a field command, had volunteered his services within days of learning of the Isandlwana defeat and was appointed to take over. Meanwhile Chelmsford assembled his forces. With many more troops under his command than were available for the initial invasion of Zululand, Chelmsford was soon ready to mount a fresh invasion. His ultimate intention was to engage the Zulu army – preferably near the king's royal homestead at Ulundi.

Chelmsford and his staff had learned much from their previous mistakes and the two huge columns now began the slow haul towards Ulundi; as they progressed they would establish a chain of fortified supply posts to guard their lines of advance. Chelmsford planned for three substantial forts to be built along his route, Forts Newdigate, Marshall and Evelyn. These would be garrisoned by small detachments of infantry and mounted troops; those detailed for this task would strongly resent missing the anticipated British victory at Ulundi.

On 29 March Crealock's First Division crossed the Tugela river at the site of Fort Pearson. Two nearby deserted Zulu homesteads, at emaNgweni and Hlalangubo, were partially destroyed. Apart from these two minor successes, the First Division achieved little but experienced all the depredations suffered by the earlier column under Colonel Pearson. There were too few wagons to enable stores and equipment to be moved at the speed required and the high mortality rate among the overworked trek oxen and mules merely added to the problem. There were no arrangements in place to deal with dead animals, so they were abandoned on the roadside to rot in the heat; their effluent duly polluted the water-courses and swarms of flies infested the men's food. Disease among the animals brought disease to the men and dysentery, enteric fever and typhoid rapidly weakened the force. The slow progress and military ineffective-ness of 'Crealock's Crawlers', as they were popularly known, was unavoid-able, making their contribution to the reinvasion of Zululand minimal.

For the northerly Second Division to advance as planned, Chelms-ford urgently needed to repossess the wagons abandoned following the disaster at Isandlwana. Many of these fully serviceable wagons still littered the battlefield and had been ignored by the Zulus so, on 21 May, the cavalry division rode to Isandlwana and recovered forty-five undamaged wagons; at the same time a token attempt was made to bury the dead in the immediate area of the shattered camp, and this part of the mission was successful although the summer rains would undo much of their work, necessitating further burials. Colonel Glyn of the 24th Regiment had instructed the burial party to leave the bodies of the 24th until the regiment could return to Isandlwana to bury its own.

All the while, King Cetshwayo watched helplessly as the three British columns moved inexorably towards the Zulu border. Many Zulus were now openly reluctant to gather round the king as they realized that their defeat was inevitable. The initial attempt in May to regroup the Zulu army had met with partial success, perhaps due to a rumour that swept across Zululand that those warriors surrendering would be castrated and their wives given to the soldiers. However, as the British advanced ever closer, greater numbers rallied to the king's call to arms. A number of Zulu chiefs were disillusioned with war and in anticipation of defeat, Prince Makwendu kaMpande, one of Cetshwayo's junior brothers, had already surrendered himself and his family to Crealock. He was later followed by Prince Dabulamanzi, the commander at Rorke's Drift, who along with Mavumengwana kaGodide, a commander at Isandlwana, established a diplomatic relationship with Crealock; more defections along the coastal regions were rumoured and some chiefs declared that they were unable to fight as their *imizi* were overcrowded with wounded. King Cetshwayo called an urgent meeting of chiefs and all agreed to commence negotiations with the British – only to have them thwarted by Chelmsford.

Meanwhile the end of May saw the Second Division assembled along the banks of the Ncome river near Koppie Alleen. They were joined on 31 May by Chelmsford and crossed the border into Zululand, as did Wood to his north; the reinvasion of Zululand now began in earnest. Wood's Flying Column saw its first action during the morning of 5 June when a reconnaissance patrol of irregular cavalry chanced upon a large Zulu force occupying the base of eZungeni hill overlooking the Upoko river. The irregulars approached the Zulus and commenced sporadic fire into the Zulu position whereupon the Zulus, vastly outnumbering the irregulars, retaliated by advancing on them in their classic 'horns' attack formation; realizing they were in peril of being surrounded, the irregulars rapidly retreated. The sound of firing alerted a nearby troop of 17th Lancers who rushed to the scene; this would be the very first engagement in Zululand for the Lancers and all were 'keen as mustard' to bring further honour to the regiment by routing the Zulus.[10] Like many before them, the Lancers did not understand Zulu tactics and deployed using the classic cavalry tactic of charging in line. The Zulus may have been impressed as the cavalry repeatedly swept past them but it was impossible for the Lancers to engage the Zulus. The terrain was totally unsuitable for cavalry and the Zulus held their ground, taking casual potshots at the riders as they swept by. The regiment then took its first loss when a Zulu marksman, using a Martini-Henry rifle, shot and killed Lieutenant Frith, the regiment's adjutant. The sudden and unexpected loss of this popular young officer brought the action to an abrupt halt and, carrying Frith's body with them, they returned to camp.

The Second Division established Fort Newdigate near the Nondweni river in order to rest the men and allow supplies to be brought forward. While at Fort Newdigate Chelmsford and his staff learned the cost of relying on so many inexperienced troops: following a false alarm one night, nervous sentries fired a number of shots into the darkness which brought the whole column to an immediate state of readiness. In the mistaken belief that they were under a serious Zulu attack the infantry opened fire, followed by the artillery who opened with indiscriminate shelling of the surrounding area. By the time it was realized that there was no attack eight men had been wounded and several horses were killed in the one-sided firefight. The incident nearly killed a recent recipient of the Victoria Cross, Lieutenant Chard, who was on picket duty occupying a forward shelter trench with his detachment. During the confusion rifle fire had been directed at Chard's position in the mistaken belief that the Zulus held it. Chard and his men threw themselves into the shallow trench; they survived unscathed and one can only wonder as to the exchange of views once normality had been restored. Exercising patriotic restraint, those war correspondents present chose not to report the incident.

The column marched on to Mthonjaneni, only 17 miles from Ulundi. Here Chelmsford formed a strongly entrenched base camp and garrisoned it with some of the Colonial volunteers and the 1/24th, much to the disappointment of their commanding officer, Colonel Glyn. Leaving his cumbersome wagon train and spare animals, Chelmsford took the remainder of his force and marched on towards Ulundi; now only the Emakosini valley, the 'place of kings' and burial sites of Cetshwayo's ancestors, lay between Chelmsford's invasion force and the king's royal homestead at Ulundi. King Cetshwayo tried repeatedly to call a halt to the invasion but all his attempts were deliberately ignored by Chelmsford; only the final battle at Ulundi would satisfy the British. Zulu home-steads along the route of advance were burnt to the ground and their cattle driven back to the army slaughterers. On 26 June a British force attacked along the Emakosini valley destroying royal homesteads; at one, esiKlebheni, they destroyed the *inkatha ye sizwe ya'kwaZulu*, the sacred coil of the nation that dated back to the time of King Shaka; it was the national symbol of unity and its destruction was a serious omen to the king. They also burned every hut and village in sight and destroyed vast amounts of mealies. This attack cleared the path to the Mthonjaneni heights overlooking the White Mfolozi river; Ulundi was now visible through the smoky haze in the middle distance.

Still optimistic that he could halt the British, King Cetshwayo sent two of his royal envoys, Nkisimane and Mfunzi, to treat with Chelms-ford; as a gesture they brought with them the Prince Imperial's sword, taken as booty from his body on 1 June. The envoys sought terms required for a Zulu surrender. Chelmsford informed the envoys that he required the surrender of all British arms captured at Isandlwana and gave them until 3 July for the king's reply. Knowing full well that the king could not possibly comply with this ultimatum because the Martini-Henry rifles were now spread across the Zulu kingdom, Chelmsford continued his advance to the White Mfolozi river where he consolidated his army's position and prepared his troops for the defeat of the Zulus. Chelmsford was under no illusion: he desperately needed the vindication for Isandlwana that this final battle would bring. Only then could he return to Britain with his reputation intact – but knowing he still had to answer to Parlia-ment, the press and the public for his previous defeats and losses. Chelms-ford was acutely aware of his predicament and wrote to the Secretary of State for War, Colonel Frederick Stanley, on this very issue:

> As it is more than probable with such a large number of newspaper corre-spondents in camp, that many false impressions may be circulated and sent home regarding our operation ... Their presence in the camp will make no difference to myself, and you may depend upon my pursuing

'the even tenour of my way', uninfluenced by the knowledge that I am surrounded by those who will not be sparing in their criticism if everything is not rearranged exactly to their liking.[11]

With the column steadily approaching Ulundi, Chelmsford received news from London that Sir Garnet Wolseley had replaced him; this was the government's response to his earlier plea to be replaced. Now that Chelmsford was on the verge of victory the news came as a psychological setback, but within days he learned that all was not lost as Wolseley was being thwarted in his attempt to take command. Wolseley's intention of being landed by boat at a location only one day's ride from the column failed due to stormy weather, and his boat had to return to Durban, leaving Wolseley no option but to chase after the column on horseback. Wolseley's misfortune made Chelmsford even more determined to press on with the attack on Ulundi; only then could he resign with honour. Wolseley nevertheless put Chelmsford under even greater pressure when on 30 June he telegraphed to him:

Concentrate your forces immediately, undertake no operations and flash back your moves. Astonished at not hearing from you.[12]

Aware of Wolseley's temporary inability to join the column, Chelmsford merely acknowledged receipt of the message. King Cetshwayo was also in a delicate position; when the envoys, Nkisimane and Mfunzi, returned to brief the king, they were prevented by the king's own advisers from reporting back to him. Like Chelmsford, King Cetshwayo and his advisers needed this battle. Surrender to the British was not an option for the Zulu king; he knew he must suffer a military defeat in order to retain his credibility and bargaining position after the battle.

For the British soldiers, now camped only 5 miles from the Zulu army at Fort Nolela, sometimes mistakenly referred to as Fort Victoria, their anxiety was proportionately matched by their inexperience. Both sides were now concentrated for battle and it was impossible for the nervous soldiers not to be aware of the Zulus. During daylight, British water-collecting parties came under sporadic Zulu rifle fire from the far river bank and at night the sounds of Zulu chanting and battle preparations could be clearly heard. Late on 3 July, King Cetshwayo attempted one last call for peace: as a desperate gesture he sent a herd of his finest cattle towards Chelmsford's camp but the warriors guarding the river, the uKhandempemvu, indignantly sent them back – they wanted to fight the British invader. Chelmsford was later to write of the incident, 'A large herd of white cattle was observed being driven from the King's Kraal towards us but was driven back again shortly afterwards.'[13]

CHAPTER 15

The Battle of Ulundi

A bloody but barren victory.[1]

JOHN WILLIAM COLENSO

On 3 July Chelmsford dispatched Colonel Buller with a strong mounted force of some 500 mounted men from the 1st Squadron Mounted Infantry, the Frontier Light Horse, Transvaal Rangers, Baker's Horse, Natal Light Horse, and the Edendale Troop of the mounted black auxiliaries. Buller's main objective was to reconnoitre the terrain and locate a suitable site for the final battle; he was also to ascertain the Zulu dispositions. The Mahlabatini plain, with Ulundi and its vastly sprawling conglomeration of hundreds of huts at its hub, stretched between two distant ranges of hills and Buller was especially interested in a small rise just 1 mile from the king's homestead. As Buller approached the grassy plain he detached sixty men of the Transvaal Rangers under Commandant Raaf to serve as a rearguard.

Uncharacteristically, Buller was led into a carefully prepared Zulu ambush near the Mbilane stream when a party of Zulu scouts suddenly appeared from the waist-high grass about 200 yards from him and then ran off towards the king's homestead. Buller's men gave chase. Buller's ADC, Captain Sir Thomas Fermour-Hesketh, shouted out that he saw another body of Zulus hiding in the grass ahead. Buller ordered his men to halt and as they reined in, some 4,000 Zulus, under the command of Chief Zibhebhu, rose up around them. The Zulu trap had been sprung, albeit prematurely; the Zulus had plaited and woven grass into a series of ropes, specially designed to trip the horses, which they rapidly pulled in to tighten. Buller's men managed to extricate themselves before the ropes could entrap them but the flanks of Zulus were already rushing to surround them. Another group of Zulus armed with captured Martini-Henry rifles then fired a volley from about 50 yards' distance which panicked several of the horses. Sergeant Fitzmaurice of the 1/24th Regiment, attached to the Mounted Infantry, fell and became trapped beneath his wounded horse; two troopers, Pearce of the Frontier Light Horse and Peacock of the Natal Light Horse, were shot and killed outright. Trooper Raubenheim of the Frontier Light Horse was mortally wounded and fell from his horse.

Captain D'Arcy of the Frontier Light Horse immediately rode back to where Raubenheim was lying on the ground. D'Arcy dismounted and, while holding the reins of his now frightened horse, helped him to his feet. D'Arcy then hauled the wounded trooper up onto his horse behind him. With the leading Zulus almost upon them the terrified horse managed a few yards and threw both riders. Though severely winded by the fall, D'Arcy rapidly remounted but was forced to abandon Raubenheim to his fate – his body was later found cut up by the Zulus for their *muti* or medicine.[2] Nearby, Lord Beresford and Sergeant O'Toole of the Frontier Light Horse had seen Sergeant Fitzmaurice fall and both dashed to his aid; with O'Toole dismounted and pushing Fitzmaurice onto the horse, Lord Beresford managed to get Fitzmaurice to hold onto him and galloped off to safety, though O'Toole barely escaped with his life. For their gallantry D'Arcy, Lord Beresford and O'Toole received the Victoria Cross. The bravery of Sergeant Major Simeon Kambula of the Edendale Troop, who determinedly held off a group of charging Zulus, was also recognized with the award of the Distinguished Conduct Medal.

Buller's men were forced to ride for their lives and near the kwa-Nodwengu homestead they were reinforced by Raaf's men who poured volleys into the pursuing Zulus. The fleeing riders managed to recross the river to safety and the Zulus withdrew. For the soldiers about to go into battle, the level of the Zulus' spirited attack left them in no doubt that the following day was not to be a foregone conclusion. That night the Zulu army completed its noisy and ritual preparations for battle, which added to the anxiety of the British, few of whom slept. It is known that King Cetshwayo departed from Ulundi just before dawn.

Lord Chelmsford and his men planned to cross the river to meet the Zulus at Ulundi for what all hoped would be the final battle. The newly reconstituted and inexperienced 1/24th Regiment was to be held in reserve, two companies already having been left at Fort Marshall, and the remaining five would be held at Fort Nolela. The regiment's soldiers were displeased at not being able to avenge their defeat at Isandlwana but Chelmsford was not prepared to take completely inexperienced soldiers into a major battle; they would have to be content with watching from afar.

It was from King Cetshwayo's dusty and impoverished capital at Ulundi that Britain's sophisticated political and military domination across South Africa had been so suddenly and seriously challenged. Situated on the Mahlabatini plain just 55 miles from the site of the inconceivable Zulu victory over Lord Chelmsford's force at Isandlwana, Ulundi consisted of an estimated 1,500 huts spread over an area later measured to be no more than 90 acres in total with the king's personal quarters, the *ikhanda*, located centrally. Another nine *amakhanda* were located within 2 miles of Ulundi. Movement through Ulundi was via a labyrinth of passageways radiating out from the royal household which dominated the capital. During the three weeks leading up to 4 July, the population of Ulundi had swollen by the influx of some 20,000 warriors responding to the king's call to resist the British invasion. Now most of the women, children and other non-combatants had begun to move away towards the protection of the surrounding hills to the north and east; carrying their bundled possessions, they clogged the tracks through the bush in their desperation to escape the consequences of the forthcoming battle.

At 4 a.m. on the morning of 4 July Chelmsford's 5,000 men camped around Fort Nolela were roused from their sleep and as dawn broke at 6 a.m. they set off in one column towards Ulundi; it was the largest force deployed by Chelmsford for any battle during the Zulu War. At 6.45 a.m. and unopposed by the Zulus, this cumbersome force waded across the shallow White Mfolozi river and then, in a tightly packed column, marched towards the previously reconnoitred small rise in the middle of the Mahlabatini plain. All the while, Buller's riders patrolled the high ground along the route. To protect the slow-moving column, mounted men rode out to cover the column's front and flanks while the 17th Lancers covered the rear. The cumbersome column enclosed Chelmsford's headquarters staff and the ammunition and entrenching-tool carts, as well as the Royal Artillery's guns, although these were positioned so as to enable them to come into action on each face without delay. With the sprawl of huts that was Ulundi now in view less than 3 miles distant, the Zulus could be seen forming up in opposition to the advancing column; visibility over the Zulu army's position was still partially obscured by drifting smoke from a thousand Zulu campfires and from the early morning mist hanging over the Mbilane stream that wound its way between the two armies. Many thousands of Zulus could also be seen assembling on the more distant hilltops to the north. Chelmsford ordered the advancing British column to 'form square', which it did, turning slowly and menacingly to face the advancing Zulus. A few minutes later the British gained the high ground they sought and settled down to await the expected Zulu charge.

The assembled Zulu army was to the north and east of the square, in the direction of Ulundi, and totalled over 15,000 men with another 5,000 along the hills in reserve; all were formed up in regimental order and began to advance steadily for their first attack. Just as Chelmsford had anticipated, the Zulus were relying on their traditional attack formation and their 'horns' or flanks began to encircle the square. All the Zulu regiments that had fought in the previous battles were present and command at Ulundi appears to have been shared between Chief Mnyamana Buthelezi, Chief Ziwedu and Chief Ntshingwayo kaMahole

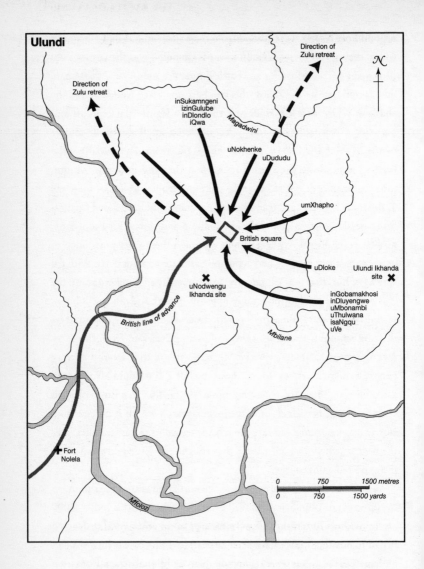

Ulundi

Direction of Zulu retreat

Direction of Zulu retreat

N

inSukamngeni
izinGulube
inDlondlo
iQwa

uNokhenke

uDududu

Magadwini

umXhapho

British square

uDloke

Ulundi Ikhanda site ✕

inGobamakhosi
inDluyengwe
uMbonambi
uThulwana
isaNgqu
uVe

✕ uNodwengu
Ikhanda site

British line of advance

Mbilane

✚ Fort
Nolela

Mfolozi

| 0 | 750 | 1500 metres |
| 0 | 750 | 1500 yards |

(the victor of Isandlwana), while the vigorous Chief Zibhebhu kaMaphitha of the Mandlakazi commanded the left horn. A captured Zulu prisoner commented:

> All the army was present today. We had very sick hearts in the fight when we saw how strong the white army was, and we were startled by the number of horsemen.[3]

The Zulus' advance slowed down as it approached the square. Chelmsford presumed this indicated their reluctance to fight so at 8.20 a.m. Buller and his mounted troops moved out of the square and, using Buller's proven tactic of provocation, rode to within 100 yards of the massed Zulu force and raked its leading ranks with several volleys of rifle fire. This blatant and bloody taunt enraged the Zulus, who charged; Buller and his men rapidly withdrew back into the relative safety of the square, which enabled the artillery and riflemen to commence volley fire. The men forming the square were prepared for the imminent onslaught; the infantry were lined up in four ranks, two kneeling and two standing, with the artillery pieces and Gatling guns sited at the corners of the square and in the centre of the sides.

Battle commenced about 8.45 a.m. with the mounted men on the right and left of the square becoming the first to be committed. The most determined Zulu attack came from the left horn under the command of Chief Zibhebhu. Watching the attack alongside Chelmsford's staff was the war correspondent Melton Prior, who clearly believed that the battle was not at all one-sided:

> I ran down to where the 21st and 58th Regiments were heavily engaged with some Zulus, said to be 6000 strong and 30 deep, who were charging, and it was then that I heard Lord Chelmsford say to the troops, 'Men, fire faster; can't you fire faster?' Now it is not my business to question the wisdom of this remark, but I cannot help contrasting it with Lord Wolseley's well-known order, 'Fire slow, fire slow!' However, the Zulus who charged this corner did not succeed in breaking it; the terrific fire of our

men made them stagger, halt, and fall back in a straggling mass, leaving a
heap of dead and dying on the ground.[4]

For a period of twenty minutes the British rate of fire was so steady and
accurate that the Zulus were unable to get close enough to inflict any
serious damage upon the British line. Another journalist present, Charles
Norris-Newman, wrote that

the Zulus were checked by the heavy, regular and well sustained fire from
the various regiments, which swept the plateau, and gradually brought
the Zulus to a stand, checked by the withering effects of that hail of
bullets, which did such murderous execution as all their efforts could
not prevail.[5]

Chelmsford was especially pleased with the behaviour of the infantry,
until now relatively untried; the men were steady and their firing was well
controlled on all sides of the square. Volley firing by sections was employed
throughout the battle although on several occasions it was necessary to
wait between volleys for the volley smoke to clear. For their part, the
Zulus were unable to inflict much damage to the British square even
though they possessed several hundred Martini-Henry rifles taken from
Isandlwana. Their usual firearms, a collection of antiquated flintlock and
percussion rifles, were never a threat to the British although Chelmsford
was clearly ready for considerable casualties. He wrote:

The fire of the enemy from a few minutes to nine to 9.20 was very heavy,
and many casualties, I regret to say, occurred, but when it is remembered
that within our comparatively small square, all the cavalry, mounted
men, natives, hospital attendants, etc. were packed, it is a matter of
congratulation that they were not heavier.[6]

At about 9 a.m. it became apparent to the British that the Zulus were
becoming disorganized and their enthusiasm to attack the British wall of
fire began to wane; they nevertheless stood their ground in the face of
repeated Martini-Henry volleys, the barrage from the Royal Artillery's

7 and 9 pound guns and from the column's two Gatling guns. A number of Zulus had managed to get to within 30 yards of the British line, but under such a hail of fire they could not sustain their attack. As Melton Prior recalled,

A bullet banged into one of our native allies close to us and rolled him over. By the way, it was very funny to see these men lying flat on the ground, with their shields covering their backs. Another bullet killed a horse behind us and made him jump at least three feet in the air. Then all at once there appeared to be a perfect hailstorm of bullets in our direction, and we both wriggled on our knees, until one in particular passed between us with a nasty 'phew', and my friend exclaimed, 'My God, Prior, that was close.'[7]

The attack soon began to falter and it was evident to the British that the Zulus were beaten; many warriors took what cover they could in the long grass and some brave individuals crawled back towards the soldiers to return fire. However, large numbers began to leave the battlefield and this only served to weaken the resolve of those further back and previously keen to engage the British. With the Zulu attack controlled, Chelmsford again sought to inflict the maximum number of casualties upon the Zulus and, as at Khambula and Gingindlovu, he ordered Buller and his mounted troops, along with the 17th Lancers, out of the square to harass the retreating Zulus. Chelmsford wrote:

The fire from the Artillery and Infantry was so effective that, within half an hour, signs of hesitation were perceivable in the movements of the enemy: I then directed Colonel Drury-Lowe to take out the 17th Lancers, passing out by the rear face he led his regiment towards the Nodwengu Kraal, dispersing and killing those who had not time to reach the shelter of the Kraal or the bush below, then wheeling to the right charged through the Zulus who, in full flight, were endeavouring to reach the lower slopes of the mountains beyond.

Numbers of the enemy in this direction who had not taken part in the

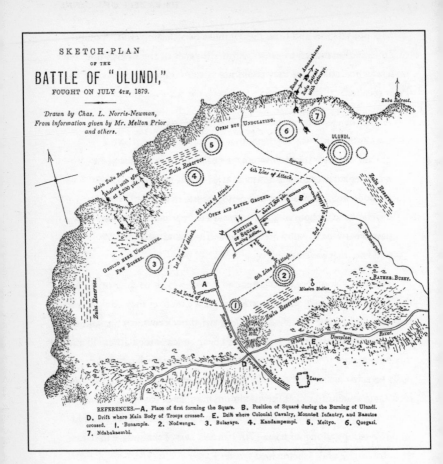

SKETCH-PLAN

OF THE

BATTLE OF "ULUNDI,"

FOUGHT ON JULY 4TH, 1879.

Drawn by Chas. L. Norris-Newman,
From information given by Mr. Melton Prior
and others.

REFERENCES.—**A.** Place of first forming the Square. **B.** Position of Square during the Burning of Ulundi. **D.** Drift where Main Body of Troops crossed. **E.** Drift where Colonial Cavalry, Mounted Infantry, and Basutos crossed. **1.** Bonampis. **2.** Nodwenga. **3.** Bulaxayo. **4.** Kandampempi. **5.** Meityo. **6.** Quegazi. **7.** Ndabakaambi.

actual attack were now firing and momentarily strengthened by those fleeing were enabled to pour in a considerable fire on the advancing Lancers below them. Our cavalry did not halt however until the whole of the lower ground was swept and some 150 of the enemy killed: many of those they had passed in their speed, had collected in a ravine to their rear, these were attacked and destroyed by our mounted natives.[8]

The Lancers attacked with great enthusiasm; they were still smarting from their previous failed clash against the Zulus when they lost their adjutant, Lieutenant Frith. This time they could charge across open country and they fell upon the Zulus, showing no mercy as they speared and hacked the fleeing and wounded warriors. The Lancers nevertheless took some casualties; the most notable was Captain the Hon. Wyatt-Edgell who was shot dead. Their commanding officer, Colonel Drury-Lowe, wrote of the pursuit with professional pride:

The pursuit was carried out in a most determined manner by five troops of the 17th Lancers and 24 men of the King's Dragoon Guards (one troop remained inside the square unknown to me). The Zulus fled in every direction and were pursued for a distance of some three miles across the slope of the hills before mentioned, very many being killed with the lance, which proved their decided superiority to the sword in pursuit. It would, I think, be invidious to point out any particular officer or man, when all, I think, showed the same eagerness to reach the enemy, and rode with the greatest determination into the scattered Zulus, for the most time under a galling fire from the hills, where the enemy formed themselves into groups and kept up an incessant fire.[9]

Chelmsford's mounted irregulars then joined the fray and, mindful of the massacre of their colleagues at Isandlwana, trotted among the scattering Zulus shooting them with impunity. One of the Edendale Troop was seen to shoot and wound a warrior and then set about questioning him; having got the answers he sought, the trooper shot the warrior dead.[10] Many warriors lay down in the grass in the hope of escape, knowing that they would be out of range of the riders' swords; but once the immediate area around the square was secured, the Native Contingent was released to kill any wounded or hiding Zulus. The horror of indiscriminate killing continued for another two hours and extended for several miles in all directions until the fleeing Zulus had either escaped or been killed. Major Robinson was a witness to the assegaing of wounded Zulus and requested a correspondent accompanying him not to comment on the slaughter 'or they will think us awful brutes, as bad as we did the Bashi-bazouks'.[11] The Zulu reserves that had occupied the slopes of the surrounding hills were beyond the reach of the cavalry so the 9 pound guns were moved from the rear and front faces of the square to shell them.

It was immediately clear to the men forming the square that the victory had been a decisive one. For Chelmsford, it meant relief from the months of tension he had laboured under since Isandlwana. It was all the more sweet because he had been able to achieve his victory before Sir Garnet Wolseley could take command.

As soon as the last groups of Zulus had been forced back over the hills Chelmsford ordered the destruction by shellfire of King Cetshwayo's royal homestead. With Chelmsford's fighting square still intact, orders were then given for the column's dead to be buried and the casualties tended to. An hour later the column marched forward for half a mile to the Mbilane stream, passing down the same grass slope where Buller's men had been ambushed the day before. After eating a midday meal, the column retraced its steps back to Fort Nolela on the far bank of the White Mfolozi river. The final battle of the Zulu war had lasted just forty minutes. On 20 September the *Graphic* commented:

> Our cavalry ... galloped out in pursuit, and mowed them down on the hill-sides in every direction. It was a brilliant half-hour's work, but much as we may congratulate ourselves, upon the gallant behaviour of our own men, we cannot help feeling some measure of admiration for the determined gallantry of their savage opponents.

The wide-ranging patrols of Lancers began to set fire to the surrounding royal homesteads while others, including Bengough's NNC, continued to track down wounded and hiding Zulus; the ongoing sound of sporadic gunfire evidenced the hunt and execution. Chelmsford then gave his officers permission to ride into Ulundi itself. A race ensued and Lord Beresford was the first into the royal homestead and according to Melton Prior, was nicknamed 'Ulundi Beresford' for his daring dash. The scamper into Ulundi nevertheless resulted in further tragedy for Chelmsford when his interpreter, the Hon William Drummond, disappeared. He was last seen riding through the vast array of huts and to the great concern of those who knew him, all attempts to find him failed; his assagaied and burned body was not found until several months later.

The British ransacked the king's huts and then set fire to Ulundi; those looking for treasure were disappointed for there was nothing of value to loot. All the while the cavalry routed the fleeing Zulus for another hour, killing every warrior they could find. All mounted troops were then recalled back to the square; but not before they had killed about 1,500 Zulu warriors. As was usual following a successful battle, Chelmsford addressed his gathered men and thanked them for their efforts. The entire force then about-turned and with Ulundi now well ablaze, began to march back towards the White Mfolozi river with the band playing 'Rule, Britannia!' and the 'Royal Alliance March'; they passed the battlefield and its glinting rows of expended ammunition cases – later estimated to have amounted to over 35,000 rounds of Martini-Henry ammunition. By the evening the British were all safely back in camp and Chelmsford could relax for the first time in many months.

CHAPTER 16

Beginning of the End

The death of 10,000 Zulus ... defending their hearths and homes.[1]

W.E. GLADSTONE

The Zulu war was over; it had cost the British 76 officers and 1,007 men killed plus a similar number of colonial and black Natal auxiliaries. A further 17 officers and 330 men had died of disease and a further 99 officers and 1,286 men were invalided away from the campaign. Exact figures for Zulu losses are impossible to assess; they certainly lost 10,000 warriors killed in action and conservative estimates suggest that a similar number probably died from their injuries.

Chelmsford had no intention of chasing after King Cetshwayo or remaining in Africa longer than was necessary; capturing the king and restoring normality to Zululand would be thankless tasks, tasks that would occupy Wolseley and his staff for many weeks if not months. Chelmsford was fully aware that before Wolseley could report anything of detriment to him he would already be back in London, and with Ulundi being portrayed by his staff as a brilliant victory, the glory would be his to enjoy.

At Ulundi there was no clearing of the battlefield; for many weeks only deserted and smouldering villages evidenced the once thriving heart of the Zulu nation. The dead bodies of slain Zulus remained where they had fallen and these were left to the predators or to rot and shrivel in the sun. The British roughly estimated that not fewer than 1,500 Zulus had died in the battle for Ulundi while Buller suggested that his mounted men increased the death toll by yet another 500 during the far-ranging Zulu rout. Even after natural scavengers had done their work, skeletons and human bones littered the battlefield for many years. Macabrely, the only attempt to clear the area occurred when an enterprising Natal trader arranged to collect sacks of bones for onward shipment to Durban; they were then sorted for grinding into bone meal but the project came to a halt when the citizens of Durban realized what was happening and strongly opposed this commercial use of human remains.

The replacement Second Division commander for the reinvasion, Major General Henry Hope Crealock, was given a mandate similar to that given to Colonel Pearson except that he was to establish strongly fortified staging posts along his advance and to use these as a springboard to destroy two large Zulu homesteads before supporting the First Division's advance on Ulundi. Having established two forts named Crealock and Chelmsford, he ran into the same problem that dogged the British throughout the campaign, namely lack of wagons and oxen. The new posts had to be laboriously supplied but only at the expense of overworking the already exhausted draught animals, many of which died. The putrefying carcasses left at the side of the busy track made conditions very unpleasant and, as a result, men began to fall sick in increasing numbers.

In order to hurry supplies forward, a pontoon bridge was constructed across the Tugela river and a suitable beach for landing supplies was established 30 miles up the coast and named Port Durnford. A third post, Fort Napoleon, was constructed as Crealock slowly advanced further inland. Because of his logistical problems, Crealock's progress had been painfully slow and he had little influence on the main events happening further north. Even though he destroyed the two large military homesteads and accepted the surrender of many of the enemy, he was inevitably castigated for being slow and ineffective. General Wolseley, who had arrived just too late to prevent Chelmsford from finally defeating the Zulus at Ulundi, dismissed Crealock's efforts by suggesting that 'the First Division might as well have been marching along the Woking and Aldershot road'.

On the return march it was evident to the troops that the Zulus were a formidable force and they were greatly unnerved by them. Pearson's force was camped near the deserted mission station at eMvutsheni when they were joined by a number of John Dunn's followers. That evening Dunn's black scouts were manning the outer camp picket when, in the early hours of darkness, a picket of the 91st Regiment mistakenly sounded the alarm. Dunn's men scurried back to the safety of the camp, only to stumble onto a line of waiting bayonets. Mistaken for Zulus, a number were seriously injured and several died of their wounds.

The British regular forces that had taken Ulundi then marched out of Zululand and left its people, particularly those whose homes had been along the invasion route, to their fate. On 6 July the column was struck by severe storms; the hail was fierce enough to kill hundreds of oxen, and numerous horses died while the soldiers took cover where they could. The abnormal conditions released a plague of snake-like worms into the British position; some were over 3ft long and 1in thick, which added to the troops' woe.[2] The men were cheered with extra supplies of rum and on the 10th the weather cleared. Chelmsford journeyed on to Cape Town where he received an enthusiastic reception from the European population for whom Ulundi had eradicated the memories of earlier disasters. Wolseley later commented that 'since his [Chelmsford's] fight he is all cock-a-hoop. Poor fellow, I can understand his feelings and am anxious to let him down easy'. Chelmsford sailed home on RMS *German* in the company of Wood and Buller, his most effective and reliable commanders, although both had earlier confided to Wolseley that they objected strongly to Chelmsford's associating with them and thereby giving the impression that 'they were in the same boat and going home because the war was over'.[3]

It could only be a matter of time before King Cetshwayo was found and captured. Indeed, it was one of the king's former friends, Mnyamana, who initially betrayed him by warning the British that the king was hiding in the Ingome forest. With so many bands of Zulus left wandering about the country, the potential for a resumption of conflict, albeit on a small scale, nevertheless continued to smoulder. Indeed, neither the loss of the battle nor the burning of Ulundi was particularly significant to the Zulus. Ulundi could have been rebuilt quickly and the northern abaQulusi remained bitterly opposed to any suggestion of surrender. Had it not been for King Cetshwayo's earlier sending a secret emissary to the abaQulusi ordering the cessation of hostilities, the war would certainly have continued. The colonial elements of Wood's column were placed under the command of Lieutenant Colonel Baker-Russell, 13th Hussars, with orders to break up these bands and pacify the north-west part of the country, especially the abaQulusi Zulus. Wolseley instructed that Baker-Russell was to be supported by Swazi forces but these turned out to be uncooperative, being more nervous of future retribution from the Zulus than of ignoring Wolseley. British troops in the Transvaal under the command of Lieutenant Colonel Villiers were then given similar instructions with the additional task of controlling the Zulus along the Pongola river.[4]

On 24 August Wolseley learned that the abaQulusi intended to continue opposing the remaining British; while he was considering this new threat the fugitive King Cetshwayo ordered all Zulus, including the abaQulusi, to surrender. Once the remaining groups of Zulus heard that the king had been captured, most sought to make peace. The remnants under Chief Manyanyoba also sought to give themselves up but their attempt to surrender coincided with an order to Villiers from Wolseley that he should 'clear Manyanyoba out'. On Villiers's orders troops under Colonel Black marched out to Manyanyoba's stronghold overlooking the Ntombe river where a group of warriors promptly surrendered; the troops then advanced towards a number of caves where the remaining warriors, women, children and animals were hiding. Unfortunately one of the warriors in a cave inadvertently discharged his rifle whereupon the warriors who had just surrendered were immediately slaughtered by their guards who suspected a trap. The surrender of Manyanyoba and his people came to a halt and the troops marched back to camp.

On 28 August the king was tracked down to a remote village by one of the searching parties, led by Major Marter. There was little the king could do – other than to surrender. Major Marter treated his prisoner with dignity though two of the king's servants were shot when they tried to escape. On 31 August the king was brought by cart to Wolseley's camp overlooking the scarred remains of Ulundi. Arrogant as ever, Wolseley declined to meet with the king, merely sending him a message that he would remain a captive of the British – at that the king's resolve left him and he was seen to crumple dejectedly. On 4 September King Cetshwayo was taken by sea from nearby Port Durnford and exiled to the Cape.

The British troops returned to deal with Manyanyoba on 5 September and attempted to smoke the Zulus from their caves, without success. On 8 September the troops returned and destroyed the caves with dynamite, notwithstanding that they were still sheltering many Zulus. On 22 September Manyanyoba, unprepared to take further losses, surrendered to the British; he and his surviving followers were escorted to the Batshe valley near Rorke's Drift where they sought to settle.

At home the British nation cheered; starved of good news and needing a lift, the public welcomed home the worn-out regiments that had suffered so greatly during the mismanaged campaign. There were plenty of heroes to fête and their names became known in every household. Queen Victoria, after years of refusing to involve herself in the nation's affairs, was pleased to pin decorations and orders on the fresh tunics of her brave soldiers and for several weeks the country enjoyed being proud of its army until memories faded and fresh news succeeded old. As Kipling perceptively wrote:

> It's Tommy this, and Tommy that,
> And chuck 'im out, the brute!
> But it's Saviour of 'is Country,
> When the guns begin to shoot ...

Now public opinion at home polarized against the war. Disraeli refused to receive Chelmsford who had cost the country so much and brought discredit to the British government. Some newspapers continued to pillory Chelmsford, popular songs mocked him and even some of his fellow peers were critical. But it was those who really mattered, the Horse Guards and Queen Victoria, who rallied to his support. Chelmsford was showered with honours; his rank of lieutenant general was confirmed and the Queen used her influence to have him appointed Lieutenant of the Tower. He later became a full general and Colonel of the Sherwood Foresters and then of the 2nd Life Guards. After his retirement, honours still came Chelmsford's way. Queen Victoria appointed him Gold Stick, an honour that was carried over when her son, Edward, succeeded her. He also made the ageing general a GCVO. On 9 April 1905, at the age of 78, Lord Chelmsford had a seizure and died while playing billiards at the United Services Club. So died a man with many admirable attributes but who was thrust into a position for which he was not intellectually equipped. Instead of being a long-forgotten Victorian general, he is still remembered as the man ultimately responsible for the Victorian army's greatest military defeat.

There was to be no redemption for Sir Bartle Frere either; he was recalled home, his credibility ruined for ever, though he defended his position to the bitter end. Even on his deathbed his last words echoed his belief that he was right: 'Oh, if only they would read *The Further Corre-spondence* they must understand', referring to his official justification for the war.[5]

On 29 May 1884 he died, probably of influenza. He was buried in St Paul's Cathedral, though no politician was invited to accompany the procession. His coffin was led into the cathedral by two dukes, one field marshal and three major generals. Queen Victoria was represented along with an array of lords, knights and ordinary soldiers. Later a statue of Frere was erected on the Thames embankment, paid for by public subscription.

After King Cetshwayo's capture on 28 August, he was taken by ship to the Cape where he remained until he was taken to England in 1882. Under the determined guidance of Bishop Colenso, King Cetshwayo had formally requested permission to meet Queen Victoria in order to outline his claim for reinstatement as King of Zululand. On 14 September 1881 permission for the visit was telegraphed to Sir Hercules Robinson, the High Commissioner in South Africa. The king's visit was delayed by British officials in South Africa who were worried by the implications of his return to authority in Zululand. Nevertheless, the following August King Cetshwayo arrived in London where he was enthusiastically received by crowds of curious Londoners. On 14 August 1882 the king formally met Queen Victoria at Osborne House on the Isle of Wight, and after returning to London had further discussions with her officials.

Queen Victoria urged her government to facilitate King Cetshwayo's repatriation; in due course the king was returned to South Africa to await permission for his return to Zululand. He then had to wait until 7 December for British permission to regain the Zulu monarchy but with the permission came news that shocked him: two large swathes of Zululand had been disposed of. One was an area to be known as the Zulu Native Reserve under the control of John Dunn and Chief Hlubi while the other area had been allocated to Chief Zibhebhu, chief of the Mandlakazi Zulus and a former rival of the king. Cetshwayo reluctantly signed the agreement and the following January he was permitted to return to Ulundi with a view to rebuilding his shattered nation. Meanwhile Zululand was in turmoil. On 2 July 1883 Zibhebhu mounted a full-scale attack against the king and his followers. The royalists were heavily defeated and over sixty of the most important chiefs loyal to King Cetshwayo were killed. These included Ntshingwayo, who had commanded at Isandlwana and Khambula, and Sihayo, whose sons had precipitated the British ultimatum. In addition to the firing of the royal *amakhanda*, all King Cetshwayo's property, including presents from Queen Victoria, flamboyant uniforms and trinkets, was seized and removed by Zibhebhu's men. King Cetshwayo was wounded and his new homestead was burnt to the ground. He was forced to flee to Eshowe where he sought protection from the British Resident Commissioner.

King Cetshwayo died following a meal on 8 February 1884, probably poisoned by his own people. To prevent his grave from becoming a future rallying point for Zulu dissenters, he was buried in an isolated and beautiful part of the Nkandla forest at Nkunzana near the Mome gorge.

Without doubt the Zulu people regarded Cetshwayo as a great king. Certainly he was highly intelligent and following his capture by the British he impressed all those who met him, including Queen Victoria. King Cetshwayo's heir was his youngest son, Dinuzulu. His inheritance was a country in ruins; villages and homesteads were burnt to the ground and cattle and crops destroyed or plundered.

When he returned to England Wolseley fared no better; both the people and the government were by now unconvinced by his treatment of the Zulu people. The *Broad Arrow* publicly noted his quiet return and wondered whether to praise or condemn him. The usual public trimmings of glory were conspicuously absent although he received the CB, a title he had rejected four years earlier. It is most likely that this very public rebuff was due to the influence of those in high places who continued actively to protect Lord Chelmsford.

CHAPTER 17

Aftermath of the Zulu War

*Zululand, having been conquered by us, according to Zulu law,
really belongs to Her Majesty the Queen.*[1]

SIR GARNET WOLSELEY

The *raison d'être* for the British invasion of Zululand was to overthrow barbarism and King Cetshwayo in order to protect the European population of Natal against the threat of an imminent Zulu invasion. In reality, this was not as singular or to the point as it seemed. Beneath the veneer of this apparently laudable crusade lay more practical and commercial causes, including the subjugation of the Zulu people in order to facilitate the British policy of Confederation in South Africa – itself a smokescreen to allow European commercial interests, in both Natal and the diamond fields, who needed access to the Zulu workforce. Almost as important, Frere considered the defeat of the Zulu army vital to protect the growing number of Boers settling in Zululand while at the same time it would confirm Britain's military invincibility to any potential adversary. It would also ensure the vainglorious Frere and Chelmsford honourable places in history.

It still remains difficult to identify any legitimate reason for Britain going to war with the Zulus. It is therefore not surprising that by March 1881, nearly two years after the war, the defeated Zulu king struggled to find any justification for the war and while held prisoner at the Cape he dictated a letter to the Governor, Sir Hercules Robinson, in an attempt to understand recent events. In his inimitable way King Cetshwayo poignantly wrote, 'Mpande did you no wrong, I have done you no wrong, therefore you must have some other object in view in invading my land'.[2] That 'other object' continues to elude the majority of historians who study the Zulu War and who still rely heavily or exclusively on the Zulu refusal to comply with the British ultimatum of December 1878 as the justification for war. Many historians' sources are based on contemporary accounts that were highly subjective purely because it was inevitable that they were written by surviving senior British officers with important reputations to preserve; and with regard to the unexpected defeats, sufficient scapegoats abounded, some obligingly now dead from loyally following their commanders' orders. Apart from private letters and reports from those involved, official military accounts of the day tended to rely on the official *Narrative of Field Operation*, but that narrative refrained from any allusion to controversy. Perhaps the most honest explanation can be credited to Laband and Thompson in their *Field Guide to the War in Zululand* in which they state that 'there is still no general agreement on the causes of the Anglo Zulu War', although the sustained Boer migration into Zululand was clearly the precipitate cause of the war.

In retrospect, Frere's reasons for the Zulu War were widely accepted by the white population of Natal. Initially the overriding and terrifying assumption that a bloodthirsty Zulu invasion of Natal was imminent can today be seen as little more than an official excuse for war. Understandably, Natal's European settlers took their pre-war cue from the British who directly influenced the Natal newspapers to regard the war as inevitable, yet there is evidence that few actually considered it desirable. However, once the war began, support for the official Frere line strengthened immeasurably. Frere's propaganda had been successful; the white population believed they had been spared an appalling fate at the hands of invading Zulu *impis*; more importantly, much money was to be made from supplying Chelmsford's army.

Nevertheless, there were many who resolutely believed that the war had been an unnecessary evil. The Bishop of Natal, John William Colenso, known to the Zulus as 'Sobantu' – 'Father of the People' – preached that the Zulu nation under Cetshwayo had presented no real threat to Natal. Nevertheless, the High Commissioner, Sir Bartle Frere, and the Secretary of State for Native Affairs in Natal, Sir Theophilus Shepstone, had deliberately provoked the conflict to further their wider ambitions for South African Confederation. There can be little doubt that Colenso was right in his damning assessment and that Isandlwana and all the other defiant battles were nothing more sinister than brave acts of self-defence by the Zulu king and his army.

Tragedies abound in any war. Perhaps the most obvious in this war was the absence of any intention by the British to pursue their policy of Confederation once the war was won; instead, they withdrew from Zululand. Not satisfied with victory, their victorious invasion force deliberately wasted the land along their lines of withdrawal. They then exiled the Zulu monarch to remove any form of national leadership and departed from Zululand leaving the impoverished Zulus to their fate.

The reason for this lack of purpose was clear; circumstances had changed since the first invasion six months earlier. Disraeli's government was on the verge of collapse as a direct consequence of the war and with it went Britain's political enthusiasm for further colonial development or military adventure in southern Africa. Worse still, the setbacks experienced by Britain in the Zulu War sent a clear message to her brooding adversaries, especially to the Boers in the Transvaal and Orange Free State; if the British lion could be seriously mauled by a force of part-time black warriors, they reasoned, a well-prepared European force would undoubtedly fare even better.

Defeating the Zulus was one thing – holding them down was another. Following the battle of Ulundi, Sir Henry Bulwer suggested to Wolseley that Zululand should be divided into four independent chiefdoms, later increased to thirteen, and the whole country placed under the supervision of a British adviser. A number of influential people with vested interests, including traders, missionaries and local officials, were all eager to advise Wolseley on the method of control. During Wolseley's stay in Zululand while awaiting the capture of King Cetshwayo, an exercise referred to as 'Catchewayo' by the troops, he sought advice from anyone who had detailed knowledge of the Zulus and in typical Wolseley style, he pitted one against the other. He wrote:

> I worked them all separately as far as possible in obtaining news for me
> & [I] then compare their statements: I have a horror of being in the hands
> of any one man especially if that one be not an English officer.[3]

Whether or not that was a reference to John Dunn is not clear but there can be little doubt that Dunn, traitor to his former friend King Cetshwayo, was looking after his own interests and was slowly but surely managing to have increasing influence upon Wolseley. Dunn had earlier been forced to flee from Zululand following the outbreak of war and had then joined Chelmsford's Intelligence Department. Wolseley liked Dunn and he accepted that Dunn knew more about the Zulus and Zululand than anyone from whom Wolseley sought advice. Dunn appeared to be the archetypal Englishman: he wore expensive European clothes, spoke as eloquently as any senior officer, and he had the ability to mix socially at the highest level, notwithstanding his proclivity to having numerous Zulu wives and concubines. Needing his counsel but clearly perplexed by Dunn, Wolseley wrote:

> He is a power in Zululand and I intend making as much use of him as
> possible. My idea is to increase his powers by making him paramount
> Chief over the District of Zululand lying along the Tegula [Thukela] &
> Buffalo Rivers frontiers of Natal. I shall thus secure the civilizing influence
> of a white man over the district of Zululand nearest to us, and he and his
> people will be a buffer between us and the barbarous districts of Zululand
> beyond. He is at heart more a Zulu than an Englishman, but he has none
> of the bloodthirsty and conquering instincts of the Zulu people.[4]

He went on,

> I have never met a man who was more of a puzzle to me than Dunn. He has
> never been in England & most of his life has passed in Zululand without any
> English or civilised society, and yet in his manners he is every way the
> Gentleman. He is quiet, self-possessed and respectful without any servility
> whatever, and his voice is soft and pleasant. He is much more of the English
> Gentleman than any of the self-opinionated & stuck up people who profess
> to be 'our leading citizens' in Natal. He leads a curiously solitary life, but he
> says he enjoys it thoroughly, being in every way his own King, without any
> policeman in his dominions to serve him with a writ or lay rough hands
> on him for taking the law into his own hands. He has as many wives &
> concubines as he wishes to keep & he has a clan about him who are all
> ready to obey his slightest nod. He pays periodical visits to Natal & has his
> books, letters & newspapers sent to him regularly. I wish I dared make [him]
> King of Zululand, for he [would] make an admirable ruler: however I am
> giving him the largest District in the country, an arrangement that I believe
> will be the small end of the wedge [of] civilisation inserted into it.[5]

John Shepstone, Acting Secretary for Native Affairs in Natal, also
strongly influenced Wolseley notwithstanding that Wolseley privately
despised Shepstone. Due to Shepstone's extensive knowledge of all the
senior Zulus, he prepared a list of Zulu chiefs whom he considered fit for
appointment as the thirteen new regional chiefs. Theophilus Shepstone,
brother of the Acting Secretary, was certainly instrumental in the preparation of his brother's list: the majority of those selected were prepared
to accept the Zulu royal house as nothing more than the total cause of
their nation's downfall. On this subject, Wolseley wrote:

> Such breaking up of the cohesion of the country will, I firmly believe,
> preclude for the future all, or almost all, possibility of any reunion of its
> inhabitants under one rule.[6]

Having considered all the advice, Wolseley prepared to enforce a strict
settlement on the defeated Zulus. On a very hot 1 September 1879, 200 of

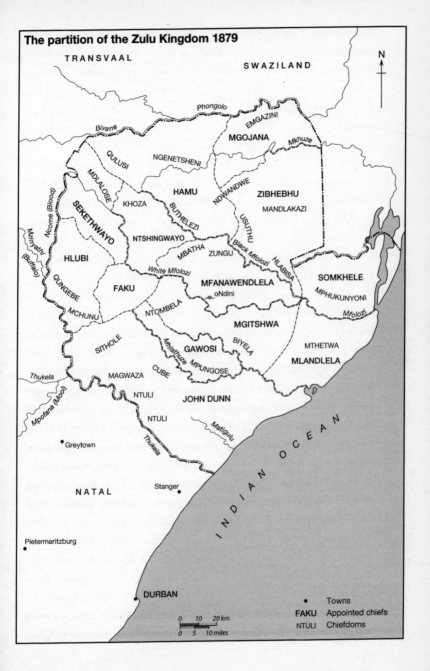

The partition of the Zulu Kingdom 1879

TRANSVAAL

SWAZILAND

N

Phongolo

Bivane

EMGAZINI

QULUSI

MGOJANA

NGENETSHENI

Mkhuze

MDLALOSE

HAMU

NDWANDWE

ZIBHEBHU

Ncome (Blood)

KHOZA

SEKETHWAYO

BUTHELEZI

MANDLAKAZI

Mzinyathi
(Buffalo)

NTSHINGWAYO

USUTHU

HLUBI

MBATHA

ZUNGU

Black Mfolozi

HLABISA

White Mfolozi

SOMKHELE

QUNGEBE

FAKU

MFANAWENDLELA

MPHUKUNYONI

MCHUNU

oNdini

Mfolozi

NTOMBELA

MGITSHWA

SITHOLE

BIYELA

MTHETWA

Thukela

MAGWAZA

GAWOSI

MLANDLELA

Mhlathuze

MPUNGOSE

CUBE

NTULI

JOHN DUNN

Mpofana (Mooi)

NTULI

Matigulu

Thukela

• Greytown

NATAL

Stanger

INDIAN OCEAN

• Pietermaritzburg

DURBAN

	Towns
FAKU	Appointed chiefs
NTULI	Chiefdoms

0   10   20 km
0   5   10 miles

329

the most senior Zulu dignitaries and chiefs were summoned to the newly established British headquarters at Ulundi where Wolseley addressed them concerning the fate of Zululand. Through his interpreter, John Shepstone, the gathered assembly were brusquely informed that their captured king was being sent into exile at the Cape and would never be permitted to return to Zululand. They were then informed that Zululand was to be divided into thirteen independent chiefdoms each ruled by a Zulu chief selected and appointed by the British, each chief to have command under the overall supervision of a British administrator. There was not to be the remotest possibility that any one individual, of royal birth or otherwise, would be able to rise up in the image of King Shaka to reunite the Zulus. As was generally expected, John Dunn was awarded the largest and most influential chieftainship in Zululand, along the border with Natal, in return for his loyal services to the British during the campaign.

It is generally accepted that the British invasion of Zululand quickly and severely disrupted the Zulus' economic structure and caused massive loss of life. Their military defeat would now ensure the destruction of their political system. Wolseley knew only too well that over several decades, the royal house had inextricably penetrated all aspects of Zulu social life to the extent that King Cetshwayo, through his previously loyal chiefs, exercised total control over the Zulu people. Power in the hands of one king, in the mould of Shaka or Cetshwayo, was now to be impossible.

Without exception, the thirteen new chiefs were men who had either fought for the British or had deserted King Cetshwayo prior to his capture; none could exercise much control over his people. Chiefs were appointed with the deliberate intention of creating political disharmony and rivalry. One of the appointed chiefs was a complete outsider; in recognition of his service to the British by providing mercenaries for the Natal government, a Sotho chief, Faku, was appointed chief of the district near Rorke's Drift, previously dominated by Chief Sihayo. On appointment, Faku ordered Sihayo to leave his district, together with his son Mehlokazulu. Chief Mnyamana, Cetshwayo's chief councillor, was likewise offered a remote territory but refused to accept it. Various interpretations are given for this; many Zulus assert it was out of loyalty to the exiled king. His own explanation to the Boundary Commission was that

> I honestly considered that I was going to be given a tract of country which, though amply large enough for my extensive following, yet, it did not include one-third of the land where my kraals were situated.[7]

Mnyamana knew that part of his own northern area, the land of the abaQulusi, was to be allocated to Chief Hamu. This settlement was Hamu's reward for defecting to Colonel Wood's Northern Column during the campaign. For these reasons Mnyamana refused to sign the paper as he did not see his way to govern a people who were unlikely to respect him as their chief. The remainder of Mnyamana's chiefdom was therefore given to Ntshingwayo and in consequence, the second most powerful man in Zululand (after King Cetshwayo) was excluded from the settlement. Ntshingwayo in turn was reluctant to accept the district because it contained so many Buthelezi and Mdlalose people, as well as another chief's (Sekethwayo's) personal homestead. Sekethwayo was appointed over a district further to the west.

Only four of these thirteen carefully selected chiefs were present at the meeting where the agreement was signed; among the stipulations was the obligation to respect their new boundaries, to abolish the Zulu military system and ensure the right of the people to seek employment beyond Zululand. This latter requirement was especially destructive to Zulu society as it encouraged a migration of male Zulus to areas of strong British commercial interest, especially farms in Natal and the more distant diamond fields located to the north near present-day Johannesburg. The Zulus were also forbidden to import firearms or become involved in any form of trade that did not have its origin in British-controlled Natal or the Transvaal, a stipulation of immense financial value to Chief Dunn. Capital punishment without trial was forbidden; land could not be sold, traded or purchased without British permission and the chiefs were to keep the peace and apply the law according to the 'ancient laws and customs' of their people, so long as these laws did not offend the sensitivities of the British administrator, although, for some weeks, no one could be found to accept this poisoned chalice. In October a Mr Wheelwright was appointed to the civilian position of British Resident in Zululand, a post that attracted an annual salary of £600 plus an expense account of £100. He was tasked with the role of being the 'eyes and ears' for the British government and monitoring the thirteen chiefs. He had no voice or power, the position lacked any credibility and this thankless task soon proved impossible – he resigned.

Melmoth Osborn, formerly a senior Natal official and close friend of Theophilus Shepstone and at this time serving in the Transvaal, was persuaded to consider the task; he accepted and was duly appointed as the British Resident Administrator of Zululand. He was soon to discover that the position lacked any real authority other than to offer advice to the new chiefs and to oversee them if it appeared that they were acting beyond the terms of their appointments. Wolseley clarified the situation when he wrote:

> I have been careful to make it clear that we intend to exercise no
> administrative authority over the country, and that we wish to disturb
> the existing conditions of life and government only where, as in the cases
> of the military system and the barbarous practices of witchcraft, these
> conditions were irreconcilable with the safety of British subjects in South
> Africa, or with the peace and prosperity of the country itself.[8]

The inevitable result of Wolseley's deliberately unreasonable settlement was that Zululand was quickly plunged into chaos, the country lacking leadership, control and supplies. Within weeks Zulu fought against Zulu as the new borders of the country and individual chiefdoms indiscriminately cut across both the social and the political groupings that had developed during the previous fifty years.

Wolseley further instructed that King Cetshwayo's relatives must abandon their homes and move into Chief Dunn's territory along the border with Natal, an order that was simply ignored as Dunn was considered to be a traitor for supporting the British against his former friend and ally, the king. Wolseley also instructed the appointed chiefs to collect all royal cattle and firearms and deliver them to the British Resident. Of all Wolseley's diktats, this most irritated the Zulus; after all, cattle were virtually the currency of the Zulu economy. King Cetshwayo owned most of Zululand's cattle, which made him the most powerful man in the kingdom; his royal herds were easily recognized by their whiteness, indicating their ownership, and due to their large number they were distributed through many royal households and represented the livelihood and sustenance of many ordinary people who tended the herds. Wolseley's instructions merely gave those newly appointed chiefs who felt sufficiently confident the legal opportunity to seize the king's cattle and plunder from those Zulus who had previously been loyal to King Cetshwayo. This disruption quickly developed into a crippling and very destructive civil war and more Zulus died during the immediate period following the Zulu War than in the war itself.

To give his draconian plan the cloak of respectability, Wolseley appointed a second Boundary Commission to demarcate both the new external border of Zululand and the thirteen internal boundaries. The Commission was instructed to ignore his earlier assurances that the Zulus would be left in full possession of their land. The northern limit of the kingdom was to be moved southwards to the Pongola river to exclude the abaQulusi and Emagazini people, together with most of Hamu and Mnyamana's people. In the north-east the new boundary would follow the Lubombo mountains and the former territory; land that was now excluded from the new Zululand would be given back to the Tongas.

Wolseley's determination and confidence increased further once King Cetshwayo was imprisoned at Cape Town. The new Boundary Commission was given instructions to lay down the borders of the chiefdoms following, where possible, natural physical features. As soon as the plans were finalized, Wolseley invited the Commission to inform the chiefs of Zululand that

> Having been conquered by us, according to Zulu law, [Zululand] really belongs to Her Majesty the Queen, but as Her Majesty has no wish to increase her dominions in South Africa, as an act of grace to the Zulu people, she has now parcelled out the country into independent chieftainships. It is, therefore, for her officers, on her behalf, to decide the extent of territory that is by her favour to be allotted to each Chief. This was a right freely exercised by Cetywayo, as well as by his predecessors, and it is a right which devolves upon the Great Queen by right of conquest, and that must not be disputed.[9]

Wolseley deliberately ignored the findings of the earlier 1878 Boundary Commission and additionally reduced the Zulus' western boundary, to the benefit of the Transvaal.

When the Boundary Commissioners informed Wolseley that some of the appointed chiefs were unsuitable, he typically suppressed their report. In due course a number of settlement errors became obvious, but Wolseley merely commented that the fault lay with the Zulus' unwillingness to comply with the settlement's terms. In reality, the new borders of the country and the boundaries of the chiefdoms ensured that established clan groups were now placed under different clan chiefs and long-standing rival groups came under the same appointed chief. Many Zulus found themselves under appointed chiefs whom they considered to be inferior or uninterested in their responsibilities; many of these disaffected Zulus then responded by ignoring or resisting the new chiefs.

When the matter of growing unrest was brought to Wolseley's attention, he instructed the Boundary Commission to inform the growing number of disaffected Zulus that they were free to move to another chief's territory; but the Zulu people were not unlike any other people – they were bonded to the districts where they had been born, which their ancestors had won by farming or warring. The Zulu people were only to be moved from their districts as a last resort; they were not prepared to move merely to satisfy white attempts at political or economic manipulation.

Wolseley had very effectively subjugated the Zulu nation and his hurried and hard-headed settlement satisfied the immediate needs of the home government in a moment of crisis but, in less than two years, the overall situation in Zululand was doomed to deteriorate to such an extent that the Colonial Office would have to abandon the arrangement. The growing unrest would become so serious that uncontrollable violence on a wide scale would threaten British interests as well as the very structure of Natal. With the conjunction of these elements, the inevitable spectre of rebellion began to fester throughout the nation; it would soon erupt into a decade of violence and civil war that would more effectively destroy the basis of Zulu royal power than the British invasion had done. British officials claimed that the ordinary people had retained possession of most of their land but by losing their king and their ability to raise an army, they lost the means to defend Zululand. Natal settlers now greedily looked at Zululand for its fertile farmland and abundant labour force, and the old Zulu order had finally collapsed.

After King Cetshwayo's death, his young son and heir, King Dinuzulu, desperately attempted to salvage the royalist cause. Sporadic violence continued for four more years during which King Dinuzulu secured Boer help to defeat Zibhebhu, but which cost the lives of a number of prominent supporters of the old order. In 1884 the Boers murdered Prince Dabulamanzi who had commanded at Rorke's Drift. King Dinuzulu was continually harassed by the colonial authorities and was eventually goaded into supporting armed resistance against the British in 1888. He was defeated, and sent into exile on St Helena.

Yet, unbeknown to the main participants, the debacle of the Zulu War had a hidden and lethal sting in the tail; the war had convinced the watching Boer politicians and generals that the British Army was not invincible. Encouraged by widespread discontent against British interests throughout the Transvaal, the Boer community made secret preparations to resist further British influence. Only six months later they commenced military action against the British at Majuba; it was a conflict that brought early disasters to the British and which developed into an even bloodier campaign, the two Boer Wars.

Meanwhile, disease and a six-year famine severely damaged the Zulus' ability to feed or re-establish themselves. This ongoing crisis was followed in 1897 by the rinderpest epidemic, which virtually destroyed their remaining cattle, and then, just as they began the long process of restocking their herds, the deadly east coast fever obliterated the young animals. Under British domination, the Zulu social structure had virtually collapsed; the young men became migrant labourers and headed from Zululand towards the growing towns and cities. Then, in 1904, the authorities created black reserves and moved the Zulu population into the most unproductive areas. Those who resisted were classified as squatters and were duly evicted to the reserves – leaving the best land to the white settlers.

In 1906 the authorities levied and enforced a prohibitive 'hut tax' on the population. Many Zulus living in Natal took up arms to protest at the harsh levels of taxation imposed upon them. One of the few Zulu chiefs to openly support the protestors was Mehlokazulu kaSihayo. Mehlokazulu had served throughout the Zulu War as an officer in the iNgobamakhosi regiment, and in 1906 he joined forces with the rebel leader, Bambatha. But the balance of power had swung even more in favour of the Europeans and the rebel army was crushed at the battle of Mome Gorge where both Bambatha and Mehlokazulu were killed. Zululand's turmoil resulted in a ferocious civil war, from which it never properly recovered.

TODAY, THE BATTLEFIELDS of Zululand remain largely as they have been since 1879. The Swedish Mission Society reoccupied its property at Rorke's Drift once the war was over, and demolished the ruins of the old buildings. However, two of the present-day buildings which stand on the site are built on their original foundations and replicate Witt's house and storeroom. The coastal site of Gingindlovu has long been covered in sugar cane, introduced by European settlers in the early part of the twentieth century. Nevertheless, the remains of Pearson's entrenchments are still visible at Eshowe and the hills around Nyezane are unchanged, while in the northern sector the battlefields of Hlobane, Khambula and Ntombe remain as they were. The clay hut floors of King Cetshwayo's royal Ulundi settlements have survived, baked to brick when the British razed the complex; the king's private quarters have been carefully reconstructed. It is a phoenix raised from the ashes and today the site is a fitting memorial to the pride of the old Zulu kingdom.

Recent research into the Zulu War of 1879 has radically altered perceptions of the conflict and broader threads of South African history have begun to develop. To the British at the time, the war seemed to be a triumph of European civilization over African savagery; today the war can be seen within the context of the systematic reduction of independent African groups in South Africa in the face of expanding power of the developing settler economy.

Modern writers' interpretations of the war have reflected these changes. The shock felt by the British at the Zulu victory at Isandlwana created a particular image of the Zulu people in British folklore. It is only in the last twenty years that scholars have come to understand something of the Zulu perspective of the events of 1879. Today's histories of the Zulu War present a more even-handed view of the conflict. Many issues remain unresolved and historians remain divided, especially regarding the war on the ground. Isandlwana attracts particular controversy, retaining an aura of mystery mainly because of the magnitude of the battle and because surviving accounts, reports and maps are often conflicting.

The first feature film about the Zulu War, *Symbol of Sacrifice*, was made in 1918 and recreated many of the events of 1879 in a way designed to arouse a patriotic response from its audiences. The film was unusual for its time in that its plots included both British and Zulu characters. In 1964 the popular feature film *Zulu*, based on the events at Rorke's Drift, was released. In 1979 *Zulu Dawn* expanded on this view, presenting the battle of Isandlwana as a classic example of British Imperial folly, but the film lacked the power and conviction of its predecessor. It was not until the 1980s that dramas such as *Shaka Zulu* again portrayed Zulu characters at the centre of their own history.

The Zulu War, although not the starting point, can be seen as the turning point for late Victorian imperialism. In the years that followed, the legacy of the Zulu War permeated the culture of an expanding British empire to such an extent that it has vigorously accompanied both Zulu and British culture into the twenty-first century.[10]

AFTER THE ZULU WAR, a steady stream of visitors made their way to the battlefields; that stream continues to this day. Most of the early visitors were disturbed to discover that the battlefield of Isandlwana was still littered with debris from the battle – smashed boxes, derelict wagons, rotting clothing and, most distressing, scattered bleached human bones. Following a number of protests from visitors, the Governor General of Natal instructed one Alfred Boast to organize the cleaning of the site. The task took one month and was completed on 9 March 1883. Boast listed no fewer than 298 cairns marking graves, each containing upwards of four bodies. He even removed the skeletons of the artillery horses killed in the ravine during the flight along the Fugitives' Trail although some cairns have since been found to contain the bodies of both men and horses.[11] The bodies of Captain Anstey and Durnford were reburied by their families, Anstey at Woking and Durnford at Pietermaritzburg. Over the years a number of regimental and family memorials were erected at Isandlwana; in March 1914 a memorial to the 24th Regiment was erected by the regiment. It was not until 2001 that a memorial to the Zulus was built at Isandlwana.

It has to be a total triumph of mankind that today, of all the visitors to Zululand it is the British who are the most numerous and popular with the local people. After everything the Zulu people have endured in the name of Christianity, modernization, socialization and progress, the majority of Zulus continue to live in their timeless way, yet hold the British in high regard – one warrior nation respecting another.

Appendices

Chelmsford's Memo

The following notes on engaging the enemy are from a memo published under the direction of Lord Chelmsford. Such a set was found on the body of Colonel Durnford RE following the battle of Isandlwana. The memo is reproduced exactly.

Although the Zulus will often meet their enemy in a fair fight in the open, like all savages they are fond of ambuscades and other ruses.

In going through bush, remember that the natives will often lie down to let you pass, and then rise and fire on you.

In moving through bush advance and rear guards and flanking parties are necessary.

They should look well under the bushes, and notice all footmarks and sounds, such as the cracking of bushes, &c, and note whether the twigs have been lately bent or broken, or the grass trodden down, all indications of men having recently passed. When the bush is too thick for flanking parties, the leading file should turn to the right and enter the bush as far as he can, kneel, and look well under the bushes; the next file, after about five paces, turn to his left, and the next to his right, and so on. The whole body may do this or only the advanced guard, according to circumstances. As the rear of the force in question approaches, the files rise in succession and close by sections, moving along between the halted sentries, and when the foremost of these is reached the process is repeated.

When waylaying or surprising an enemy make no noise until the enemy finds you, rise, and move, not along the path, but just inside the bush.

When moving near an enemy, or reconnoitring, do not return to the camp by the route you left it.

A common ruse with the natives is to hide a large force in the bush and show a few solitary individuals to invite an attack. When the troops enter the bush in pursuit of the latter the hidden men rise and attack them.

In advancing through bush a herd of cattle is seen feeding with only a small guard, which runs as soon as our troops appear. The mounted men push on to capture the former, and when they are well separated from the rest, the natives, who were hidden all the time in the bush, rise and cut them off before the infantry can come to their rescue.

Native advance guards and flanking parties cannot be trusted, the former will cluster together, and the latter will often lie down.

Natives always know when an enemy is in the bush, but they often forget to report it, thinking the white men know as well as themselves.

The Boers found that the Zulus could not stand repeated cavalry charges on the flanks, and that a very effective method of attack was to gallop upon their flanks, dismount, and fire into them; retreating to reload, or when attacked.

When the wagons of a force are parked at night, if the Zulus attack they always try to make the cattle, which are kept within the park, stampede, in order to break a hole in the line of defence.

The same applies to cavalry, who should take every precaution against their horses being stampeded by a sudden attack.

Composition of the Opposing Forces

Isandlwana

Brevet Lieutenant Colonel Pulleine commanded the Imperial No. 3 Centre Column at Isandlwana which consisted of 68 officers and 1,800 men made up from his 1/24th (Warwickshire) Regiment, N Battery 5th Brigade Royal Artillery, 5th Field Company Royal Engineers, 5 companies of the 1st Battalion 2/24th (Warwickshire) Regiment, 1 company of the 2nd Battalion 2/24th (Warwickshire) Regiment plus detachments from the 90th Foot, the Army Service Corps, Army Hospital and Army Pay Corps. Colonial troops under his command included detachments of the Mounted Infantry, Natal Volunteer Corps, Natal Carbineers, Newcastle Mounted Rifles and the Buffalo Border Guard, the 3rd Regiment NNC and elements of the Natal Native Pioneer Corps.

The total Zulu fighting force was about 25,000 with another 10,000 supporters. They were commanded by chieftains Ntshingwayo kaMahole Khoza and Mavumengwana kaNdlela Ntuli and included 13 full *amabutho* (regiments).

Rorke's Drift: British forces engaged in the defence of the mission station

Unit	Officers	Wounded	ORs	Sick	Killed	Wounded	Remarks
In command	Lt Chard						
Staff							
Royal Artillery			4	3			
Royal Engineers			1				
2nd/3rd Regiment Buffs			1				
1/24th Regiment			11	5	3	2	1 died of wounds
2/24th Regiment	Lt Bromhead		98	17	8	5	1 died of wounds
Commissariat Department	Mr Dalton, Mr Byrne and Mr Dunne	Mr Dalton	1		1 (Mr Byrne)		
Army Medical Department	Surgeon Reynolds		3				
Chaplain's Department	Revd George Smith						Civilian
90th Regiment			1	1			
Natal Mounted Police			3	3	1		
Natal Native Contingent	Lt Adendorff		6	6	2	2	
Ferryman			1				Civilian Daniels
	8	1	131	35	15	9	

Rorke's Drift: Zulu forces engaged in the attack on the mission station

These consisted of elements of the uThulwana, iNdluyengwe, iNdlondlo and uDloko regiments. The overall commander was Prince Dabulamanzi kaMpande, the king's half-brother.

Nyezane

Major Tucker was in command of 5 companies of the 80th Regiment stationed at nearby Luneburg. At the scene of the defeat, there were 103 non-commissioned men under the command of Captain Moriarty.

British casualties were high and consisted of 1 officer, 1 doctor, 64 soldiers and 15 black levies killed; the 20 missing soldiers were presumed drowned in the river.

The size of the Zulu force can only be estimated; reports state that between 800 and 3,000 warriors took part. Prince Mbilini kaMswati was in command. Zulu casualties were comparatively light and amounted to 25 Zulu bodies found at the river crossing.

Hlobane

British troops were under the command of Colonel Buller and amounted to 675 officers and men representing the Royal Artillery Rocket Battery plus the following Colonial troops: the 2nd Battalion. Wood's Irregulars, Frontier Light Horse, Border Horse, Transvaal Rangers together with Dutch burgers under Piet Uys and his two sons. British casualties were enormous compared with Zulu losses: a total of 15 officers and 79 men plus some 140 black troops of Wood's Irregulars were lost. The second force that attacked the lower terrace was commanded by Lieutenant Colonel Russell's force. This force amounted to 640 officers and men including Royal Artillery and Mounted Infantry supported by the following colonial troops: the Natal Native Horse, Kaffrarian Rifles, 1st Battalion Wood's Irregulars and a 200-strong detachment of Prince Hamu's disaffected Zulus.

The Zulus consisted of 2,000-plus warriors from the abaQulusi tribe supported by Mbilini's clan and the uMcijo and iNgobamakhosi regiments. Zulu casualties are unknown but not significant.

Khambula

British troops at Khambula were commanded by Colonel Wood VC and totalled 2,086 officers and men, representing the following units: the Royal Artillery, Royal Engineers, 1/13th (Somerset) Light Infantry, the 90th Light Infantry and Mounted Infantry. Colonial troops were made up from Baker's Horse, Border Horse, Frontier Light Horse, Kaffrarian Rifles, Mounted Basutos, Raaf's Transvaal Rangers and Wood's Irregulars.

British and Colonial casualties were low and amounted to 3 officers and 26 men killed with 5 officers and 50 men wounded – all but two from Martini-Henry rifles captured from the British at Isandlwana.

The Zulu force consisted of some 20,000 warriors and was commanded by two senior *indunas*, Ntshingwayo and Mnyamana Buthelezi. The right horn consisted of the iNgobamakhosi; the left horn, the uMcijo; the centre force, the uDloko, uDududu, iMbube, uThulwana and iNdlondlo. Most of these units had fought at Isandlwana. Units of the local abaQulusi from Hlobane joined the main Zulu force.

Zulu casualties amounted to at least 1,200 killed around the battlefield. Many more died from their injuries.

Ulundi

Lieutenant General Lord Chelmsford was in overall command. The 2nd Division column was commanded by Major General Newdigate, the Flying Column (formally the Northern Column) was commanded by Brigadier General Sir Evelyn Wood. The 2nd Division included units of the King's Dragoon Guards, the 17th (Duke of Cambridge's Own) Lancers, Royal Artillery, the 2/21st Royal Scots Fusiliers and the 58th (Rutland) Regiment. The Flying Column included units from the Royal Artillery, Royal Engineers, 1/13th Light Infantry, the 80th (Staffordshire) Regiment, the 90th Light Infantry, the Army Medical Department, Hospital Corps and Mounted Infantry. The Colonial forces consisted of the 2nd Battalion

NNC, Shepstone's Horse, Bettington's Horse, Wood's Irregulars, Natal Native Pioneers, Transvaal Rangers, Frontier Light Horse and the Natal Native Horse. The total force amounted to 5,317 white troops and 1,152 native troops. In the battle their casualties amounted to 3 officers and 10 men killed, with 69 men wounded.

The total Zulu force is estimated at 20,000 warriors and consisted of elements of various regiments under the command of Ziwedu, Cetshwayo's brother. He was supported by three battle-experienced *indunas*, Mnyamana Buthelezi (the Zulu prime minister), Prince Dabulamanzi (commander at Rorke's Drift) and Ntshingwayo Khoza (commander at Isandlwana). Their casualties are difficult to assess as accounts vary; an average suggests that about 1,500 dead warriors were found around the battlefield. Buller claimed that a further 500 were killed during the far-ranging pursuit.

The *Referee's* poem on Rorke's Drift

RORKE'S DRIFT
There was an old soldier named Dan'el
He fought until his clothes were in rags,
So the Government gave him a flannel,
And also a new pair of bags.

And the news it went over the Channel,
Through Europe it's chaff for the wags,
That we honour our heroes in flannel,
And clothe their achievements in bags.

'Tis a blot on our glorious annals,
Oh, who were the elderly hags,
Who suggested those charity flannels
And ordered those beggarly bags?

When the public its jury empanels,
'Twill suggest, ere the interest flags,
That the Tories for skirts take the flannels,
And they might put their heads in the bags.

Deaths Caused by Disease at Fort Melvill

Figures are as follows – gaps denote information unknown:

Regiment or Corps	Brigade or Battalion	Regimental No.	Rank and Name	Age	Date of death	Cause of death
24	2		Private J. Williams		05.02.79	Dysentery
24	2		Private G. Evans		23.02.79	Fever
24	2	1407	Private Farr		04.03.79	Fever
24	2	1320	Private C. Foster		06.03.79	Fever
24	2		Private P. Murphy		08.03.79	Fever
24	2	1146	Private T. Jones	25	10.03.79	Fever
24	2	1067	Sergeant D. Jones	21	10.03.79	Fever
24	2	1605	L Corporal C. Frower	19	12.03.79	Fever
RE			Sapper J. Russell		20.02.79	Fever
Newcastle Rifles			Trooper Dixon		12.01.79	Drowned
24	2	605	Colour Sergeant W. Cuthbert	23	12.03.79	Fever
24	2	1046	L Corporal J. Haslam		18.03.79	Fever

This number excludes 2nd Lieutenant Franklin of the 24th who, while seriously ill, was moved to Helpmekaar on 22 February. He died shortly after arriving there and is buried in the Helpmekaar cemetery. Initially the soldiers' bodies were buried in the Rorke's Drift cemetery alongside those who had died in the fighting; when the total reached 25, the remainder were buried in a small cemetery across the river from the fort which, over the years, became totally overgrown and forgotten. It was even omitted from military maps of the area, possibly due to the fact that it contained the bodies of fever cases rather than those killed in battle. During 2001 the cemetery was restored and repaired.

APPENDIX E

Award of Zulu War Medals

Queen Victoria was a great believer in bestowing rewards for loyalty and merit, especially in the military where every campaign during her reign saw the issue of specially designed medals and ribbons in recognition of brave or loyal service. Although Queen Victoria had instituted the Distinguished Conduct Medal for other ranks at the start of the Crimean War, she acknowledged the need for an award for outstanding bravery, one that could be bestowed regardless of rank. The resulting bronze cross, fashioned from the metal of captured Russian guns from Sebastopol, was first presented in June 1857, but there were very few opportunities to win this coveted award. Those officers who did found the road to promotion considerably easier and, as a consequence, many volunteered for active service with the possibility of a VC in mind. Considering the short duration of the Zulu War and its long periods of inactivity, the number of VCs awarded was exceptionally high. Apart from the politics involved, there was another reason. The Zulus did not possess artillery or effective firearms and so most of the fighting was highly visible and close combat, perfect warfare for the brave.

The award of so many VCs to one regiment for the Rorke's Drift action was unprecedented although more VCs were awarded in total for each of the following battles:

19 for Inkerman; 5 November 1854 – 10 hour battle

20 for Great Redan; 18 June 1855 – battle lasted 5 hours

12 for Great Redan; action on 8 September 1855

17 for Sikandar Dagh; action on 16 November 1857

Figures kindly supplied by the Victoria Cross Society.

Zulu War Medals in campaign order

ISANDLWANA   22 January 1879

Victoria Cross. Private S. Wassall 80th Regiment.

Note

a In 1907 two further awards were made to Lieutenant Coghill and Lieutenant Melvill of the 24th Regiment who died after crossing back into Natal from Isandlwana. At the time of the Zulu War there was no provision for posthumous awards.

b In 1882 Trooper Barker of the Natal Carbineers was recommended for the VC by Maj. Gen. Sir Evelyn Wood VC for his actions at the Buffalo river. The recommendation was rejected.

RORKE'S DRIFT   22 January 1879

Victoria Cross. Lieutenant J.R.M. Chard RE; Lieutenant G. Bromhead, 2/24th Regiment; Surgeon J.H. Reynolds, Army Medical Department; Acting Commissary J.L. Dalton, Commissariat and Transport Department; Corporal W.W. Allen, 2/24th Regiment; Corporal F.C. Schiess, Natal Native Contingent; Privates F. Hitch, A.H. Hook, R. Jones, W. Jones and J. Fielding (alias Williams) of the 2/24th Regiment.

Distinguished Conduct Medal. Colour Sergeant F. Bourne, 2/24th Regiment; Corporal F. Attwood, Army Service Corps; Wheeler J. Cantwell, Royal Artillery and Private W. Roy, 1/24th Regiment.

Note Corporal M. McMahon of the Army Service Corps was also awarded the medal but it was subsequently withdrawn following his conviction for theft and desertion.

An interesting postscript concerning Chard's Victoria Cross occurred in 1999. Stanley Baker, who played Chard in the film *Zulu*, acquired Chard's pair of medals at auction in 1972. Although the campaign medal was genuine, the Victoria Cross was catalogued as a copy and, as a consequence, Baker paid the comparatively modest sum of £2,700 for the pair. On Stanley Baker's death, the Cross changed hands three times until it ended up, lodged for safety, with Spinks of London who decided to check the nature of Chard's 'copy' medal; its metallic characteristics were tested by the Royal Armouries. The test results were compared with those of the bronze ingot kept at the Central Ordnance Depot, from which all Victoria Crosses are cast. The tests revealed that the 'copy' had come from this same block and there was no doubt that it was the genuine article. No price can be put on this authenticated VC belonging to such a famous recipient.

NTOMBE RIVER   12 March 1879
Victoria Cross. Sergeant A.C. Booth, 80th Regiment.

HLOBANE 28 March 1879
Victoria Cross. Brevet Lieutenant Colonel R.H. Buller, 60th Rifles; Major W. Knox-Leet, 1/13th Regiment; Lieutenant H. Lysons, 90th Regiment; Private E. Fowler, 90th Regiment.
Distinguished Conduct Medal. Corporal W.D. Vinnicombe, Frontier Light Horse; Trooper R. Brown, Frontier Light Horse; Private J. Power, 1/24th Regiment; Bugler A. Walkinshaw, 90th Light Infantry.

Note Captain Duck of the Veterinary Corps, for bravery at the Devil's Pass, was recommended by Buller for the VC. It was turned down on the grounds that 'he should not have been there'.

KHAMBULA   29 March 1879

Victoria Cross. Lieutenant E.S. Browne, 1/24th Regiment.

Distinguished Conduct Medal. Troop Sergeant Major Learda, Natal Native Horse; Acting Sergeant E. Quigley and Private A. Page, 1/13th Regiment.

MFOLOZI RIVER   3 July 1879

Victoria Cross. Captain Lord W.L. Beresford, 9th Lancers; Captain C.D. D'Arcy and Sergeant E. O'Toole, Frontier Light Horse.

Distinguished Conduct Medal. Troop Sergeant Major S. Kambula, Natal Native Horse.

ULUNDI   4 July 1879

Distinguished Conduct Medal. Colour Sergeant J. Phillips, 58th Regiment and Gunner W. Moorhead, Royal Artillery.

The alternative gallantry award was the **Distinguished Conduct Medal**, which carried a gratuity of £15 for sergeants, £10 for corporals and £5 for privates. The Zulu War saw as many as twenty-three Victoria Crosses awarded compared with just fourteen DCMs. One wonders why only five DCMs were awarded for the defence of Rorke's Drift when there were so many acts of gallantry displayed. Indeed, one could argue that some of the Victoria Crosses awarded for this action probably merited the DCM instead. But then other motives were at work to lessen the impact of Isandlwana on the British public. The Rorke's Drift recipients of the 'Silver Medal', as it is sometimes known, were Corporal Francis Attwood, Army Service Corps, Gunner John Cantwell, Royal Artillery, the celebrated Colour Sergeant Frank Bourne 2/24th and Private William Roy 1/24th who was one of the defenders of the hospital. Private Roy left the army but could not settle; he emigrated to Australia where his health deteriorated. In 1887 a military concert was held in Sydney for his benefit as he was 'almost blind and helpless'. He lived out the remainder of his life in an institution. The fifth recipient was Corporal Michael

McMahon, Army Hospital Corps, who subsequently had his award taken away for theft and desertion.

The **South Africa Medal** was given to all who were involved in the war effort and covered the period from 25 September 1877 to 2 December 1879. Army Order 103 dated 1 August 1880 specifically excluded the award of clasps to those who did not cross into Zululand. Curiously, those members of B Company who fought at Rorke's Drift but did not cross the border into Zululand nevertheless received bars to their medals, whether by omission or design is not known.

Bromhead's Letters

Both of the following Bromhead letters are unabridged and unaltered.
For further details see my book *Rorke's Drift* (Cassell 2002).

Bromhead's letter to Lieutenant Godwin-Austen

Rorke's Drift

19th February 1879

My Dear Austin, [sic]

I can't tell you how grieved I was to hear on the return of the Column on
the 23rd of January that your brother had been left in that fateful camp. He
had been attached to B Co at Freetown and we got on so jolly together
that he told me he should ask the Col. to let him stay with the Company,
but I am sorry to say it was not to be. The night before the Column
transport crossed the river it came out in orders that B Company were to
remain here and your brother was sent back to G Company and Griffiths
who was Company Officer as usual was posted to the Company. Your
brother who was knocked up from over work at the ponts, where he had
been working day and night, to get troops across the river had to go sick,
but still he march [sic] with the Column. I have not got over the dreadful
news we received yet, in fact can hardly believe it. We had an awful night of
it here as you may fancy. We heard the camp had been taken, and were
also afraid that the Column had received a heavy blow, and the Zulus came

at us in such force and with such fierce pluck. I thought we should never pull through it, but the Company behaved splendidly [word illegible] as our ammunition held out and we held them back till daylight. We were on the Natal side of the Buffalo but can do nothing as far as I can see until we are fitted up again. I hope they are going to send us out some more troops or you wont [sic] see many of us again. The Zulus are so strong we stand a poor chance against them, as it is we expect to be attacked any day.

I hope the wound is better, and that you do not suffer from it.

Yours sincerely,

G. Bromhead

Bromhead's letter to his sister

This was written towards the end of February and it received limited publicity in Britain:

I fear you will be very anxious about me as no doubt we are rather in a fix. I am getting over the excitement of the fight and the sickness and fury at our loss. It is not so much the poor fellows being killed as the way the savages treat them. Having been left alone we have built a mud fort, which I think we ought to hold against any amount of Zulus, till we get help from England. I send you a paper with the report of the fight and the remarks of the General on the behaviour of my company which are flattering. If the Government gives all the steps [promotions] of the poor fellows killed I shall most probably get my company into the 1st Battalion who are to go home directly after the war is finished. I have not got over the wonder of there being one of us left. God was very good to us in giving us a little time to get up a defence, or the black fellows would have taken us by surprise, which they will find hard to do now.

Lord Chelmsford's Telegram

From: Lieut General Lord Chelmsford KCB

To: Rt. Hon Secretary of State for War

I regret to have to report a very disastrous engagement which took place
on the 22nd instant between the Zulus and a portion of No 3 Column left
to guard a camp about 10 miles in front of Rorke's drift – the former came
down in overwhelming numbers and, in spite of the gallant resistance
made by six companies of the 24th regiment, 2 guns, 2 Rocket – tubes,
104 mounted men and about 800 natives, completely overwhelmed them.
The camp, containing all the supplies ammunition and transport of No 3
Column, was taken, and but few of its defenders escaped. Our loss, I fear,
must be set down as 30 officers and about 500 non commissioned officers,
Rank and File of the Imperial troops and 21 officers and 70 Non Commissioned officers and Rank and File of the Colonial Forces.

A court of enquiry has been ordered to assemble to collect evidence
regarding this unfortunate affair, and will be forwarded to you as soon as
received.

Full particulars, so far as can be obtained, have been sent in my
despatch of this day's date which will reach you in the next mail. It would
seem that the troops were enticed away from their camp, as this action
took place about one mile and a quarter outside it –

The effects of the reverse have already been very serious. Two whole regiments of natives have deserted and it is to be feared, that the rest will follow.

A panic is spreading broadcast over the Colony which is difficult to allay.

Additional reinforcements must be sent out: At least three Infantry regiments and two cavalry Regiments with horses are required and one more Company of Engineers.

The Cavalry must be prepared to act as Mounted Infantry and should have their Carbines slung on their shoulder, and a sword shorter than the regulation pattern fastened to the saddle.

Chelmsford.

Courtesy of the National Army Museum

Map of the Excavation of Isandlwana in 2000

ORIGINAL GRAVE SITES

A to B: Site of camp, 22 January 1879

1/24th Regiment

Mounted Camp (Mounted infantry, Natal Carabiniers, N.M.P., N.M.R.)

Col. Harness's battery

2/24th Regiment

Natal Native Contingent

Natal Native Contingent

C   Col. Durnford, R.E., Capt. Wardell (1/24th Regt), Lt Dyer (2/24th Regt), Lt Scot (Natal Carabiniers), Lt Bradstreet (N.M.R.), Quartermaster Hitchcock (N.M.R.), 1 Officer unrecognisable (24th Regt), and about 150 men (mostly 24th Regt) buried here.

D   Capt R Younghusband (1/24th Regt), 2 unrecognisable officers (24th Regt), and about 60 men (24th Regt) buried here.

E   Black's Kopjie

       About 100 white bodies buried on nek below, close to road, also many single bodies along road which runs at head of camp as far as B.

F   Isandlwana Rock

G to H Signs of heavy fighting and determined stand having been made here. Kraal at G full of dead Zulus. Colour Sgt Wolf and 20 men (24th Regt) found amongst rocks just above G. The southern crest line from G to H strewn with empty cartridge cases. Guns of R.A. were firing for some time from point H to kraals at I which were afterwards found full of dead Zulus.

ARCHAEOLOGICAL AREAS OF INVESTIGATION IN 2000

Potential firing line of artillery

Zulu *Umutzi* (homestead) to fron tof camp

Main British camp

Cairns of Royal Artillery gunners and final position of guns (after escape from 1)

Density of expended Martini-Henry ammunition cases (Lt Pope's last stand?)

Line of expended Martini-Henry ammunition cases – probable true position of British line

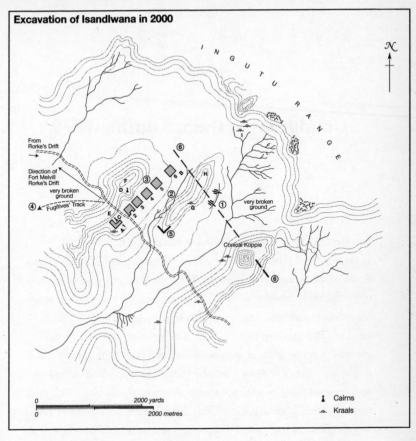

Excavation of Isandlwana in 2000

I N G U T U   R A N G E

N

From Rorke's Drift

Direction of Fort Melvill Rorke's Drift

very broken ground

④ Fugitives' Track

F
D
③
⑥
⑥ B
H
E
②
L
C
A
1 2 3 4 5
⑤
Q

very broken ground

①

Conical Koppie

⑥

| 0 | | 2000 yards |
| 0 | | 2000 metres |

Cairns

Kraals

Courtesy of 2nd Lieutenant Andrew Greaves RA, then an archaeology student at Oxford University.

Conditions in Camps during 1879

Prevalence of fever at Helpmakaar and Rorke's Drift

In the middle of February fever made its appearance at Helpmakaar and Rorke's Drift. Immediately after the disastrous affair at Isandlwana, these two important strategic positions were immediately placed in a more secure state of defence, and revetments were extemporized with sacks of mealies. The garrison troops, both European and native, were now crowded together without tents or shelter, except that afforded by a few tarpaulins. Over 1,000 men were at Helpmakaar exposed to cold and rain, some sleeping on wet mealie bags, others on the damp ground, their nights sleepless from constant alarms, and subjected to the noxious exhalations given off from the decomposing grain and a soil saturated with urine. The danger of rotting grain and mealies was frequently represented to the military authorities, but to little purpose, military necessity ruling paramount. Under these unfavourable conditions a low vital tone quickly supervened, indicated by malaise and loss of appetite, the young and weakly men being soon attacked with fever, diarrhoea and dysentery.

The fort at Rorke's Drift was similar in many respects to that of Helpmakaar, there being the same overcrowding, excessive fatigue, exposure to the cold and rain, and to the emanations of fermenting mealies and want of sleep, inducing a depressed condition of the vital powers highly favourable to the invasion of febrile attacks.

Notes

PREFACE

1 J.S. Rothwell, figures from *Narrative of Field Operations Connected with the Zulu War of 1879* (London 1881).

2 Norman Etherington, *Anglo Zulu Relations 1856–1878 – New Perspectives* (University of Natal Press 1981). Total of seventy-two colonial wars – figures from Niall Ferguson, BBC 2003.

CHAPTER 1 **Early Settlers in South Africa**

1 H.E. Marshall, *South Africa* (London 1915), referring to Drake's secret circumnavigation from east to west after having discovered the Cape Horn passage to the Pacific Ocean. By 1879 a total of sixty-three European vessels were lost between the Cape and Durban – see J. Smail, *With Shield and Assegai* (Cape Town 1969).

2 L. Van der Post, *The Heart of the Hunter* (Penguin 1923).

3 By the early 1800s the largest non-white group at the Cape consisted of Boer-owned slaves and their descendants. The majority of these slave people had been taken from Madagascar, Ceylon, India and the East Indies, the most popular being black men from Madagascar for physical labour while the other nationalities were prized for their domestic skills.

4 J.B. Peires, *House of Phalo* (Johannesburg 1981)

5 John Milton, *The Edges of War – A History of Frontier Wars 1702–1878* (Juta & Co., Cape Town 1983)

6 Johannes Meintjes, *The Voortrekkers* (Corgi 1973)

7 The *umfecane* was the period of internecine clan fighting pre 1825, not attributable to King Shaka. One curious result of the *umfecane* relates to the feared man-eating attributes of the lion. The San have long related that because there were so many dead or maimed human bodies readily available, lions acquired their liking for human meat. Prior to the *umfecane*, lions avoided contact with the San.

8 Anglo Zulu War Historical Society Journal 1, June 1997 p. 33.

9 Graham Leach, *The Afrikaners* (Mandarin 1989) quoting Prof. Liebenberg's *Myths Surrounding Blood River and the Vow*.

10 J. Laband and P. Thompson, *Field Guide to the War in Zululand and the Defence of Natal* (University of Natal Press 1979).

CHAPTER 2 **The Zulus, Defenders of the Buffalo River**

1 Anglo Zulu War Historical Society Journal 1, June 1997, introduction.

2 A.T. Bryant, *The Zulu People* (Shuter and Shooter 1949). See reference to *ukuSula isiKuba*.

3 Some modern writers have used the term 'assegai' to mean a stabbing spear. In fact, the word 'assegai' has nothing to do with the Zulu language. The word is Berber and was widely used by the Spanish and Portuguese and was later adopted by the French and English. In fourteenth-century French, such a weapon was known as the 'archegaie' while in English, Chaucer used the term 'lancegay'. The word 'assegai' never existed south of the Sahara.

4 T.V. Bulpin, *Shaka's Country* (Howard Timmins, Cape Town 1952), quoting Fynne's diary.

5 Ibid.

6 John Dunn, a local trader of English extraction, had allied himself to Chief Mbulazi and escaped only by swimming the river; Dunn helped some of Mbulazi's men to safety. Zulus avoided swimming at all times for cultural reasons – Cetshwayo's men forced the survivors into the river or put them to death. See AZWHS Journal 1 June 1997.

7 So many Zulu men had crossed the Tugela into Natal during King Mpande's reign that the *amabutho* system became seriously depleted. Throughout Zululand the king's weakening control encouraged up-and-coming clan leaders to develop their own power bases which resulted in the 1850s civil wars. King Cetshwayo operated a system of border patrols to deter would-be escapers.

CHAPTER 3 **The Zulu Military and Their Tactics**

1 George Chadwick, *The Zulu War of 1879* (Natal Educational Activities Association, undated).

CHAPTER 4 **Trade, Diamonds and War**

1 Louis Creswicke, *The Zulu War* (E.C. Jack, Edinburgh 1900).

2 Enclosure in Dispatch No. 12, 26 February 1864 p. 43. This also included the area surrounding the Boer town of Utrecht as Zulu territory.

3 Parliamentary Papers C.1748 p. 24.

4 *The Zulu War*.

5 Parliamentary Papers, C.1776 p. 150.

6 Louis Creswicke, *The Political Web* (E.C. Jack, Edinburgh 1900).

7 Frances Colenso, *History of the Zulu War and Its Origins* (Chapman & Hall Ltd, London 1880).

8 *The Zulu War*.

9 Damian O'Connor, *The Zulu and the Raj* (Able Publishing 2002).

10 The Zulus would not have appreciated tables and chairs; they had no documents to put on tables and preferred to sit on mats. There is an old Zulu saying that 'Only Englishmen and chickens sit upon perches.'

11 *The Zulu War* (quoting Sir Henry Bulwer). Similar situations had arisen during 1878; the British reaction had been to return offenders to Zululand – in November 1878 the British opinion was that such occurrences were not the responsibility of King Cetshwayo as the act 'had not been with his concurrence or even cognisance'. See Parliamentary Papers C.2222 p. 173. Further, Sihayo's errant son, Mehlokazulu, was never

charged with any offence relating to the alleged murder of Sihayo's wives – on the grounds that there 'was no evidence to maintain the charge'. See *Daily News* 30 October 1879.

12 R.W.F. Droogleever, *The Road to Isandlwana* (Greenhill Books 1992).

13 Letter dated 1878, Anglo Zulu War Historical Society Journal 1, June 1997, p. 27.

14 Parliamentary Papers C.2222 p. 176.

15 Parliamentary Papers C.2308 p. 16.

16 Sir Reginald Coupland, *Zulu Battle Piece Isandhlwana* (Collins 1948).

17 Paul Thompson, *The Natal Native Contingent in the Anglo Zulu War* (University of Natal Research Fund 2003). See also Parliamentary Papers C.2308 pp. 69 and 70 evidencing multiple warnings of a Zulu attack and protesting that the warnings were ignored.

18 Lieutenant Archibald Milne RN, from his *Report on Proceedings* (Public Record Office).

19 *The Zulu and the Raj*.

CHAPTER 5 **The British, Invaders of Zululand**

1 Public notificaton by Sir Bartle Frere dated 11 January 1879. See Parliamentary Papers C.2242 p. 24.

2 *Précis of Information Concerning Zululand* (War Office 1879). See Colonel Bray – p. 140.

3 By the end of the war, the invasion force used over 27,000 oxen and nearly 5,000 mules to reach Ulundi for the final battle. (Figures from the War Office *Précis*.)

4 See Appendix A.

5 John Laband, *Lord Chelmsford's Zululand Campaign 1878–1879* (Army Records Society 1994), Vol. 10 p. xxxv, Introduction.

6 *Lord Chelmsford's Zululand Campaign*.

7 Memorandum by Lieutenant General Lord Chelmsford, 23 October 1878.

8 *Natal Witness*, 1 January 1879.

9 *Natal Witness*, 5 January 1879.

CHAPTER 6 **The Five Invading Columns**

1 Lt. Gen. Chelmsford to Sir Bartle Frere, 6 January 1879, quoted in *Lord Chelmsford's Zululand Campaign 1878–1879* (Army Records Society 1994).

2 In 1873 the Gatling gun had been present during the Ashanti War but not used in action.

3 Parliamentary Papers C.2242 p. 26.

4 Frances Colenso, *History of the Zulu War and Its Origins* (Pietermaritzburg 1880).

5 *History of the Zulu War and Its Origins.*

6 Letter to his mother, 11 November 1878. See also *The Road to Isandlwana* by R.W.F. Droogleever for the life of Colonel Durnford.

7 The Hon Gerald French, *Lord Chelmsford and the Zulu War* (Unwin Brothers 1939).

8 *History of the Zulu War and Its Origins* p. 266.

9 *Natal Witness*, 5 January 1879.

10 Parliamentary Papers C.2242 p. 27, 28.

11 Anglo Zulu War Historical Society Journal 9, June 2001.

12 See Chapter 7 note 2.

13 *History of the Zulu War and its Origins.*

14 Parliamentary Papers C.2242 p. 24.

15 Originally spelled *Helpmekaar* by the Boers and subsequently as *Helpmakaar* by British settlers and troops. In Dutch it means 'help one another' whereas it was popularly known as 'help m' cart up' by the British troops due to the steep hill climb to the settlement. This work retains the original spelling throughout (except in quoted passages).

16 A.H. Swiss, *Records of the 24th Regiment* (London 1882).

17 *Natal Witness*, 5 January 1879.

CHAPTER 7 The First Invasion of Zululand, 11 January 1879

1 *Natal Mercury*, December 1878, commenting on the British invasion force.

2 Dispatch from Lord Chelmsford at Pietermaritzburg to Col. Wood, 23 November 1878.

3 The following is an extract from the official orders issued by Lord Chelmsford in November 1878. Item 145 deals with '*Cattle and other prize*' and reveals why all ranks had a vested interest in the price obtained from the contractors.

Item 145. The following rules, having reference to the capture of cattle, or other prize, will be adhered to by all forces serving under the orders of the Lieutenant-general commanding – On any cattle or other prize being taken, the officer commanding the corps or party making the same will at once report the circumstances and number or nature of the prize to the officer in charge of the operations, who will thereupon determine what troops will share, and will appoint prize agents to arrange for the disposal of the cattle, &c., and to distribute the proceeds according to the following scale, viz. –

Private or trooper – 1 share.

NCO – 2 shares.

Captain or subaltern – 3 shares.

Field officer – 4 shares.

Officer in command of the operations – 6 shares.

Officers of the staff – shares according to their rank.

4 Parliamentary Papers C.2454 p. 183 re Milne's report.

5 Hamilton-Browne, *A Lost Legionary in South Africa* (Werner Laurie, London 1890).

6 Anglo Zulu War Historical Society Journal 3, June 1998. The decision not to laager caused a serious rift among certain senior officers when, on 14 January, Major William Dunbar of the 2/24th was detailed to take his company and some native troops to the Batshe valley between Rorke's Drift and Isandlwana to repair the old wagon road. Ordered to pitch his tents beneath a rock outcrop close to Sihayo's homestead and among heavy thorn bushes, Dunbar was obliged to mount strong guards every night with men who had been working all day. When Chelmsford, Col. Glyn, their respective staff officers and an escort rode up to inspect the work, Dunbar asked for permission to move his camp. In the discussion that followed, Chelmsford's senior staff officer, Lt. Col. John Crealock, seems to have lost his temper and remarked impatiently, 'If Maj. Dunbar is afraid to stay there, we could send someone who was not.' Dunbar, a big, imposing man, walked off in a rage and resigned his commission; it was several hours before Chelmsford could persuade him to withdraw his resignation. The embarrassment caused to both Chelmsford and Glyn and to all the officers of the 24th should not be underestimated. On the very same day Inspector George Mansell of the Natal Mounted Police had lookouts placed along the top of the Nqutu plateau overlooking Isandlwana. Major Clery, a former professor of tactics and the senior staff officer of the 1/24th, later withdrew the lookouts on the grounds that they served no useful purpose.

7 AZWHS Journal 3, June 1998.

8 Charles Norris-Newman, *In Zululand with the British throughout the War of 1879* (W.H. Allen 1880).

9 *Lord Chelmsford's Zululand Campaign 1878–1879* (Army Records Society), Vol. 10.

10 *The Natal Carbineers 1855–1911*, edited by Rev. Stalker (Davis & Son, Pietermaritzburg 1912).

11 Ron Lock, *Blood on the Painted Mountain* (Greenhill Books 1995). Also, during a formal archaeological survey of Isandlwana battlefield in summer 2000 by Glasgow University and the South African authorities, it was discovered that the British front line was approximately 200 yards

further from the camp than previously supposed. The new position suggests it was covering the dead ground to its immediate front and puts the front line out of sight of Pulleine's HQ tent and even out of sight of the main British camp at Isandlwana. This hypothesis is based on the location of clusters of spent Martini-Henry ammunition cases and ammunition-box straps.

12 A. Greaves and B. Best, *The Curling Letters of the Zulu War* (Pen & Sword 2001).

13 Frank Emery, *The Red Soldier* (Jonathan Ball, Johannesburg 1977).

14 Ibid.

15 *The Curling Letters of the Zulu War.*

16 Appendix to *Field Exercises – Rifle and Carbine Exercises and Musketry Instructions* issued by Horse Guards (War Office) July 1879.

17 *Field Exercises – Rifle and Carbine Exercises and Musketry Instructions.*

18 George Mossop, *Running the Gauntlet* (Nelson 1937). Furthermore, an examination of some of the contemporary paintings of the time, often painted from descriptions given by actual combatants, clearly reveals palls of smoke on various Zulu War battlefields. This effect can be seen in, among others, C.E. Fripp's painting *Isandlwana*, De Neuville's *Rorke's Drift*, Lt Evelyn's two sketches *Nyezane*, Crealock's *Final Repulse* of Gingindlovu, Orlando Norie's watercolour *Kambula* and the equally famous *Illustrated London News*'s *Square at Ulundi*.

Marching the troops about the battlefield also affected their ammunition; Maj. Gen. Newdigate was so concerned about the frailty of Martini-Henry ammunition that he wrote to the War Office, 'Numerous complaints were made about the ball-bags; the weight of the cartridges makes the bags open, and when the men double the cartridges fall out.' Buller also wrote that the bullets easily became detached from the cartridges. For further details see my *Isandlwana* (Cassell 2001).

19 *The Curling Letters of the Zulu War.*

20 In due course the dogs became so savage that the Buffalo Border Guard stationed at Fort Pine had to shoot them.

CHAPTER 8 **An Appalling Disaster**

1 Trooper Richard Stevens, Natal Mounted Police, as quoted in the *Natal Colonist*, 17 April 1879.

2 Numerous Zulu accounts. The red jackets were dyed from the extract of the root of the madder plant.

3 A. Greaves and B. Best, *The Curling Letters of*

the Zulu War (Pen & Sword 2001).

4 Adrian Greaves, *Isandlwana* (Cassell 2001).

5 Revd John Stalker, *The Natal Carbineers 1855–1911* (Davis & Son, Pietermaritzburg 1912).

6 This is also supported by:

a Chelmsford in his personal dispatch dated 23 January 1879; he confirmed that on returning to Rorke's Drift, he saw 'large bodies of Zulus … which had been on the Natal side of the Buffalo River burning Kraals etc'.

b Major Mainwaring who wrote in his memoirs, 'On arriving at Rorke's Drift, we saw the house in flames, also far over the country we observed various homesteads ablaze. This led us to believe that the Zulus had invaded Natal' (Cairo 1895).

c See Chapter 6 note 2; confirming Chelmsford's intelligence of Zulu intention to cross into Natal.

d Some of the Zulus who crossed into Natal had taken part in either the battle or post-battle looting of the camp at Isandlwana as the filial (crown piece) of one of the 2nd Battalion colours, lost at Isandlwana, was subsequently found in the garden of a looted and burned-out farm situated on the Natal side of the Buffalo river, some 4 miles from Rorke's Drift.

7 Sir Reginald Coupland, *Zulu Battle Piece Isandhlwana* (Collins 1948).

8 C.T. Atkinson, *The South Wales Borderers* (Cambridge University Press 1937). In 1879 colours were still used in battle to rally troops and this policy continued through to the first Boer War. It appears that at the battle of Laing's Nek the 58th went into battle with both colours flying – the colours were carried by Lieutenants Baillie and Peel. Both officers and their colour parties came under concentrated fire. In the following confusion, Baillie tripped and fell; the colour was taken to safety by Sergeant Bridgestock. Lieutenant Hill tried to assist Baillie who was then hit and killed. Hill left Baillie and rescued another soldier for which he was awarded the VC. Such was the rate of Boer fire on the colour parties that in 1882 a War Office order was promulgated throughout the British Army that colours would never again be carried into battle.

9 Michael Glover, *Rorke's Drift* (Wordsworth Military Library 1997). Note – if Adendorff fought at Rorke's Drift, he was the only person to see action at both Isandlwana on 22 and Rorke's Drift on 22–23 January. Likewise, the Rorke's Drift lists prepared by Dunbar and Bourne make no mention of him. Glover states that Adendorff was later arrested at Pietermaritzburg. The

desertion of Captain Stevenson at Rorke's Drift was also fresh in everyone's mind.

10 Ian Knight, *The Zulu War Then and Now* (Plaistow Press 1993).

11 *The Zulu War Then and Now.*

12 Anglo Zulu War Historical Society Journal 2, December 1997.

13 Robert Hope, *The Zulu War and the 80th Regiment of Foot* (Churnet Valley Books 1997).

When he left the army, Wassall moved to Barrow-in-Furness and lived with his brother William at 18 Exeter Street. He was for a time employed in the electrical department of the Barrow shipyard. He married Rebecca Round on 10 April 1882 at the Parish Church of St Matthew. They were blessed with seven children, all of whom later married. Wassall died at the age of 70 and is buried at St James's Church, Barrow-in-Furness in the same grave as his wife. Their graves were unmarked until 1985 when a fine marble headstone was erected by his regiment.

14 *The Natal Carbineers 1855–1911.*

CHAPTER 9 Rorke's Drift, 22–23 January 1879

1 Letter from Gunner Howard RA, February 1879.

2 Boys were permitted to join the Regular Army, but those under the age of 17½ were enlisted as 'boy soldiers' and only entitled to half pay until reaching that age. Curiously, Colour Sergeant Bourne receives no mention in Donald Morris's classic *The Washing of the Spears*.

3 Chelmsford wrote that it was 'the non-arrival of this detachment that caused Major Spalding to go to Helpmakaar to hasten its departure'. He went on, 'I refer to this latter point in justice to Major Spalding as I have heard that remarks have been made relative to his absence from this post at the time'. Chelmsford's letter dated 19 May 1879.

4 a *Through the Zulu Country* by Bertram Mitford (1881) who heard accounts from Zulus quoting the words of King Cetshwayo: 'Go and drive them across the Umzinyati [Buffalo river] right back to Natal.'

b Major Bengough's report to Chelmsford – see note 17 to Chapter 4.

c In a post-war discussion between Mr J. Gibson, a magistrate in Zululand, and King Cetshwayo's brother, Chief Undabuko, there was no suggestion that to cross the border would have contravened the king's orders; and according to Undabuko, 'seeing that portion of the army which had not been engaged cross the border, [he] called to

members of his own regiment, the Mbonambi, to join them but they declined on the ground that it was necessary to return to the field of battle to attend to their wounded'. As reported in *The Zulu War* by David Clammer (Pan Books 1975).

d Muziwento recounted that during the lull in fighting at Isandlwana, his men were exhorted to fight by the call of their commander, 'Never did the king give you the command "Lie down upon the ground". His words were "Go, and toss them to Martizburg".' See John Laband, *Fight Us in the Open*, KwaZulu Monuments Council (Shuter and Shooter 1985).

5 John Laband, *Rope of Sand* (Jonathan Ball, Johannesburg 1995). The 'house of Jim' refers to James Rorke, after whom Rorke's Drift was named.

6 Numerous primary sources reveal that Dalton strongly assisted with the command during the battle at Rorke's Drift – only to revert to his official subservient duties the following day. Although his role was acknowledged by Chard, Dalton's role was overlooked in official reports and his actions officially 'downgraded' when medals were awarded. It is popularly believed that Dalton had been a sergeant major in the 85th Regiment. He left the 85th in March 1862 having achieved the rank of sergeant. He then transferred to the Commissariat Staff where he reached the rank of 1st class staff sergeant before he retired in 1871 with the Long Service and Good Conduct Medal for nearly twenty-two years' service. He then emigrated to South Africa. For further evidence on this aspect, see Chapter 14. See also *Padre George Smith of Rorke's Drift* by Canon Lummis MC.

7 Anglo Zulu War Historical Society Journal 14, December 2003, quoting Captain Tongue who described the barrier: 'the hospital was connected to the remainder of the defences by a low breast-work of mealie sacks two high'.

8 During the following day Witt and his wife each learned from different sources that the Zulus had killed the other. Convinced by the news, both made their way to Durban in abject sadness – only to meet each other on the outskirts of the town.

9 Chard wrote of certain actions of Adendorff but others who knew all the men involved credited Attwood with these actions for which Attwood was awarded the DCM at Pietermaritzburg on 15 November 1879. Accounts of the time reveal that Adendorff disappeared into obscurity although, later, news reached Rorke's Drift that both Vane and Adendorff had been arrested at Pietermaritzburg

for desertion. Chard's report that Adendorff had 'stayed to fight' had already received some publicity and so it appears that the matter of Adendorff's disappearance was quietly dropped.

10 Adrian Greaves, *Rorke's Drift* Appendix B (Cassell 2002).

11 Corporal Anderson was buried with those killed at Rorke's Drift. By shooting him, the soldiers of the 24th had dealt with the matter to their satisfaction. Captain Stevenson was detained by the British two days later and returned to Rorke's Drift. He was informally 'court-martialled' and dismissed from his position but then appointed Captain 3rd Troop, Natal Horse; present at Ulundi, and during the siege of Pretoria (medal and clasp for 1877–8–9); Assistant Inspector, Gold Coast Police, August 1881; Government Secretary and Superintendent of Police, Gambia, December 1886.

12 *Rorke's Drift* Appendix E.

13 See *Pall Mall Gazette and The Defence of Rorke's Drift* – account of the painting by A. De Neuville 1879, reprinted in AZWHS Journal 13, June 2003.

14 AZWHS Journal 4, December 1998 – Colonel Bourne's BBC radio transcription. In December 1936 the BBC conducted a radio interview with Colonel Bourne about the battle of Rorke's Drift. In the programme he was asked about the rifles used by the Zulus; Bourne (then Colour Sergeant) was adamant that the Zulus attacking the outpost had used British Martini-Henry rifles captured earlier in the day at Isandlwana. He stated:

> The Zulus had collected the rifles from the men they had killed at Isandlwana, and had captured the ammunition from the mules which had stampeded and threw their loads; so our own arms were used against us. In fact, this was the cause of every one of our casualties, killed and wounded, and we should have suffered many more if the enemy had known how to use a rifle. There was hardly a man even wounded by assegais – their principal weapon.

Many historians have queried Bourne's account that the Zulus possessed Martini-Henry rifles but Bourne was probably correct; they undoubtedly came from Isandlwana, although not from the main battle. They came from two comparatively minor encounters when the 4,500 Zulus detailed for the reserve at Isandlwana swept behind the mountain and overran two isolated groups of British soldiers, Dyson's troop and the RE detach-

ment, before successfully blocking the British escape route from Isandlwana. They then formed part of the Zulu force that harried the camp survivors along the fugitives' trail before eventually moving on to Rorke's Drift.

15 *Rorke's Drift* Second 'Chard Report', see Appendix A.

16 Major Spalding wrote:

> OC No. 3 Column ordered Capt Rainforth's Company 1/24th Regiment from Helpmekaar to Rorke's Drift for the purpose of taking up and entrenching a position commanding and defending the ponts on the Buffalo River.
>
> I know of no other orders touching the erection of work for such a purpose.
>
> This company should have been in the required position on the 20th January the day of the departure of No. 3 Column from Rorke's Drift for Isandhlwana. They did not arrive on that day nor even on the 21st. Seeing this, on the 22nd I rode over to Helpmekaar with a written order in my pocket directing Capt Rainforth positively to reach the points by sundown on that day. I met his company together with that of Major Upcher of the same Regiment on their march down to Rorke's Drift. I accompanied them. The intelligence from Isandhlwana met us on the way.

17 Statement taken at Pietermaritzburg, *British Battles on Land and Sea* (Cassell 1898).

18 Letter from Gunner Howard RA, February 1879.

19 Readers may have noticed the emphasis placed on horses in contemporary letters, diaries and journals relating to nineteenth-century warfare. Harness understood the position and importance of horses and gave meticulous attention to this aspect of his command. Through 1878 Stuart Smith, Harness's captain, scoured southern Africa to buy suitable horses. On 6 March of that year Harness wrote that his captain had returned the previous day with forty-eight horses at an average cost of £24 13s. 7¼d. The artillerymen who mastered the care of horses in southern Africa – with small feeds and the use of every opportunity for grazing – criticized the failure of the regular cavalry to adapt to local conditions during the Zulu campaign. On 19 July 1878 Harness wrote that he congratulated himself on the condition of the horses, and, 'if we get through the march as I hope we shall, it will be a creditable thing to the officers and men of the battery'. Colonel J.T.B. Brown RA complimented

Harness on the condition of his horses on another march, to Ulundi, almost a year later: 'Lieutenant-Colonel Harness's horses were all native, and principally bought in the Orange Free State and Old Colony, before there had been so great a demand. They were useful and handy horses for the light guns, and Harness had them so well trained that they were very little trouble. A few mounted men used to drive them to water, or out to feed just like a herd of cattle instead of having a man to every two or three horses.'

20 *Lord Chelmsford's Zululand Campaign*, letter dated 8 February 1879.

21 Laband and Thompson with Sheila Henderson, *The Buffalo Border* (University of Natal 1983).

CHAPTER 10 Post-battle: A Deep Sigh of Relief

1 Anglo Zulu War Historical Society Journal 14, December 2003 quoting Captain Tongue of the 24th Regiment.

2 Donald Morris, *The Washing of the Spears* (Simon & Schuster, New York 1965) (first edition)

3 For detailed archaeological notes, see Adrian Greaves, *Rorke's Drift* Chapter 17 (Cassell 2002).

4 Hamilton-Browne, *A Lost Legionary in South Africa* (Werner Laurie, London 1890).

5 Ibid.

6 Ibid.

7 Ibid.

8 Horace Smith-Dorrien, *Memories of Forty-Eight Years Service* (John Murray, 1925).

9 From Curling's original Zulu War letters, courtesy the AZWHS.

10 Norman Holme, *The Silver Wreath*, reference Private 913 James Ashton.

11 *A Lost Legionary in South Africa*, also
(i) Chelmsford denied allegations of massacred Zulus by quoting his 1878 Regulations for Field Forces which stated: 'Natives will be treated with kindness. Commanding Officers will exert their influence with all ranks to prevent there being in any way molestation or oppression.'
(ii) Following the publication in the British press of letters from Sergeant Jervis, 90th Light Infantry, and Private Snook, 13th Light Infantry, reporting the massacre of hundreds of Zulu wounded following the battle of Khambula, numerous questions were asked in the British Parliament. For the full reports, see House of Commons Hansard, 3rd Series, vol. 246 cc. 1708–1718 of 12 June 1879; vol. 247 cc. 693–694 of 26 June 1879 and vol. 247

cc. 723–724 of 26 June 1879, and F. Emery, *The Red Soldier* Johannesburg 1977 (Jonathan Ball). Although the British military commanders in Zululand initially denied the routine killing of Zulu wounded, reports and letters from participants in subsequent battles confirmed the policy – especially following the battles of Khambula on 26 March and Ulundi on 4 July 1879.

12 Greaves, *Rorke's Drift*, Appendix A, quoting Chard's second report. Also, officers were cautious in expressing their views, possibly because they knew that the facts were being manipulated for political reasons. See AZWHS Journal 14 for the letters of Captain Tongue – which include the line concerning press reports, 'Look out in the Standard towards the end of the month and you will see an almost [underlined in letter] accurate account of doings of the 21st, 22nd, & 23 Jany, we have got it together; therefore, dare not say all we think or know.'

13 AZWHS Journal 4, December 1998.

14 *A Lost Legionary in South Africa*.

15 S. Clarke, *Zululand at War 1879* (Brenthurst Press 1984).

16 *A Lost Legionary in South Africa*.

17 Blue Book C-2318 Enclosure 1.

18 Ibid. Enclosure 2.

19 Ibid No. 9D.

20 Ibid. No 11.

21 *The Red Soldier*

22 D. Child, *Zulu War Journal Col. Henry Harford, C.B.* (Shuter and Shooter 1978).

23 Glyn's correspondence. By kind permission 24th Regimental Museum, Brecon.

24 These bodies are buried at a recently (2002) restored cemetry on the north bank of the Buffalo river at Rorke's Drift.

25 Charles Reynolds, *A Civil Surgeon*, diary entry dated 27 January 1879 (private publication).

26 A. Greaves and B. Best, *The Curling Letters of the Zulu War* (Pen & Sword 2001).

27 *Précis of Information Concerning Zululand* (War Office 1879).

28 Letter from Col. Pickard to Col. Wood, 14 October, quoted in Ian Bennett's *Eyewitness in Zululand* (Greenhill 1989).

29 Ian Knight, *The Sun Turned Black* (Windrow & Greene 1992).

30 AZWHS Journal 2, December 1997. When Wolseley presented Bromhead with his Victoria Cross, he did so in the mistaken belief that he was presenting the award to Bromhead's brother who had served with Wolseley in Ashanti. Wolseley was

apparently bemused by Bromhead's lack of recognition. See *Life of Lord Wolseley* by Morris and Arthur, 1924.

31 Letter from Wolseley dated 16 July 1879. See WO327386 (awards to Commissary Dalton and Dunne).

32 No 1 HRH'S Schedule quoted in *Eyewitness in Zululand*.

CHAPTER 11 Enquiry and Cover-Up

1 Telegram from Chelmsford to the Secretary of State for War. See Appendix G.

2 Blue Books C.2242.

3 Ibid.

4 Ibid.

5 Curling's letters courtesy Anglo Zulu War Historical Society.

6 Smith-Dorrien letters. By kind permission 24th Regimental Museum, Brecon.

7 Curling's letters courtesy AZWHS.

8 Ian Knight, *Reasons of Defeat at Isandlwana 1879* (Military Illustrated 1986). Account by Muziwento, a Zulu warrior.

9 Statement of Mehlokazulu – by kind permission of David Rattray.

10 Parliamentary Papers C.2242.

11 The Hon Gerald French, *Lord Chelmsford and the Zulu War* (Unwin Brothers 1939).

12 Unpublished papers of Lt Cochrane. Courtesy of the AZWHS.

13 John Laband, *Lord Chelmsford's Zululand Campaign 1878–1879* (Army Records Society 1994).

14 *Times of Natal*, 5 January 1887.

15 AZWHS Journal 4, December 1998, referring to Durnford's original orders from Chelmsford.

16 A. Greaves and B. Best, *The Curling Letters of the Zulu War* (Pen & Sword 2001).

17 *Lord Chelmsford's Zululand Campaign*, Vol. 10.

18 AZWHS Journal 2, December 1997.

19 Glyn papers. By kind permission 24th Regimental Museum, Brecon.

20 Adrian Greaves, *Rorke's Drift* (Cassell 2002) p. 177.

21 *The Curling Letters of the Zulu War*.

22 *Hansard* February and March 1879 – Members of Parliament lamented Royal involvement before Parliament had been informed of Isandlwana.

23 Ibid.

24 *The Curling Letters of the Zulu War*. Curling moved to Wesselstrom in the Transvaal early in

October 1879 where he remained until the end of November. During this period, he heard that he had been promoted captain and posted to a battery in 'Caubal – in time to earn another medal'. He hoped that he would be able to secure home leave before sailing to India, but it was not to be and in a letter dated 25 January 1880 from Pinetown, he wrote that he expected to sail for India and the Afghan war on 4 February. In a letter he wrote during this period he mentions that of his fifty men, ten were in hospital and one had died a few days earlier, all from fever. Curling served in the Afghan war, in India, Aldershot, and in 1896 was Lieutenant Colonel OC RA in Egypt. He retired to Kent where he became a respected Justice of Peace.

CHAPTER 12 The Coastal (No. 1) Column

1 Howard Whitehouse, *A Widow-Making War: The Diaries of Capt. Warren Wynne* (Paddy Griffiths Associates, 1995).

2 The Gatling gun had been present during the Ashanti War of 1873, but not used in action. Prior to the Zulu War the Gatling gun had been issued only to the navy; it had originally been designed as a ship-mounted weapon to give covering fire to naval landing parties.

3 The Zulus failed to synchronize their attack and were soon driven off with heavy losses. Their casualties are estimated at 500 dead with a similar number wounded. By comparison with the Zulus, British casualties were light with two officers of the NNC and eight men killed, one officer and fifteen men wounded. This engagement is especially significant as it took place at about the same time and on the same day as the Zulu attack on Chelmsford's Centre Column at Isandlwana and Wood's Northern Column near Hlobane – which belies the view widely held by authors and historians that the Zulus would, for cultural and religious reasons, avoid fighting on 22 January, the day of the dead moon. This theory overlooks the evidence that the Zulus engaged the British on 22 January at four different locations, at Isandlwana, Rorke's Drift, and Nyezane and at Hlobane. With regard to Isandlwana, these theorists would claim the Zulus attacked because they were surprised by a British patrol; there is sufficient evidence that the Zulu attack on Isandlwana was well under way when first encountered by the British patrol. See Chapter 2.

See also the Zulu War diary of Surgeon L. Reynolds dated 22 January in which he wrote, 'A partial eclipse; it was prophesied the Zulus would make an attack today, which proved to be the case.'

4 *A Widow-Making War.*

5 John Laband, *Fight Us in the Open* (University of Natal, Pietermaritzburg, 1985).

6 Ibid.

7 Ian Castle and Ian Knight, *Fearful Hard Times* (Greenhill 1994).

8 Anglo Zulu War Historical Society Journal 4, December 1998.

9 The Hon Gerald French, *Lord Chelmsford and the Zulu War* (Unwin Brothers 1939).

10 *Fearful Hard Times.*

11 *A Widow-Making War.*

CHAPTER 13 **The Northern Column**

1 A. Greaves and B. Best, *The Curling Letters* (Pen & Sword 2001).

2 See *British Battles on Land and Sea* (Cassell 1898), p. 244.

3 Anglo Zulu War Historical Society Journal 5, June 1999.

4 After the Zulu War, Booth became a sergeant instructor with the local rifle company until his retirement in 1898. His total army service was 33 years 182 days. Sadly, he did not live to enjoy a long retirement for he died of rheumatic fever in 1899.

5 R. Hope, *The 80th Regiment of Foot* (Churnet Valley Books 1997).

6 For full extract, see *Narrative of Field Operations Connected with the Zulu War of 1879* (London 1881).

7 The citation reads:

For his gallant conduct on the 12th March 1879, during the Zulu attack on the Ntombe River, in having when considerably outnumbered by the enemy, rallied a few men on the south bank of the river, and covered the retreat of fifty soldiers and others for a distance of three miles. The officer Commanding 80th Regiment reports that, had it not been for the coolness displayed by this non-commissioned Officer, not one man would have escaped'.

8 Lindsay Reyburn, *The 1879 Zulu War Diaries of RSM F.W. Cheffins* (private printing, Pretoria 2001).

9 AZWHS Journal 6, December 1999 – article by Ron Lock.

10 G. Mossop, *Running the Gauntlet* (Thomas Nelson & Son 1937).

11 Ibid.

12 Letter dated 31 March 1879 later published in the *Illustrated London News.*

13 As quoted in *Natalia,* December 1997 (Natal Social Library).

14 Major Knox-Leet successfully lobbied influential friends at the War Office for the VC.

15 Private John Snook's letter to his landlord at Tiverton, reproduced in Frank Emery's *The Red Soldier* (Jonathan Ball, Johannesburg 1977).

16 Private Joseph Banks, 90th Light Infantry, letter published in The *Dover Express,* 6 June 1879, and reproduced in *The Red Soldier.*

17 Ian Knight, the *Battle of Khambula,* AZWHS Journal 9, June 2001.

18 Sir Evelyn Wood, VC, *Midshipman to Field Marshal* (Methuen 1906), Vol. 2.

19 Account by an unidentified British participant, quoted in D.C.F. Moodie's *The History of the Battles and Adventures of the Boers, the British, and the Zulus in Southern Africa from 1495 to 1879* (1879), also reproduced in *The Red Soldier.*

20 Same correspondent, ibid.

21 Report of the *Natal Mercury's* correspondent, 'Khambula Camp, April 1st 1879', 9 April 1879.

22 AZWHS Journal 13, June 2003, letter from Private John Snook, 1/13th Regiment.

23 Correspondent with Wood's column, report marked 'Camp Khambula, 31st March 1879', reproduced in *Natal Mercury* of 12 April 1879.

24 *The Red Soldier* quoting Sergeant Jervis, 90th Regiment – letter to his brother.

CHAPTER 14 **The Second Invasion, 31 May – 4 July 1879**

1 A. Greaves and B. Best, *The Curling Letters of the Zulu War* (Pen & Sword 2001).

2 John Laband, *Lord Chelmsford's Zululand Campaign 1878–1879* (Army Records Society 1994).

3 *The Zulu War and Colony of Natal* (Natal Provincial Administration 1979). (From a conversation with Sir Bindon Blood.)

4 *The Curling Letters of the Zulu War.*

5 Ibid.

6 Anglo Zulu War Historical Society Journal 7, June 2000

7 Ibid. The prince's mother, Eugénie, known throughout childhood as 'carrot top', was brought up and educated in England by Villiers, Fourth Earl of Clarendon and Foreign Secretary. Villiers, probably Eugénie's father, continued his relationship with Eugénie's mother until late in their lives. It was Villiers who eventually introduced Eugénie to Napoleon III.

8 Charles Norris-Newman, *In Zululand with the*

British throughout the War of 1879 (W.H. Allen, London 1880).

9 AZWHS Journal 6, December 1999.

10 Keens of London supplied mustard to the troops during the Zulu War.

11 Lord Chelmsford's Zululand Campaign 1878–1879.

12 The Hon Gerald French, Lord Chelmsford and the Zulu War (Unwin Brothers 1939).

13 Lord Chelmsford's Zululand Campaign 1878–1879.

CHAPTER 15 The Battle of Ulundi

1 John William Colenso, Colenso Papers, 25 July 1879; see also J. Guy, The Destruction of the Zulu Kingdom (Longman 1979).

2 Contrary to popular belief, there is no evidence that Trooper Raubenheim was tortured. His body was found mutilated on 4 July where he had fallen – see Maj. Gen. W.C.F. Molyneux's Campaigning in South Africa and Egypt (London 1896). The grass had been trampled where Zulus had gathered around the body to cut off certain body parts. There are no authenticated examples of torture employed by the Zulus during the Anglo-Zulu War.

3 Melton Prior, Campaigns of a War Correspondent (London 1912).

4 Ibid.

5 Charles Norris-Newman, In Zululand with the British throughout the War of 1879 (W.H. Allen, London 1880).

6 British Parliamentary Papers, C.2482. Chelmsford's official dispatch.

7 Campaigns of a War Correspondent.

8 Parliamentary Papers C.2482.

9 Parliamentary Papers C.2482. Drury-Lowe, official report.

10 Account in the Cape Argus, reproduced in Frank Emery's The Red Soldier (Jonathan Ball, Johannesburg 1977).

11 J. Laband, The Battle of Ulundi (KwaZulu Monuments Council 1988).

CHAPTER 16 Beginning of the End

1 Damian O'Connor, The Life of Sir Bartle Frere (Able Publishing 2002).

2 From the genus Caecilian (legless amphibians). Caecilians closely resemble burrowing snakes, but do not have external scales. They range in size from inches to several feet, with diameters up to an inch or two. Caecilians are carnivorous creatures, eating insects, insect larvae and worms. Some caecilians are oviparous (egg layers), some

viviparous (live bearers), and a few are ovoviviparous (the eggs hatch inside the mother and the young live in her until maturity). Many landbound caecilians live their life burrowed underground. There are no known species in Europe, North America, Australia or Antarctica.

3 Sir Garnet Wolseley's South African Journal, 12 July 1879.

4 On 4 August Wolseley wrote in his journal that he would 'like to let loose the Swazis upon these northern tribes at once but I have to think of the howling Societies at home who have sympathy with all black men'. Wolseley despised Villiers whom he described as 'the arch adulterer'; see A. Preston, The South African Journal of Sir Garnet Wolseley (Cape Town 1973), entry 18 July 1879.

5 W. Worsfold, Sir Bartle Frere: A Footnote to the History of the British Empire (London 1923). The 'Further Correspondence' relates to personal letters in the Blue Books which Frere believed, until his dying day, vindicated him.

CHAPTER 17 Aftermath of the Zulu War

1 Colonial Office Papers 879/16, 204, No. 151.

2 A. Preston, The South African Journal of Sir Garnet Wolseley (Cape Town 1973).

3 Ibid.

4 Ibid. John Dunn, a local trader and known as a white Zulu chief, had befriended King Cetshwayo prior to the war. He became an influential adviser to King Cetshwayo who appointed him to the rank of chief and gave him title to land bordering the Tugela river. Dunn then changed sides for the duration of the war, reverting to the Zulus post-war.

5 Ibid.

6 British Parliamentary Papers C.2482.

7 Colonial Office Papers 879/16, 204, No. 49.

8 Colonial Office Papers 879/16, 204, No. 123.

9 Colonial Office Papers 879/17, 215, No. 151.

10 A. Greaves and I. Knight, A Review of the South African Campaign of 1879 (Debinair Publishing 2000).

11 These cairns were carefully excavated and repaired by the official archaeological team from Glasgow University during 2000. See map at Appendix H.

Bibliography

Anglo Zulu War Historical Society Journals 1–16

British Battles on Land and Sea (Cassell, 1898)

Lord Chelmsford's Zululand Campaign (Army Records Society), Vol. 10 (1994)

Précis of Information (War Office, 1879)

Parliamentary Papers 1878–1906 (C 2222–2295)

Atkinson, C.T., *The South Wales Borderers 24th Foot 1689-1937* (Cambridge, 1937)

Bryant, A.T., *The Zulu People* (Pietermaritzburg: Shuter & Shooter, 1949)

Bulpin, T.V., *Shaka's Country* (Capetown: Howard Timms, 1952)

Castle, Ian and Knight, Ian, *Fearful Hard Times* (Greenhill, 1994)

Chadwick, George, *The Zulu War of 1879* (The Natal Educational Activities Association, undated).

Clarke, Sonia, *Invasion of Zululand* (Brenthurst, 1979)

Colenso, Francis, *History of the Zulu War and its Origins* (Chapman & Hall, 1880)

Colenso, John William, Colenso Papers, 25 July 1879; see also J. Guy's *The Destruction of the Zulu Kingdom* (Longmans, 1979)

Cope, Richard, *The Ploughshare of War* (University of Natal Press, 1999)

Cory, George (ed.), *The Diaries of the Rev. Francis Owen* (Cape Town, 1926)

Creswicke, Louis, *The Zulu War* (Edinburgh: E.C. Jack, 1900)

Cunynghame, Sir A, *My Command in South Africa* (Macmillan, 1879)

Emery, F, *The Red Soldier* (London, 1977)

Etherington, Norman, *Anglo Zulu Relations 1856–1878 – New Perspectives* (University of Natal Press, 1981)

French, The Hon. Gerald, *Lord Chelmsford and the Zulu War* (Unwin, 1939)

Gon, P., *The Road to Isandlwana* (London, 1979)

Greaves, A. and Best, B., *The Curling Letters* (Pen & Sword, 2001)

Greaves, A. and Knight, I., *A Review of The South African Campaign of 1879* (Debinair, 2000)

Greaves, Adrian, *Fields of Battle: Isandlwana* (Cassell, 2001)

— *Rorke's Drift* (Cassell, 2002)

Guy, J.J., *A note on firearms in the Zulu kingdom with special reference to the Anglo-Zulu War 1879*
    Journal of African History (4):557-570

Hamilton-Browne, G., *A Lost Legionary in South Africa* (London: Werner Laurie, 1890)

Hope, R., *The 80th Regiment of Foot* (Churnet Valley Books, 1997)

— *The Zulu War and the 80th Regiment of Foot* (Churnet Valley Books, 1997)

Knight, Ian, *Reasons of defeat at Isandlwana 1879* (Military Illustrated, 1986)

— *The Zulu War Then and Now* (Plaistow Press, 1993)

— *The Sun Turned Black* (Watermans, 1995)

— *There Will Be An Awful Row At Home About This* (Shoreham, 1987)

Laband, J. and Thompson, P.S. with Sheila Henderson, *The Buffalo Border* (University of
    Natal Press, 1983)

Laband, John, *Lord Chelmsford's Zululand Campaign* (Alan Sutton Publishing, 1996)

— *Rope of Sand* (Johannesburg: Jonathan Ball, 1995)

Leach, Graham, *The Afrikaners* (Mandarin, 1989)

Meintjes, Johannes, *The Voortrekkers* Corgi (1973)

Milton, John, *The Edges of War – A History of Frontier Wars 1702–1878* (Capetown:
    Juta & Co., 1983)

Montague, W.E., *Campaigning in South Africa* (Blackwood, 1880)

Maurice, Sir F and Arthur, Sir G., *The Life of Lord Wolseley* (London, 1924)

Morris, Donald, *The Washing of the Spears* (New York: Simon & Schuster, 1965)

Mossop, George, *Running the Gauntlet* (Nelson, 1937)

Newman-Norris, Charles, *In Zululand with the British throughout the War of 1879*
    (London: W.H. Allen, 1880)

O'Connor, Damian, *The Life of Sir Bartle Frere* (Able Publishing, 2002)

— *The Zulu and the Raj* (Able Publishing, 2002)

Paton, Glennie and Penn Symons, *Records of the 24th Regiment* (London, 1892)

Peires, J.B., *House of Phalo* (Johannesburg, 1981)

Preston, A., *The South African Journal of Sir Garnet Wolseley* (Cape Town, 1973)

Prior, Melton, *Campaigns of a War Correspondent* (London, 1912)

Reyburn, Lindsay, *The 1879 Zulu War Diaries of RSM F.W. Cheffins* (Pretoria: Private
    printing, 2001)

Reynolds, Charles, *A Civil Surgeon* (Private publication, 2003)

Smail, J., *With Shield and Assegai* (Cape Town, 1969)

Stalker, John, *The Natal Carbineers* (Davis & Son, 1912)

Swiss, A.H., *Records of the 24th Regiment* (London, 1882)

Van der Post, L., *The Heart of the Hunter*, (Penguin, 1923)

Whitehouse, Howard, *A Widow-Making War: The Diaries of Capt. Warren Wynne*
    (Paddy Griffiths Associates, 1995)

Wilmot, A., *The Zulu War* (London, 1880)

Wood, Sir Evelyn, *Midshipman to Field Marshal* (Methuen, 1906), Vol. 2

Worsfold, W., *Sir Bartle Frere; a Footnote to the History of the British Empire* (London,
    1923)

Index